MAKING SENSE OF

LEAN
SIX
SIGMA

PROCESS
IMPROVEMENT

MAKING SENSE OF

LEAN SIX SIGMA

PROCESS IMPROVEMENT

ROBERT SETIADI, PhD

First Edition   01-06i

ISBN: 978-0-6489636-0-8
Libraries Australia ID 68360453

A catalogue record for this
work is available from the
NATIONAL
LIBRARY   National Library of Australia
OF AUSTRALIA

This book is dedicated to my amazing wife Henny
and my little ones Andrew and Alice.

CONTENTS

GETTING TO KNOW
THE BASICS

01. PREFACE

Making Sense of Lean Six Sigma Process Improvement is a comprehensive introduction to the principles and frameworks of Lean Six Sigma. Six Sigma principles help organisations to improve processes, increase consistency and customer satisfaction, whilst Lean principles help to identify and remove non-value-added waste in a process, minimising cost and maximising profits.

Breaking down the fundamentals of data-driven methodology, Lean techniques and Six Sigma principles so that even complete beginners can understand, this book seeks to provide readers with a down-to-earth and thorough look at the fundamental ideas underpinning the Lean Six Sigma process.

One of the major challenges for newcomers to learn Lean Six Sigma is that most learning pathways would require them to take an expensive course or learn from multiple books and other sources. Designed to help readers get to grips with Lean Six Sigma without having to spend huge amounts of money on courses and tons of books, this book is written to provide a one-stop learning solution. *Making Sense of Lean Six Sigma Process Improvement* is a must-read for any executives, managers, entrepreneurs and industry professionals who want to implement the highly effective principles of Lean Six Sigma in their business to streamline their processes and transform their businesses. In addition, this guide arms professionals preparing for IASSC and ASQ Lean Six Sigma certification exams with the essential knowledge they need to go from zero to exam-ready and receive recognition for their skills so that they can start implementing Lean Six Sigma's powerful improvement tools to achieve real-world benefits and gain more experience.

The skill level of a Lean Six Sigma practitioner is measured using belt colour. *Yellow Belt* indicates a basic level of understanding about Lean Six Sigma concepts, sufficient for team members involved in a Six Sigma project. *Green Belt* indicates good level of knowledge to lead Six Sigma project on a part-time basis. *Black Belt* indicates a strong working knowledge of Lean Six Sigma capable of leading complex projects on full-time basis. *Master Black Belt* is the highest level of Lean Six Sigma skills; it shows full mastery of all concepts and those achieving it usually take on the role of training others.

In summary, this book is designed to help readers:
- Understand the principles of Six Sigma;
- Learn about Lean principles and how they work together with Six Sigma;
- Appreciate the benefits of implementing Lean Six Sigma;
- Learn the tools of process improvement and when to use them;
- Implement the knowledge in their work;
- Study and prepare for Lean Six Sigma certification exams.

There is no prerequisite for reading this book other than willingness to learn. Basic understanding about management principles and descriptive statistics are recommended, but not required. Most topics will be discussed in simplified forms, with brief explanation of underlying knowledge when necessary.

This book has 38 chapters divided into 7 sections. Quick reading for high-level understanding of the overall topics will take approximately 30-40 hours, whereas comprehensive reading to master all topics will take between 1 to 3 months, depending on your time commitment. Lean Six Sigma is a highly demanding topic to study, but the potential it helps to unlock is well worth the hard work.

A challenging aspect in organising this book is the fact that so many topics are interconnected; explaining a certain topic requires a basic understanding of some others and explaining those other topics requires even more concepts. Accordingly, this book is structured to start with the simplest concepts, and then builds on them in the following chapters. Hence, if this is your first time learning about Lean Six Sigma, it is strongly recommended to read this book in sequential order. However, depending on your goal in reading this book, you might want to review the table of topics in Chapter 05 where you can see which topics and chapters are relevant for different roles and/or different Belt levels for certification exams. Indeed, the very early concept of this book actually started from the author's study notes when preparing for the Lean Six Sigma Black Belt certification exam. Combined with years of experience and months of research, the study notes evolved into the structure of this book.

The first section gives the basic knowledge about Lean Six Sigma to serve as a foundation for the following sections. Sections 2 to 6 discuss each phase of DMAIC methodology (Define, Measure, Analyze, Improve and Control). These are the 5 phases followed by Six Sigma for process improvement. Topics on Lean principles relevant to each phase are integrated within each section.

Define phase aims to define set a clear and measurable goal of process improvement. *Measure phase* focuses on collecting data by measuring aspects of the current process to identify a list of possible factors (X) impacting target outcome (Y). *Analyze phase* works on the collected data and perform hypotheses to confirm X factors to be improved. *Improve phase* performs experiments to find optimal value combinations of X to achieve best possible Y that meets the improvement goal. *Control phase* executes the improvement and sets up a methodical mechanism to control the process.

Major topics such as Measurement System Analysis, Hypothesis Testing, Design of Experiment and Statistical Process Control are split into smaller chapters to help with focus and structure. Each topic can be found under the relevant phase in DMAIC sections.

The last section presents a summary of all the previous topics in DMAIC, followed by chapters on Kaizen event and Design for Six Sigma (DFSS) using DMADV methodology. Reference tables for some of the techniques discussed in this book can be found in the last chapter.

Before we begin, please note the following publishing features. Firstly, examples are used throughout the book to help with explanations of certain topics and calculations. These examples are made for the purpose of explaining concepts and may not necessarily reflect real world data. It is also worth noting that many other books on Six Sigma use Minitab Statistical Software to perform analysis; however, this book focuses more on explaining concepts and calculations so that you can perform them by hand instead of using tools. After you understand the process and reasoning behind a calculation, it will be easy to pick up any tool of your choice.

Keywords are styled in *italics*. Key concepts are presented in rectangle box or underlined to help with quick discovery. All statistical formulae are presented using consistent symbols across the book. Please be aware that other books or materials might use slightly different symbols for different purposes.

Finally, this book is written in Australian English, which means you will see *optimise* instead of *optimize*, *colour* instead of *color*, *centre* instead of *center* and so on. However, one exception is given for the term *Analyze phase* as one of the phases of DMAIC. Since this term represents a phase name of a globally recognised methodology, it will be written in its original form using US English.

02. UNDERSTANDING QUALITY

Suppose there are 2 restaurants in a neighbourhood: Restaurant A and B. Restaurant A offers only 8 choices of dish in their menu. The food always arrives fast after a customer's order. The taste of their cooking is slightly above average, but the taste they produce for all customers at any time is quite consistent. Restaurant B offers 58 choices in their menu, but it usually takes longer for the food to arrive. When certain chef is on duty in Restaurant B, the food quality is top notch. However, they have 3 different chefs and the other 2 often produced overcooked protein or soggy salad.

Bob is a famous food critic. One day, Bob visited both Restaurant A and Restaurant B. At the time of Bob's visit, the good chef is on duty at Restaurant B, so Bob is very impressed with the food he eats. In his review, Bob writes big praises for Restaurant B, and not so much for Restaurant A.

Jane and Sam walk around Restaurant A and B after a business meeting with their company's partner. Sam showed Jane the food magazine he just bought with great article on Restaurant B from a famous food critic. Jane, a Six Sigma Black Belt, observes both restaurants and realises that Restaurant A is full of customers despite having average review from the food critic, while there are only a few customers in Restaurant B.

Things become clearer when Jane and Sam decide to get takeaway food from both restaurants. The food from Restaurant B is overcooked and under-seasoned, making the food from Restaurant A tastes so much better by comparison.

Jane explains to Sam that Restaurant A is more successful in maintaining the consistency of their products. Restaurant B, while having an exceptional chef, is unable to consistency reproduce the food quality because their other chefs are not as capable. Restaurant A also does better with the shorter waiting time because they choose to offer 8 menu choices, allowing their kitchen to work faster and more efficient. From Six Sigma perspective, Restaurant A produces smaller variation in their cooking, so that customers know they can always expect certain level of quality. From Lean perspective, faster cooking time means they are better in optimising their processes in the kitchen, pulled by customer demands.

The vast majority of businesses earn their income from producing certain number of products or services regularly to customers. Quality as perceived by customers is not simply defined by their best ever unit of products. One excellent unit means very little to a brand's reputation if customers could not expect to get product or service at the same quality level with every purchase.

There are many different ways to measure quality. A researcher could conduct a survey to all customers visiting Restaurant A and B in a particular day and ask them to rate the food in the scale of 1 to 10, then calculate the average score. A question might be raised that the scores of customers buying different menu are not actually comparable. This is called sampling problem.

Calculating average is not always the best way to measure quality. In fact, it rarely is. For example, Restaurant A gets scores of 6, 7, 7 and 6 from 4 customers; Restaurant B gets 4, 9, 3, 10 scores. They have the same average of 6.5, but looking at the number, it is clearly shown that Restaurant B has significantly higher variation in their scores because of cooking inconsistencies. A measure of standard deviation will give value of 0.5 for Restaurant A and value 3.04 for Restaurant B, quantitatively showing the measurement of inconsistencies from both restaurants.

Kano Model

Let us start the journey to understand quality by studying a very useful tool called Kano Model. This tool was published in 1984 by Dr. Noriaki Kano from Tokyo University of Science.

According to Kano Model, there are 5 categories of customer preference attributes:
- *Essentials*: attributes that must exist in a product or service
- *Dissatisfiers*: attributes that must not exist in a product or service.
- *Satisfiers*: reasonable expectations of performing features.

- *Delighters*: unexpected quality factor that will delight customer when they find it.
- *Indifferent*: features that are neither good nor bad, has no impact to customer's satisfaction.

Essentials are also known as basic quality attributes. The absence of essential attributes will make customers feel dissatisfied, but the presence of these will not bring satisfaction. In the prior example of restaurant quality, one essential attribute would be *properly cooked protein*. If a customer's order arrives with overcooked protein, customer will feel dissatisfied. However, receiving food that is not overcooked does not automatically bring satisfaction because it is perceived as the minimum standard of quality by the customer.

Dissatisfiers are the opposite of essentials. They are known as reverse quality, attributes that are not supposed to exist in a product or service. If a customer finds it, he will be dissatisfied. Yet the absence of it will not bring satisfaction. An example of this attribute is pieces of broken cooking utensil in the food served to customer.

Satisfiers are quality attributes considered as reasonable expectations by the customers. The presence of these factors will bring customer's satisfaction. For example, well-seasoned protein with delicious sauce will make a customer happy.

Delighters are positive surprise factors, things that customers do not expect but will bring them delight if they get it from a product or service. The absence of these attributes will not bring down the satisfaction level. A regular customer comes in, orders some food, then gets a slice of cake as bonus because the restaurant manager knows it is the customer's birthday. This will bring delight, making the customer more than satisfied and will increase loyalty.

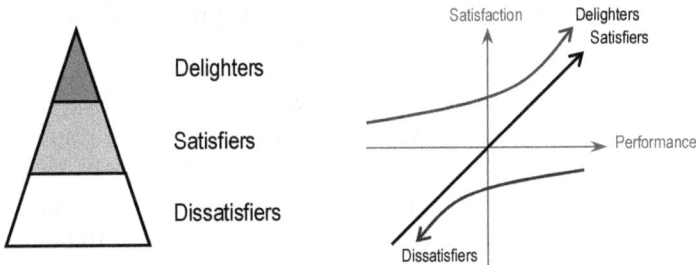

Figure 02-1 Kano Model

Higher level of attribute factors will be rendered ineffective (or at least less effective) if the level below is not met. For example, well-seasoned protein (satisfier attribute) will not be effective to bring satisfaction if the food is overcooked (essential attribute is not met).

Customers' expectations of a family restaurant will be fairly different from customers of a fine dining restaurant with Michelin-star. What customers expect from a restaurant back in 1950s are very different from the expectations in the year 2020. It is very important for any business to know their own customers in order to offer the kind of products and services that customers are willing to pay for.

Voice of the Customer (VOC) and Critical to Quality (CTQ)

To achieve success, a business needs to know what its customers want. Without customers, there will be no demand, there will be no profit to make and there will be no business.

A customer might walk into a restaurant with a requirement that he wishes to eat food that does not contain certain allergen (such as eggs or peanuts). This is an example of *Voice of the Customer*, often referred as VOC.

In everyday cases, requirement from one customer does not necessarily represent what is desired by the majority of other customers. Hence the study of Voice of the Customer is an in-depth process of capturing customer's expectations, preferences, experiences and aversions. Depending on the industry, business might choose to focus on the requirements that represent the majority, or they might opt to cater to individual requests.

Knowing what customers want is only one side of the equation. The other side is to know how much customers are willing to pay for a particular product or service. This is particularly important when designing new products or services. If this price that customers are willing to pay is under a limit that is profitable for a company, it is wise not to offer the product/service in the first place.

In 2001, a company launched a product of two-wheeled personal transportation device called Segway. The product looks like something that came out from a science fiction movie and naturally it became hot conversation topic for a while. People were curious, people admired the product. The founders predicted that the company would sell 10,000 units per week, yet it only managed to sell 10,000 units within its first two years. The reality was roughly 1% from the business prediction.

Admiring a product does not equal to wanting the product. Wanting the product does not equal to willingness to pay a product's asking price. One unit of Segway was priced at $5,000 in its early days, then it went down to $4,000 later. Even the reduced price is still way beyond what average people can save in a few months. Most people would decide to spend that money on products that they *need* instead of what they *want*. Another factor is the concerns around the product's safety, but that is an entirely different topic.

There are many possible methods to capture VOC. A company can conduct surveys, interviews, focus groups or dedicated team for continuous market research.

Surveys are useful when there are reasonably big number of customers and they might have wide variety of views. Well-executed survey could be a powerful tool to gather as-is conditions and the underlying drivers. It is usually not possible to gather survey responses from all customers. Gathering responses from a subset of customers chosen through a sampling method could produce results with certain degree of statistical confidence without spending too much time and cost.

Interviews can be used to gather deeper insights at the cost of more time and effort per respondent when compared to surveys. An individual interview focuses on one interviewer and one respondent at each time. Panel interview involves multiple individuals from different roles in a company and one interviewee. Group interview involves multiple respondents at the same time, usually to save time. Sometimes, observing respondents' reaction during group interview could lead to valuable information beyond the interview questions.

Focus group is used to obtain even deeper analysis of customers' thoughts and expectations. A session of focus group is normally attended by 5 to 15 customers along with small number of management representatives including front-line people who deal directly with customers. Focus group session is moderated, possibly with some visualised data for reference, and generally should take up to 3 hours. This technique can be beneficial if there is certain degree of confidence that invited customers are either having strong influence on other customers or they really represent the general population of all customers.

After properly obtaining what customers really want and willing to pay for, the next step is to translate it into a different form called *Critical to Quality* (CTQ).

VOC is written using the language of customers, often they are not directly measurable. CTQ is written using business process' point of view. CTQ translates VOC into specific and measurable requirements that can be used in process analysis to determine whether customers' requirements have been fulfilled.

For example, VOC of [no egg allergen in my food] from a restaurant customer can be translated into multiple CTQs:

- No egg ingredients for this specific customer.
- No cross-contamination from cooking process.
- No cross-contamination from plating and handling processes.

CTQ can be defined as attributes of a process to make products or services that has direct and significant impact to quality, both actual and as perceived by customers. It drives the efforts of achieving a product or service that can satisfy (and hopefully delight) customers.

In Lean Six Sigma study, the definition of supplier and customer are expanded beyond the traditional understanding. Every process is seen as requiring inputs and producing outputs. The business process in a company might have several sub-processes with one's output becomes the input of another. For each process, any entity that provides the input is called the process' supplier. Any entity that receives the output is called customer.

Using the expanded definition, we now have 2 types of customers: external and internal. *External customers* are customers in traditional sense, they are entities outside a business that pays money to obtain product or service. *Internal customers* are any entity within an organisation that receives the output from any sub-process.

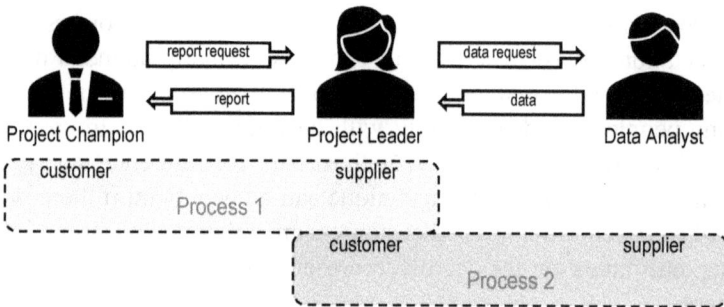

Figure 02-2 Supplier and customer in a process

A *project champion* (senior executive) requests a report from project leader. *Project leader* assigns *data analyst* to produce the (raw) data for the report and then transforms the data into presentable report for *project champion*. *Project leader* is a customer to *data analyst*; therefore, *data analyst* needs to capture what is needed by *project leader* (internal VOC) and make it into technical request (internal CTQ) to ensure the correct data is produced. Similarly, *project champion* is a customer to *project leader*, and thus the process to transform internal VOC into internal CTQ is critical to ensure good quality of report.

Other than VOC, a Six Sigma practitioner needs to understand about *Voice of the Business* (VOB). As the name indicates, VOB captures the stated and unstated needs of the company, shareholders, business owners. Common forms of VOB are financial data, company profits, operational costs, viability of business, brand power and customer loyalty. In ideal situation, VOB should be in line with VOC. However, some conflicts between VOC and VOC might arise because of pricing decision, difference views in quality requirements, inaccurate forecasts or competitions from other businesses.

Cost of Poor Quality (COPQ)

A manufacturing company realises that they receive a lot of complaints from their customers because their products failed to meet the qualification standards. To address this problem, a senior director established a new division to check product quality before shipment to customers. Defective items are classified into two categories. If they can be improved, items will be sent back for rework. Otherwise, they are put in scrap category.

After implementing the quality control division, customer complaint decreases. However, when analysing the annual cost report, the senior director realises that the cost of improving product quality adds more than 20% of their production cost.

The above description is a classic example of *Cost of Poor Quality*, commonly shortened as COPQ. When a production system fails to meet quality standard at the first attempt, it incurs additional costs. A rework wastes time and efforts for the fix. A scrap wastes the entire cost of materials, time and efforts to make the defective item.

There are two types of COPQ: visible and hidden. *Visible COPQ* are costs that are easily measurable, usually through loss of sales, defective items and inefficient process. *Hidden COPQ* are things that are not directly associated to cost or company spending, but they contribute to negative impacts to the business.

Visible COPQ can be classified as:
- *Internal failure cost*. This happens when defective units are identified by a process before reaching customers. Defective units could cause

rework (fixable) or scrap (not fixable), both will incur costs that can be avoided if the process could produce non-defective items in the first go.

- *External failure cost.* This happens when defective units have reached the customers and returned through warranty claims.
- *Appraisal cost.* This is the cost to ensure that every item meets requirements standard before reaching customer. Common methods of appraisal include quality inspections or audits.

Having low number of warranty claims from customers do not necessarily indicate well performing process. If many defective units are regularly found during quality check, large number of scrap and rework will drive up the production cost.

Hidden costs of poor quality do not directly associate with certain spending. Examples of hidden costs are lost customer loyalty, longer production time, cost of downtime and so on.

The opposite of COPQ is *Cost of Quality* (COQ). As the name suggests, COPQ is the cost of producing good quality products or services. There are two components of COQ:

- *Production cost.* This is the normal production cost without considering quality.
- *Prevention cost.* This is the cost for efforts to prevent poor quality from happening.

Instead of spending more after a defective item is made, prevention efforts are focused to prevent or minimise defects during the first attempt of production. Any spending on prevention will reduce the cost on failures, both internal and external. Failure costs should get closer to zero when a process generates 100% non-defective products.

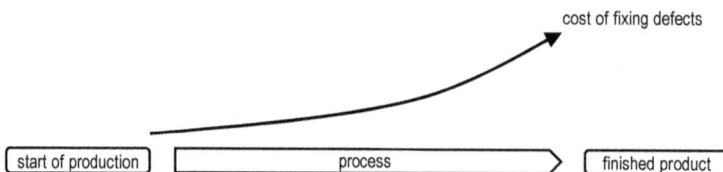

Figure 02-3 Cost of fixing defects

A simplified process illustration uses a straight horizontal line where the left-side end represents the start of production and the right-side end represents completed product. A defect could be identified at any point in the horizontal line. The cost incurred by the defect will get higher as the production process moves to the right. This means, the sooner a defect is caught, the less cost it is going to incur.

The most effective way to reduce failure cost is by assuring quality at every point where work is performed so that no defect passes downstream. This concept is known as *quality at the source*, which will be discussed in later chapters about Lean.

03. SIX SIGMA PRINCIPLES

In Six Sigma, quality is measured by how well a process is able to consistently produce outputs that meet requirements. There are two key words in this statement: *consistent* and *meet requirements*. It is important for a product or service to be good, yet it is equally important that a process is able to produce such goodness consistently.

Six Sigma process improvement aims to improve a process so that it is capable to produce outputs that meets specifications with minimum variation. The goal of Six Sigma effort is to minimise variations down to an acceptable level. A process is said to have six sigma capability level when it produces no more than 3.4 defect parts (non-conforming feature) for every million opportunities.

As a philosophy, Six Sigma strives for perfection by being proactive. It focuses on preventing defects instead of detecting it after production. As a performance matrix, Six Sigma measures the capability of a process to stay within customer specifications with minimum variation. As a methodology, Six Sigma offers *DMAIC* (*Define, Measure, Analyze, Improve, Control*) methodology for process improvement and *DMADV* (*Define, Measure, Analyze, Design, Verify*) methodology for designing new process, product or service.

Brief History of Process Improvement

The long history of process improvement started back in the late 1800s when *Eli Whitney* promoted the feasibility of making interchangeable parts. In 1910, *Henry Ford* invented assembly line standard production flow in car

17

manufacturing. This invention revolutionised the automotive industry and reshaped many other industries with mass production.

In 1896, *Sakichi Toyoda* invented the principles of *Jidoka*, loosely translated as intelligent automation for his textile business. His son, *Kiichiro Toyoda* introduced flow production method using chain conveyors (1927). Kiichiro is the founder of Toyota Motor Corporation, and who changed the focus of textile business started by his father into automobiles production. Kiichiro's concepts on automation and eliminating production waste would later become the foundations of *Just-In-Time* (*JIT*) manufacturing. JIT is the pillar of Toyota production, revived and developed by *Taiichi Ohno* in 1950.

Water Shewhart developed *PDCA* cycle in 1931. He also introduced statistical process control and control charts. PDCA cycle starts with *Plan* phase to identify opportunities and plan for change, *Do* phase to implement on small scale, *Check* phase to use data to analyse the results and *Act* phase to implement the change on wider scale.

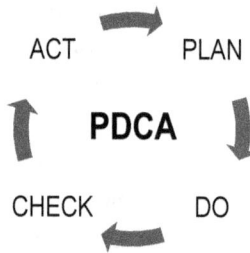

ACT → PLAN

↑ **PDCA** ↓

CHECK ← DO

Figure 03-1 PDCA cycle

Philip Crosby started zero defects concept in 1957, then *Armand Feigenbaum* started the concept of Total Quality Control (TQC) in 1961. *Joseph Juran* developed managerial processes called Juran Quality Trilogy (planning, control, improvement). This trilogy coined the idea of continuous process improvement.

Kaoru Ishikawa (1985) developed *cause-and-effect* diagram, known as Ishikawa diagram or fish diagram. His other contribution was the concept of CWQC (Company Wide Quality Control). This management philosophy seeks continuous improvement in the quality of performance of all the processes within a company.

Edward Demings (1986) introduced a list of 14 points of improvement steps focused on change in management attitude. Those 14 points are: demonstrate commitment, learn new philosophy, understand inspection, stop making decisions, improve constantly, institute training, institute leadership, drive out fear, optimise the efforts, eliminate exhortations, enumerate business objectives, remove barriers, encourage education and take action.

Bill Smith (Motorola, 1987) introduced the term *Six Sigma* to indicate performance measures. He is credited as the father of Six Sigma and the co-founder of Six Sigma along with Mikel Harry who formulated the Measure, Analyze, Improve and Control approach to achieve Six Sigma level of quality. Later on, General Electric (GE) added the Define phase into the methodology, making it *DMAIC*.

The term Lean was created by *James Womack* in 1990. Back to the beginning of the twentieth century, the inventions of Henry Ford and Eli Whitney were considered to pioneer some early ideas of Lean. Even though several aspects of Lean have been introduced since Jidoka and JIT, the term Lean manufacturing and the formal definition of Lean principles was published in 1991 by *James Womack, Daniel Jones* and *Daniel Roos*.

In 1995, *Jack Welch* from General Electric adopted Six Sigma, making it as the central focus of his business strategy. During his time as CEO, the company's revenue increased fivefold to reach $130 billion.

Throughout its history, Six Sigma has demonstrated massive power in improving the quality of mass production, together with the integration of Lean principles to help Six Sigma to cover more areas of improvement. In 2000, a group of 14 developers produced the *Agile Manifesto*, starting the new concept of Agile. This new idea answers new challenges of a dynamic market in many industries. Agile picked up steam and went mainstream in the 2010s, and still evolves today. There is no reason that Lean Six Sigma and Agile could not co-exist together. In fact, some of their principles complement each other, allowing improvements to be achieved across different kinds of challenges.

Process Variation

Have you ever tried to compare two cupcakes of the same flavour bought at the same day from the same café? Even though they are offered as the same products, putting them on a kitchen scale will mostly reveal slight difference in weight between the two. If the cupcakes come with sprinkles, very likely that they would not have the exact number of sprinkles. That is a simple example of variation. Does that make us upset as customer? Most people would say no because minor differences in cupcakes are within our reasonable expectation as customer.

It is considered as common sense that no two cupcakes would be exactly identical down to the smallest detail. However, most people assume and expect that products manufactured by machines are precisely identical. In reality, they are not. The variations might be too small for human eyes to distinguish and they may or may not impact the functionalities of the product.

Variations can be caused by random causes or special causes. Metal expands when heated, so the temperature might affect a unit's exact measurement, this is an example of random cause (also known as common cause). As long as the variation is still within tolerance, random variation is generally accepted as part of normal process execution. Error in machine calibration or extreme temperature that is not expected in normal range are examples of special cause of variation.

Total elimination of variation is theoretically not possible. However, efforts of process improvement are focused to bring down variation as low as possible to an acceptable level.

A process is classified as stable if such process is able to produce predictable performance that meets certain criteria, such as average of certain output dimension. It must remain stable over time and consistently achieving targets.

Normal Distribution

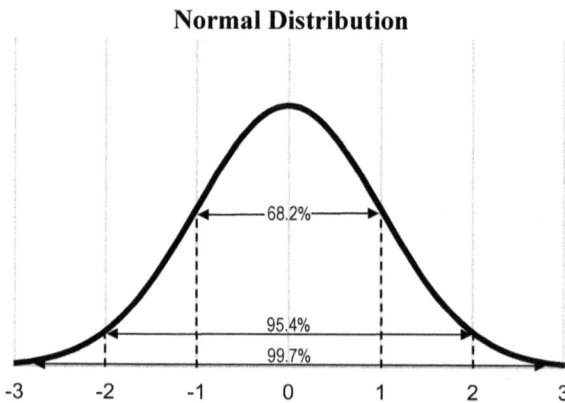

Figure 03-2 Normal Distribution Curve

Process variation in Six Sigma is measured using descriptive statistics of *average* and *standard deviation*. Dataset with Normal Distribution (see Figure 03-2) has the following characteristics:

- 68.2% of data points are within one standard deviation from average.
- 95.4% of data points are within two standard deviations from average.
- 99.7% of data points are within three standard deviations from average.

If the specification limits of a system are located at the points of plus and minus three standard deviations from average, it means that 99.7% of data are considered good and the remaining 0.3% will not meet specifications (see Figure 03-3). Such process is called a 3σ (Three Sigma) process because standard deviation is commonly represented with σ (sigma) symbol.

Lower Specification Limit   Upper Specification Limit

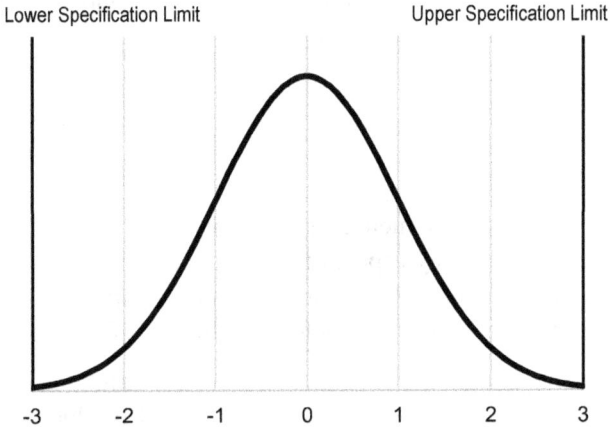

-3   -2   -1   0   1   2   3

Figure 03-3 Three Sigma process variation

Lower Specification Limit   Upper Specification Limit

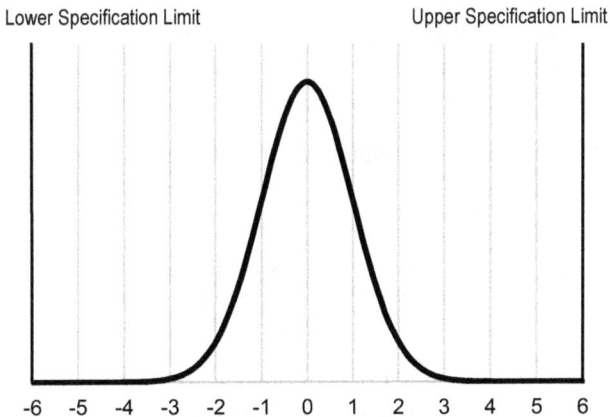

-6   -5   -4   -3   -2   -1   0   1   2   3   4   5   6

Figure 03-4 Six Sigma process variation

Process is said to achieve 6σ (Six Sigma) level if variations as large as ± 6 times of standard deviation are still within the specification limits of expected output. To put in simple numbers, if a cutting process needs to produce 3 metres cable and the specification limits are between 2.994 to 3.006 metres, it means a process needs to have average production of 3 metres and maximum standard deviation of 0.001 metre. If standard deviation is greater than 0.001, 6 times standard deviation plus and minus average would fall outside the specification limits and the process would not qualify as Six Sigma level. Standard deviation commonly uses sigma symbol in statistics, this is how the term Six Sigma came from.

Staying within specification limit does not always guarantee customer satisfaction. According to *Dr. Genichi Taguchi*, any variation from the expected result already causes gradual customer dissatisfaction following exponential increase. This theory is commonly known as *Taguchi Loss function*.

Six Sigma Metrics

Measurements of Six Sigma metrics use the concepts of defect, defective and good output. A *defect* is any aspect of a product or service that fails to meet specifications' requirement. One particular unit of product or service is *defective* if it contains one or more defects. Otherwise, it is a *good output*.

In some practical situations, a production system might implement more complex decisions to determine whether one unit of product is defective or not. For example, defects might be categorised as hard defect and soft defect. One single *hard defect* makes a unit immediately classifies as defective, but a unit might be allowed to have up to n *soft defects* before it gets classified as defective. Unless when stated otherwise, this book assumes all defects are hard defects and therefore a unit with one defect is considered as defective.

Defects Per Unit is defined as total number of defects found in specific dataset divided by the number of units. This measurement is commonly known as DPU.

$$DPU = \frac{total\ number\ of\ defects}{total\ number\ of\ units}$$

Defects Per Opportunities (DPO) is defined as total number of defects found in specific dataset divided by total number of defect opportunities.

$$DPO = \frac{total\ number\ of\ defects}{total\ number\ of\ defect\ opportunities}$$

Defects Per Million Opportunities (DPMO) is defined as total number of defects units found in specific dataset divided by total number of defect opportunities multiplied by one million. It is basically DPO times one million. DPMO is one of the key measurements used in Six Sigma.

$$DPMO = \frac{total\ number\ of\ defects}{total\ number\ of\ defect\ opportunities} \times 1{,}000{,}000$$

Parts Per Million Defective (PPM) is defined as total number of defective units found in specific dataset divided by the number of units. This measurement is used when the number of defective products is small.

$$PPM = \frac{total\ number\ of\ defective\ units}{total\ number\ of\ units} \times 1{,}000{,}000$$

Suppose a production system is manufacturing dice. A dice has six sides of equal size and each of them has to be marked with one to six dots. There are 8 *defect opportunities* identified for one unit of dice:
- Side 1 is not properly marked with one dot.
- Side 2 is not properly marked with two dots.
- Side 3 is not properly marked with three dots.
- Side 4 is not properly marked with four dots.
- Side 5 is not properly marked with five dots.
- Side 6 is not properly marked with six dots.
- The size of the dice is bigger or smaller than specification limits.
- The weight of the dice is higher or lower than specification limits.

Production results of a certain hour is described as follows:
- 475 units of dice has no defect.
- 5 units of dice has 3 sides incorrectly marked (3 defects).
- 5 units of dice has 2 sides incorrectly marked (2 defects).
- 10 units of dice has 1 side incorrectly marked (1 defect).
- 2 units of dice has 1 side incorrectly marked, the size is too big, and the weight is too heavy (3 defects).
- 3 units of dice are lighter than weight specification limit (1 defect).

Total number of units in this sample is 500, with 25 of them defective. The total number of defects is 44. Each unit has 8 defect opportunities, so 500 units have $8 \times 500 = 4{,}000$ defect opportunities. Using these numbers, we can calculate:

$$DPU = \frac{44}{500} = 0.088$$

$$DPO = \frac{44}{4000} = 0.011$$

$$DPMO = \frac{44}{4000} \times 1,000,000 = 11,000$$

$$PPM = \frac{25}{500} \times 1,000,000 = 50,000$$

One defective unit might have one or multiple defects. To measure process performance, using the number of defects will give more accurate indications compared to the number of defective units. Even though a defective unit with one defect and another unit with ten defects might end up to the same pile of scrap, ten defects show more variations compared to one defect. This is the reason why DPMO is the metric commonly associated with the calculation of Six Sigma level of system capability.

Sigma Level and DPMO

Sigma level has direct correlation with the expected DPMO of a process. When a process performance is measured right after the completion of Six Sigma project, the standard deviation value is the result of a system that has been controlled recently. Such performance is called *short-term performance* and usually will not stay the same in the long run.

Even though a process performs very stable under observation, changing environmental conditions and other common factors will increase standard deviation of a process in the long run, reducing sigma level by 1.5. This is commonly referred to as *sigma shift*. The new sigma level is called the *long-term performance*.

$$\sigma_{lt} = \sigma_{st} - 1.5$$

Six Sigma project aims to reach 6σ during project execution because the expected *long-term performance* is actually 4.5σ. Sigma levels normally listed in DPMO tables are sigma level of short-term performance, but the actual correlation happens between DPMO and Sigma Level of long-term performance.

The calculation of expected DPMO from sigma level can be performed quickly using NORM.S.DIST function in Excel 2010 or newer. The *true* parameter is to tell the function to calculate normal cumulative distribution instead of normal density.

$$DPO = (1 - NORM.S.DIST(\sigma_{lt}, TRUE))$$

$$DPMO = (1 - NORM.S.DIST(\sigma_{lt}, TRUE)) * 1000000$$

The following table shows sigma levels and the expected DPMO:

Sigma Level (short-term)	Sigma Level (long-term)	DPMO	% Good
0.0	−1.5	933,193	6.6807201%
0.5	−1.0	841,345	15.8655254%
1.0	−0.5	691,462	30.8537539%
1.5	0.0	500,000	50.0000000%
2.0	0.5	308,538	69.1462461%
2.5	1.0	158,655	84.1344746%
3.0	1.5	66,807	93.3192799%
3.5	2.0	22,750	97.7249868%
4.0	2.5	6,210	99.3790335%
4.5	3.0	1,350	99.8650102%
5.0	3.5	233	99.9767371%
5.5	4.0	32	99.9968329%
6.0	4.5	3.4	99.9996602%
6.5	5.0	0.29	99.9999713%
7.0	5.5	0.02	99.9999981%
7.5	6.0	0.001	99.9999999%

If DPMO is known, sigma level can be calculated using NORMSINV function in Excel.

$$\sigma_{lt} = (NORMSINV(1 - DPMO/1000000))$$

Many companies operate with process performance between 3σ to 4σ. A process is said to have achieved 6σ (Six Sigma) level if it produces no more than 3.4 DPMO. To put in perspective, improving process performance from 3σ to 6σ is equal to reducing defects (per million opportunities) from 66,807 to 3.4. That is a very significant difference.

DMAIC

DMAIC is the term used to describe the Six Sigma process improvement methodology. Each letter represents one phase in the methodology: *Define, Measure, Analyze, Improve* and *Control*.

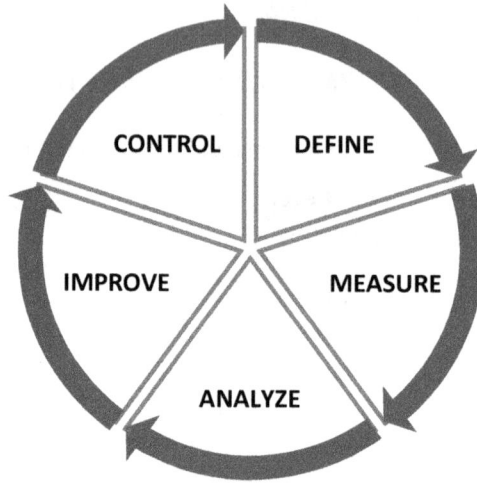

Figure 03-5 DMAIC methodology

Define phase is the first phase of Six Sigma process improvement project. The focus of this phase is to prepare and finalise Project Charter, which contains project name, description, business case, measurable objectives, scope and key milestones.

Measure phase focuses on collecting data to enable data-driven analysis in all subsequent phases. Before data is collected, it is important to conduct Measurement System Analysis (MSA) to make sure that the measurements used to collect data are accurate and precise. Trustable data is the fundamental condition to perform statistical analysis. No useful conclusion can be reached using wrong data. Garbage in, garbage out.

Analyze phase uses data collected from previous phase to come up with a list of factors impacting the result of a measurement that needs to be improved. Hypothesis testing is used to perform statistical analysis in this phase.

Improve phase takes on the factors discovered in prior phase and work to find the best values of those factors to reach the optimised result of the goal parameter as specified in project charter. Several techniques from DOE (Design of Experiments) are used depending on the case. After finding solution, pilot implementation is performed to validate the solution and identify implementation risks.

Control phase involves the creation of control plan and response plan, followed by full-scale implementation. Using control plan, relevant stakeholders will be able to monitor if the process is running in control and when to step in with response plan if special variation is detected.

The first two phases of Define and Measure focus on *problem definition*. Analyze phase uses *statistical analysis* to answer hypothesis questions. Improve and Control phases work on *problem solution*.

Y = f (X)

Six Sigma process improvement is about improving process so that its results are centred (or near centred) around specification limits and the variations (measured using standard deviation) are controlled to stay as minimum as possible. The result parameter for this improvement is called Y, also known as the dependent factor. The independent factors in a process that affect the outcome are referred to as X. Both X and Y must be measurable or countable. Six Sigma principles could not improve things that cannot be measured nor counted.

Six Sigma formula takes the form of $Y = f(X)$. It basically states that Y is the result of a function of X. There could be multiple X factors affecting the same Y variables, more about this will be discussed in later parts of this book.

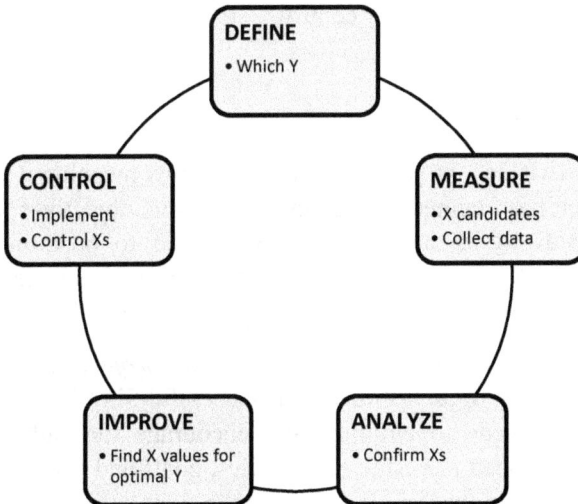

Figure 03-6 $Y = f(X)$ in DMAIC phases

Using $Y = f(X)$ formula, Six Sigma process improvement tries to explain how the process inputs and controls (independent X factors) interact and how they can be used to predict the outcome of Y. Understanding the correlation between Y and Xs opens the possibility of process tuning to increase process capability.

Outcome Y is often called *dependent variable* or *criterion* because its value depends on the combination values of Xs. Input X is often called *independent variables* or *independent factors* or *predictor* because its values help to predict the result of Y.

Phases of DMAIC:

- *Define phase*: Six Sigma project defines which Y outputs need to be improved.
- *Measure phase*: At this point Six Sigma project team does not know yet which X factors are actually impactful for Y. Some decision-making tools can be used to shortlist the possible Xs. Collect data of X candidates and Y from existing process. Use this data to confirm the Y.
- *Analyze phase*: Analyse the data collected in prior phase. Confirm which Xs are proven to have significant impact on Y. Obtain some understanding about the f formula.
- *Improve phase*: Calculate and confirm f formula. Generate potential solutions (values of Xs to optimise Y). Choose best solution and implement pilot test to confirm.
- *Control phase*: Implement the solution. Establish Control Plan to ensure that Xs stay under control.

Six Sigma Roles

Six Sigma DMAIC is a project-based methodology, meaning it has clear start and end date, it has planned budget and measurable objectives, it has project team that needs to be managed and supported to perform the process improvement work effectively. A Six Sigma project is managed by a project leader, under the guidance and support of project champion.

From the top, every Six Sigma project needs *project sponsor* from top executives within an organisation. For a successful Six Sigma improvement, project sponsor needs to embrace and encourage the right mindset and behaviours. They need to ensure that metrics, goals and rewards are aligned. They need to confirm that employees have the right level of skills.

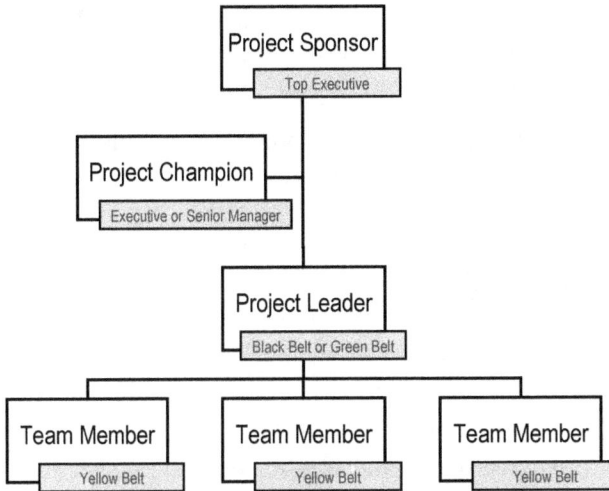

Figure 03-7 Six Sigma roles

Project sponsor views Six Sigma projects as means to achieve specific goals. When multiple potential projects are in the pipeline, project sponsor establishes selection criteria to evaluate and select proposed projects. After project is selected, project sponsor assigns project champion for the project and continuously provide resources as needed.

Project champion is management team's point person for a particular Six Sigma project. To increase the chance of success, project champion needs to be someone from executive or senior manager level with enough power and respect to ensure progress and remove impediments.

Process owners or *subject matter experts* (SME) are key stakeholders from the management of operations that carry out the process to be improved. They hold critical part in Six Sigma project to make sure that process changes are implemented properly, and process control is followed to sustain the improvements.

There are four skill levels of Six Sigma practitioners: Yellow Belt, Green Belt, Black Belt and Master Black Belt. *Yellow Belt* level is generally needed for the team members of Six Sigma project. By achieving Yellow Belt, a team member demonstrates that s/he is aware of Six Sigma concepts to perform his/her specific tasks within the team effectively.

Green Belt practitioner possesses sufficient skills and knowledge to use Six Sigma processes and tools. Someone from Green Belt level usually perform part-time leadership of Six Sigma projects.

Black Belt practitioner is considered as Subject Matter Expert for all Six Sigma processes and tools. S/he carries out the role of full-time leadership of multiple Six Sigma projects.

Project leader of a Six Sigma project could be a practitioner with Green Belt or Black Belt qualification. Generally Black Belts are assigned more projects with higher complexity compared to Green Belts. By doing full-time work, Black Belt focuses only on Six Sigma projects as the main priority of his/her work role. Green Belt usually takes on Six Sigma responsibilities on part-time basis, meaning s/he has other responsibilities related to his/her main skills in the cross-functional team. Throughout this book, the term *Belt* is used to refer to project leader with Green Belt or Black Belt qualification.

Master Black Belt is the highest level of skill in Six Sigma. Someone with this qualification usually takes on the role to train and coach Black Belts and Green Belts. If an organisation regularly has multiple Six Sigma projects running in parallel, Master Black Belt could perform the role to administer Six Sigma program. If really needed, Master Black Belt can directly lead a complex Six Sigma project with high impact to the organisation.

Coaching stakeholders is another responsibility of Master Black Belt. If there is no Master Black Belt within an organisation, Black Belt holding the role of project leader might perform coaching tasks.

Stakeholders are usually more interested about the business or operational impacts from a Six Sigma project rather than the details of Six Sigma tools used in the project. Six Sigma coach needs to bring stakeholders as part of the journey, ensuring they understand about the adaptive characteristics of Six Sigma project and relate key steps and key decisions to operational impacts. Stakeholders need to understand the basic concepts of data-based decision-making and its powerful potential.

The process of coaching stakeholders can be performed during individual interactions or in a formal setting of *gate review*. In Six Sigma project, gate review is a combination of status review, risk reporting, plan approval and alignment discussion. Start each session by explaining the focus and goals to be achieved within this phase.

04. LEAN PRINCIPLES

Lean is the removal of waste. The basic idea of Lean is to deliver only what is needed at the right time without anything extra. It aims to achieve near-perfect process with continuous improvement mindset.

There are five principles of Lean: *define value*, *map value stream*, *create flow*, *establish pull* and *seek perfection*.

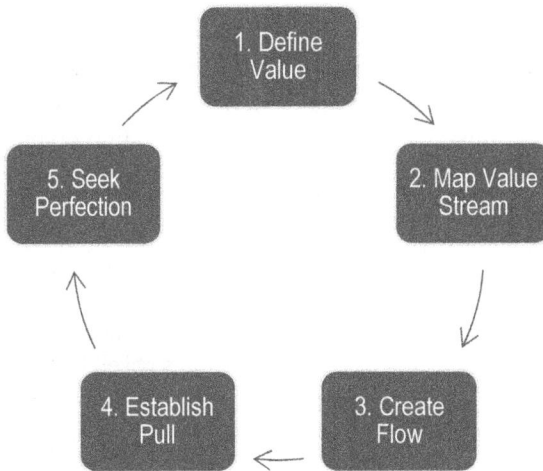

Figure 04-1 Five principles of Lean

Value is anything that customers are willing to pay for. The first principle (***define value***) is achieved by obtaining Voice of the Customer (VOC) through various methods such as surveys, interviews or focus group.

Second principle (*map value stream*) uses the VOC as reference point and identify all activities that contributes to creation of those values. Activities that do not add value nor needed to enable value are considered as waste and needs to be eliminated.

After all process waste are eliminated, the third principle (*create flow*) analyses the flow of the remaining activities to see if there are any factors of inefficiencies, such as delays or obstacles.

According to *Eliyahu Goldratt's theory of constraint*, the output of a value stream is only as fast as the slowest processing step, known as bottleneck or constraint. Increasing flow means addressing each point of bottleneck until it performs as fast as other steps in the value stream.

Inventory is considered as waste with one of the largest costs in most production systems. Once process has a good flow, the next principle is to *establish pull*. Customer demand pulls the order, product or transaction flows throughout the value stream from suppliers to customers with minimum possible inventory. Lean also aims to minimise *Work In Progress* (WIP), defined as all parts of unfinished product still in production process or waiting to be processed. By minimising inventory and WIP, Lean principle enables *Just-In-Time* (JIT) flow for a value stream, a condition where product or service is processed, created and delivered just as they are needed at the rate of customer demand.

The last principle (*seek perfection*) is considered as the most important of all. Even though Lean tries to reach near-perfect system, it believes that there is always something more to improve. Lean organisation embraces continuous improvement as integral part of its culture.

Cycle Time, Lead Time and Takt Time

To achieve the five principles of Lean, a process needs to have optimised workflow capable to process products or services based on pull from customer demand. Lean uses three measurements for workflow optimisation: *cycle time*, *lead time* and *takt time*.

Cycle time is the time needed to complete the production of a single count of product or service from start to finish. This measurement is defined as the length of production time divided by the number of items completed. If a manufacturing process is capable to finish 300 bolts every minute (*production rate*), the cycle time of such process is 60 seconds divided by 300 units of bolt = 0.2 seconds. Production of one unit of bolt takes 0.2 seconds of Cycle Time.

Lead time is the time needed to complete production of a single count of product or service from the time of customer demand until the product or service reaches the customer. Different from cycle time which focuses only on the production time, lead time takes into account the administrative steps, waiting time and fulfilment steps for the product or service to reach the customer.

Takt time is the time needed to satisfy the rate of customer demand, also known as the pull. A restaurant manager counted that there are 20 customers in one hour (*takt rate*). Takt time is 60 minutes divided by 20 customer = 3 minutes per customer.

Still referring to the example from takt time, the head chef said that kitchen has the ability to serve 30 customers in one hour. This means the cycle time is 60 minutes divided by 30 customers = 2 minutes per customer. It seems that the restaurant is doing alright to meet customer demand. Further observations reveal that it takes 1 minute for an order to be typed into the point of sales system, 75 seconds for the order to reach the kitchen and another minute for the waiter to serve the food. The restaurant's cycle time is able to meet demand, but the lead time is longer than takt time. This is not an ideal situation from Lean perspective and can be improved by optimising the ordering system.

Elements of Waste

Lean technique focuses on identifying activities within a process and classify them into value-added, non-value-added and enabler activities. An activity is *value-added* if it changes the form, state or function of a product or service in such a way that customer is willing to pay for it. An *enabler* is an activity that does not directly adds value, but it is required for another activity that adds value.

In a restaurant, a certain ingredient is stored in special room far from the kitchen. 60% of the menu uses this ingredient and members of kitchen team have to walk to the special room to obtain this ingredient at least 10 times a day. It takes around 12 minutes to walk there and another 12 minutes to return to the kitchen. The 24-minutes activity of walking is an example of *non-value-added* activity because it does not add any value to the customers. It can be avoided if the restaurant could renovate an empty room next to the kitchen to become the new location of this special room.

Taiichi Ohno defined seven elements of waste, commonly known as *muda*, loosely translates as uselessness. These elements are *Transportation,*

Inventory, Motion, Waiting, Overproduction, Overprocessing and *Defect*. The 8th element (*Skill Underutilised*) was added later in the 1990s, making it eight waste categories with acronym TIMWOODS. Another version of waste category uses DOWNTIME acronym: *Defects, Overproduction, Waiting, Non-used Talent, Transportation, Inventory, Motion, Extra Processing*.

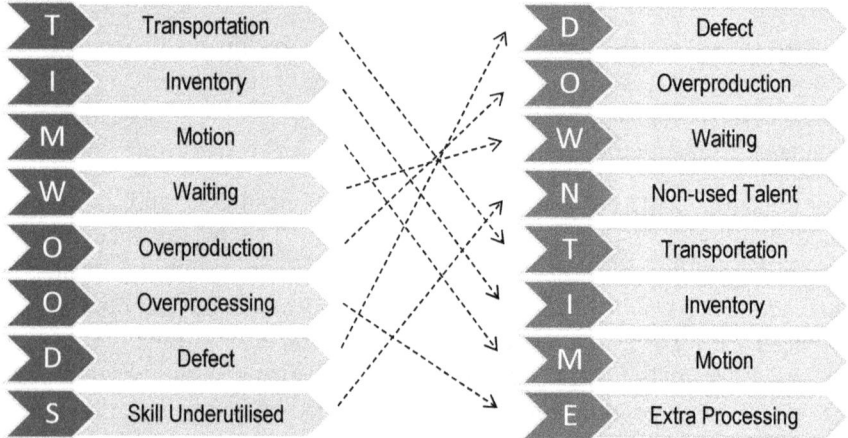

Figure 04-2 Elements of Waste

Transportation waste is the unnecessary movement of all parts, products, tools and equipment, also known as *conveyance waste*. The process of transporting items only has value to the customer when the transport happens from production site to customer's hand. Many other transportation activities that happen within a production process are considered as waste because these do not add value from customer's perspective.

Inventory waste is the cost of storing products because production speed is higher than customer demand. Inventory includes the storing of unfinished products in WIP queue or finished products completed before customer demand. Some types of perishable items might no longer suitable to achieve the expected quality after being stored for too long. Efforts are required to store, organise and retrieve items in inventory. Storing unfinished parts in inventory might delay the discovery of defects, increasing the possibility of rework or scrap.

Motion waste is the movement of people, tools or machines involved in production. This includes any excessive movement that people need to do as part of their production tasks, such as walking, bending and lifting. For operators, this waste is often linked with health and safety issues. For Tools and machines, this waste focuses on the motion that they need to perform as part of the production. Examples for this waste are walking to get material, rearranging something that was not right the first time, relying on human to do repetitive heavy lifting work to a distance.

Waiting waste happens when a process (or sub-process) cannot proceed with work because material or equipment is not ready, causing some people or machines to stay idle. This waste is usually caused by process components operating at different speed.

Overproduction waste is a situation when production speed is higher than the rate of customer demand. Lean principles prefer *Just-In-Time* philosophy (making products or services as they are pulled by customer demand) instead of Just-In-Case mentality of producing more than what is needed.

There are 3 techniques to prevent Overproduction waste:
- Calculate takt time and adjusting cycle time to match it.
- Use Kanban system to minimise the amount of WIP.
- Reduce batch size to reach Single-Piece-Flow.

Overprocessing waste is a situation that occurs when a production system does more work than what is necessary as indicated by customer demand. In the context of manufacturing, this could be some work to achieve higher precision than what is needed in specification limits or adding more features that customers do not perceive as value. In the context of general process, overprocessing could happen when there are too many required steps to obtain approval for everyday activities, double efforts of data entry and complex forms that gathers unnecessary data.

Defect waste happens when a product or service has one or more aspects that fail to meet the requirement. The failure point is called a *defect* and the unit with at least one defect is called *defective*. Defective units would incur costs because they could need rework or become scrap. An ideal Lean system aims to achieve zero defect. A Six Sigma process allow no more than 3.4 defects per million opportunities.

Skills underutilised waste is the waste of human potential. This type of waste could happen if an organisation is structured in such a way to prevent the use of expertise from people who does the actual production work. When employees on production site are forced to blindly follow orders, it is said that their skills might become underutilised.

Newer Lean theories added *Space waste*. It happens when the use of either physical space or digital storage does not add value to a production system, yet those have cost associated with keeping them. The addition of this waste category brings the acronym into TIMWOODS+S or DOWNTIMES.

Kanban

Originated from the 1940s when Toyota started its *Just-In-Time* production system, *Kanban* uses board for visual work coordination between parts of the system. It is a powerful system because it provides visibility so that people know when and how many parts they need to product. This is very useful to minimise WIP and promote focus.

Kanban system organises pieces of work into columns. The simplest of columns to start using Kanban are *To Do*, *In Progress* and *Done*. There are other names for the To Do column, such as Backlog, Requests or Queue, but they represent the same idea.

Pieces of work are represented by cards as representation. The movements of these pieces serve as *signals* for others involved in the process. Kanban board can be physical or digital board. As long as all the relevant people are able to access it without difficulties, Kanban board radiates information on real-time basis, allowing much better coordination.

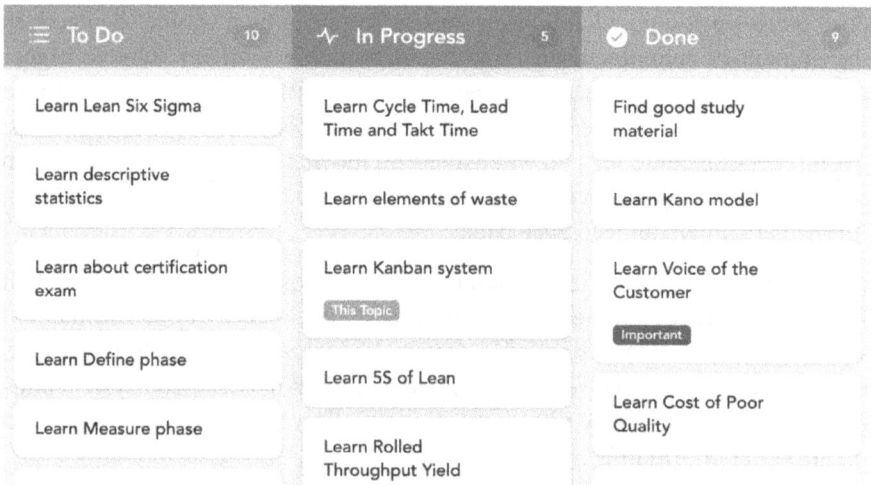

≣ To Do 10	⌁ In Progress 5	✓ Done 9
Learn Lean Six Sigma	Learn Cycle Time, Lead Time and Takt Time	Find good study material
Learn descriptive statistics	Learn elements of waste	Learn Kano model
Learn about certification exam	Learn Kanban system **This Topic**	Learn Voice of the Customer **Important**
Learn Define phase	Learn 5S of Lean	
Learn Measure phase	Learn Rolled Throughput Yield	Learn Cost of Poor Quality

Figure 04-3 Example of Kanban board

Kanban method originated from manufacturing industry in the physical form of actual board. It steadily evolved to take on more complex challenges in the modern digital world. Kanban has been widely adapted by Agile community. Many Scrum practitioners use Kanban as a technique to manage their iterations. Digital Kanban tools such as Jira and Trello allow remote team to work together with effective collaboration.

A well-implemented Kanban system will help to achieve:
- Workflow visualisation
- Limiting Work In Progress (WIP)
- Better flow management and control
- Solid teamwork where everyone is on the same page
- Effective feedback loop
- Transparency
- Positive collaboration

5S of Lean

One of Lean implementation methods is called *5S of Lean*. The term 5S originally came from 5 Japanese words *seiri, seiton, seiso, seiketsu* and *shitsuke*. In English adaptation, the 5S of Lean becomes *Sort, Straighten, Shine, Standardise* and *Sustain*. Some modern implementations add *Safety* as the sixth S.

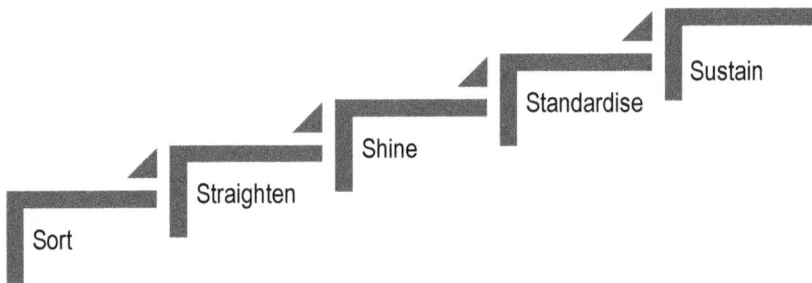

Figure 04-4 5S of Lean

Sort activity is implemented by separating tools and equipment at work into frequently used, infrequently used and unneeded. One way to start the process is by gathering members of a targeted group (unit or department) and guide them to label each item in work area with green, amber and red labels. Green label means an item is frequently used for work. Amber label is used for items that are useful, but the use frequency is low (such as periodic use, monthly or perhaps quarterly) so that such items do not need to overcrowd the everyday working space. Finally, unneeded items are given red labels.

Straighten activity is also known as *set in order*. It continues the work from *sort* activity by neatly arrange the tools and equipment based on the labels. Frequently used items need to be stored in locations that are easy to access during work activities. Items of infrequent use are properly labelled, categorised and stored in a safe location.

Shine activity uses a special event dedicated for clean-up. This activity ensures all items are clean, organised, well-functioning (not broken) and easily accessible.

Standardise activity aims to maintain and monitor the activities of *sort*, *straighten* and *shine*. This activity creates standard operating procedure so that the cleanliness and orderliness that have been achieved do not fall back to the previous mess. Visual reminders are often used to help people to comply, such as signs, posters, floor markings, shadow boards and organising labels.

Sustain activity is the hardest to achieve of 5S. This activity is about keeping the 5S running as part of new organisational culture. *Sustain* is an active effort to involve everyone in the organisation to take positive part in ensuring the success of 5S.

Safety activity focuses to eliminate or mitigate risks in work location by arranging things in certain ways. For example: all chemicals with potential safety risks must be labelled with consistent warning, dangerous equipment can only be used by trained operators, areas with safety risks must be locked outside working hours with clear procedure on who is responsible for access.

Even though 5S started as a tool to help with physical items, it is fully applicable for digital work. *Sort* activity could be utilised to separate digital files, records, bookmarks and tools into frequently used, infrequently used and unneeded. *Straighten* activity could be utilised to put them in order and identify areas of improvement. *Shine* activity organises how digital items are stored and cleans up items that are no longer needed. *Standardise* and *sustain* activities aim to maintain the activities and making them sustainable.

In the era of cloud infrastructure, lower pricing structure is often available for data storage with infrequent use, this could lead to significant saving if an organisation properly classifies and organises its digital files. Many companies use multiple tools and services and keep on paying the costs even after they are no longer needed. Having a clear organisation of digital files, records, bookmarks and tools allow team members to work more effectively and reduce the amount of (non-essential) administrative tasks.

Rolled Throughput Yield (RTY)

An ideal Lean system produce the right output right from the start. Any defect produced by a system would always result in wasteful activities. The measurement of *First Time Yield* (FTY) calculates the proportion of good units produced divided by the number of units went into the start of production.

$$FTY = \frac{good\ units\ produced}{units\ at\ the\ start\ of\ production}$$

Example:

Suppose there are four processes (A, B, C and D) in a production system. The number of inputs, good output, rework and scrap for each process are shown in the figure below. For every process, the number of good outputs is the number of inputs minus the number of rework and scrap.

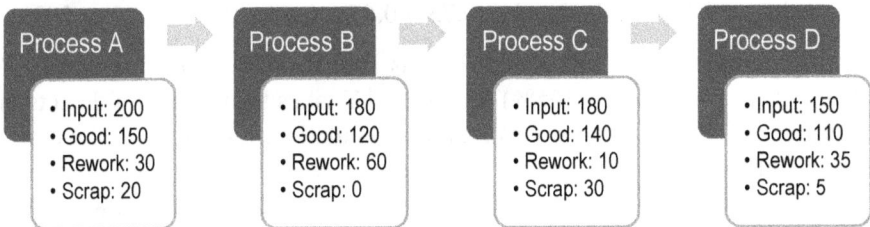

Process A	Process B	Process C	Process D
• Input: 200	• Input: 180	• Input: 180	• Input: 150
• Good: 150	• Good: 120	• Good: 140	• Good: 110
• Rework: 30	• Rework: 60	• Rework: 10	• Rework: 35
• Scrap: 20	• Scrap: 0	• Scrap: 30	• Scrap: 5

Figure 04-5 Example for FTY and RTY

The entire system starts with process A working on 200 units and produces 110 good units at the end of process D. The FTY is 110 divided by 200 = 0.55 or 55%

FTY can also be calculated using DPU (*Defect Per Unit*)

$$FTY = e^{-DPU}$$

- DPU is the total number of defects divided by total number of units inspected.
- e is a mathematical constant known as Euler's number; the value is 2.7183.

Rolled Throughput Yield (RTY) is defined as the probability of a unit to pass all processes without any defect. It is calculated as the local FTY of process A times the local FTY of process B times the local FTY of process C times the local FTY of process D.

$$RTY = FTY(A) \times FTY(B) \times FTY(C) \times \cdots \times FTY(n)$$

Rolled Throughput Yield Loss (RTYL) is the opposite of RTY.

$$RTYL = 1 - RTY$$

Using the same example, the yield rates for each process are:
- Yield rate of process A = 150 / 200 = 0.75
- Yield rate of process B = 120 / 180 = 0.67
- Yield rate of process C = 140 / 180 = 0.78
- Yield rate of process D = 110 / 150 = 0.75

The value of RTY is calculated as $0.75 \times 0.67 \times 0.78 \times 0.75 = 0.29$ or 29%.

In the example above, calculated RTY is significantly lower than the FTY value of the entire system (55%) because RTY takes the number of defects in each process (rework and scrap) into the calculation. Even though the entire system ends up producing 110 good units, several of them went through rework process during production. Lean principles aim to create a process having RTY value of one or near one.

One Piece Flow

The basic idea of *one piece flow* is creating a production process that starts with customer demand, then one piece of product (or service) is produced with an optimised system with no waste and RTY value of one and it can finish the whole process before the next customer demand. The system produces one unit of item when customer for one with 100% confidence that it will be done right the first time. Other sources might refer to this as *single piece flow* or *continuous flow*.

The characteristics of *one piece flow* system:
- It is pulled by customer demand, one production at a time.
- The production system has RTY value of one, or at least near one.
- Zero waiting time, very low number of WIP.
- No overprocessing.
- Quality is built into the system.
- Production lead time is equal to takt time.

Simplified comparison between traditional flow with batch & queue vs. *one piece flow* is presented in Figure 04-6. Pieces (units or product) are produced in batches of 8, each batch require 8 minutes to complete.

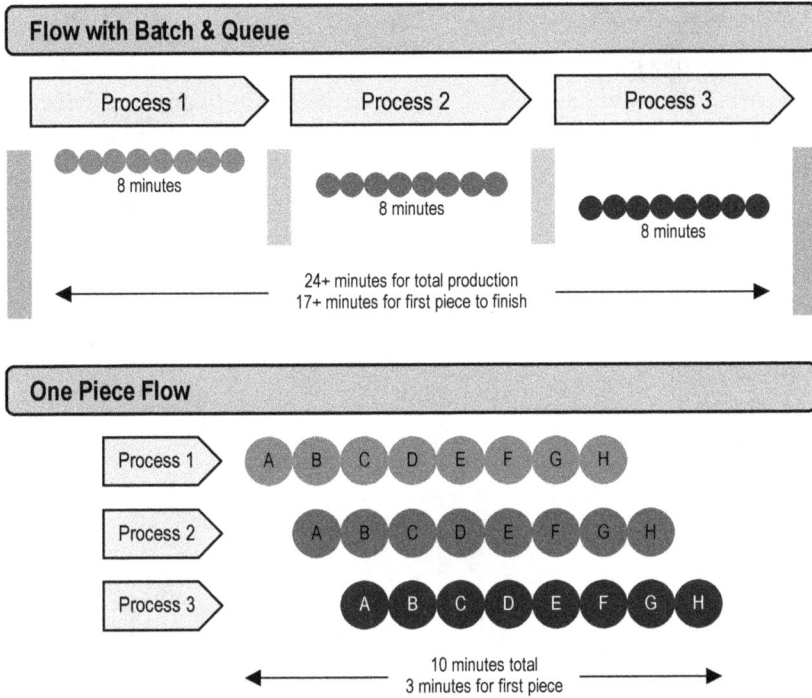

Figure 04-6 Comparison of flow with batch & queue vs. one piece flow

There are 3 processes in the production system. Each process needs the same amount of time to work on every batch. No final piece will be produced before Process 1 and Process 2 finish their work on all pieces in a batch, resulting that the first piece of product will be available after 17 minutes. Total production of 8 pieces would require 24 minutes. Depending on how the batches are moved between processes, there could be additional processing time in-between.

Using *one piece flow*, after Process 1 finishes with piece A, Process 2 immediately starts processing the piece. While Process 2 is working on piece A, Process 1 starts working on the next piece, that is piece B. Piece A will flow throughout all three processes within 3 minutes and ready to fulfill customer's demand. Another piece (B, then C, then D and so on) will be available every minute. The whole processes of 8 pieces require total time of 10 minutes instead of 24.

One piece flow requires highly efficient coordination and consistency to pull off. This model is good in theory, but not always applicable in all real-world scenarios. In cases when only one piece at a time is not possible due to production constraints, a very small batch size can be considered provided it still matches customer demand.

Even though *one piece flow* has many theoretical benefits, this method is easy to go wrong. If any of the processes in Figure 04-6 fails to produce defect-free piece in the first go, then whole production will be impacted. When things go wrong, the cost will be high, including the possibility of losing customer loyalty. It is up to each organisation to decide on the risk level they are willing to take and maintain the fine balance between ideal condition and practical challenges.

05. LEAN SIX SIGMA

Both Lean and Six Sigma are techniques for process improvement. Lean focuses on eliminating waste and building production flow that is pulled by customer demand. Six Sigma focuses on improving process to meet requirement specifications, align the centre of results in the middle, reduce variation and sustain the improvements. Both techniques are useful for different use cases and they are strong complement for each other.

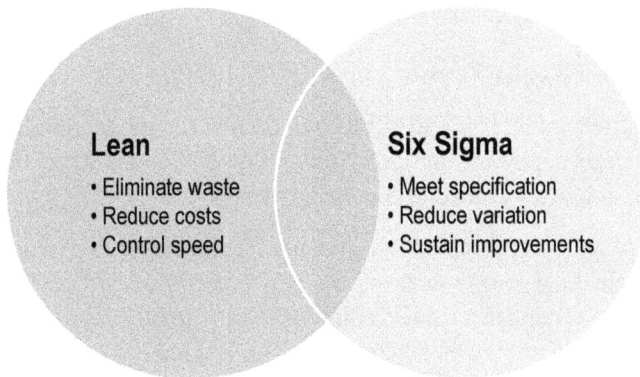

Lean
- Eliminate waste
- Reduce costs
- Control speed

Six Sigma
- Meet specification
- Reduce variation
- Sustain improvements

Figure 05-1 Six Sigma and Lean

Lean Six Sigma methodology uses principles from Lean and Six Sigma to cover more possible root causes of a problem. If a problem occurs because high percentage of products do not meet specifications, Six Sigma project is started to improve the process. If a problem occurs because too many steps in production system actually do not add any value for the customer, a Lean process is executed to eliminate waste.

In Lean's *one piece flow*, pieces are moved through each process of the production system with zero waiting, one piece at a time. To achieve this, all processes in the system should be able to consistently produce good outputs at the speed of customer demand with very minimum variation. Minimising variation is achievable through Six Sigma process improvement.

Similarities of Lean and Six Sigma:
- Lean and Six Sigma aim to improve process.
- Lean and Six Sigma rely on data.
- Lean and Six Sigma focus on customer.
- Lean and Six Sigma follow structured methodology with clear steps and tools.

Differences between Lean and Six Sigma:

Lean	Six Sigma
analyses value-added activities	starts from VOC and CTQ
optimises process flow	increases accuracy and precision
eliminates waste	minimises variation
calculates flow and customer demand	uses statistical analysis
tools: Takt, 8 waste, Ishikawa diagram, JIT, Kanban, 5S, RTY, Kaizen event	tools: MSA, hypothesis testing, DOE, SPC charts, control plan

Choosing the Right Framework

There are three main frameworks of Lean Six Sigma methodology: *Lean Kaizen, Six Sigma DMAIC* and *Six Sigma DMADV*. Each framework has its specific use and often can complement each other.

If drivers of performance can be obtained using collective knowledge of certain people in the organisation, a Lean project is the preferred way to achieve improvement. The most common Lean project takes the form of a **Kaizen event**, also known as Kaizen workout. Kaizen is a Japanese word that can be translated as *change for the better*.

In cases when drivers of performance are unknown, **Six Sigma DMAIC project** is the preferred way for process improvement because this framework has the right tools to analyse root causes based on collected data. As the name suggest, this framework has five phases: *Define, Measure, Analyze, Improve* and *Control*. DMAIC is data-driven methodology which conduct statistical analysis to determine which values of factors bring the best outcome.

Both Kaizen event and DMAIC take an existing process and improve on them. The third framework in Lean Six Sigma is **DMADV** or **Design for Six Sigma (DFSS)**. This framework is very powerful to design a new product, service or process. The first three phases of DMADV are identical to the first three phases in DMAIC: *Define*, *Measure* and *Analyze*. The last two phases in DMADV are *Design* and *Verify*.

Certification Exam

Studying Lean Six Sigma is not something that can be done in a day or two. Quick reading for high-level understanding of the overall topics in this book will take approximately 30-40 hours. Comprehensive reading to master all topics will take between 1 to 3 months depending on your time commitment and the level of knowledge you already have about some quality tools and statistical analysis.

The level of knowledge of a Lean Six Sigma practitioner is usually measured with Belt level: Yellow Belt, Green Belt, Black Belt and Master Black Belt. *Yellow Belt* indicates a basic level of understanding about Lean Six Sigma concepts, sufficient for team members involved in a Six Sigma project. *Green Belt* indicates good level of knowledge to lead Six Sigma project on a part-time basis. *Black Belt* indicates a strong working knowledge of Lean Six Sigma capable of leading complex projects on full-time basis. *Master Black Belt* is the highest level of Lean Six Sigma skills; it shows full mastery of all concepts and those achieving it usually take on the role of training others.

How does one get acknowledged to possess the skills to a certain level? There are few possible ways.
- *First party declaration*. One could finish Lean Six Sigma self-study, then self-declare that s/he has obtained knowledge to the level of Black Belt, for example. This is the easiest path, but with the lowest credibility. Unless a person already has solid existing reputation from the beginning, most people will not acknowledge self-declaration of skill without objective proof.
- *Second party declaration*. The next option is to take training from certain provider, could be a training centre or an individual Master Black Belt. On the completion of course, the training provider produces certificate that declares one has met the requirements of certain Belt level. This method is better than self-declaration, but it still comes with question on objectivity. A training provider has financial motive to pass a participant regardless of his/her actual skills and the training material

does not necessarily follow what is considered as industry standards.

- **_Third party declaration_**. A candidate takes certification exam from independent body that does not provide the training or study material. This method provides the most objective assessment of someone's actual skill level.

There is no single official certification body for Six Sigma. However, certifications from *IASSC* (*The International Association for Six Sigma Certification*) and *ASQ* (*American Society for Quality*) are highly respected by the industry and considered as good standards. Other popular certification bodies include *Villanova University*, *CQI* (*Chartered Quality Institute*) and *IISE* (*Institute of Industrial and Systems Engineers*).

It is important to note that IASSC provides certification for Lean Six Sigma while other certifying bodies provide certification for Six Sigma with no direct mention of Lean, even though their body of knowledge might include aspects of Lean. This book covers 100% of IASSC body of knowledge for Black Belt and majority of ASQ body of knowledge, especially on the DMAIC methodology.

IASSC offers certification exams for Lean Six Sigma Yellow Belt, Green Belt and Black Belt. Certification exams can be taken in one of its testing centres (PearsonVue) located in 165 countries or through on-demand web-based exam (proctored). The cost of certification exam in testing centres vary by country. On-demand web-based exam costs the same worldwide, cheaper than exam in testing centre.

	Yellow Belt	**Green Belt**	**Black Belt**
Cost (web-based)	USD $195	USD $295	USD $395
Exam retake	USD $195	USD $295	USD $395
Graded questions	60	100	150
Non-graded questions	6	10	15
Total exam questions	66	110	165
Time	2 hours	3 hours	4 hours
Pass rate	70%	70%	70%

Table 05-A IASSC certification exams

All IASSC certification exams are strictly closed book. It means test takers cannot bring any reference material to the exam. There is one exception: IASSC provides one PDF files with the statistical formulas and reference tables. Those are not really useful unless one already knows how to use them in the first place. Non-programmable calculator is allowed. This information on IASSC exam is accurate on the day this book was written, please refer to

IASSC website to check the latest information.

ASQ offers certification exams for Six Sigma Yellow Belt, Green Belt, Black Belt and Master Black Belt. Certification exams can be taken in one of its test centres (Prometric) around the world or through remote proctoring web-based exam. Paper-and-pencil exam is available twice a year in high-demand cities only. The cost of certification exam is the same for remote proctoring web-based and testing centre. ASQ members get a discount on exam costs.

	Yellow Belt	Green Belt	Black Belt
Cost (non-members)	USD $394	USD $438	USD $538
Exam retake	USD $184	USD $238	USD $338
Graded questions	75	100	150
Non-graded questions	10	10	15
Total exam questions	85	110	165
Time	2 hours 30 mins	4 hours 18 mins	4 hours 18 mins

Table 05-B ASQ certification exams

The pass rate for ASQ exam is 550 out of possible 750 points. Paper-and-pencil exams have slightly different exam duration because they do not have the non-graded questions. To be certified as Master Black Belt, a candidate needs to pay $650 for portfolio review plus $2,229 for exam fee.

All ASQ certification exams are open book. Test takers must bring their own reference materials, along with non-programmable calculator. Some levels of ASQ certification have job experience as part of the requirements. This information on ASQ exam is accurate on the day this book was written, please refer to ASQ website to check the latest information.

Regardless of which certification body you choose, always start your learning journey by visiting the certification body's website and download their official *body of knowledge*. It has the list of all topics they expect a person holding certain Belt level should know, according to their standard. Make sure that your learning journey covers all items from that list.

Useful tips for the preparation before exam day:
- Prepare yourself with the core knowledge of Lean Six Sigma.
- Decide on certification body.
- Decide on belt level to pursue.
- Find out about exam cost.
- Decide on exam location.
- Visit the website of the certification body and download the official *body of knowledge*.

- Evaluate if there are some topics you have not covered yet.
- Read about exam rules specific to the certification body that you chose. Find out if the exam is closed book or open book. Find out if calculator or other tools are allowed.
- If books or reference materials are allowed, decide on which materials to use during exam. Choose material that you are able to quickly find what you need.
- Find out exam duration and how many questions in the exam. Your biggest enemy during exam is time. The duration might seem a long time at the beginning, but it will quickly run out once you start working on the questions.
- Calculate how many questions you need to finish every 15 minutes. This will help you to stay on track during exam. Always set a target to finish all questions within 65% of the exam duration because some questions are harder than others and need more time.
- Pay attention if the exam description says that there will be certain amount of non-graded questions. You will not know which questions are non-graded, so you still need to answer all questions to the best of your ability. As example, for black belt exam there are 15 non-graded questions. For a four-hours exam, those 15 questions will take approximately 20-30 minutes of your time, so count those questions in your time planning.
- Take practice exams, at least 3 different sets, preferably from different sources. This will help you to get a feel of the difficulty level of the exam as well as time management. Note that most practice exams do not include non-graded questions, so you need to reduce the target time because in real exam you will need to answer more questions.
- Check if the certification body offers official practice exam. It is highly recommended to take.
- Register for exam and choose the date and time. Remember that this is a hard exam requiring serious concentration, so try not to choose certain time when you are usually not able to concentrate.
- One day before exam, check the exam venue. If you register for an exam in physical venue, drive to the location to confirm location, parking options, etc. If you choose online-proctored exam, do a system check using the computer that will be used during exam.

Useful tips for exam day:
- Make sure you get enough rest the night before.
- Prepare all the items that you need, such as reference material, calculator, photo ID.

- If you choose to take exam in physical venue, arrive at least 15 minutes before exam time. This will give you some time to calm down and focus.
- If you choose to take exam via online-proctored system, have everything ready at least 15 minutes before. Make sure the aircon or heating system in the room is set at comfortable level. Doing hours of exam in uncomfortable room can do significant damage to your concentration ability.
- Make sure you understand the rule on restroom breaks (if any), use that strategically. If you do exam from home, every time you return from restroom break, you may need to show the proctor the situation of your desk and four sides around. This could take valuable time.
- Do not spend too much time on one question. If it is too hard, note down the question number, take a quick guess and move on. If you have extra time later, you can always revisit the question.
- Read the questions carefully. Many wrong answers come from simple mistakes in reading and understanding the questions.
- Some questions may appear harder than it actually is. Not all information or numbers presented in a question have to be used in the calculation. Understand the problem correctly, apply the right technique and believe in yourself.
- Review all outstanding questions before doing the final submission.
- Finally, good luck!

Table of Topics

The following table lists all topics covered in this book with their relevance for each Belt level and project champion role (suitable for executives and senior managers). This table is only for general recommendation. Both certification bodies might revise their standards at any time. It is strongly recommended to obtain the latest version of *body of knowledge* from their websites.

- ★ required to master this topic.
- ☆ required to understand basic principles of this topic.
- Δ optional but recommended to read about the basics.

Topic	Chapter	Champion	Black Belt		Green Belt		Yellow Belt	
			IASSC	ASQ	IASSC	ASQ	IASSC	ASQ
Understanding Quality	02	★	★	★	★	★	★	★
Kano Model	02	★	△	★	△	★	△	△
Voice of The Customer	02	★	★	★	★	★	★	☆
Cost of Poor Quality	02	★	★	★	★	★	★	☆
Six Sigma Principles	03	★	★	★	★	★	★	★
History of Process Improvement	03	△	★	★	★	★	★	★
Process Variation	03	☆	★	★	★	★	★	★
Six Sigma Metrics	03	☆	★	★	★	★	★	★
Sigma Level DPO, DPMO and PPM	03	☆	★	★	★	★	★	★
Basic Concepts of DMAIC	03, 35	☆	★	★	★	★	★	★
Y = f (X)	03	☆	★	★	★	★	☆	☆
Six Sigma Roles	03	☆	★	★	★	★	☆	☆
Lean Principles	04	★	★	★	★	★	★	★
Cycle Time, Lead Time, Takt Time	04	☆	★	★	★	★	★	★
Elements of Waste	04	☆	★	★	★	★	☆	☆
Kanban	04	☆	★	★	★	★	☆	☆
5S of Lean	04	☆	★	★	★	★	☆	☆
Rolled Throughput Yield	04	☆	★	★	★	★	★	★
One Piece Flow	04	☆	★	★	★	★	☆	☆
Combining Lean and Six Sigma	05	☆	★	★	★	★	★	★
Choosing the Right Framework	05	★	★	★	★	★	★	★
Descriptive Statistics	06	☆	★	★	★	★	★	★
Probability Distribution	07	△	★	★	☆	☆	☆	☆
Check Sheet	08	△	★	★	★	★	★	★
Cause-and-Effect Diagram	08, 14	☆	★	★	★	★	★	★
Flow Chart	08	☆	★	★	★	★	☆	☆
Scatter Plot	08	△	★	★	★	★	☆	☆
Histogram	08	△	★	★	★	★	☆	☆
Pareto Chart	08	△	★	★	★	★	☆	☆
Control Chart	08, 31	☆	★	★	★	★		△
Box Plot	08	△	★	★	★	★	☆	☆
Dot Plot	08	△	★	★	★	★	☆	☆
Define Phase	09, 12	★	★	★	★	★	★	★

Topic	Chapter	Champion	Black Belt		Green Belt		Yellow Belt	
			IASSC	ASQ	IASSC	ASQ	IASSC	ASQ
Project Selection	09	★	★	★	★	★	★	★
Project Charter	10	★	★	★	★	★	★	★
High Level Process Map	11	☆	★	★	★	★	★	★
Detailed Process Map	11	△	★	★	★	★	☆	☆
Swimlane Process Map	11	△	★	★	★	★	☆	☆
SIPOC Diagram	11	△	★	★	★	★	★	★
Measure Phase	13	★	★	★	★	★	★	★
5 Whys	14	☆	★	★	★	★	★	☆
XY Matrix	14	△	★	★	★	★	★	☆
Multi-voting	14	△	★	★	★	★	★	☆
Failure Modes and Effects Analysis	14	△	★	★	★	★	★	☆
Process Capability	14	☆	★	★	★	★	★	★
Measurement System Analysis	15	☆	★	★	★	★	★	☆
Data Collection and Sampling	16	☆	★	★	★	★	★	★
Analyse Phase	17	★	★	★	★	★	☆	★
Lean Measures	18	☆	★	★	★	★		☆
Value Stream Mapping	18	☆	★	★	★	★		☆
Statistical Data Analysis	19	☆	★	★	★	★		☆
Visual Analysis	19	☆	★	★	★	★		☆
Descriptive vs. Inferential	19	☆	★	★	★	★		☆
Confidence Interval	19	☆	★	★	★	★		
Univariate, Bivariate, Multi-variate	19	△	★	★	★	★		
Hypothesis Testing	20	☆	★	★	★	★		☆
Alpha and Beta Risks	20	☆	★	★	★	★		☆
Test Statistics vs. Critical Value	20	△	★	★	★	★		☆
P-Value	20	△	★	★	★	★		☆
Data Normality Test	20	△	★	★	★	★		
Test Selection	20	☆	★	★	★	★		
Correlation	21	△	★	★	★	★		☆
Linear Regression	21	△	★	★	★	★		☆
Non-Linear Regression	21		★	★	★	☆		☆
Multiple Regression	21		★	★	★	△		△
One Proportion Test	22	△	★	★	★	★		

Topic	Chapter	Champion	Black Belt		Green Belt		Yellow Belt	
			IASSC	ASQ	IASSC	ASQ	IASSC	ASQ
Two Proportions Test	22	△	★	★	★	★		
Chi-Squared Test	22	△	★	★	★	★		
One Sample Variance Test	23	△	★	★	★	★		
F-Test	23	△	★	★	★	★		
Bartlett's Test	23	△	★	★	★			
One Sample T-Test	23	△	★	★	★	★		
Two Samples T-Test	23	△	★	★	★	★		
Paired Sample T-Test	23	△	★	★	★	★		
One-way ANOVA	23	△	★	★	★	★		
One Sample Wilcoxon Test	24		★	△	★			
One Sample Sign Test	24		★	△	★			
Mann-Whitney Test	24		★	★	★			
Mood's Median Test	24		★	△	★			
Kruskal-Wallis Test	24		★	★	★			
Friedman Test	24		★	△	★			
Improve Phase	25	★	★	★	★	★	☆	★
Pull-based System	26	☆	★	★	★	★		△
Error Proofing (Poka Yoke)	26	△	★	★	★	★		☆
Six Thinking Hats	26	△	△	△				
Design of Experiments	27	☆	★	★		☆		
Trial and Error	27	△	★	★				
One Factor At A Time (OFAAT)	27	△	★	★				
Full Factorial Design	28	△	★	★		△		
Replication and Repetition	28	△	★	★		☆		
Factorial Design Mathematical Model	28		★	★				
Response Surface Design	28	△	★	★		☆		
Fractional Factorial Design	29	△	★	★		△		
Balanced & Orthogonal	29		★	★				
Confounding Effects & Resolution	29		★	★				
Control Phase	30	★	★	★	★	★	★	★
Control Plan and Response Plan	30	☆	★	★	★	★	☆	☆
Implementation Planning	30	☆	★	★	★	★		
Cost and Benefit Analysis	30	★	★	★	★	★	☆	☆

Topic	Chapter	Champion	Black Belt		Green Belt		Yellow Belt	
			IASSC	ASQ	IASSC	ASQ	IASSC	ASQ
Statistical Process Control (SPC)	31	☆	★	★	★	★	△	☆
Special Cause Variations	31	☆	★	★	★	★	△	☆
I-MR Chart	32	△	★	★	★	★		△
Xbar-R Chart	32	△	★	★	★	★		☆
Xbar-S Chart	32	△	★	★	★	★		
C Chart	33	△	★	★	★	★		
U Chart	33	△	★	★	★	★		
NP Chart	33	△	★	★	★	★		
P Chart	33	△	★	★	★	★		
CuSum Chart	34		★	△	★			
EWMA Chart	34		★	△	★			
Kaizen Event	36	☆	★	★	★	☆		☆
Design for Six Sigma (DFSS)	37	△	△	★				

Table 05-C Topics in Lean Six Sigma

06. DESCRIPTIVE STATISTICS

Descriptive statistics is a study of statistics to describe the summarised characteristics of data. Many aspects of Lean Six Sigma methodologies and framework uses descriptive statistics to help with understanding data. This chapter provides the necessary basic knowledge for new learners, or it can serve as a refresher for those with prior experience.

There are two basic categories of descriptive statistics:
- Measures of central tendency.
- Measures of data variability.

Measures of central tendency focuses on the values of mean, median and mode. Collectively, these values will quickly give some idea about where the values in a dataset are centralised around. However, it will not give any indication of data variability. For data variability, measures of standard deviation, variance, minimum, maximum, range, skewness and kurtosis are obtained.

Data Types

Statistics is a study of collecting and analysing data, specifically quantitative data. It is only natural to start the discussion on descriptive statistics with good understanding on the types of quantitative data.

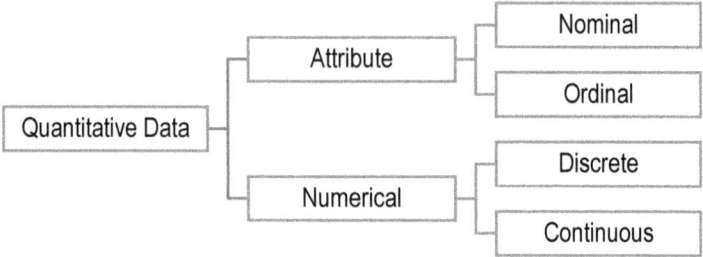

Figure 06-1 Quantitative data

First, not all data are quantitative. Some data are simply describing information that is observed subjectively. This type of data is called *qualitative data*. Examples of qualitative data:

- Fried noodle tastes great.
- That flower smells good.

Quantitative data is loosely defined as anything that can be listed, ordered, counted or measured. The simplest version of quantitative data is *attribute data*, which can be nominal or ordinal. Attribute data is also known as *categorical data*.

Nominal data is any data that comes from a list and there is no meaning about the order of items in that list. This type of data is often confused with qualitative data. If a membership registration form has a question of "what is your favourite sport?" and new members can fill in anything, that is qualitative data. Instead of allowing anything to be written, the form could instead offer a list of sports: tennis, basketball, baseball, soccer, cricket and others. New members can choose one of the sports or choose the last option is their favourite sport is not in the list. There is no meaning behind listing tennis as the first item because the order of the list can be rearranged without changing the meaning of the question. The answer collected from it becomes a nominal data.

Ordinal data is any data that come from an ordered list. A popular example of this data type is when a survey form asks people about their satisfaction level.

- 1 means very unsatisfied
- 2 means unsatisfied
- 3 means neutral
- 4 means satisfied
- 5 means very satisfied

For ordinal data, the order of the list means something. The choice of [very satisfied] is meant to have the highest number. It does not make sense to change the value 3 into [very satisfied] and value 5 into [neutral].

There are two types of numerical data: discrete and continuous. *Discrete data* is something that can be counted, for example: head or tail in coin flip, number of visitors and number of defective items. A store can have 10 visitors or 11 visitors, but it cannot be 10.4 visitors.

Continuous data is something that can be measured, for example: length of an item, weight of an item and temperature. A child can weigh 15 kg or 15.5 kg or 15.5555 kg.

In statistics, continuous data can be organised into ordered units that have the same difference. If the ordered units have an absolute zero value, the data is called *ratio data*, otherwise they are *interval data*.

Good example of data that can be collected as *ratio data* is height. Height can be categorised as 0 m, 0.5 m, 1 m, 1.5 m, etc. The data of 0 metre is absolute zero because it really means no height, or the height does not exist.

On the other hand, temperature can also be categorised as -2°C, -1°C, 0°C, 1°C, 2°C and so on. It seems that it has value zero, but it is not absolute zero because 0°C does not mean there is no temperature. There is a temperature and its value happen to be zero. When converting Celsius into Fahrenheit or Kelvin, the value of the same temperature will get translated into different number. This is an example of *interval data*.

Mode, Mean, Median and Percentile

Starting from the simplest measurement of central tendency, **Mode** is the value most frequently appear in a dataset. There can be more than one Modes in a dataset.

This dataset A will be used for the following parts of this chapter:

5	5	5	6	6	8	8	20	25	32

In dataset A, value 5 appears three times, which is the highest frequency compared to all other values. The mode of dataset A is 5.

Mean is the average of all values in a dataset. To calculate mean, we simply add all the values, then divide by the count of values.

Formula to calculate mean:

$$\mu = \frac{\sum x_i}{N}$$

Calculating the *mean* value of dataset A:

$$\mu = \frac{5 + 5 + 5 + 6 + 6 + 8 + 8 + 20 + 25 + 32}{10} = 12$$

For some data with specific characteristics, *trimmed mean* is often calculated instead of normal mean. Trimmed mean removes the top X% and the bottom X% of data before calculating mean.

For example, 10% *trimmed mean* of dataset A:

$$\mu = \frac{5 + 5 + 6 + 6 + 8 + 8 + 20 + 25}{8} = 10.375$$

Median value is the value located in the middle of a dataset that has the values sorted from the smallest to largest. Mathematically, median is the $((N + 1)/2)^{th}$ value. If the number of values in a dataset is an even number, this middle point will fall between two values, median is calculated as the average of those values.

$$Md = x_{(N+1)/2}$$

In the example with dataset A, $((N + 1)/2)$ is 5.5, median is located between 5th and 6th value. Therefore, median is the average of values 6 and 8. Median value of dataset A is 7.

Percentile is a statistical term to indicate how a value compares to all other values in the same dataset. Percentile is commonly expressed in percentage value. Percentile rank of 75 (represented with symbol R) means a value that is greater than or equal to 75% of the values in dataset. Median is always equal to 50 percentiles because it splits all values in a dataset into two equal parts.

$$Pr(R) = x_{(N+1) \times R}$$

Using the same example, the 75th percentile of dataset A is:
- The $(10 + 1) \times 0.75 = 8.25^{th}$ value of dataset A.
- That is the 8th value plus 25% of the distance between 8th value and 9th value.
- The 8th value is 20 and the 9th value is 25.
- Distance between these values is 5.

- 25% of 5 is 1.25.
- Therefore, 75th percentile of dataset A is 22 + 1.25 = 23.35.

25th percentile is known as *first quartile* or *lower quartile*. 75th percentile is known as *third quartile* or *upper quartile*. *Interquartile range* (IQR) is a measure of data dispersion between lower and upper quartile. Small IQR shows that data is concentrated around median. Large IQR indicates spread out data.

An *outlier* is a value that has abnormal distance from other values in a dataset, usually defined as:

- any value less than first quartile minus (1.5 × IQR) or
- any value greater than third quartile plus (1.5 × IQR).

Minimum, Maximum and Range

Minimum, Maximum and Range are the simplest measurements to indicate a dataset's variability. *Minimum* is the smallest value in a dataset; *Maximum* is the biggest value. *Range* is the difference between maximum and minimum values.

Example:

- In dataset A, the minimum value is 5. Maximum value is 32.
- Range is 32 − 5 = 27.

The collection of minimum, first quartile, median, third quartile and maximum values are called the *five-number summary* of a dataset.

Variance and Standard Deviation

Standard deviation is a measure of how spread out the values in a dataset from its mean. Standard deviation is calculated as the square root of *Variance*, which is the sum of squared difference between each value and mean, divided by the count of values.

Standard deviation is represented using the symbol of σ (sigma). Variance is commonly written as σ^2.

Formula for variance of population:

$$\sigma^2 = \frac{\Sigma(x_i - \mu)^2}{N}$$

Standard deviation is the square root of variance. The formula of standard deviation for population:

$$\sigma = \sqrt{\frac{\Sigma(x_i - \mu)^2}{N}}$$

As example, variance and standard deviation of dataset A can be calculated:

- $\sigma^2 = \frac{\Sigma(x_i - 12)^2}{10} = 88.4$

- $\sigma = \sqrt{\frac{\Sigma(x_i - 12)^2}{10}} = 9.4$

Why do we need to square the difference between each value and the mean to calculate variance?

The simple answer is that applying square weighs values far from mean more heavily.

The mathematical answer will be explained using the help of dataset B and C:

Dataset B	96	100	104	104	96
Dataset C	107	102	99	100	94

- Dataset B and C have the same mean value: 100.
- By quick observation, one should be able to see that dataset C has more variability because it has values that deviates further from the mean.
- Option 1: calculate the sum of differences divided by N

$$SoD_B = \frac{(96-100)+(100-100)+(104-100)+(104-100)+(96-100)}{10} = \frac{0}{10} = 0$$

$$SoD_C = \frac{(107-100)+(102-100)+(99-100)+(100-100)+(94-100)}{10} = \frac{0}{10} = 0$$

This is not a good calculation to measure variability because the differences are cancelling each other.

- Option 2: calculate the sum of absolute differences divided by N

This measurement has a name: *Mean Deviation*.

$$MD = \frac{\Sigma|x_i - \mu|}{N}$$

$$MD_B = \frac{|96-100|+|100-100|+|104-100|+|104-100|+|96-100|}{10} = \frac{16}{10} = 1.6$$

$$MD_C = \frac{|107-100|+|102-100|+|99-100|+|100-100|+|94-100|}{10} = \frac{16}{10} = 1.6$$

Good measurement of variability should be able to show that dataset C has more variability compared to dataset B. However, both datasets have the same mean deviation value.

Mean deviation is not capable to differentiate the variability of datasets B and C because it does not weigh far differences more heavily.

- Option 3: calculate the sum of squared differences divided by N

$$\sigma_B^2 = \frac{(96-100)^2+(100-100)^2+(104-100)^2+(104-100)^2+(96-100)^2}{10} = 3.2$$

$$\sigma_C^2 = \frac{(107-100)^2+(102-100)^2+(99-100)^2+(100-100)^2+(94-100)^2}{10} = 8.8$$

Variance calculation using sum of squared differences is able to show that dataset C has higher variability than dataset B because it weighs values far from mean more heavily.

Skewness

Skewness is a measure of asymmetry. If value distribution on the right side of mode looks identical to the value distribution on the left side of mode, it is said that such distribution is *symmetrical*, having skewness value of zero.

Skewness formula is calculated as:

$$Sk = \frac{1}{N}\sum \left(\frac{x_i - \mu}{\sigma}\right)^3$$

Or in the case of sample dataset:

$$Sk = \frac{1}{n-1}\sum \left(\frac{x_i - \bar{x}}{S}\right)^3$$

The nominator of skewness formula is raised to the third power, so it can have positive or negative value. The denominator is positive because σ and S are always positive.

- Negative skewness value indicates data distribution skewed to the left.
- Positive skewness value indicates data distribution skewed to the right.

The side of skewness is the side where longer tail occurs, not the side where the peak appears to be.

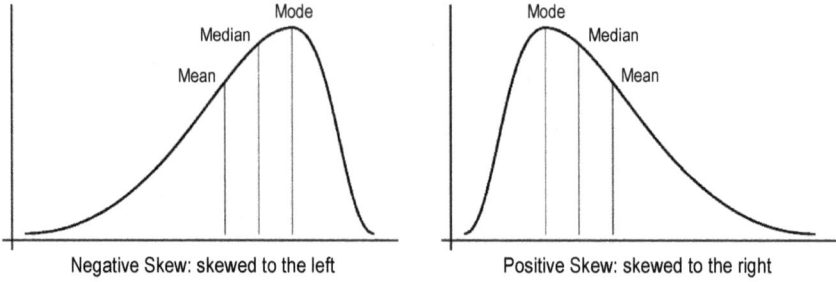

Figure 06-2 Skewness

Another measure of skewness using percentile:

$$Sp = \frac{90\ percentile - median}{median - 10\ percentile}$$

When measured using percentile, a symmetrical distribution has the Sp value of 1.

- Values between 0 and 1 indicates data distribution skewed to the left.
- Values greater than 1 indicates data distribution skewed to the right.

Kurtosis

Kurtosis is a measure of *peakness* and *tailedness* level of value distribution within a dataset. Normal distribution has kurtosis value = 3, known as *mesokurtic*. Mesokurtic is considered as baseline value for kurtosis.

Value distribution that looks flatter (less peaked) and lighter tails has kurtosis value < 3, known as *platykurtic*. On the other hand, value distribution with higher (more concentrated) peak and longer tails has kurtosis value > 3, known as *leptokurtic*.

The formula of kurtosis value of population:

$$K = \frac{1}{N}\sum \left(\frac{x_i - \mu}{\sigma}\right)^4$$

Kurtosis value of sample dataset:

$$K = \frac{1}{n-1}\sum \left(\frac{x_i - \bar{x}}{S}\right)^4$$

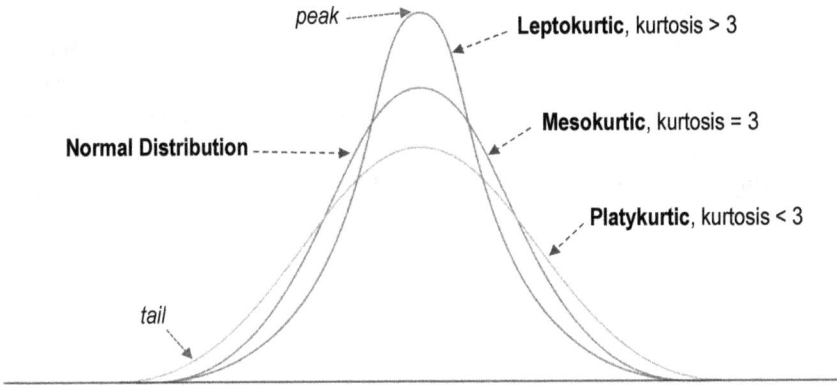

Figure 06-3 Kurtosis

Excess kurtosis is the value of kurtosis minus 3. Some books and articles prefer to use excess kurtosis because its value of zero for normal distribution is considered more intuitive. Microsoft Excel function KURT and popular statistical software Minitab use excess kurtosis in their calculations.

Central Dogma of Statistics

Population in statistics is loosely defined as a set of every members in a particular topic of interest. *Sample* is a subset of population, chosen with certain sampling method in the hope that studies on the characteristics of sample will represent the characteristics of the population it was taken from.

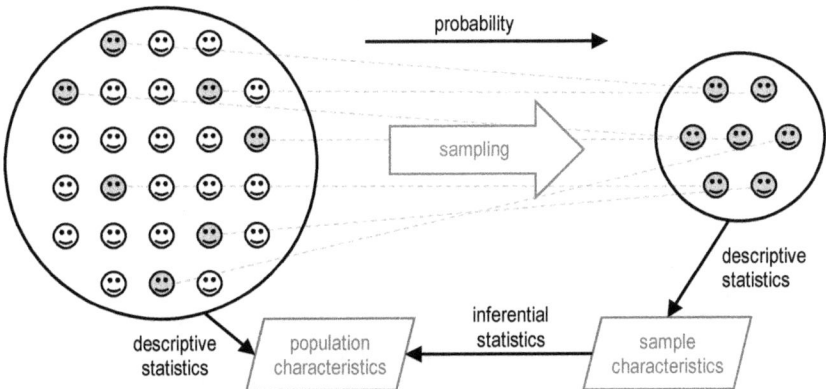

Figure 06-4 Central Dogma of Statistics

Central Dogma of Statistics explains the connection between population, sample, descriptive statistics, probability and inferential statistics. *Descriptive statistics* is used to describe the characteristics of a dataset. Such dataset can be population or sample. *Sample* is used when *population* data is not available, and it is not feasible to obtain. The process of sampling uses the theory of *probability*. *Inferential statistics* is used to predict the characteristics of population based on the descriptive statistics applied to sample dataset.

07. PROBABILITY DISTRIBUTION

In statistics, *probability distribution* is the likelihood that certain value will occur. This applies to both discrete and continuous data. This chapter presents quick explanations on five types of probability distribution:
- Uniform distribution (discrete and continuous)
- Binomial distribution (discrete)
- Normal distribution (continuous)
- Poisson distribution (discrete)
- Exponential distribution (continuous)
- Geometric distribution (discrete)

Uniform Distribution

Uniform distribution is the simplest form of probability distribution where all outcomes are equally likely. For discrete data, the probability for each is one divided by the number of possible values. For continuous data, the probability is one divided by range of values.

Probability of uniform distribution for discrete data with n possible values within interval a to b:

$$U(x = k; n) = \begin{cases} 1/n, & x \in [a \text{ to } b] \\ 0, & x \notin [a \text{ to } b] \end{cases}$$

Probability of uniform distribution for continuous data from minimum value a to maximum value b:

$$U(x = k; a; b) = \begin{cases} 1/(b-a), & a \leq x \leq b \\ 0, & x < a \text{ or } x > b \end{cases}$$

A dice has six sides. When we roll a dice, the possible outcomes are 1 to 6 with equal chance. The possibility to get each of the possible value is 1/6. Outcome 5.4 is not possible because dice outcome is discrete. The possibility to get 7 as the outcome is zero.

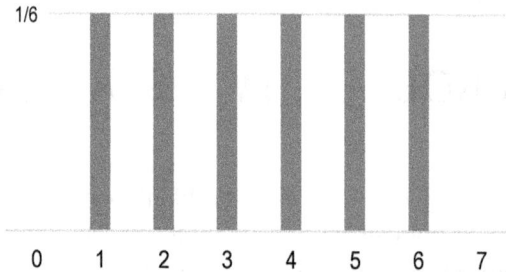

Figure 07-1 Uniform distribution for discrete data

An ice cream shop sells ice cream to 20 to 100 customers per day. Assuming uniform distribution, what is the probability that today's customer count falls between 30 to 40?

- Target range is $30 \leq x \leq 40$.
- $a = 20; b = 100$.
- $U(30 \leq x \leq 40; 20; 100) = (40 - 30) \times \frac{1}{(100-20)} = 0.125$.
- Probability of today's customer count falls between 30 to 40 is 12.5%.

Binomial Distribution

Binomial distribution is a discrete probability distribution with two possible values: success or fail. The probability to achieve successful result is indicated by variable P. Variable n is the number of trials. The simplest version of binomial distribution is called *Bernoulli distribution*. It is a special case of binomial distribution with only one trial.

Binomial distribution of x with n trials and success probability P is:

$$b(x = k; n; P) = {}^n_x Comb \times P^x \times (1 - P)^{(n-x)}$$

For Bernoulli distribution, since n is equal to 1:

$$b(x; 1; P) = \begin{cases} P, & x = 1 \\ 1 - P, & x = 0 \end{cases}$$

As a refresher, permutation of r from n means the number of possible set of samples with r items can be chosen from population with n items. If we have a population set of {A, B and C}, the possible combinations of samples with two items are:

- For sampling with replacement, there are nine possible permutations: {A, A}, {A, B}, {A, C}, {B, A}, {B, B}, {B, C}, {C, A}, {C, B} and {C, C}.
- For sampling without replacement, there are six possible permutations: {A, B}, {A, C}, {B, A}, {B, C}, {C, A} and {C, B}.

Formula for permutation with replacement:

$$_r^n PermR = n^r$$

Formula for permutation without replacement:

$$_r^n Perm = \frac{n!}{(n - r)!}$$

Exclamation mark is symbol for factorial. $x!$ means $1 \times 2 \times \cdots \times x$.

By applying the values of r and n into the formula, the number of permutations can be calculated:

- For sampling with replacement: $_2^3 PermR = 3^2 = 9$.
- For sampling without replacement: $_2^3 Perm = \frac{3!}{(3-2)!} = 6$.

Note than in permutation results above, {A, B} and {B, A} are considered two different samples. That is because permutation cares about the sequence of items in the selected samples.

Combination is permutation without caring about the sequence of items in the samples. The order of items does not matter, resulting in usually smaller number of possible samples when compared to permutation.

Formula for combination with replacement:

$$_r^n CombR = \frac{(r + n - 1)!}{r! (n - 1)!}$$

Formula for combination without replacement:

$$\begin{matrix}{}^n_r Comb\end{matrix} = \frac{n!}{r!\,(n-r)!}$$

By applying the values of r and n into the formula, the number of combinations can be calculated:

- For sampling with replacement: ${}^3_2 CombR = \frac{(2+3-1)!}{2!\times(3-1)!} = 6$.

  Samples: {A, A}, {A, B}, {A, C}, {B, B}, {B, C} and {C, C}.

- For sampling without replacement: ${}^3_2 Comb = \frac{3!}{2!\times(3-2)!} = 3$.

  Samples: {A, B}, {A, C} and {B, C}.

Unless otherwise stated, sampling without replacement is the default assumption for permutation and combination.

Back to binomial distribution, let us consider an example. Suppose there is a game where people would roll a dice. A player wins if the outcome is side-6. Any other results are considered as lose. What is the probability that someone will win exactly 3 times from 10 times of rolling the dice?

- The probability of winning in each trial is 1/6 because a dice has six faces.
- $P = 1/6 = 0.1667$.
- There are ten times of dice rolling, $n = 10$.
- $x = 3$.
- $b\left(x = 3; 10; \frac{1}{6}\right) = {}^{10}_3 Comb \times \left(\frac{1}{6}\right)^3 \times \left(1 - \frac{1}{6}\right)^{(10-3)} = 0.155$
- The probability of someone wins exactly 3 times is 15.5%

The cumulative probability for discrete distribution can be calculated using the following principles:

$$f(x < k) = \sum_{i=min}^{k-1} f(x = i)$$

$$f(x \le k) = \sum_{i=min}^{k} f(x = i)$$

$$f(x > k) = 1 - f(x \le k)$$

$$f(x \geq k) = 1 - f(x < k)$$

For binomial distribution, substitute $f(x)$ with $b(x; n; P)$. The *min* value for binomial distribution is zero.

Example for cumulative probability:
What is the probability of someone win maximum 2 times out of 10 games?

- Winning maximum 3 times means winning 0 or 1 or 2 times.
- The total probability is $b\left(x \leq 2; 10; \frac{1}{6}\right) = \sum_{i=0}^{2} b\left(x = i; 10; \frac{1}{6}\right) = b\left(x = 0; 10; \frac{1}{6}\right) + b\left(x = 1; 10; \frac{1}{6}\right) + b\left(x = 2; 10; \frac{1}{6}\right)$
- $b\left(x = 0; 10; \frac{1}{6}\right) = {}^{10}_{0}Comb \times \left(\frac{1}{6}\right)^{0} \times \left(1 - \frac{1}{6}\right)^{(10-0)} = 0.1615$
- $b\left(x = 1; 10; \frac{1}{6}\right) = {}^{10}_{1}Comb \times \left(\frac{1}{6}\right)^{1} \times \left(1 - \frac{1}{6}\right)^{(10-1)} = 0.3230$
- $b\left(x = 2; 10; \frac{1}{6}\right) = {}^{10}_{2}Comb \times \left(\frac{1}{6}\right)^{2} \times \left(1 - \frac{1}{6}\right)^{(10-2)} = 0.2907$
- Total probability = 0.7752 or 77.52%

Normal Distribution, Z Score and Central Limit Theorem

Normal distribution is continuous probability distribution where the majority of items are centred around the peak and the values further away from mean gradually decreases in both directions. Most situations in real life follow this model to a certain degree, hence the name.

Known characteristics of *normal distribution*:
- Mean, median and mode values are the same.
- Distribution chart looks like the shape of a bell, known as *bell curve* or *Gaussian curve*.
- Total area under the curve is equal to 1, which is 100% of all values in dataset.
- Symmetrical, not skewed, skewness value is 0.
- Kurtosis value is 3, excess kurtosis is 0.
- 68.2% of data points are within one standard deviation from mean.
- 95.4% of data points are within two standard deviations from mean.
- 99.7% of data points are within three standard deviations from mean.

The formula for *f(x)* in normal distribution:

$$f(x) = \frac{1}{\sigma\sqrt{2\pi}} \times e^{\frac{-(x-\mu)^2}{2\times\sigma^2}}$$

For standard normal distribution with $\mu = 0$ and $\sigma = 1$

$$f(x) = \frac{1}{\sqrt{2\pi}} \times e^{-1/2(x^2)}$$

e is a constant (2.71828) called *Euler's number*.

Z score is defined as the distance in terms of standard deviation between a value and the mean in a dataset with normal distribution. If a value is equal to mean plus $2 \times$ standard deviation, then it is said that the Z score is 2.

- Positive Z score indicates value above mean.
- Negative Z score indicates value below mean.

Formula of Z score:

$$Z = \frac{x_i - \mu}{\sigma}$$

Central Limit Theorem

Random samples taken from a population (with replacement) having mean μ and standard deviation σ will be close to normal distribution if the sample size is sufficiently large, even if the population itself does not follow normal distribution.

Central Limit Theorem (CLT) is the foundation of many other theories in statistical sampling and hypothesis test. These are critical parts of a Six Sigma DMAIC project and will be discussed in more details in later parts of this book.

Poisson Distribution

Poisson distribution is a discrete probability distribution model for the number of times an event occurs within a fixed interval of time or space. This measure calculates the possibility of x events occur during the interval if the average occurrence is λ (*lambda*).

Formula for Poisson distribution:

$$Ps(x = k; \lambda) = \frac{\lambda^x \times e^{-\lambda}}{x!}$$

e is a constant called *Euler's number*. The approximate value is 2.71828.

Example 1:

The average number of people visiting a local library is 20. What is the probability that 25 visitors will come to the library today?

- The average number of customers per day (λ) is 20.
- The target value is $x = 25$.

- $Ps(x = 25; 20) = \frac{20^{25} \times e^{-20}}{25!} = 0.0446$

- The probability that 25 people will visit the library today is 4.46%

The cumulative probability using Poisson distribution is the sum of probabilities of all accepted values.

Example 2:

In average, a librarian sends 5 late return reminders by email per day. What is the probability of sending maximum of 3 reminders today?

- The average number of reminders per day (λ) is 5.
- The target value is $x \leq 3$.

- $Ps(x \leq 3; 5) = \sum_{i=0}^{3} Ps(x = i; 5)$

- $Ps(x \leq 3; 5) = Ps(x = 0; 5) + Ps(x = 1; 5) + Ps(x = 2; 5) + Ps(x = 3; 5) = 0.1247$

- The probability that librarian will send maximum of 3 reminders today is 12.47%

Exponential Distribution

Exponential distribution is a continuous probability distribution model for the time between specific events. It is often used together with Poisson distribution because of their complementary characteristics: Poisson distribution counts the number of events, exponential distribution measures the time between the events.

The average time between events is measured as λ (*lambda*). The target time is x and it cannot be negative value for exponential distribution. e is *Euler's number* constant (2.71828).

$$Ex(x = k; \lambda) = \begin{cases} \dfrac{e^{\left(\frac{-x}{\lambda}\right)}}{\lambda}, & x \geq 0 \\ 0, & x < 0 \end{cases}$$

71

Other books or courses might use *decay parameter* $m = 1/\lambda$ in the formula:

$$Ex\left(x = k; \frac{1}{m}\right) = \begin{cases} me^{-mx}, & x \geq 0 \\ 0, & x < 0 \end{cases}$$

Example 1:

In average, players need 5 minutes to finish a certain level in a game. What is the probability that a random player will take 4 minutes to finish the level?

- Average of 5 minutes, $\lambda = 5$ and $m = \frac{1}{5} = 0.2$.
- Target value of $x = 4$.
- $Ex(x = 4; 5) = 0.2 \times e^{-(0.2 \times 4)} = 0.0899$
- The probability that a random player finishes the level in 4 minutes is 0.0899 or 8.99%.

Cumulative of exponential distribution is calculated as the probability of having $0 \leq x \leq k$, or from k point to the left of chart down to zero because x cannot be negative value.

$$Ex(x \leq k; \lambda) = \begin{cases} 1 - e^{\left(\frac{-x}{\lambda}\right)}, & x \geq 0 \\ 0, & x < 0 \end{cases}$$

Example 2:

The average time needed to finish a certain level in a game is 5 minutes. Calculate the probability of a random player finish the level between 3 to 4 minutes.

- Average of 5 minutes, $\lambda = 5$ and $m = \frac{1}{5} = 0.2$.
- Target value of $3 \leq x \leq 4$.
- $Ex(3 \leq x \leq 4; 5) = Ex(x \leq 4; 5) - Ex(x \leq 3; 5)$
- $Ex(3 \leq x \leq 4; 5) = \left(1 - e^{-(0.2 \times 4)}\right) - \left(1 - e^{-(0.2 \times 3)}\right)$
- $Ex(3 \leq x \leq 4; 5) = 0.5507 - 0.4512 = 0.0995$
- The probability that a random player finishes the level between 3 to 4 minutes is 0.0995 or 9.95%.

Cumulative of exponential distribution of k-or-above is defined as $x > k$, or from k point to the right of chart, up to infinity.

$$Ex(x > k; \lambda) = \begin{cases} e^{\left(\frac{-x}{\lambda}\right)}, & x \geq 0 \\ 0, & x < 0 \end{cases}$$

Example 3:
The average time needed to finish a certain level in a game is 5 minutes. Calculate the probability of a random player finish the level in more than 6 minutes.

- Average of 5 minutes, $\lambda = 5$ and $m = \frac{1}{5} = 0.2$.
- Target value of $x > 6$.
- $Ex(x > 6; 5) = e^{-(0.2 \times 6)} = 0.3012$
- The probability that a random player finishes the level in more than six minutes is 0.3012 or 30.12%.

Geometric Distribution

Geometric distribution is a discrete probability distribution in counting the number of trials until achieving the first success. This distribution is considered as the discrete counterpart of exponential distribution. Exponential distribution measures time (continuous) vs. geometric distribution counts the number of trials until next success (discrete).

Every count of trials in geometric distribution is a single entity of *Bernoulli trial*. Comparable to binomial distribution, each trial has probability of success equal to P. Assuming that every trial is independent, the probability that k^{th} trial is the first success is measured in geometric distribution as:

$$G(x = k; P) = P \times (1 - P)^{k-1}$$

Counting the number of trials until the first success means the minimum value of x is 1. This happens when the first trial is already successful. Therefore, the value of x cannot be negative or zero.

Example:
Suppose there is a game where people would roll a dice. A player wins if the outcome is 6. Any other results are considered as lose. What is the probability that someone will win the first time on the 5th attempt?

- The probability of winning in each trial is 1/6 because a dice has six faces.
- $P = 1/6 = 0.1667$.
- $G\left(x = 5; \frac{1}{6}\right) = \frac{1}{6} \times \left(1 - \frac{1}{6}\right)^{5-1} = 0.0804$.
- The probability of winning the first time on the 5th attempt is 8.04%.

Still using the dice example, what is the probability that someone will have the first win in maximum 3 attempts?

- Cumulative formula for discrete distribution is used with *min* value 1.
- $G\left(x \leq 3; \frac{1}{6}\right) = \sum_{i=1}^{3} G\left(x = i; \frac{1}{6}\right).$
- $G\left(x \leq 3; \frac{1}{6}\right) = G\left(x = 1; \frac{1}{6}\right) + G\left(x = 2; \frac{1}{6}\right) + G\left(x = 3; \frac{1}{6}\right).$
- $G\left(x = 1; \frac{1}{6}\right) = \frac{1}{6} \times \left(1 - \frac{1}{6}\right)^{1-1} = 0.1667.$
- $G\left(x = 2; \frac{1}{6}\right) = \frac{1}{6} \times \left(1 - \frac{1}{6}\right)^{2-1} = 0.1389.$
- $G\left(x = 3; \frac{1}{6}\right) = \frac{1}{6} \times \left(1 - \frac{1}{6}\right)^{3-1} = 0.1157.$
- $G\left(x \leq 3; \frac{1}{6}\right) = 0.4213.$
- The probability of someone winning the dice game in maximum 3 attempts is 42.13%.

Others

Other notable distributions:

- *Bimodal distribution* is a continuous probability distribution with two peaks of different heights. It represents multiple independent conditions. Similarly, *multimodal distribution* has multiple peaks of different heights.
- *Log-normal distribution* is a continuous probability distribution with asymmetrical and heavily skewed curve. It shows logarithmic distribution of a related normal distribution and is commonly used to represent machine down time.
- *Weibull distribution* is a continuous probability distribution that represents multiple effects, such as failure rates during a product's lifetime. The curve of Weibull distribution is asymmetrical and could be a mix of exponential and log-normal curves. It is powerful to model slow wear and tear in normal circumstances.

08. BASIC TOOLS OF QUALITY

Lean Six Sigma projects use *seven basic tools of quality* to help with identifying issues. These tools help Six Sigma practitioners during problem solving sessions by allowing systematic approach to analyse the situation. Seven basic tools of quality do not have the power to resolve complex problems that require significant statistical analysis, but it will be useful for an organisation to catch and address long hanging fruits.

The seven basic tools of quality are:
1. Check sheet
2. Cause-and-effect diagram
3. Flow chart
4. Scatter plot
5. Histogram
6. Pareto chart
7. Control chart

This chapter also discusses box plot and dot plot. They are not part of seven basic tools of quality, but they are useful and commonly used in Lean Six Sigma.

Check Sheet

Check sheet (also known as *tally sheet*) is a basic quality tool to collect data, most commonly quantitative count of certain events. It uses rows and columns to classify data into clusters and provide quick visual representation.

Technical support department of an online shopping company wishes to compare the help requests that they receive each day for each category. The following check sheet shows the help requests and the total for each row and column.

Description	Mon	Tue	Wed	Thu	Fri	Total
Problem with login	⁇⁇ ⁇⁇ /	///	⁇⁇	⁇⁇ ⁇⁇	////	33
Cart & payment issues	⁇⁇	⁇⁇ ⁇⁇	⁇⁇ ////	⁇⁇ //	⁇⁇ ⁇⁇ //	43
Return & warranty	⁇⁇ ///	⁇⁇ ///	///	⁇⁇ ⁇⁇ //	⁇⁇ ///	39
Loyalty membership	⁇⁇ /	⁇⁇	⁇⁇ ⁇⁇	////	⁇⁇ ⁇⁇	35
Total	30	26	27	33	34	150

Table 08-A Example of check sheet

Cause-and-Effect Diagram

Cause-and-effect diagram is a quality tool to find and show possible causes of a problem. This tool was invented by *Dr. Kaoru Ishikawa*, also known as *fishbone diagram* or *Ishikawa diagram*. The name fishbone diagram is inspired by the shape of this diagram that looks like skeleton fish. A horizontal line in the middle is pointing to problem statement written on the right side. From this middle line, a few "bones" branch out. Each bone represents one analysis category, along with the findings in that category.

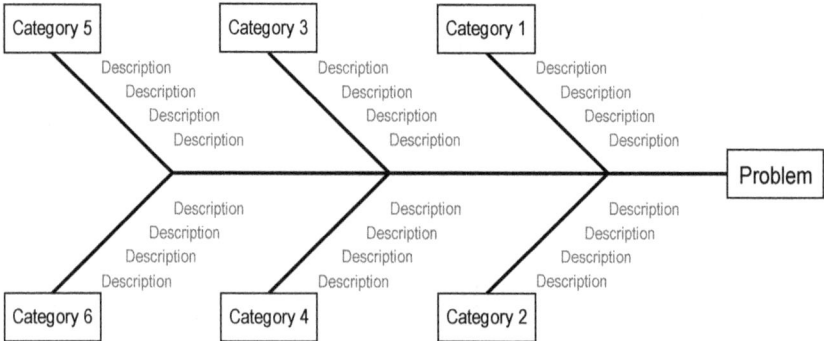

Figure 08-1 Cause-and-effect diagram

Figure 08-1 shows an example of cause-and-effect diagram with six categories. A Belt (Lean Six Sigma practitioner with Green Belt or Black Belt qualification) may choose to create categories unique to the problem or can follow one of the popular fishbone categories.

There are three popular fishbone categories:
- *4S diagram*: Suppliers, Skills, Surrounding, Systems
- *6M diagram*: Man (personnel), Methods, Machine, Material, Measurement, Mother Nature (external environment).
- *8P diagram*: Product (service), Price, Place, Promotion, Personnel, Process, Physical Evidence, Productivity.

4S and 8P diagrams are commonly used in service industry. 6M diagram is popular with manufacturing. Influenced by its root of origin from Japan, cause-and-effect diagram is written and read from right to left.

Due to their similar purpose, *5 whys* technique is often used together with cause-and-effect diagram. This technique uses nested questioning to drill down the root cause of a particular problem. Suppose there is a problem A in production system. The first why would ask why A happens. If the answer is B, then ask why B happens. Repeat these five times and there is a good chance that a potential root cause is among the mentioned answers.

Flow Chart

Flow chart is a common tool to document the process flow in a system using well-defined shapes to represent consistent meaning.
- Oval represents start and end.
- Rectangle represents process.
- Rectangle with rounded edges represents alternate process.
- Parallelogram represents input and output.
- Diamond indicates decision point.
- Line with arrow shows relationships between entities.

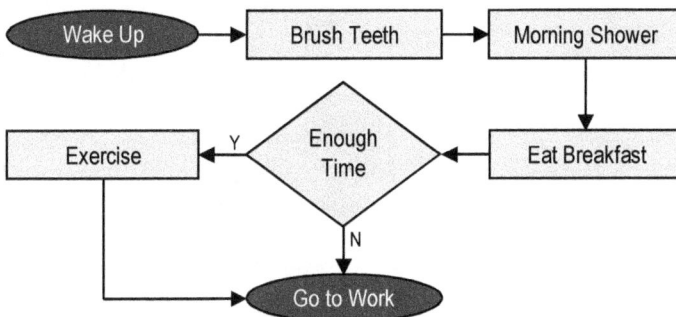

Figure 08-2 Flow chart example: morning activities before work

77

As a visual representation tool, flow chart is a powerful tool to understand how a system works, the sequence of processes, how decisions are made and the boundaries of operational units.

Scatter Plot

Scatter plot is a visual tool to represent the values of two different variables. It uses x-axis and y-axis to map values in a Cartesian plane, making it easier to identify correlation trend or outliers. This tool is also known as *XY graph*, *scatter chart* or *scatter diagram*.

A restaurant specialised in selling hot soup tries to analyse their daily sales versus the noon temperature of that day. They collected data for 2 weeks with the following results:

Temp °C	Sales	Temp °C	Sales
28.8°	$ 4,885	22.5°	$ 5,950
26.1°	$ 4,335	18.9°	$ 6,030
28.5°	$ 3,890	33.2°	$ 3,100
37.4°	$ 2,330	27.2°	$ 4,505
28.5°	$ 4,990	26.5°	$ 4,820
18.6°	$ 6,375	19.2°	$ 6,225
31.5°	$ 3,960	23.4°	$ 5,285

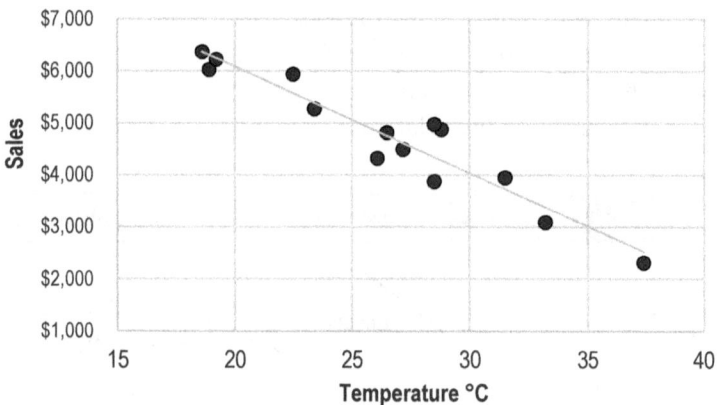

Figure 08-3 Scatter plot example: hot soup restaurant

78

The scatter plot of hot soup restaurant's data shows *negative correlation* between temperature and sales. The higher the temperature, there is a common pattern that sales on that day will likely go smaller. This trend line is known as *line of best fit* or *regression line*.

Note that scatter plot does not consider the sequence of data. The fact that 26.1° day comes after 28.8° day is not represented in the plot/chart. Scatter Plot simply takes the values of X (temperature) and map it against the values of Y (sales).

Histogram

Histogram is a visual quality tool using *bar chart* to represent the distribution of data. The term histogram and its formal description were introduced by *Karl Pearson* in 1895. However, *William Playfair* was credited as the first person to use it, along with his inventions of bar, line and area charts back in 1786.

The most common use of histogram is to present the counts of continuous data grouped into several range groups. If the data distribution is normal, histogram will show bell-shaped bars with *average (means)* in the middle.

School XYZ collects data of their students' test results. There are 100 students, the lowest score is 37 and the highest score is 100. Data are grouped into eight clusters. The mapping of data count is presented with a histogram.

Test Scores in School XYZ

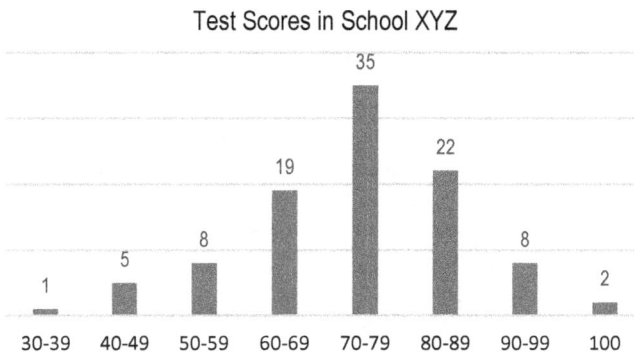

Figure 08-4 Histogram example: test scores

Pareto Chart

Pareto chart is a quality tool showing frequencies in bars and cumulative percentage in line graph. This chart was introduced by *Vilfredo Pareto* with a theory that 80% of problems are caused by 20% of few major factors. Focusing to improve the 20% factors and resolving 80% of problems will bring major impact to the end result.

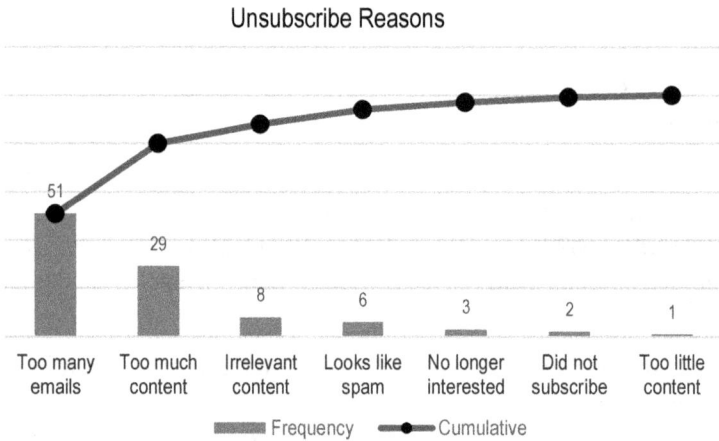

Figure 08-5 Pareto chart example: unsubscribe reasons

Control Chart

Control chart is a statistical chart showing the values of key factors in a system to see if a process is within control. It plots data values on a line chart to enable quick visualisation on how each data point is located with respect to *average* line, upper control limit line and lower control limit line. Simple version of control limits can be calculated as horizontal lines of *average* plus/minus three times *standard deviation*. Different types of control charts have different formulas to calculate control limits. This quality tool was invented by *Walter Shewhart* and often known as *Shewhart chart*.

It is important to note that control limits are different from specification limits from customer. Control limits are calculated based on system performance to try to identify if process variations occur because of common cause (random) or special cause. In Figure 08-6, the process is said to be *out of control* when it produces data point outside control limit.

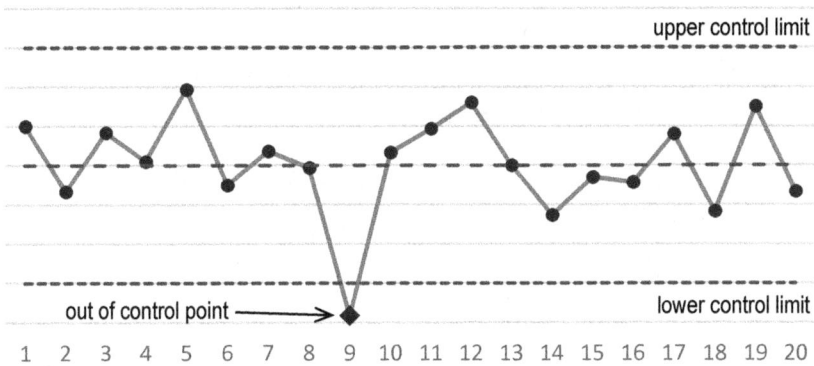

Figure 08-6 Control chart example

Each data point in control chart could represent individual observation or average value of each sub-group. There are different types of control chart, depending on data type (continuous or discrete) and the involvement of past observations in each data point. Detailed explanations on control chart are available in later chapters on the topic of *Statistical Process Control* (SPC).

Box Plot

Box plot (also known as *box and whisker plot*) is a visual tool to show the distribution and skewness of data. It shows a number of key statistical boundaries of multiple datasets, allowing quick comparison and decision making.

It is important to understand the anatomy of box plot. The box part represent area from 25th to 75th percentile of data divided by horizontal line to show median value. Mean value (average) is indicated by X mark. Outside the box, there are two whiskers representing the area from the box to the maximum and minimum values. However, if a data point is statistically far from others in a dataset, it will be marked as a separate dot outside the box and whiskers, identifying possible outlier.

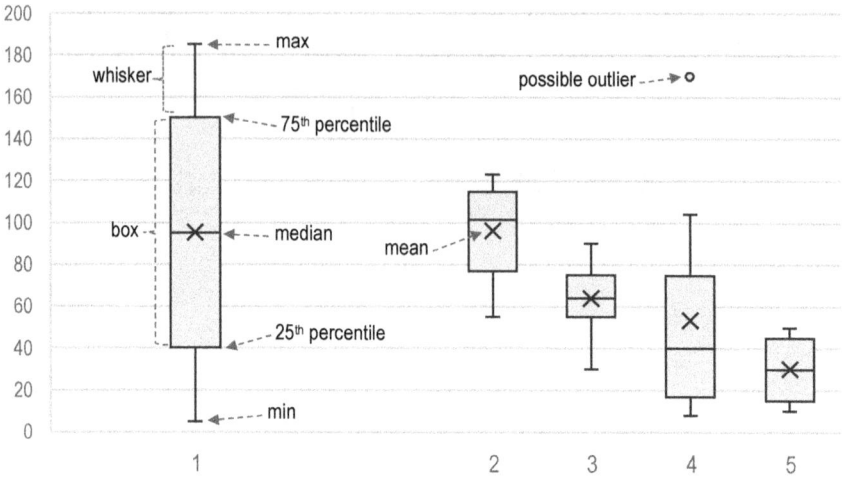

Figure 08-7 Box plot example

From the box plot in Figure 08-7, it can be observed that:

- Dataset 1 has the widest range. Data seems to be symmetrically distributed, with median point equal to mean point.
- Dataset 2 appears skewed, mean value is smaller than median value.
- Dataset 3 has the smallest box, it means the data points are concentrated around median value, which happens to be equal to mean value.
- Dataset 4 appears skewed and has potential outlier.
- Dataset 5 has very short whiskers, indicating multiple data points with close values outside the box.

Box plot makes it possible to compare data from different processes. From the example above, it can be observed that all values in dataset 2 are bigger than any value in dataset 5. Dataset 3 might have the best performance because of its smaller variation. However, this observation still needs further information (such as the size of each dataset) to make better conclusion.

Dot Plot

Dot Plot (also known as *strip chart*) is a simple statistical tool to visualise data using dots. Its concept is similar to bar chart, but it uses dots to represent one data point. This tool is suitable for small to medium dataset and useful to identify clusters and outliers.

A company gathers data on how many cups of coffee each employee drinks in a day. The result is presented in this table:

cups of coffee	0	1	2	3	4	5	6
people	8	9	6	7	3	2	5

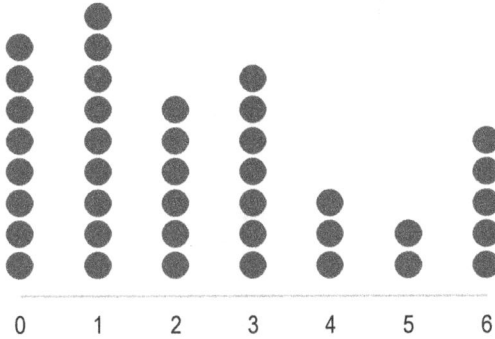

Figure 08-8 Dot plot example

DEFINE PHASE

DEFINE PHASE

09. PROJECT SELECTION

Company XYZ is a toy manufacturer (not a real company, this is just an example). The toys are popular with significant market share, but the company's profit has been stagnant for a few years and competitors are slowly increasing their market share. Jane, the CEO of XYZ, asks Tim, a Lean Six Sigma Black Belt, to analyse what can be improved so that the company's products would remain competitive.

Tim spends some time to understand the business and production process before creating a list of possible projects. There are some principles to help with identifying possible improvements:

- Measure the current process. This should be the first step because one cannot improve something that cannot be measured. To be able to confirm improvement, we need to compare measurement before and after.
- Analyse available data and reports.
- Find gaps and shortfalls in the process.
- Compare production results against requirements from Voice of the Customer (VOC) as written in Critical to Quality (CTQ). If these are not available, start with aspects that are clearly not appreciated by customers.
- Discover variability problems in production. Even if the average of production falls within the range of customer specifications, high variability will make significant portion of production results fall outside the range.
- Identify recurring problems, if any.

- Use *gemba walk* to directly observe production process. Learn about the process flow from the actual place where it happens. Find non-value-added steps (waste) and identify possible improvements.
- Identify process waste: transportation, inventory, motion, waiting, overproduction, overprocessing, defect and skill underutilised.
- Compare takt rate against cycle time and lead time.
- Analyse warranty claims, recalls, customer complaints.
- Identify the visible and hidden costs of process inefficiencies.
- Brainstorm with Subject Matter Expert (SME) in each area, find out their thoughts on what needs to be addressed.
- Read employee suggestion, if any. Find if the suggestion is backed by data. Some of them already have genuinely good ideas on things to improve.

To qualify to be considered for Six Sigma DMAIC project, a problem must be a *recurring* problem. Single occurrence problem that does not happen again is not within the domain for Six Sigma project because it is not considered as the systemic result of a process.

Not all potential improvements will end up being addressed by *Six Sigma DMAIC* projects. Remember that DMAIC is a process improvement methodology. It needs an existing process to improve. Therefore, if one of the problems discovered is the need to design an entirely new product, then it is not the right problem for DMAIC.

Another consideration is whether drivers of performance for a particular problem is already known. If the factors impacting performance is already known or can be obtained by tapping the knowledge from some people within the organisation (could be department managers, SMEs, field experts, operator supervisors, etc) then a *Kaizen event* is a better methodology to address the problem Six Sigma DMAIC is a powerful methodology of process improvement if the drivers of performance for a problem is unknown and need further analysis from data.

Back to the company XYZ example, Tim might discover the following problems:
- Production process had to stop production a few times a month because some parts are depleted and new batch from supplier has not arrived yet.
  Analysis: This is a *waiting waste* in Lean principles.

- XYZ has two production facilities located far from each other. Some toy models require production processes in both facilities. Parts and unfinished products need to be transported back and forth three times during production.

Analysis: This is a *transportation waste* in Lean principles.

- There is significant number of complaints from the customers that they are not happy with the packaging of some toys because they are too difficult to open even for parents. Upon investigation, such packaging actually requires more production efforts and simpler packaging would save costs and make customers happy.

   Analysis: This is an *overprocessing waste*, a production effort that does not add value as perceived by customers.

- Four types of toys have higher than 35% return rate.

   Analysis: This is an example of a problem that is identified by both Lean and Six Sigma principles. From Lean perspective, this is a *defect waste*. From Six Sigma perspective, this is a failure to meet customer demand because of production accuracy or variability issues. If the factors causing the defects are unknown, Six Sigma DMAIC project can be used to improve the situation.

Problems identified as non-value-added steps (waste) of Lean could be addressed by having a Kaizen event or data-backed discussions with decision makers and key stakeholders. Problems related to process accuracy and variability are listed as potential Six Sigma DMAIC projects.

Any company usually have multiple problems at the same time. Solving all of those would be ideal, but sometimes not feasible due to the limited availability of time, cost and resources for the problem solving or process improvement activities. Most of the time, a company would have to select which projects get to start first based on their priorities.

Remember that Six Sigma project uses $Y = f(X)$ formula. According to *Pareto principle*, 20% of the causes (the X factors) are causing 80% of the problems (the Y outcomes). Project selection needs to identify which projects would be useful to control these 20% of the causes so that 80% of the problems will get resolved.

There are several aspects to be considered for project selection:

- *Cost and benefit analysis*. Compare the estimated cost of running the project compared to the potential benefits once it is completed. The benefits of a project could be additional revenue or cost saving.

- *Degree of urgency*. Some problems have strict due date beyond a company's control such as new regulation from the government that will start on certain date.

- *Alignment with company goals.* Some improvements might provide strategic benefits for the company to reach its main goals while some others might only have minimal impact.
- *Alignment with customers' perceived value.* Projects that will bring improvement to product (or service) value as perceived by customers should get higher priority.
- *Estimated completion time.* Most companies want to see short term results before they would invest for longer-term investment on bigger projects. Unless for exceptional circumstances, most DMAIC projects are expected to complete in less than six months.
- *Safety impact.* If a certain problem could put employees or customers in danger (safety issues), then a problem is critically important to address.
- *Operational impact.* Executive leadership of a company might choose projects based the operational impacts to minimise disruptions. For example: a company might choose to do major operational changes in November because it might impact their production capacity to fulfil the demand for Christmas and New Year shopping.
- *Resource impact.* Project selection needs to consider the availability of protect team members and key stakeholders.
- *Data availability.* Six Sigma DMAIC is a data-driven project. Some data might already be available while others need to be collected during project execution. This is additional time and efforts, which will translate to project cost. Projects with most data already available might be considered to start first. If output data from a project is needed for another project, it might be beneficial to execute them in the right sequence.

Project selection is commonly performed by *steering committee* or *project sponsors* involving top executive and senior management in a company, with assistance from Black Belt or Master Black Belt. A popular method for selection is by creating *project viability matrix.*

In project viability matrix, selection criteria are given weight points. The more important a criterion, the bigger weight it gets. Setting the right weight value is critically important to make sure that every critical criterion (such as safety and regulation) gets the attention it requires.

After setting the weights, each project candidate is scored on the scale of 1 to 5. Maximum score of 5 is given when there is a strong reason to raise a project's importance level based on this criterion.

Criteria	Weight	Project A	Project B	Project C
Is potential benefit bigger than cost?				
How urgent is this change?				
Is this aligned with company goals?				
Will this improve customer's satisfaction?				
Is this related to safety or regulation?				
Are the resources available?				
Is all supporting data available?				
<a criterion>				
<a criterion>				
...				
Total		**Total 1**	**Total 2**	**Total 3**

Table 09-A Project Viability Matrix

Some criteria have answers that will change depending on the timing of project selection activity. It is generally a good practice to always start with a table with empty scores for every round of project selection to capture the latest situation.

Depending on their specific constraints or situations, some companies might choose to use different mechanism for project selection. The most important thing is to ensure that decision making process is data driven and all key aspects have been put into consideration.

After one or multiple projects are selected, the next job of project sponsors is to appoint project champion as management team's point person for a particular project. Project champion is a person from executive or senior manager level with enough power and respect to ensure progress and remove impediments. Project leader is chosen with inputs from project champion. Project leader takes on a project and start the work on *project charter*.

10. PROJECT CHARTER

Solving a problem needs to start from defining the problem. There is a famous quote from Charles Kettering: "A problem well-stated is a problem half-solved."

The first phase of Six Sigma DMAIC project is the *Define phase*. As the name suggests, this phase focuses on defining the project, making sure everyone is on the same page and agree on the problem.

Project charter is the main deliverable of Define phase. It is a document containing all the key information about a Six Sigma DMAIC project. This document is a critical reference to the problem statement, goal statements, initial estimation and milestones. Project charter is required to obtain written approval to start a project. It is a *living document*, meaning it will continue to be updated as necessary through the following phases of DMAIC.

Purposes of project charter:
- Serves as a written agreement between DMAIC project team and company management.
- Facilitates discussions to align the expectations from relevant stakeholders.
- Serves as reference point on the problem definition, goal statement and project scope.
- Keeps the team focused.
- Provides high level documentation about the project.

Problem Statement

Problem statement is a statement that defines the problem. It defines why a DMAIC project is needed. As a critical statement to start a Six Sigma project, it needs to be factual (data-based) and specific.

A good problem statement has its root from *Voice of the Customer* (VOC). In simple terms, VOC is the list of things that are considered as valuable from the customer's perspective. These are things that customers want, written in their point of view.

The next step of using VOC is to convert it into *Critical to Quality* (CTQ). This is the list of quality aspects that a product (or service) needs to have in order to satisfy customer's expectations as recorded in VOC. In a Six Sigma process, CTQ is the reference point for customer specifications.

If everything goes perfect, there is no need for a DMAIC project. When problems happen, its impact needs to be quantified. *Cost of Poor Quality* (COPQ) is a measure of costs incurred when a production process fails to meet quality requirements. There are two types of COPQ: visible and hidden. Visible COPQ includes internal failure costs (the costs from defective units before reaching customers), external failure costs (after reaching customers) and appraisal costs (the costs to check whether a product or service meets the quality requirements). Hidden COPQ are the costs not directly quantified, such as loss of customer loyalty or loss of potential sales. Please refer to Chapter 02 to learn more about VOC, CTQ and COPQ.

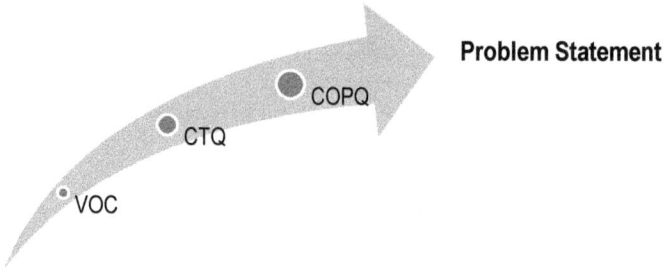

Figure 10-1 Making Problem Statement

Jumping directly to problem statement without going through the steps of VOC, CTQ and COPQ is a common mistake in writing problem statement. Following the right steps helps to produce well-defined statement, which in turn will provide strong starting point for a project.

Let us analyse some possible problem statements for a DMAIC project in toy maker company XYZ:

- *Our toy's quality is poor, people are returning our products.*
  Analysis: This problem statement does not present data to support its claim. The statement uses qualitative claim without clear proposal on how to measure it.

- *According to our product return report, too many customers are returning our products.*
  Analysis: This problem statement uses product return report as the supporting data for its claim. However, the definition of too many customers is not clear. How many is considered too many? Does the company have standard on acceptable number of returns? This statement addresses the VOC, but not the CTQ.

- *According to our product return report, 22% of our product sales are returned by customers because of defects. This is significantly higher than the acceptable return rate of 5%.*
  Analysis: This problem statement is supported by data and provides specific measurement of the current situation compared to the acceptable return rate. However, this problem statement does not specify what is the impact for the company for having such problem. This statement addresses VOC and CTQ, but not the COPQ.

- *According to our product return report, 22% of our product sales are returned by customers because of defects. This is significantly higher than the acceptable return rate of 5%. The cost of rework to fix the defects costs the company more than $300,000 per month and it is causing loss of customer loyalty and loss of potential sales.*
  Analysis: This problem statement addresses what the customer perceives (VOC), the measurement from company's perspective (CTQ) and the cost of not meeting the expected quality (COPQ). This is an acceptable problem statement, but it can still be improved further.

- *According to our product return report in the last 12 months, 22% of our product sales are returned by customers because of defects, significantly higher than the acceptable return rate of 5%. This trend started from 9 months ago. The cost of rework to fix the defects costs the company more than $300,000 per month and it is causing loss of customer loyalty and loss of potential sales.*
  Analysis: This problem statement addresses what the customer perceives (VOC), the measurement from company's perspective (CTQ) and the cost of not meeting the expected quality (COPQ). All

claims are supported by data and the statement clearly describes the time frame of the problem.

In the cases when the specific data for problem statement is not readily available, estimation based on other available data might be acceptable. Since project charter is a living document, the measures need to be updated as soon as reliable data becomes available throughout project execution.

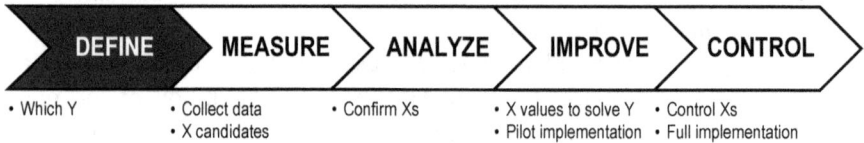

DEFINE	MEASURE	ANALYZE	IMPROVE	CONTROL
• Which Y	• Collect data • X candidates	• Confirm Xs	• X values to solve Y • Pilot implementation	• Control Xs • Full implementation

Figure 10-2 Define phase in DMAIC

Problem statement of a project must be a representation of the big Y in Six Sigma Y = f (X) formula. It marks the starting point of Six Sigma journey to work on Y by finding the candidates of X that influence Y, calculating the optimal values of Xs for best Y performance, then implementing the change.

Goal Statement

Goal statement is a statement to answer what the project is trying to achieve in order to address problem statement. This statement describes what the project tries to accomplish using five principles of *SMART* (specific, measurable, attainable, relevant and time-bound).

Specific goal statement means it defines what it is trying to resolve, not other things. If project goal tries to improve the return rate of product, it should not be expected to resolve other problems related to inventory. A specific DMAIC project initiated by Australian branch to resolve problems in Australia should not be expected to resolve problems in other countries.

Measurable goal statement means the success criteria of the project must be something that can be measured objectively after project completion. If the goal is to increase sales by 20%, it should not be expected to achieve 50% of increase.

Attainable goal statement indicates that goal is achievable given the project time frame, available resources, support from project sponsors and other constraints. Goal attainability is something that needs to be agreed on. Once committed, everyone involved will have to do their part to make best possible efforts to reach the goals that have been agreed as doable.

Relevant goal statement means that a goal needs to be aligned with the business goals. No matter how sweet a goal sounds like, it means very little if it is not aligned with the company objectives and business goals.

Time bound goal statement provides the connection between project goal and time frame when such goal needs to be achieved. Project goal could not specify 20% of sales improvement that can be achieved within infinite time. There needs to be an agreed time frame on when the expected benefits would be reflected in the company's performance.

Possible goal statements for a DMAIC project in toy maker company XYZ:

- *Reduce the return rate.*
  Analysis: This goal statement is not measurable.

- *Reduce the return rate down to 5% across all product categories.*
  Analysis: This goal statement is not time bound. There is no clear time frame on when to achieve the improvement.

- *Reduce the return rate down to 5% across all product categories within five months to increase customer loyalty and reduce rework costs.*
  Analysis: This goal statement is specific, measurable, attainable, relevant and time bound.

Components of Project Charter

Project charter is the main deliverable of Define phase. It serves as high-level requirements and project documentation from the beginning of a project. DMAIC Define phase prepares, presents, discusses and gets approval on Project Charter before the project can move on to the following phases.

An effective project charter needs to answer the *five basic Ws* about the project:

- Why is the project needed?
- What are the objectives to achieve?
- When can the project be completed?
- Who is working on the project?
- Where do the budget and resources come from?

There is no strict format about how a project charter should look like. Different organisations might come with their versions of project charter adjusted to their specific situations.

Project charter is constructed using the following components:
- Project Name
- Problem Statement
- Goal Statement
- Business Case
- Project Scope
- Project Impacts
- Timeline
- Team Members
- Approval

Problem statement and *goal statement* have been discussed in the previous parts of this chapter. These are the foundations of a project and represents the big Y in Six Sigma $Y = f(X)$ formula.

Business case explains the quantified costs and benefits of the project and explains how it is aligned with company's business goals. Project benefits could be in the form of additional revenue or cost saving. In general, benefits must be something that can be measured within no longer than one year after project completion.

Project scope defines the aspects that are covered by the projects and the ones which are not. A good statement of well-defined scope includes specific mention of out-of-scope items. This protects the team from scope creep during project execution. Scope creep happens when a project gradually takes on additional tasks outside what was originally agreed, making it harder to achieve the original goals.

Project impacts describe how the project will impact customers, employees, stakeholders and company operational. Examples of project impacts:
- Impact on customers: different mechanism to return defective product, longer warranty period, increased customer loyalty from better products.
- Impact on employees: mandatory training for employees in certain department, new recruits, downsizing, adjusted working hours.
- Impact on stakeholders: updated process for certain division, campaign project needs to be executed in parallel.
- Impact on operational: disruptions during project execution, increased or decreased production capacity during certain period, temporary rule changes.

Timeline or *project milestones* explains the expected duration of the project, broken down into phases and each key activity. It gives clear expectations on when project sponsors and stakeholders can expect to see some deliverables.

Team members lists the name of each person that will work in project team, along with their position in the project and the expected time commitment so that everyone is clear on how much time they should spend on the project as well as the time they spend in their normal responsibilities in their usual role. It is critical to make sure that the expectations are realistic. A project could not expect someone to spend 50% of their time in a project without arranging for the person to get adjusted workload for his BAU (*business as usual*) tasks.

The final part of project charter is *approval*. At the minimum, usually a Project Charter needs to be approved by project sponsors, project champion, finance department and project leader. Approval can be in the form of signature in printed document or can be a simple email with the words "Approved, please proceed." Project charter approval becomes the mandate for project team to start working.

Stakeholder Management

Working on project charter involves different people from different levels in the company. There is a delicate balance between not involving enough people and involving too many people.

Involving too many people will usually make it significantly harder to reach agreement, especially when some stakeholders have different agenda. It is also easier to get distracted into pointless argument about non-substantial issues when too many people are involved. On the other hand, not involving enough people might cause a project to start on the wrong foot by not getting the agreement or buy-in from a critical key stakeholder because she was not involved in Project Charter discussion.

RACI matrix (also known as *responsibility assignment matrix*) is a useful management tool to help with stakeholder management. It starts with a list of names and roles. Then it classifies each stakeholder into four categories: *Responsible, Accountable, Consulted, Informed*. The name RACI is taken from the first letter of these categories.

Activity	Champion	Project Leader	Finance Director	Process Owner	SME 1	SME 2	Marketing Manager
Project Charter	A,I	R	C	C	C	C	I
Process Mapping	I	R,A		C	C	C	
Some activity in Measure phase	I	R,A		C	I	I	
Some activity in Measure phase	I	R,A		C	I		
Some activity in Analyze phase	I	R,A		I	C	C	
...							

Table 10-A RACI matrix

Responsible category is assigned to stakeholders who are responsible to do certain task or involved in certain discussion. Multiple stakeholders can be responsible for the same task.

Accountable category is assigned to one person who should make sure that a task is properly completed. There can be only one accountable stakeholder for each task.

Consulted category is assigned to stakeholders whose opinions are needed for a task. This could be department managers, subject matter experts (SMEs) or someone from the senior management.

Informed category is assigned to stakeholders who needs to receive up to date information about a task. This category indicates one-way communication from project team to the individuals in this category.

Winning the support of all key stakeholders is critically important for the success of a Six Sigma project. It is also important to understand that support is not static. Involving key stakeholders as part of the work journey or at least keeping them informed will increase the likelihood of their continuous support.

Risk Management

Risk management in Six Sigma project is an integrated process throughout DMAIC phases. Each phase in DMAIC needs to complete different parts of risk management activities.

As the first phase in DMAIC, Define phase needs to complete the risk management plan along with initial set of identified risks. Risk management plan describes how risks are going to be managed, roles and responsibilities in risk management, what is expected from each role, format and frequency of risk reporting and escalation mechanism when a risk becomes significant issue.

It is important to learn from past project to avoid repeating the same mistakes. Factors causing significant issues in the past might still exist in the current situation of a company.

There are two kinds of risks to be identified in risk assessment: project risks and solution risks. *Project risks* are the risks of carrying out the project. Assessment of project risks and their mitigation plans are critically important to obtain buy-in from Project Sponsors and key stakeholders.

Examples of project risks:
- Project resources might not be able to fulfil the time commitment for the project if there are higher priority tasks from outside the project.
- Project might get delayed if key project resources take long leave.

Solution risks are the risks for the solution that the project is trying to find. These risks focus on what might go wrong after the solution is implemented instead of what could happen during project execution.

Examples of solution risks:
- Supplier might not be able to meet the revised frequencies of material deliveries according to the solution.
- Operators might revert back to old working practices. Therefore, the solution needs to include some error-proofing aspects to ensure that new practices are being followed.

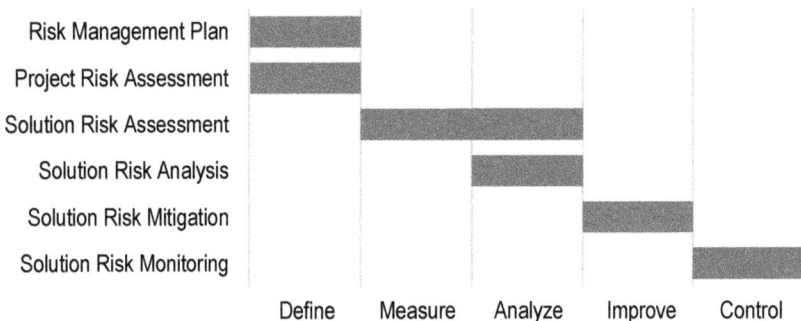

Figure 10-3 Risk management

Solution risk assessment is started during Measure phase and might continue through Analyze phase. In Analyze phase, solution risks are being analysed when team is working to confirm the factors affecting target outcome. During Improve phase, team calculates the optimal values of input factors to achieve the expected Y outcome. This process gives some visibility to what go wrong, allowing team to create mitigation strategy. Finally, solution is implemented during Control phase and risk mitigation plan is executed to monitor and control the risks.

11. PROCESS MAPPING

Process mapping is very useful to get an overall view about a process. By understanding the steps in a process, team members and key stakeholders could have the same understanding about the current situation, the weak points of a process and often some indications on what might cause a particular problem.

The most important aspect of process mapping is the journey of discovering the steps and their connections. Such information could be obtained from process documentation, SME knowledge or direct observation through *gemba walk*. A good process map should have combined information from all three sources.

There are several types of process maps.
- High level process map
- Detailed process map
- Swimlane process map
- SIPOC diagram
- Value stream mapping

A Six Sigma DMAIC project might not need all of them. The use of each map depends on the unique situation of every project and the Y outcome that needs to be analysed and improved.

High Level Process Map

High level process map is a high-level representation of the end-to-end view of a process. It is constructed using *flow chart* to show all activities in a system and their connections. Being a high-level view, it should not contain more than ten steps. If more detail is required, *process decomposition* can be performed on one or more activities, resulting in a *detailed process map.*

As a refresher, in flow chart oval represents start and end, rectangle represents sub-process or activity, diamond represents decision point and line with arrow shows relationships between entities. Please refer to Chapter 08 to review basic tools of quality.

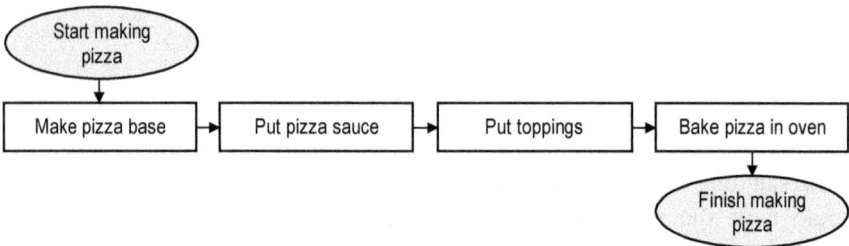

Figure 11-1 High level process map

A simple high level process map for pizza making process is presented in Figure 11-1. It does not go into details on what actually happens in the activity of [Make pizza base], but it serves the purpose of describing the end-to-end steps from the start to finish.

Detailed Process Map

Detailed process map is a flow chart describing how a system works presenting sufficient level of detail to gain understanding about the Y outcome that a project works to improve. This map is usually made by choosing some activities from *high level process map* that needs better granularity.

The start and end points of detailed process map does not have to be the start and end of the entire system. It can present only the parts that needs to be focused on.

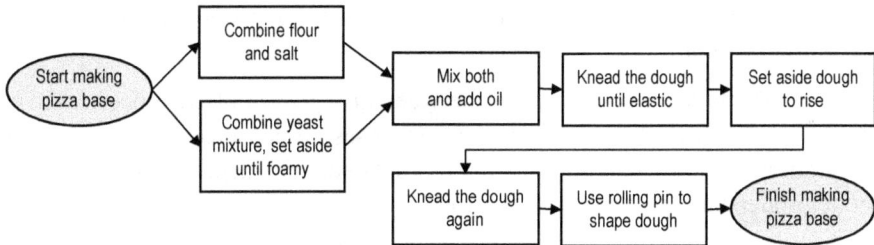

Figure 11-2 Detailed process map

Detailed process map from Figure 11-2 is the result of breaking down step [Make pizza base] from Figure 11-1. It is created for team to analyse a particular step, usually the steps related to target outcome of Y in the Y = f (X) formula.

Swimlane Process Map

Swimlane process map is a special type of detailed process map with additional information of the groups involved in the steps. This process map is commonly used to illustrate the collaboration between multiple departments in a process or production system.

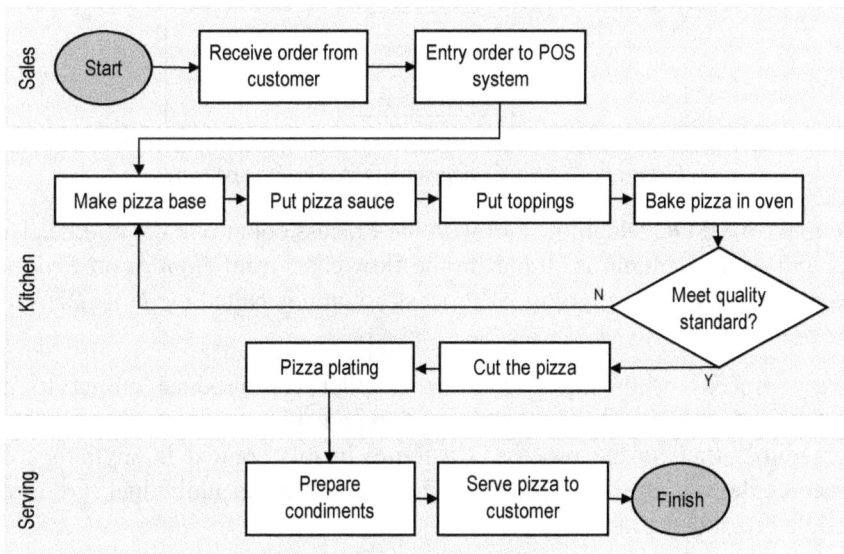

Figure 11-3 Swimlane process map

Figure 11-3 shows swimlane process map of a pizza restaurant. It gives the overall process from customer order to the time customer receives the pizza.

It shows the steps in a process and which group of people are involved in doing those steps.

With its ability to show interaction between groups, swimlane process map is a powerful tool to describe complex processes. When properly drawn, this diagram will show the communication points between departments, allowing better understanding and identification of problems.

SIPOC Diagram

SIPOC Diagram is a tool to summarize inputs and outputs of a process in the form of simple table. SIPOC is an acronym that stands for *Supplier*, *Input Process*, *Output* and *Customer*. Each of these becomes a column in SIPOC table.

Supplier	Input	Process	Output	Customer
+ Sales dept + Flour supplier + Cheese shop + Vegetable market + Butchery	+ Order information + Flour + Tomatoes + Cheese + Vegetables + Mushroom + Sausages + Salami + Pepperoni	Make pizza base ↓ Put pizza sauce ↓ Put toppings ↓ Bake pizza in oven ↓ Review quality ↓ Cut into slices	+ Hot pizza	+ Customer

Figure 11-4 SIPOC diagram of pizza making process

To make a SIPOC Diagram, start with the Process column in the middle. The content of this column is similar to the flow chart from *High Level Process Map*. The first and last points of Process column is called the *boundaries* of the process.

Every process needs input from its supplier and produce output to its customer. Supplier in this context is anything outside the process that provides something used by the process. Customer in this context is anything that receives the output of the process. These could be an individual, group of people or another process.

Suppose there is a production system with processes A, B and C. Process B takes the output from A and use it as input. Process A is the supplier for process B. The output of process B is used by process C. Therefore, process C is the customer of process B.

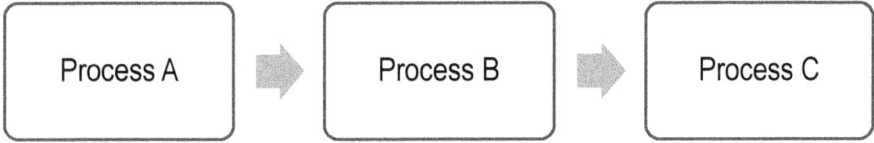

Supplier	Input	Process	Output	Customer
A	Output from A is the input for B	B	Output from B is the input for C	C

Figure 11-5 Input-output illustration

SIPOC diagram can be used in either Define phase or Measure phase in DMAIC project. It is a powerful tool to help a team to understand a process and have aligned understanding with relevant stakeholders.

12. DEFINE PHASE SUMMARY

Define phase is the first phase of DMAIC project. As the name suggests, it focuses on defining the problem that a project is trying to solve. In the terms of $Y = f(X)$ formula, Define phase aims to clearly define what is the Y outcome that needs to be improved.

The journey of Define phase starts with creating project charter. In the project charter, problem statement and goal statement are clearly articulated in a way that is specific, measurable, attainable, relevant and time bound. To write problem statement and goal statement, earlier work is needed to gather Voice of the Customer (VOC), Critical to Quality (CTQ) and Cost of Poor Quality (COPQ).

Project charter also specifies the business case to start a project, along with cost and benefits analysis. If a project has impacts to customers, employees, stakeholders or company operations, those needs to be listed so that project sponsors can make informed decision.

During Define phase, the team to work a project is established. Project charter needs to list all team members by name, their roles and the expected time commitment. The next step is to create project schedule with key milestones.

Finally, project charter needs to be approved by project sponsor, project champion, finance department and project leader. This approval serves as an authorisation gate to move to the next activities.

Along with the creation of project charter, Define phase also tries to document process maps, at least at high-level. This helps team members and key stakeholders to have the same understanding about the situation and things that need improvement.

Other deliverables in Define phase include stakeholder analysis (often written in RACI matrix) and risk management planning. Risk management in Six Sigma project is an integrated process throughout DMAIC phases. Define phase needs to complete the risk management plan along with assessment of project risks.

At the end of Define phase, the following outputs need to be completed:
- Voice of the Customer
- Critical to Quality
- Cost of Poor Quality
- Problem statement
- Goal statement
- Business case (cost and benefits analysis)
- Project team (names, roles, commitment, structure)
- Project schedule and key milestones
- Project charter approval
- Stakeholder analysis
- Risk management plan and initial risk assessment
- Process map

Project charter is a living document. Therefore, it needs to be continuously updated as new information becomes available throughout the execution of other phases of DMAIC.

MEASURE PHASE

13. UNDERSTANDING MEASURE PHASE

The second phase of Six Sigma DMAIC project is the *Measure phase*. As the name suggests, this phase focuses on obtaining data and measuring as-is performance of the system.

Let us begin the discussion on Measure phase by reviewing the five phases of DMAIC and the $Y = f(X)$ formula.

DEFINE	MEASURE	ANALYZE	IMPROVE	CONTROL
• Which Y	• X candidates • Collect data	• Confirm Xs	• X values to solve Y • Pilot implementation	• Control Xs • Full implementation

Figure 13-1 Measure phase in DMAIC

In Measure phase, the focus is to collect data so that project team can discover what are the possible X factors that impact the outcome Y. There are four steps to reach this goal:

- Perform *as-is process review*. Find factors that might impact the outcome of Y using data from the current process. These factors are called the X candidates.
- Perform *Measurement System Analysis* (MSA) to make sure that valid data can be collected.
- Make data collection plan based on X candidates.
- Collect data.

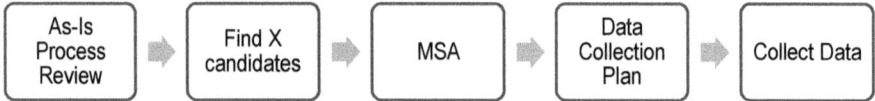

Figure 13-2 Steps in Measure phase

Through the process of collecting data, Measure phase attempts to understand the performance gap. How is the current process running? How big and how widespread is the problem factors causing Y outcome? What are the possible causes of performance issue?

Measure phase is about measuring data. Collecting "all data" is a waste of time and resources. It adds complexity to the work without adding value, so it goes against the principles of Lean. To do the most efficient data collection, a Six Sigma project team needs to know which data need be measured. In other words, team needs to collect data related to the possible X factors having *reasonable* possibility to have big impact on Y.

Measure factors could not tell which X factors have actual impact on Y performance because this phase does not perform in-depth analysis of the collected data (that will happen during Analyze phase). Instead, Measure phase uses As-Is process review to rule out factors that are clearly have no impact to Y so that there is no need to collect data related to these no-impact factors.

The end result of Measure phase is a list of shortlisted X candidates along with collected data related to these Xs. Analyze phase will take on these results, perform in-depth analysis on the data, and then come up with a list of *actual* X factors that are *statistically proven* as independent factors impacting Y.

Deliverables from Measure phase:
- Failure Modes and Effects Analysis (FMEA)
- Calculation of As-Is Process Capability
- List of potential X factors
- Measurement System Analysis (MSA)
- Data Collection Plan
- Baselined data related to Y outcome and potential X factors
- Solution Risk Assessment

14. AS-IS PROCESS REVIEW

Six Sigma DMAIC project is a process improvement project to achieve the goal statement defined in Project Charter. The goal to be achieved is the Y outcome in $Y = f(X)$ formula. The Define phase defines which Y to improve, Measure phase finds what are the possible X factors that might impact the performance of Y.

To find possible X factors, it is important to understand how to current system works. As-Is process review uses a variety of decision-making tools to shortlist possible causes that are likely to have big impact on Y. Looking from another perspective, this also means that the As-Is process review will help to rule out factors that are clearly not impacting Y performance.

This chapter discusses some tools that can be used to review the current process and find the possible causes of performance problem. The choice of tools depends on each use case and the unique situations of a problem.

Cause-and-Effect Diagram

Cause-and-effect diagram (also known as *fishbone diagram* or *Ishikawa diagram*) is a quality tool to find and show possible causes of a problem, organised into several categories. This diagram is drawn like skeleton fish and read from right to left.

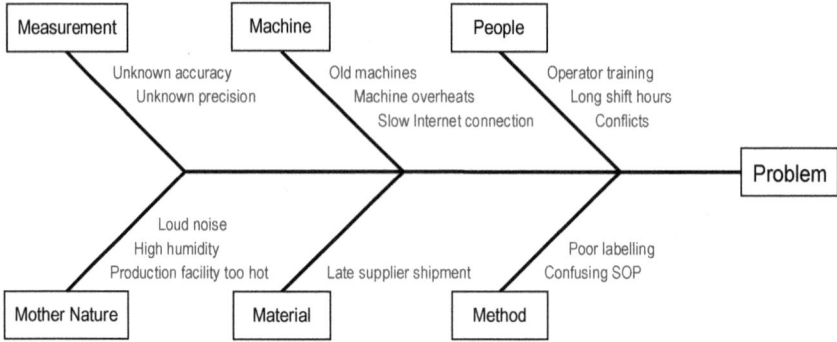

Figure 14-1 Example of cause-and-effect diagram

An example of cause-and-effect diagram is presented in Figure 14-1. It uses the 6M categories: Man (People), Method, Machine, Material, Measurement and Mother Nature (Environment). Other popular categories are 4S: Suppliers, Skills, Surrounding, Systems; and 8P: Product (service), Price, Place, Promotion, Personnel, Process, Physical Evidence, Productivity. Six Sigma team can choose one of the available sets of categories or make custom categories best suited for the project.

Cause-and-effect diagram is built from collaboration between project team, process owners and subject matter experts. Start the diagram from the right side (head of the fish) then move to the left. Write the categories and start brainstorming on the possible causes in every category.

If a potential cause might be listed in more-than-one categories, just choose one. There is no need to spend time to argue about categorisation, as long as a cause is identified and listed somewhere. All causes will be passed on to the next step as potential X factors, regardless of category in this diagram.

5 Whys

5 whys is one of the simplest tools to help with root cause identification. As the name suggest, this technique asks five times about why a problem happens, then continue with asking why the previous answer happens. This tool is powerful if the person answering the question is a capable stakeholder with good understanding about the situation.

Example of 5 whys:
- Why do we have significant cases of angry customer returning bad products?

- Because the products they purchased was broken within few days after purchase?
- Why do the products get broken so quickly?
- Because the material we use is not durable.
- Why do we use non-durable material for our product?
- Because the usual material becomes too expensive for our production cost, so we choose an alternative material that is cheaper.
- Why do we choose the cheaper material that is not durable as replacement?
- Because that was the best option from the 3 candidates presented by purchasing manager.
- Why did we limit ourselves to those 3 candidates?
- Because only purchasing manager has the authority to approach potential supplier.

The simple sequence of asking why five times helps to uncover the layers of symptoms leading to the root cause, or at least getting closer to the root cause. The repetition of five times asking is just a rule of thumb, it can be adjusted as needed.

XY Matrix

XY matrix is a visual tool for understanding how some factors in the process (Xs) impacts a specific measure of outcome (Y). This tool uses the specifications derived from Voice of the Customer (VOC) and Critical to Quality (CTQ).

There is no standard format of XY matrix. Common versions of this tool put items from VOC and CTQ as columns (what customers want) and list some factors in the process as rows (how the process tries to fulfill what customer wants).

The simplest version of XY matrix is a table with yes/no status, showing whether a particular process factor contributes to a particular item of customer expectation or not. This version keeps XY matrix as an objective tool to show connections without trying to put values on them.

		What Customers Want (Y)		
		Attractive Design	Vibrant Colours	Durability
Production Factors (X)	Strong Material			yes
	Strong Adhesive			yes
	Top Quality Paint		yes	
	Advanced Machinery	yes	yes	yes
	Custom Moulding	yes		yes
	Market Research	yes		
	Famous Designer	yes	yes	
	Superhero Character	yes		

Table 14-A Example of simple XY matrix

Table 14-A shows an example of simple XY matrix from a company selling toys for children. It has identified that their customers want toys with attractive design, vibrant colours and also durable. A team has identified eight factors contributing to the quality requirements that customers want. If a particular factor contributes to a customer requirement, the value yes is added into the matrix. DMAIC project is trying to solve the problem of unhappy customers returning the products because of poor durability. This XY matrix helps to show that team needs to look into four possible X factors: strong material, strong adhesive, advanced machinery and custom moulding.

The more sophisticated version of XY matrix shows quantitative values indicating the strength of connections between X and Y. Furthermore, it can also put different weights on different customer expectations.

		What Customers Want (Y)			Total	%
		Attractive Design	Vibrant Colours	Durability		
	Weight	8	6	9		
Production Factors (X)	Strong Material			9	81	11.9%
	Strong Adhesive			8	72	10.5%
	Top Quality Paint		9		54	7.9%
	Advanced Machinery	4	7	8	146	21.4%
	Custom Moulding	7		6	110	16.1%
	Market Research	6			48	7.0%
	Famous Designer	9	6		108	15.8%
	Superhero Character	8			64	9.4%
	TOTAL				683	

Table 14-B Example of quantified XY matrix

Table 14-B presents an example of quantified XY matrix. Instead of showing yes/no, it presents the quantified value of each connection between X and Y using scale from 1 (minimum impact) to 9 (maximum impact). Every item of customer requirement can be assigned different weights to indicate their importance level. The company can quickly see that advanced machinery is the most important factor in their production process, impacting 21.4% of the perceived quality. If the project is to improve general quality of the product, this is the strongest X candidate to focus on. However, the project currently ongoing is specifically trying to improve product durability, so it takes strong material as the top candidate for X.

Doing quantified XY matrix with numerical values is a double-edged sword. It can be powerful because it quickly identifies the strongest possible X factors, but it can also be counter-productive if the decisions about the connection values are arbitrary. Six Sigma is a data-driven approach of process improvement. Therefore, creating quantified values without strong data evidence could lead to incorrect conclusions.

Different scoring systems can be chosen as alternative to reduce the impact of arbitrary values. Instead of using numbers 1 to 9, ordinal values of *high*, *medium*, *low* can be used to differentiate the levels of impact.

Multi-voting

Multi-voting is a consensus tool to help a team to narrow down a list with many items into manageable few. This tool is used when group judgement is considered necessary.

To use multi-voting, a group of people gathers at the same time, could be physically or digitally. Everyone is presented with the same list of possible options, then each of them gets a number of votes.

The number of votes for each person in multi-voting follows this simple formula:

$$votes\ per\ person = \frac{number\ of\ people}{3}$$

If there are 14 people in a group that needs to decide using multi-voting, each person gets $14 / 3 = 4.67 \approx 4$ (rounded down). Every member of the group can choose 4 items from the list that they believe are the most important or impactful. Alternatively, they can also put multiple votes on one item.

The votes on every item are counted, then sorted from the items with the highest number of votes. Team decides on how many items should be part of the narrowed down list.

Failure Modes and Effects Analysis (FMEA)

Failure Modes and Effects Analysis (FMEA) is a tool to identify risks of failures in existing (As-Is) process and their causes and effects. Understanding the risks in current process helps to understand what could go wrong, how likely it could happen and how severe is the impact.

FMEA starts with a list of possible failures. Afterwards, high-level analysis is performed to find out the causes and effects of those failures.

There are two main types of FMEA:

- *Design FMEA* is risk analysis performed during design phase of a product or service.
- *Process FMEA* is risk analysis performed on existing or new process. This is the type of FMEA most commonly used in DMAIC methodology.

Both types of FMEA focus on identifying risks of failure and applying *Risk Priority Number* (RPN) to them. Risk Priority Number is a value calculated from three components:

- *Severity.* The severity of a failure in 1 to 10 scale, 10 is the most severe.
- *Occurrence.* The likelihood of failure in 1 to 10 scale, 10 means guaranteed failure.
- *Detection.* The probability of <u>not</u> detecting a failure before a product (or service) reaches customer. This uses 1 to 10 scale, 10 means zero probability of detecting the failure.

Risk Priority Number is the multiplication of these components:

$$RPN = Severity \times Occurrence \times Detection$$

Every risk (potential failure) has RPN number between 1 to 1000. The largest number means a risk makes the process most vulnerable. If this risk is related to one of the X factors impacting Y, team needs to give priority to mitigate the risk first.

#	Failure Mode	Failure Effects	S E V	Failure Cause	O C C	Current Controls	D E T	R P N
1	Toy has sharp parts	Could cause injury to children using the toy	9	Production defect	3	Quality check	4	108
2	Included battery doesn't work	Toy will not work without battery replacement	3	Defective part (battery)	2	None	10	60
...								

Table 14-C Example of FMEA table

Table 14-C shows an FMEA table from a company selling toys for children. There are two failure modes identified. The effects of the failure are described, along with the cause and current ways to control. Subjectivity is the biggest weakness of this technique. One value difference in one of the Severity, Occurrence and Detection scores could cause significant changes to the RPN. The scoring process must follow objective standards for the technique to work effectively.

FMEA risks can and should be mitigated. Changing Severity score is usually unlikely. Instead, team needs to focus on reducing Occurrence score by improving process quality and reducing Detection score by increasing the possibility of detecting a failure before it reaches customer. Improving process is achieved by reducing standard deviation, making a process more consistent. Detecting failure is achieved by implementing Statistical Process Control.

#	Failure Mode	Before Mitigation						After Mitigation					
		Failure Effects	S E V	Failure Cause	O C C	Current Controls	D E T	R P N	Failure Effects	S E V	Failure Cause	O C C	Improved Controls	D E T	R P N
1															
2															
...															

Table 14-D Example of FMEA table with mitigation analysis

In Table 14-D, an improved FMEA table has two parts: before and after mitigation. It analyses the risk of failures in the system as-is, and what it would be after the process is improved and process controls are implemented. The second half of this table (after mitigation columns) can be estimated in Measure phase and revised in Control phase.

Process Capability

Process capability is a measure to compare process performance against specification requirements. The higher process capability, the higher the chances that a process will produce something that meets requirements.

Specification requirements is obtained from Voice of the Customer (VOC) that is quantified into Critical to Quality (CTQ). Customers of a coffee shop has an expectation that coffee is served hot. This requirement from customer is an example of VOC. This is translated into CTQ as "coffee must be served between 70°C and 80°C".

Upper specification limit (USL) is the highest acceptable value of a particular measure of a product. In this case: coffee temperature. The USL of the process is 80°C. *Lower specification limit* (LSL) is the lowest acceptable value for that measure. LSL is 80°C for the coffee shop example. Middle point between USL and LSL is called the *T point* $\left(\frac{USL-LSL}{2}\right)$.

There are four indicators of process capability:
- *Cp* is the best-case performance of a process using short-term data.
- *Cpk* is the actual performance of a process using short-term data.
- *Pp* is the best-case performance of a process using long-term data.
- *Ppk* is the actual performance of a process using long-term data.

99.7% of data points from a process happen within plus minus 3 standard deviation from mean. In the calculation of process capability, this is called *system spread*. The value of system spread is 6 times standard deviation because the range from minus 3 standard deviation to plus 3 standard deviation is 6 standard deviation.

Long-term data is the data on system performance throughout its lifetime. This is considered as the population data of system performance. The standard deviation of population is represented with σ symbol. Short-term data is a subset of population data that represents data from more recent times, this is considered as sampling. Standard deviation of sample dataset is represented with S symbol.

Pp is measure of best-case performance of a process using long-term data. It is calculated as:

$$Pp = \frac{USL - LSL}{6\sigma}$$

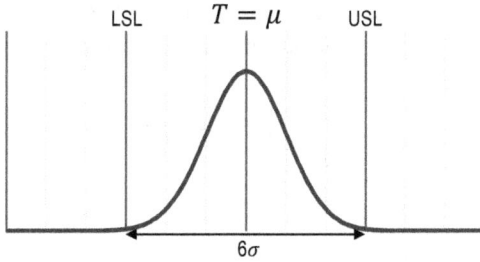

Figure 14-2 Process capability with Pp=1

Being a measure of best-case performance, *Pp* assumes that process means is equal to the middle point between USL and LSL. Figure 14-2 shows a process centred inside USL and LSL with process mean (μ) equal to *T point*. This is an example of a process with *Pp* value = 1 because USL − LSL is equal to 6 times population standard deviation.

Ppk is measure of actual process performance using long-term data. It does not assume that process is situation right in the middle of specifications. This measure calculates the shortest distance between mean (μ) and one of the specification limits and divide it by 3 times standard deviation:

$$Ppk = min \left[\frac{USL - \mu}{3\sigma} ; \frac{\mu - LSL}{3\sigma} \right]$$

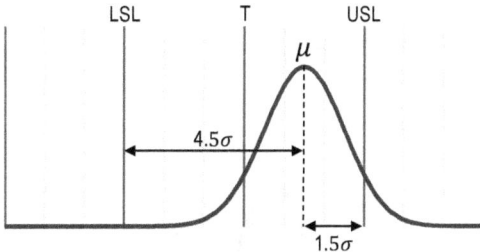

Figure 14-3 Process capability with Ppk = 0.5

Process illustrated in Figure 14-3 is not situated in the middle of USL and LSL. Process mean is closer to USL and the distance is equal to 1.5 times of standard deviation. This means that process is more likely to produce output higher than USL compared to output lower than LSL. In this figure, the calculation of $Ppk = min \left[\frac{1.5\sigma}{3\sigma} ; \frac{4.5\sigma}{3\sigma} \right] = 0.5$.

Cp is measure of best-case performance of a process using short-term data. Just like *Pp*, *Cp* assumes process mean (μ) is equal to the middle point between USL and LSL.

$$Cp = \frac{USL - LSL}{6S}$$

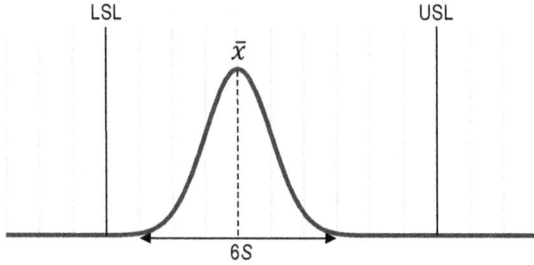

Figure 14-4 Process capability with Cp = 1.6667

In Figure 14-4, the range from LSL to USL is equal to ten times standard deviation. *Cp* assumes that $\bar{x}$ is in the middle of LSL and USL, regardless of where it is actually located. The value of $Cp = 10S / 6S = 1.6667$.

Cpk measures the actual process performance using short-term data. Similar to *Ppk*, it calculates the shortest distance between mean ($\bar{x}$) and one of the specification limits and divide it by 3 times standard deviation.

$$Cpk = min \left[\frac{USL - \bar{x}}{3S} ; \frac{\bar{x} - LSL}{3S} \right]$$

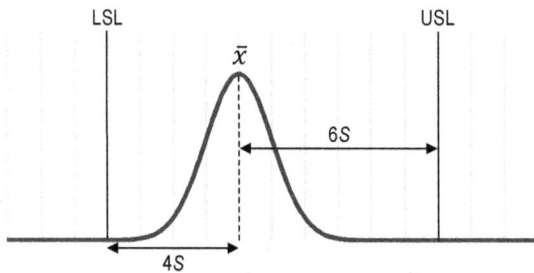

Figure 14-5 Process capability with Cpk = 1.3333

Process performance in Figure 14-5 is identical from Figure 14-4. However, in the calculation of *Cpk*, the fact that process mean ($\bar{x}$) does not located in the middle point between LSL and USL makes a difference. Since $\bar{x}$ is closer to LSL and the distance is 4 times standard deviation (*S*), this is the value that goes to the calculation of $Cpk = \min\left[\frac{6S}{3S}; \frac{4S}{3S}\right] = 1.3333$.

The connections between process capability indicators:
- *Ppk* is equal to *Pp* if μ is equal to *T point*.
- *Cpk* is equal to *Cp* if $\bar{x}$ is equal to *T point*.
- *Capability Ratio (Cr)* is the inverse of *Cp*. Formula for $Cr = \frac{1}{Cp}$

Compared to other indicators, *Cpk* is arguably the most important because it uses recent data and actual process performance. Bigger *Cpk* value means better process performance.

Sigma level (short term) of a process is calculated from *Cpk*.

$$\sigma_{st} = Cpk \times 3$$

The minimum level of acceptable Sigma Level for short-term performance is 4. This could go down to 2.5 sigma in the long-term according to *sigma shift* theory.

To achieve minimum sigma level of 4, the minimum value of *Cpk* is 1.3333. This is called the minimum *Cpk* for a capable system.

Value interpretation of *Cp*, *Cpk*, *Pp* and *Ppk*:
- Less than 1: system is not capable.
- From 1 to 1.3333: system is potentially capable.
- From 1.3333 to 2: system is capable.
- 2 or greater: system is Six Sigma capable.

For attribute data, *Cpk* is measured from the value of DPMO of short-term data. As refresher, please review the following definitions:
- *Defect* is any aspect of a product or service that fails to meet requirement.
- *Defective* is a unit that contains one or more defects.
- *Opportunity* is a characteristic in a product or service that could pass or fail requirement.
- *Defects Per Unit* (DPU) is the total number of defects divided by the number of units.
- *Defects Per Opportunities* (DPO) is the total number of defects divided by total number of defect opportunities.
- *Defects Per Million Opportunities* (DPMO) is DPO times one million.

Sigma level can be obtained from DPMO table (see Chapter 03) or calculated using NORMSINV function in Excel.

$$\sigma_{st} = (NORMSINV(1 - DPMO/1{,}000{,}000)) + 1.5$$

Calculating *Cpk* from Sigma Level:

$$Cpk = \sigma_{st} / 3$$

Another notable indicator of process capability is *Cpm*. Instead of using the standard deviation from sample data, *Cpm* calculates its own standard deviation using *T point* instead of sample mean.

$$S_{Cpm} = \sqrt{\sum_{i=1}^{n} \frac{(x_i - T)^2}{n - 1}}$$

Cpm is calculated as:

$$Cpm = \frac{USL - LSL}{6 \times S_{Cpm}}$$

In order to demonstrate that DMAIC project successfully increase process performance, project team must be able to compare Process Capability before and after the improvement.

Process capability before improvement is measured from As-Is process performance review during Measure phase. If data for the calculation are not readily available, this can be performed after data collection.

15. MEASUREMENT SYSTEM ANALYSIS (MSA)

Six Sigma DMAIC methodology is a data-driven process improvement methodology. Every phase of this methodology uses data to achieve its purposes. If the data used for calculations are invalid, then the entire conclusion and proposed solution will become meaningless. Garbage in, garbage out.

Suppose a café has a rule that coffee must be served at 75°C. Café owner assigns someone to visit at random times to measure coffee temperatures. After four weeks of data collection, the recorded number seems to have high variance. However, café owner found out that data collector uses one of two available thermometers at random every visit. One of the two thermometers is not accurate. All data collected within four weeks are now considered invalid and cannot be used to make decision.

Measurement System Analysis (MSA) is the first recommended step during Measure phase to ensure that data to be collected are accurate and precise. Every process has error and measurement is a process. Therefore, it is not realistic to expect measurement system with absolute zero error. What can be done is determining an acceptable level of error. If the magnitude of error is higher than acceptable level, measurement system needs to be changed or adjusted before data collection.

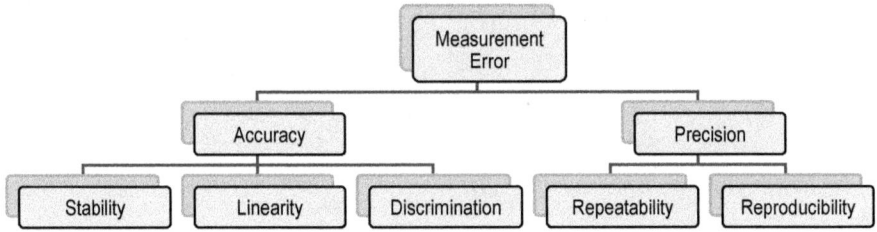

Figure 15-1 Measurement error

Accuracy and Precision

A measurement is ***accurate*** if the average of its results is the same as the true value. The difference between a measurement and its true value is called *bias*. If true value is not known and difficult to obtain, estimated true value can be calculated from the average of best available measurements. *Calibration* is the effort to bring measurement results closer to the true value.

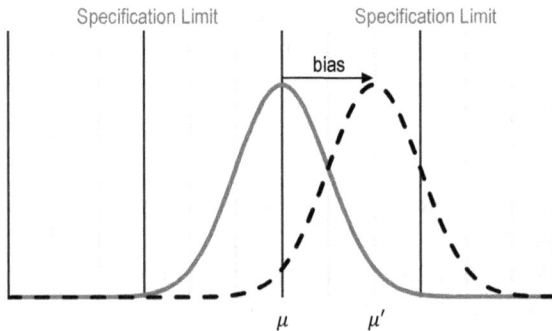

Figure 15-2 Normal distribution affected by bias

In the illustration of normal distribution curve, measurement bias shifts the curve to the left or right. If the difference is significant, it could bring a system to reject good product or the other way around.

Stability	Linearity	Discrimination
Measurement results are consistent across time.	Measurement results are consistent across operating range.	Gauge resolution is capable to differentiate at least 15 levels of values across normal range.

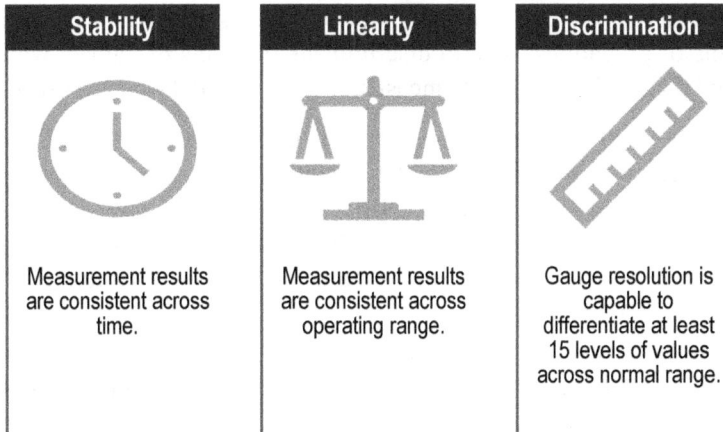

Figure 15-3 Stability, linearity, discrimination

Assessment of accuracy involves three aspects: stability, linearity and discrimination. Measurement is **stable** if its distribution stays the same over time (μ and σ). A particular entity would still measure the same regardless if it is measured at noon or midnight, measured today or next month or next year.

If a measurement tool (often referred to as *gauge*) produces different results at different times, the cause of the variation should be analysed. The cause could be noise factors or controllable factors. This type of inaccuracy is resolved by establishing *gold standard* as reference point for calibration.

Measurement system is **linear** if it has the same bias over the operating range of the gauge. For example: a certain scale is accurate when measuring items above 30kg. Anything lighter than 30kg causes measurement bias.

Linearity is a common problem in measurement because each gauge/tool usually has an ideal range. This type of accuracy problem is resolved by *choosing the right tool* for certain use. Most room thermometers are not able to measure temperature higher than 100°C but cooking thermometers can.

Discrimination is a measurement tool's ability to detect small changes. For example, a kitchen scale has measurement range up to 10kg with 1-gram increments. This 1-gram increment is called the discrimination ability of the kitchen scale. This scale is sufficient to measure the weights of cooking ingredients, but it is not the right tool to measure the weights of gold jewellery that requires a tool that can measure 0.1 grams difference. If a 15.7 grams necklace and another one that weighs 15.9 grams are both measured as 16 grams, then the lack of discrimination ability of the gauge causes accuracy problem.

As a general rule, a measurement tool for continuous data must have minimum 10 levels of gradations (able to discriminate 10 levels of values) within the expected range it is supposed to measure. This is called the gauge's *resolution*.

Number of Distinct Categories (NDC) is a measure to ability of a measurement tool to distinguish data. NDC value 1 means a gage is not capable to differentiate anything. NDC value 2 means gage is capable to classify data into two groups, such as big and small. NDC value 3 means it has ability to discriminate data into 3 parts, such as big, medium and small. The higher NDC the better.
- NDC value below 3 is considered unacceptable.
- NDC value between 3 and 13 is marginally acceptable depending on use case.
- NDC of 14 or greater is considered acceptable.

$$NDC = \sqrt{2} \times \frac{\sigma_{part}}{\sigma_{gage}}$$

Measurement bias can be caused by *gauge bias* or *operator bias*. In the case of operator bias, it may be due to insufficient training or unclear standard operating procedure. Some gauges need some amount of time to stabilise before it shows the final value. Collecting the value before the gauge is ready is an example of operator bias.

A measurement is **precise** if multiple measurements on the same entity shows consistent value. There are two types of precision:
- *Repeatability* is the consistency of measurement results when an entity is measured multiple times by the same operator.
- *Reproducibility* is the consistency of measurement results when an entity is measured multiple times by different operators.

Call centre operators have a responsibility to classify the reason of someone's call into one of five categories. A Black Belt wants to measure the precision of their classifications, so he makes multiple phone calls with exactly the same enquiry.
- The first call is answered by Jake and gets recorded in category A.
- The second call is answered by Kim and gets recorded in category B. This is a reproducibility problem because different operators are not able to produce the same category for the same item.
- The third call is answered by Jake again and gets recorded in category C. This is a repeatability problem because the same operator is not able to produce the same category for the same item.

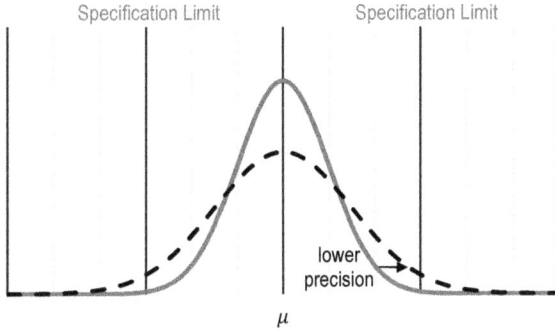

Figure 15-4 Normal distribution affected by low precision

Measurement accuracy focuses on the *mean* of measurement results compared to the true values. Precision focuses on the variation of measurement results. It tries to discover the probability distribution of obtaining consistent results throughout the process. In other word, it focuses on *standard deviation* of the process.

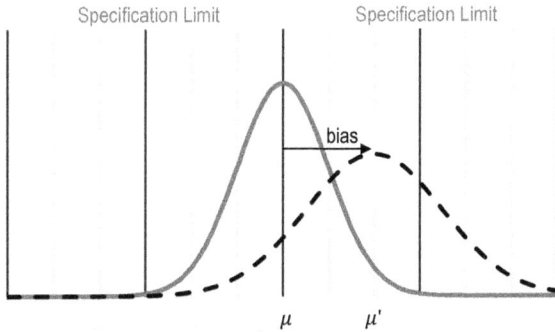

Figure 15-5 Normal distribution with bias and low precision

Since a process has variation and measurement has errors (from bias and variation), total variation is a formula of:

$$Total\ Var = Process\ Var + Measurement\ Bias + Measurement\ Var$$

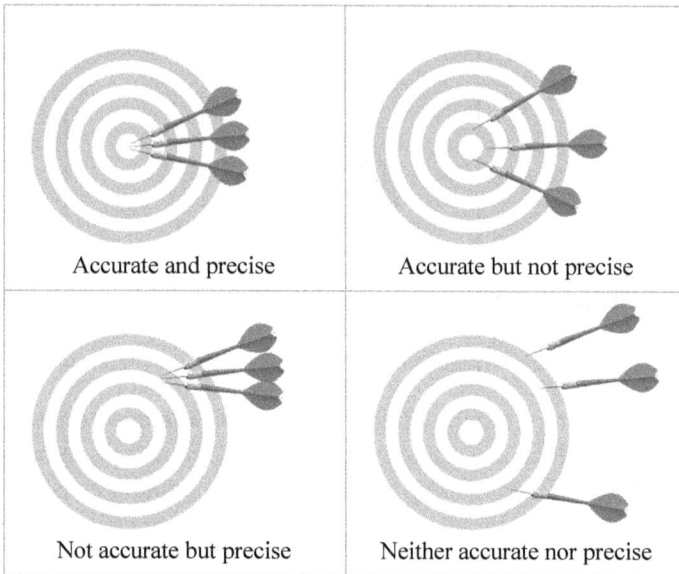

Figure 15-6 Illustration of accuracy and precision

To collect usable data, a measurement system needs to be accurate and precise. Figure 15-6 illustrates how accuracy and precision impact the result of a dart game.

Gage R&R

Gage R&R (Repeatability and Reproducibility) is a study to evaluate the precision of a measurement system for continuous data. This study does not address the problem of accuracy. It focuses on calculating variations in measurement process, involving equipment and operator.

To align with the terms from AIAG (Automotive Industry Action Group), the following part of this book will use the words:
- *Part* for items to be measured.
- *Equipment* for measurement tools or gauge.
- *Appraiser* for people doing the measurement.

There are two types of Gage R&R study: crossed study and nested study. In *crossed study*, every operator measures all items multiple times. *Nested study* assumes all items in a group are identical, so not all combinations of operator-item are tested. Nested study is sometimes chosen if the cost of doing crossed study is too high. It is strongly recommended to choose crossed study if it is feasible to do so. The Gage R&R discussion in this chapter uses crossed study.

Basic principles of Gage R&R:

- Equipment accuracy has been validated before performing Gage R&R. This includes observing stability, linearity and discrimination.
- It is recommended to use ten parts or more.
- If applicable, appraisers need to be trained before the study.
- Each part is measured three times by the same appraiser to calculate repeatability.
- Each part is measured multiple times by three different appraisers to calculate reproducibility. It is important to choose appraisers from the actual team that does the work in normal production process.
- Parts to be measured needs to include parts within and outside CTQ specifications. In other words, good parts and defective parts.
- Parts must be measured in random order and appraisers should not be able to identify the parts being measured to ensure objectivity. Data collection system needs to be established so that all measurements are recorded correctly despite the random order.

For the following discussions:

r	is the number of trials
a	is the number of appraisers
n	is the number of parts

Equipment Variation (EV) is a measure of variation within observations of one individual appraiser. It represents repeatability. EV is the standard deviation of measurement results within appraiser. If a Gage R&R study only does two or three trials per part per appraiser, standard deviation is not a good measure. Therefore, this formula is used to calculate EV:

$$EV = K_1 \times \bar{\bar{x}}_{Range}$$

$\bar{\bar{x}}_{Range}$ is the mean of measurement ranges for each appraiser.

K_1 is a constant value:

Trials (r)	K_1
2	0.8862
3	0.5908

Appraiser Variation (AV) is a measure of variation between appraisers (reproducibility). AV is the standard deviation of measurement results between appraisers. If a Gage R&R study only involves two or three appraisers, standard deviation is not a good measure. Therefore, this formula is used to calculate AV:

$$AV = \sqrt{Max\left[\left(\left(Max(\bar{x}_{Appr}) - Min(\bar{x}_{Appr})\right) \times K_2\right)^2 - \left(\frac{EV^2}{n \times r}\right); 0\right]}$$

K_2 is a constant value:

Appraisers (a)	K_2
2	0.7071
3	0.5231

Part Variation (PV) is a measure of parts variation. PV is the standard deviation of parts used in the study. If a Gage R&R study only involves small number of parts, standard deviation is not a good measure. Therefore, this formula is used to calculate PV:

$$PV = \left(Max(\bar{x}_{Part}) - Min(\bar{x}_{Part})\right) \times K_3$$

$\bar{x}_{Part}$ is the mean of all measurement values for a part.

K_3 is a constant value:

Parts (n)	K_3
2	0.7071
3	0.5231
4	0.4467
5	0.4030
6	0.3742
7	0.3534
8	0.3375
9	0.3249
10	0.3146

Total Variation (TV) is the entire variation. It adds squared EV, squared AV and squared PV. Then it calculates the square root of the sum.

$$TV = \sqrt{EV^2 + AV^2 + PV^2}$$

Gage Repeatability & Reproducibility (GRR) only considers EV and AV because they represent repeatability and reproducibility.

$$GRR = \sqrt{EV^2 + AV^2}$$

GRR% is calculated as GRR divided by TV. This is the value used to determine whether a measurement system is acceptable or not.

$$GRR\% = \frac{GRR}{TV} \times 100\%$$

According to AIAG standard:
- GRR% of 10% or lower is acceptable.
- GRR% between 10% to 30% is marginally acceptable, depending on the use case.
- Anything higher than 30% is not acceptable.

Example:
The following table presents a case for Gage R&R calculation for continuous data. Three appraisers (Liz, Meg and John) are assigned to perform measurements on ten parts. They need to measure each part three times in random order. To help with controlling the random order, a Black Belt has assigned each measurement with unique experiment ID.

Appraiser	Trial	Part 1	Part 2	Part 3	Part 4	Part 5	Part 6	Part 7	Part 8	Part 9	Part 10	Mean
Liz	1	#17	#82	#30	#75	#12	#34	#48	#71	#52	#03	
	2	#78	#05	#67	#23	#60	#29	#62	#14	#24	#86	
	3	#40	#37	#15	#72	#41	#83	#09	#68	#20	#45	
	Range											
Meg	1	#64	#51	#01	$42	#63	#07	#85	#77	#33	#88	
	2	#10	#31	#79	#54	#46	#74	#65	#44	#90	#50	
	3	#43	#84	#49	#11	#19	#39	#28	#89	#55	#18	
	Range											
John	1	#80	#16	#70	#57	#35	#22	#66	#02	#27	#53	
	2	#04	#59	#32	#25	#61	#87	#13	#58	#76	#38	
	3	#69	#47	#21	#73	#06	#56	#81	#36	#08	#26	
	Range											
Part Mean												

Table 15-A Case example for Gage R&R with experiment IDs

Experiments are conducted using the sequence of experiment ID from #01 to #90. Liz, Meg and John only see the experiment ID label on the parts they are measuring without knowing whether they are actually part 1 or part 2 or part 10. This helps them to measure the parts objectively.

After all measurements are completed, Black Belt puts the numbers back into the table according the positions indicated with experiment IDs. The result of collected data can be observed in case example in Table 15-B.

Appraiser	Trial	Part 1	Part 2	Part 3	Part 4	Part 5	Part 6	Part 7	Part 8	Part 9	Part 10	Mean
Liz	1	55.5	65.1	88.1	98.5	51.5	73.2	64.8	78.1	83.4	66.7	
	2	56.9	64.3	85.2	97.4	49.2	72.7	67.3	79.6	84.3	64.2	72.6967
	3	54.4	66.9	86.8	95.8	52.8	74.9	69.6	80.9	81.9	67.3	
	Range	2.5	2.6	2.9	2.7	3.6	2.2	2.3	2.8	2.4	3.1	2.71
Meg	1	55.9	59.7	84.5	92.9	45.6	69.7	64.3	75.9	80.1	60.5	
	2	55.2	58.2	83.4	93.2	43.6	70.1	65.9	75.2	79.8	61.7	68.8367
	3	54.5	58.2	82.8	94.6	46.1	71.3	65.5	74.1	81.5	60.9	
	Range	1.4	1.5	1.7	1.7	2.5	1.6	1.6	1.8	1.7	1.2	1.67
John	1	57.7	60.1	85.6	93.6	41.7	68.6	65.3	73.4	80.2	60.9	
	2	50.3	58.5	80.1	90.1	476	75.8	72.2	70.1	80.5	55.7	69.3333
	3	53.4	65.3	78.7	99.5	52.1	70.3	60.1	80.8	88.1	63.7	
	Range	7.4	6.8	6.9	9.4	10.4	7.2	12.1	10.7	7.9	8.0	8.68
Part Mean		54.87	61.83	83.91	95.07	47.80	71.84	66.51	76.46	82.20	62.40	

Table 15-B Case example for Gage R&R with collected data

Calculation of Equipment Variation (EV):
- Each appraiser does three trials for each part. For Liz, the trial data for part 1 has range of 2.5, data for part 2 has range of 2.6 and so on. All these range values have mean of 2.71.
- Similarly, Meg's range values for each part has the mean of 1.67. It shows that Meg produces data with smaller variations for each part.
- John's range values for each part has the mean of 8.68. This shows that John's data has more variations.
- The average of 2.71, 1.67 and 8.68 is the mean of measurement ranges for each appraiser. Therefore, $\bar{\bar{x}}_{Range}$ is $(2.71+1.67+8.68)/3 = 4.35$.
- $EV = K_1 \times \bar{\bar{x}}_{Range} = 0.5908 \times 4.35 = 2.5719$

Calculation of Appraiser Variation (AV):
- The average value for all data measured by Liz is 72.6967. This is the value of $\bar{x}_{Liz}$.
- $Max(\bar{x}_{Appr}) = Max(\bar{x}_{Liz}; \bar{x}_{Meg}; \bar{x}_{John})$
- $Max(\bar{x}_{Appr}) = Max(72.6967; 68.8367; 69.3333) = 72.6967$
- $Min(\bar{x}_{Appr}) = Min(\bar{x}_{Liz}; \bar{x}_{Meg}; \bar{x}_{John}) = 68.8367$
- This shows that Liz has highest average value and Meg has the lowest.

- $AV = \sqrt{Max\left[\left(\left(Max(\bar{x}_{Appr}) - Min(\bar{x}_{Appr})\right) \times K_2\right)^2 - \left(\frac{EV^2}{n \times r}\right); 0\right]}$

- $AV = \sqrt{Max\left[\left((72.6967 - 68.8367) \times 0.5231\right)^2 - \left(\frac{2.5719^2}{10 \times 3}\right); 0\right]}$

- $AV = \sqrt{Max[3.8565; 0]} = \sqrt{3.8565} = 1.9638$

- The value of AV above zero indicates that some of the appraisers produce higher or lower values compared to others and the difference is statistically significant.

Calculation of Part Variation (PV):
- The average value for all data for part 1 is 54.87. This is called Part Mean or $\bar{x}_{Part1}$.
- Part Mean for each part: 54.87, 61.83, 83.91 and so on.
- $Max(\bar{x}_{Part}) = Max(\bar{x}_{Part1} \ldots \bar{x}_{Part10})$
- $Max(\bar{x}_{Part}) = Max(54.81, 61.83, 83.91, \ldots 62.40) = 95.07$
- $Min(\bar{x}_{Part}) = Min(\bar{x}_{Part1} \ldots \bar{x}_{Part10}) = 47.80$
- $PV = \left(Max(\bar{x}_{Part}) - Min(\bar{x}_{Part})\right) \times K_3$
- $PV = (95.07 - 47.80) \times 0.3146 = 14.8711$

Calculation of Total Variation (TV) and GRR:
- $TV = \sqrt{EV^2 + AV^2 + PV^2}$
- $TV = \sqrt{2.5719^2 + 1.9638^2 + 14.8711^2} = 15.2191$
- $GRR = \sqrt{EV^2 + AV^2}$
- $GRR = \sqrt{2.5719^2 + 1.9638^2} = 3.2359$
- $GRR\% = \frac{3.2359}{15.2191} \times 100\% = 21.26\%$
- The value of $GRR\%$ falls between 10% and 30%, making this measurement system marginally accepted according to AIAG standard.

Attribute Agreement Analysis

Attribute agreement analysis is a study to evaluate appraisal errors for attribute data. This technique analyses attribute data with two possible values: such as pass/fail, yes/no or good/defective. It has the capability to calculate problems with both accuracy and precision.

Basic principles of *attribute agreement analysis*:
- Requires 20 to 30 items.
- Each item is appraised two or three times by the same appraiser to calculate repeatability.
- Each item is appraised multiple times by three appraisers to calculate reproducibility. It is important to choose appraisers from the actual team that does the work in normal production process.
- Items to be appraised need to have 50-50 balance between possible values, or at least 70-30.

- Items must be appraised in random order and appraisers should not be able to identify the items to ensure objectivity. Data collection system needs to be established so that all appraisal results are recorded correctly despite the random order.
- If applicable, appraisers need to be trained before the study.

For the following discussions:

r	is the number of trials
a	is the number of appraisers
n	is the number of items

Repeatability is calculated from the average of consistent appraisal within each appraiser. Individual appraiser repeatability counts how many times an appraiser produces the same appraisal results for the r trials of one item. Then system repeatability calculates the average of each appraiser's individual repeatability scores.

Reproducibility calculates the consistent appraisal between appraisers. This measure compares all possible paired combinations between appraisers. For a study with three appraisers, this value compares the appraisal results of appraiser 1 and 2, then between appraiser 2 and 3, then between appraiser 1 and 3. For higher number of appraisers, there will be a combination of ^a_2Comb pairs that need to be observed.

One match is counted for each time all trials from one appraiser for one item matches all trials from another appraiser for the same item. System reproducibility sums all the match counts and divide by n times the number of combinations.

Kappa is a measure of agreement between appraisers. It compares the appraisal results of two appraisers for n items. Kappa calculates the observed counts vs. the expected counts using the following formula:

$$kappa = \frac{p_o - p_e}{1 - p_e}$$

Perfect agreement between two appraisers has kappa value of 1. The value of kappa above 0.9 indicates excellent agreement. Values between 0.75 to 0.9 shows good level of agreement. Kappa value of zero means the results of two appraisers are random. Kappa value of -1 shows perfect disagreement between two appraisers.

Accuracy is calculated by counting the number of appraisals that match the true/actual/standard values, then divide it by the total number of appraisals ($n \times r \times a$).

Miss rate is a measure of how often an appraiser would assess an item as pass when it should be assessed as fail. *False alarm rate* calculates how often an appraiser would appraise as fail when the true value is pass. Finally, *system effectiveness* is calculated as the proportion of items that all appraisers agree on all trials and the results match the actual value.

Acceptance criteria of *attribute agreement analysis* uses multiple variables:

Decision	Repeatability	Reproducibility	Accuracy	Miss Rate	False Alarm Rate	System Effectiveness
Acceptable	>90%	>90%	>90%	<2%	<5%	>90%
Marginally Acceptable	80% - 90%	80% - 90%	80% - 90%	2% - 5%	5% - 10%	80% - 90%
Unacceptable	<80%	<80%	<80%	>5%	>10%	<80%

If different variables fall into different levels of acceptance, the lowest level of acceptance is selected.

Let us consider a case example for *attribute agreement analysis*:
Three appraisers (Dan, Rein and Ella) are assigned to perform appraisals on twenty items, two trials each. The experiment is performed in random order. The following Table 15-C records the result of their appraisals.
- Column [Actual (Ac)] is the true value of an item. These are considered as the standard that appraisers need to match, but they do not have access to these values.
- There are 11 passes and 9 fails. To be considered as valid study, a set of items need to have balance between possible values (pass or fail) from 50-50 to 70-30. The proportion of 55-45 meets the balance requirement.
- Column [1&Ac] shows if the appraisal #1 matches the actual value.
- Column [2&Ac] shows if the appraisal #2 matches the actual value.
- Column [1&2] shows if the result of appraisal #1 matches the result of appraisal #2.

Item#	Actual (Ac)	Dan					Rein					Ella				
		#1	#2	1&Ac	2&Ac	1&2	#1	#2	1&Ac	2&Ac	1&2	#1	#2	1&Ac	2&Ac	1&2
1	pass	pass	pass	1	1	1	pass	pass	1	1	1	pass	pass	1	1	1
2	fail	fail	fail	1	1	1	fail	fail	1	1	1	fail	fail	1	1	1
3	pass	pass	pass	1	1	1	pass	pass	1	1	1	pass	pass	1	1	1
4	fail	fail	fail	1	1	1	fail	fail	1	1	1	fail	fail	1	1	1
5	pass	fail	fail	0	0	1	fail	pass	0	1	0	pass	pass	1	1	1
6	pass	pass	pass	1	1	1	pass	pass	1	1	1	pass	pass	1	1	1
7	pass	pass	pass	1	1	1	pass	pass	1	1	1	pass	pass	1	1	1
8	fail	fail	fail	1	1	1	fail	fail	1	1	1	fail	fail	1	1	1
9	fail	fail	fail	1	1	1	fail	fail	1	1	1	fail	fail	1	1	1
10	pass	fail	fail	0	0	1	pass	pass	1	1	1	fail	pass	0	1	0
11	fail	fail	fail	1	1	1	fail	fail	1	1	1	pass	pass	0	0	1
12	fail	fail	fail	1	1	1	fail	fail	1	1	1	fail	fail	1	1	1
13	pass	pass	pass	1	1	1	pass	pass	1	1	1	pass	pass	1	1	1
14	fail	fail	pass	1	0	0	fail	fail	1	1	1	fail	pass	1	0	0
15	pass	pass	pass	1	1	1	pass	pass	1	1	1	pass	pass	1	1	1
16	pass	pass	pass	1	1	1	fail	pass	0	1	0	pass	pass	1	1	1
17	fail	fail	fail	1	1	1	fail	fail	1	1	1	fail	fail	1	1	1
18	pass	pass	pass	1	1	1	pass	pass	1	1	1	pass	pass	1	1	1
19	pass	pass	pass	1	1	1	pass	pass	1	1	1	pass	pass	1	1	1
20	fail	fail	fail	1	1	1	fail	fail	1	1	1	fail	fail	1	1	1
Total				18	17	19			18	20	18			18	18	18

Table 15-C Case example for Attribute Agreement Analysis

Calculation of repeatability:

- Observe the [1&2] column for each appraiser. This column indicates when an appraiser produces the same appraisal results in all trials for one particular item.
- Dan produces repeatable appraisals for 19 out of 20 items. His repeatability is 19/20 = 0.95 or 95%.
- Rein's repeatability is 18/20 = 0.90 or 90%.
- Ella's repeatability is 18/20 = 0.90 or 90%.
- System repeatability is the average of the repeatability of the three appraisals: (0.95+0.90+0.90) / 3 = 0.9167 or 91.67%.

Calculation of reproducibility:

- Dan and Rein agree on all trials for 16 out of 20 items.
- Dan and Ella agree on all trials for 17 out of 20 items.
- Rein and Ella agree on all trials for 15 out of 20 items.
- Number of combinations: 3.
- System reproducibility = (16+17+15) / 60 = 0.8 or 80%.

Calculation of accuracy:

- Dan has made 18 correct appraisals (same result as standard value) in his first trial and 17 correct appraisals on his second trial.

- Similarly, Rein has made 18 and 20 correct appraisals.
- Ella has made 18 and 18 correct appraisals.
- Accuracy is the total number of correct appraisals divided by the total number of appraisals: (18+17+18+20+18+18) / 120 = 0.9083 or 90.83%.

Calculation of miss rate:
- Dan has made 1 appraisal as pass when the standard value is fail.
- Rein has made 0 appraisal as pass when the standard value is fail.
- Ella has made 3 appraisals as pass when the standard value is fail.
- Miss eate is the total number of mistakes divided by total number of appraisals that should produce fail: (1+0+3) / 54 = 0.0741 or 7.41%.

Calculation of false alarm rate:
- Dan has made 4 appraisals as fail when the standard value is pass.
- Rein has made 2 appraisals as fail when the standard value is pass.
- Ella has made 1 appraisal as fail when the standard value is pass.
- False alarm rate is the total number of mistakes divided by total number of appraisals that should produce pass: (4+2+1) / 66 = 0.1061 or 10.61%.

Calculation of system effectiveness:
- Item #5, item #10, item #14 and item #16 have one or more appraisers made mistake in one or more trials.
- It means, the other 16 items have all appraisers agree with actual value in all trials.
- System effectiveness is 16 / 20 = 0.8 or 80%.

Kappa is calculated between pairs or appraisers. In this case example, there will be kappa values for Dan-Rein, Dan-Ella and Rein-Ella. The following tables are made from comparing the appraisal results between each appraiser:

Pair #1 (observed)		Rein		
		pass	fail	total
	pass	17	2	19
Dan	fail	3	18	21
	total	20	20	40

Pair #2 (observed)		Ella		
		pass	fail	total
	pass	19	0	19
Dan	fail	5	16	21
	total	24	16	40

Pair #3 (observed)		Ella		
		pass	fail	total
	pass	19	1	20
Rein	fail	5	15	20
	total	24	16	40

For the comparison of Dan and Rein, there are 17 trials that both Dan and Rein appraised as pass and 18 trials appraised as fail. Dan and Rein had disagreement 5 times. In 2 cases, Dan appraised as pass and Rein appraised as fail. In the other 3 cases, Dan appraised as fail and Rein appraised as pass. The same analysis is performed for Dan-Ella and Rein-Ella pairs. These are the *observed counts* for kappa formula. Note that these comparisons are between appraisers without considering the actual values.

Pair #1 (expected)		Rein				Pair #2 (expected)		Ella				Pair #3 (expected)		Ella		
		pass	fail	total				pass	fail	total				pass	fail	total
	pass	9.5	9.5	19			pass	11.4	7.6	19			pass	12	8	20
Dan	fail	10.5	10.5	21		Dan	fail	12.6	8.4	21		Rein	fail	12	8	20
	total	20	20	40			total	24	16	40			total	24	16	40

For pair #2 (Dan-Ella), total values for the column pass and fail (Ella's) are 24 and 16. So the proportion is 60% and 40%. The expected value for pass-pass is the total value of pass row (Dan's) multiplied by the proportion from Ella's totals: $19 \times 60\% = 11.4$. The expected value for pass-fail is $19 \times 40\% = 7.6$. Similarly, the expected value for fail-pass is $21 \times 60\% = 12.6$ and the expected value for fail-fail is $21 \times 40\% = 8.4$.

Alternatively, the calculation of expected values can start from the total values for the rows pass and fail (Dan's). The proportion is 47.5% and 52.5%. The expected value for pass-pass is the total value of pass column (Ella's) multiplied by the proportion from Dan's totals: $24 \times 47.5\% = 11.4$. The expected value for fail-pass is $24 \times 52.5\% = 12.6$. Similarly, the expected value for pass-fail is $16 \times 47.5\% = 7.6$ and the expected value for fail-fail is $16 \times 52.5\% = 8.4$.

The tables of expected values for pair #1 (Dan-Rein) and pair #3 (Rein-Ella) can be calculated using the same technique. These are the *expected counts* for kappa formula.

Calculation of kappa for pair #1 (Dan-Rein):
- The value of p_o is the total of observed pass-pass and fail-fail, divided by the total number of comparisons.
- $p_o = \frac{17+18}{40} = 0.875$
- The value of p_e is the total of expected pass-pass and fail-fail, divided by the total number of comparisons.
- $p_e = \frac{9.5+10.5}{40} = 0.5$
- $kappa_{(Dan-Rein)} = \frac{p_o-p_e}{1-p_e} = \frac{0.875-0.5}{1-0.5} = 0.7500$

Calculation of kappa for pair #2 (Dan-Ella):
- $p_o = \frac{19+16}{40} = 0.875$
- $p_e = \frac{11.4+8.4}{40} = 0.495$
- $kappa_{(Dan-Ella)} = \frac{p_o-p_e}{1-p_e} = \frac{0.875-0.495}{1-0.495} = 0.7525$

Calculation of kappa for pair #3 (Rein-Ella):

- $p_o = \frac{19+15}{40} = 0.85$
- $p_e = \frac{12+8}{40} = 0.5$
- $kappa_{(Rein-Ella)} = \frac{p_o - p_e}{1 - p_e} = \frac{0.85 - 0.5}{1 - 0.5} = 0.7000$

Finally, the acceptance table of the measurement system:

Decision	Repeatability	Reproducibility	Accuracy	Miss Rate	False Alarm Rate	System Effectiveness
Acceptable	91.67%		90.83%			
Marginally Acceptable		80%				80%
Unacceptable				7.41%	10.61%	

Even though the repeatability and accuracy of the measurement system are high, it has clear problems with miss rate and false alarm rate. Therefore, the *attribute agreement analysis* should consider the measurement system as unacceptable.

16. DATA COLLECTION

Six Sigma DMAIC methodology is a data-driven technique for process improvement. After confirming that measurement system is acceptable, the next step in Measure phase is data collection.

Simply trying to "gather all data" is unlikely going to work well. First, collecting all data is usually not feasible due to cost and time required. Second, gathering more data than what is needed will bring unnecessary extra efforts in collection and analysis. It is against the principles of Lean because the extra data does not add value to the project.

Data Collection Plan

Data collection plan is a deliverable of Measure phase that describes the steps that must be followed when collecting data. This document helps to perform data collection efficiently and minimise potential issues from different assumptions and interpretations between team members.

Starting data collection without proper plan is usually the recipe for disaster. It is a poor approach because it will waste effort and the important data usable for process improvement may or may not get collected in the end.

Considerations in making data collection plan:
- *Understand the overall flow of process improvement.* Starting from goal statement in project charter, project team analyses the measurement of Y as the performance to be improved. Process mapping and As-Is process review helps to understand the system and come up with a list of possible factors that might impact Y.

- *Identify the questions that need answers.* The list of potential factors (Xs) that might impact Y needs to be confirmed later in Analyze phase. Collect sufficient data related to Y and potential Xs. Statistical data analysis will be used to prove or disprove hypothesis to reach conclusion. Make sure that data collection is focused on answering questions during hypothesis testing.
- *Find and confirm readily available data.* If some data are already available and have been confirmed as valid, there is no need to redo the work.
- *Find sources of data.* Sometimes, not all questions can be answered because the data cannot be obtained. Data collection process need to be realistic and cost effective. Some data will not be available in raw form but can be observed from the relations of other data.
- *Understand different types of data and how to collect them.* Collecting numerical and attribute data would require different techniques. This includes choosing the collection tool and procedures.
- *Decide how much data is needed to make statistically significant conclusion.* If it is not practical to collect the entire population of data, sampling must be considered. It is important to make sure that sample size is sufficient for hypothesis testing in Analyze phase.
- *Plan how the data is going to be used.* Some data are collected to be presented in reports visual charts; others will be used in internal analysis.
- *Make clear schedule.* List all data to be collected, who is responsible for each data collection activity and explain the timing of data collection.

If possible, data from completed products and historical records need to be collected first before data from current production process. Data collection must make efforts to minimise disruption in normal production activities.

Training is an important part of data collection. Explain to team members and operators about the data that need to be collected and the reason why they are required. Simple mistakes from misunderstanding can negate significant efforts if the collected data become unusable.

Sampling

Sample data is collected when it is not possible to measure the whole population. In the Central Dogma of Statistics presented in Figure 16-1, sampling produces dataset with smaller size that is expected to represent the population. Population characteristics can be predicted from sample characteristics using *inferential statistics*.

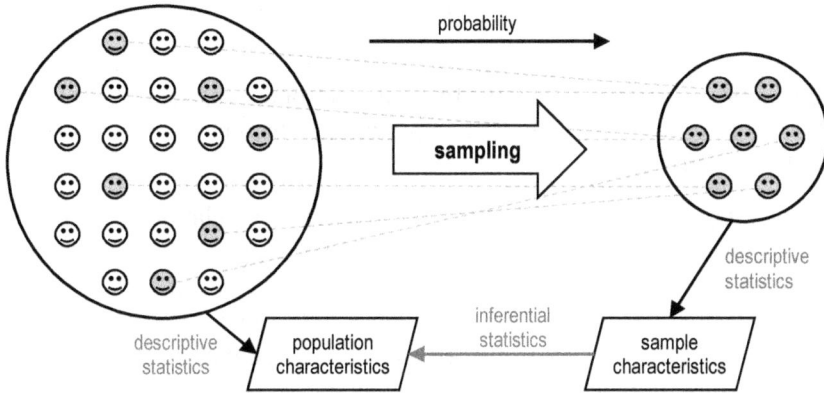

Figure 16-1 Sampling in Central Dogma of Statistics

For inferential statistics to work, sample must fulfill the following criteria:

- *Representative*. This means that sample must have enough number of items to represent all groups and patterns from the population.
- *Random*. This means that every data point in population has equal chance to be selected.
- *Relevant*. This means that data is collected for a purpose might not be suitable for other purposes.

In *probability sampling*, items in the population have non-zero probability to be selected in sample. The probability might not always be equal, depending on which technique is used for data collection. If probability sampling is not feasible (for example when items in the population cannot be enumerated), then *non-probability sampling* is used as alternative.

Techniques for probability sampling:

- Systematic sampling.
- Opportunity sampling.
- Cluster sampling.
- Stratified sampling.
- True random sampling.

Systematic sampling is sampling technique that uses the sequence of data in population. First, choose the first item from the population, then every k items afterwards. For this technique to work, the sequence of items in population must already be in random order. The value of k is decided from calculating the total number of items in the population (N) divided by the expected size of sample (n).

$$k = \frac{N}{n}$$

Opportunity sampling chooses the first n items from the population and ignore the rest. Similar to systematic sampling, this technique only works for population data with random order.

Cluster sampling identifies clusters (groups) in the population and focuses to collect sample items from selected clusters. For example: students from grade 6 are members of a cluster in the population of all students in primary school. If a project only needs data from grade 6 students, there is no need to include students from other grades. Collected data can be generalised to represent the characteristics of grade 6 students but cannot be used to generalise all primary school students.

Stratified sampling divides population into homogenous groups, then choose random items proportionally from those groups. This technique is useful to ensure that each group is represented in the sample. For example: The state of Victoria has 88 electoral districts. If a study wants to predict the results of an upcoming election, it needs to find out the number of residents within each district, then calculate the number of samples needed from each district so that the sample proportion represents the whole population of Victoria.

True random sampling ignores any groups or clusters in the population and gives every item equal and independent chance to get selected in sample dataset. This technique will work if the sample size is large enough to represent all characteristics from the population.

Techniques for non-probability sampling:
- Accidental sampling.
- Purposive sampling.

Accidental sampling is a sampling technique of collecting the easiest data or the first available data. Systematic sampling and opportunity sampling could become accidental sampling if the sequence of data in population is not random. For example, a study wants to learn about people's opinion for an upcoming election. Data collector steps out of his house and survey the first 30 people that he meets in his neighbourhood. This sequence is not really random because his neighbourhood is well known for supporting one particular political party. There is high probability that the collected data will come from people who support the candidate from the political party preferred in the neighbourhood.

Purposive sampling uses human judgement from data collector to decide which items to be included in sampling. There are several types of purposive sampling:

- *Heterogenous sampling*: items are chosen to maximise variation in the sample.
- *Homogenous sampling*: items are chosen to minimise variation in the sample.
- *Typical case sampling*: items that are considered as typical is chosen. Sample taken using this technique cannot be used to generalise the population.
- *Extreme case sampling*: items that are considered as unusual is chosen. This is the opposite of typical case sampling.
- *Expert sampling*: items are chosen based on the guidance from an expert with extensive knowledge about a particular domain.

When an item from the population is selected for sample dataset, the same item may or may not be selected again depending on the sampling type:

- Sampling with replacement.
- Sampling without replacement.

Sampling without replacement means if an item is removed from population pool after it is selected into sample dataset. The same item will not get selected again because it is no longer in the population pool.

Sampling with replacement means when an item from the population is selected into sample, it will not be removed from population pool. In other words, it receives replacement in the population so that the same item can be selected again. Because of this replacement, any item from the population can appear multiple times in sample dataset.

Sample Size

The size of sample dataset is a key parameter impacting the sample's ability to make inferences about a population. Bigger sample size is usually the better but collecting more than what is necessary to make statistical inference goes against the reason of choosing to use sample (instead of population) in the first place.

To ensure that collected sample is able to statistically represent the characteristics of a population, there are two aspects to consider when deciding on sample size:
- Confidence level.
- Precision level.

X% *confidence level* means that statistics is X% confident that certain subset of sample contains the true mean of the population. The most popular confidence level is 95%. Depending on the use case, confidence level 90%, 98% and 99% are also commonly used. Unless stated otherwise, this book uses 95% confidence level as the default assumption.

Precision level is a measure of how precise we need to make inferences about the population. For example, a precision of 0.5 means that sample is able to differentiate value of 2 and 2.5 when predicting something about the population. However, the same sample would not have the ability to differentiate 2.4 and 2.5, both will be predicted as 2.5.

Sample size (continuous data) for X% confidence level and δ precision is calculated as:

$$n = \left(\frac{Z \times \sigma}{\delta}\right)^2$$

Z in the formula is the *Z score* for X% confidence level. *Z score* is the distance in terms of standard deviation between a value and the mean in a dataset with normal distribution. This measure has been introduced in Chapter 03. As refresher, formula of *Z score*:

$$Z = \frac{x_i - \mu}{\sigma}$$

From basic normal distribution theory, we know that the range from minus σ to plus σ covers 68.2% of possible data points. For the purpose of calculating sample size, it is said that to reach 68.2% confidence level, the value of Z score is 1 because 68.2% is the probability covered by *middle area* between minus 1σ to plus 1σ.

Normal Distribution

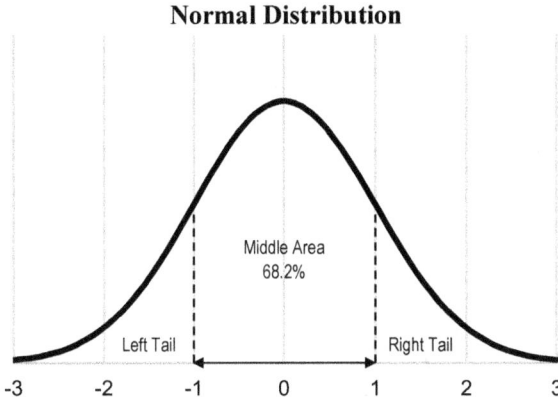

Figure 16-2 Normal Distribution Curve with Z=1

According to normal distribution theory, total area under the distribution curve is 1.

$$Left\ Tail + Middle\ Area + Right\ Tail = 1$$

The areas under normal distribution curve outside middle area are called the *tail areas*. The *left tail* covers $(1 - 0.682) / 2 = 0.159$ or 15.9%. The *right tail* covers another 15.9%.

How do we get confidence value of 68.2% from Z = 1?

The easiest way to find the value is to use *Z table* from Chapter 38. This table shows the *cumulative P-value* of all data points possibility <u>from Z score to the left</u>.

- For negative *Z score*, *P-value* is the total value of *left tail*.
- For positive *Z score*, *P-value* is the total value of *left tail* plus *middle area*.

Z	0.00	0.01	0.02	0.03	0.04	0.05	0.06	0.07	0.08	0.09
0.8	0.788145	0.791030	0.793892	0.796731	0.799546	0.802337	0.805105	0.807850	0.810570	0.813267
0.9	0.815940	0.818589	0.821214	0.823814	0.826391	0.828944	0.831472	0.833977	0.836457	0.838913
1.0	0.841345	0.843752	0.846136	0.848495	0.850830	0.853141	0.855428	0.857690	0.859929	0.862143
1.1	0.864334	0.866500	0.868643	0.870762	0.872857	0.874928	0.876976	0.879000	0.881000	0.882977
1.2	0.884930	0.886861	0.888768	0.890651	0.892512	0.894350	0.896165	0.897958	0.899727	0.901475

Table 16-A Partial Z table showing P-value for Z=1

From partial Z table in Table 16-A, the *P-value* of Z = 1.0 is 0.8413. Therefore, middle area can be calculated using the following steps:

- *Right Tail* = 1 − *P*.

151

- *Middle Area* = 1 – *Left Tail* – *Right Tail*.
- For normal distribution, *Right Tail* = *Left Tail*.
- *Middle area* = 1 – (1 – P) – (1 – P) = 2P – 1.
- *Middle area* = (2 × 0.8413) – 1 = 0.6826 or 68.26%

With good understanding on the correlation between *Z score* and confidence level, *Z score* for any X% confidence level can be looked up from the Z table after considering the tail area.

To calculate Z score for 95% confidence level for a two-tailed problem:

- 95% confidence level for means Middle Area covers 95%.
- *Left Tail* = *Right Tail* = (1 – *Middle Area*) / 2 = (1 – 0.95) / 2 = 0.025.
- *P* = *Left Tail* + *Middle Area* = 0.025 + 0.95 = 0.975.
- Find the *P-value* of 0.975 in Z table (see Table 16-B).
- The first *P-value* that is greater than 0.975 is 0.975002. It has *Z score* of 1.96.

Z	0.00	0.01	0.02	0.03	0.04	0.05	0.06	0.07	0.08	0.09
1.8	0.964070	0.964852	0.965620	0.966375	0.967116	0.967843	0.968557	0.969258	0.969946	0.970621
1.9	0.971283	0.971933	0.972571	0.973197	0.973810	0.974412	0.975002	0.975581	0.976148	0.976705
2.0	0.977250	0.977784	0.978308	0.978822	0.979325	0.979818	0.980301	0.980774	0.981237	0.981691
2.1	0.982136	0.982571	0.982997	0.983414	0.983823	0.984222	0.984614	0.984997	0.985371	0.985738
2.2	0.986097	0.986447	0.986791	0.987126	0.987455	0.987776	0.988089	0.988396	0.988696	0.988989

Table 16-B Partial Z table showing P-value for Z=1.96

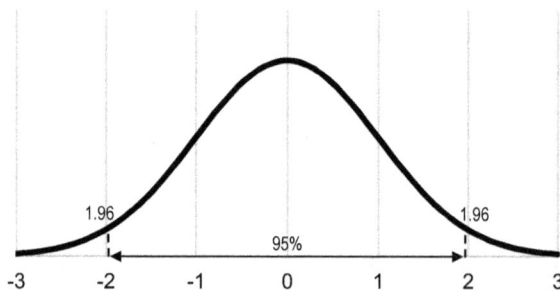

Figure 16-3 Normal Distribution for 95% Confidence Level

For quick reference, the Z scores for frequently used confidence levels:

- 90% confidence level has *Z score* = 1.65.
- 95% confidence level has *Z score* = 1.96.
- 98% confidence level has *Z score* = 2.33.
- 99% confidence level has *Z score* = 2.58.

Example 16-1:
Calculate the sample size for a population with standard deviation 50, 95% confidence level and precision to detect value differences of 5.

- $\sigma = 50$
- 95% confidence level means $Z = 1.96$.
- $\delta = 5$
- $n = \left(\frac{Z \times \sigma}{h}\right)^2 = \left(\frac{1.96 \times 50}{5}\right)^2 = 384.16$
- The value of n for sample size is always rounded up.
- Sample size is 385.

Sample size for discrete or attribute data:

$$n = \left(\frac{Z \times \sqrt{(p)(1-p)}}{\delta}\right)^2$$

Precision:

$$\delta = \frac{Z \times \sqrt{(p)(1-p)}}{\sqrt{n}}$$

p is the proportion of interest.

Example 16-2:
Sample data is collected to estimate whether defect rate of the population is 5% with precision of plus minus 0.5%. What is the required sample size to estimate such defect rate with 95% confidence level?

- $p = 0.05$
- 95% confidence level means $Z = 1.96$.
- $\delta = 0.005$
- $n = \left(\frac{Z \times \sqrt{(p)(1-p)}}{\delta}\right)^2 = \left(\frac{1.96 \times \sqrt{0.05 \times 0.95}}{0.005}\right)^2 = 7299.04$
- The value of n for sample size is always rounded up.
- Sample size is 7,300.

Sample Mean, Variance and Standard Deviation

Sample mean is the average of all values in a sample dataset. Since sample does not contain all items from the population, the average of a sample might be different from the average of population.

As refresher, the mean formula for population:

$$\mu = \frac{\sum x_i}{N}$$

Mean formula for sample:

$$\bar{x} = \frac{\sum x_i}{n}$$

In this book, *mean* of population is represented with symbol μ, read as mu. *Mean* of sample is represented with the symbol $\bar{x}$, read as x-bar. The count of values (the amount of data) in a population is represented with symbol N and the count of values in sample uses the symbol n.

Standard deviation is a measure of how spread out the values in a dataset from its mean. Standard deviation is calculated as the square root of *Variance*, which is the sum of squared difference between each value and mean, divided by the count of values.

As refresher, variance formula for population:

$$\sigma^2 = \frac{\sum(x_i - \mu)^2}{N}$$

Standard deviation is the square root of variance. The standard deviation formula for population:

$$\sigma = \sqrt{\frac{\sum(x_i - \mu)^2}{N}}$$

Standard deviation of a population is represented using the symbol of σ (sigma). Standard deviation of a sample uses the symbol S. Variance for population and sample are written as σ^2 and S^2.

To calculate variance in sample, $n - 1$ is used instead of n for the *unbiased sample variance*, this is called *Bessel's correction*. Sample S^2 is an estimation of population σ^2. Each difference between a value and mean is calculated using $\bar{x}$ (sample mean) instead of μ (population mean).

Variance formula for sample:

$$S^2 = \frac{\sum(x_i - \bar{x})^2}{n - 1}$$

Standard deviation formula for sample:

$$S = \sqrt{\frac{\sum(x_i - \bar{x})^2}{n - 1}}$$

Why $n - 1$ is used for denominator? What is unbiased sample variance?

$n - 1$ is the *degrees of freedom* for a sample. If mean value and all the values except one are known for a sample, the last unknown value can be calculated. In the case of calculating sample variance, $\bar{x}$ (sample mean) is used because μ (population mean) is not known. The sample mean generates bias, but it does not tell us the value of the bias. What we do know is that S^2 usually underestimates the estimation of σ^2 except for a few rare cases. Using $n - 1$ denominator corrects this bias.

It is easier to demonstrate this concept using an example. Suppose we have a population data with three values: 1, 3 and 5.

- $\mu = \frac{1+3+5}{3} = 3$
- $\sigma^2 = \frac{(1-3)^2+(3-3)^2+(5-3)^2}{3} = \frac{8}{3}$
- There are nine possible samples (with replacement) for $n = 2$

Possible Samples	Sample Mean	Sample Variance with n	Sample Variance with $n - 1$
1, 1	1	$\frac{(1-1)^2 + (1-1)^2}{2} = 0$	$\frac{(1-1)^2 + (1-1)^2}{1} = 0$
1, 3	2	$\frac{(1-2)^2 + (3-2)^2}{2} = 1$	$\frac{(1-2)^2 + (3-2)^2}{1} = 2$
1, 5	3	$\frac{(1-3)^2 + (5-3)^2}{2} = 4$	$\frac{(1-3)^2 + (5-3)^2}{1} = 8$
3, 1	2	$\frac{(3-2)^2 + (1-2)^2}{2} = 1$	$\frac{(3-2)^2 + (1-2)^2}{1} = 2$
3, 3	3	$\frac{(3-3)^2 + (3-3)^2}{2} = 0$	$\frac{(3-3)^2 + (3-3)^2}{1} = 0$
3, 5	4	$\frac{(3-4)^2 + (5-4)^2}{2} = 1$	$\frac{(3-4)^2 + (5-4)^2}{1} = 2$
5, 1	3	$\frac{(5-3)^2 + (1-3)^2}{2} = 4$	$\frac{(5-3)^2 + (1-3)^2}{1} = 8$
5, 3	4	$\frac{(5-4)^2 + (3-4)^2}{2} = 1$	$\frac{(5-4)^2 + (3-4)^2}{1} = 2$
5, 5	5	$\frac{(5-5)^2 + (5-5)^2}{2} = 0$	$\frac{(5-5)^2 + (5-5)^2}{1} = 0$

- The average of all sample mean is the sum of all sample mean divided by the number of possible samples.

$$\frac{1+2+3+2+3+4+3+4+5}{9} = \frac{27}{9} = 3 \quad \text{this is equal to } \mu.$$

- If the sample variance is unbiased, the average of variance values of all possible samples should be equal to population variance σ^2.
- The average of variances of all samples calculated with n

$$\frac{0+1+4+1+0+1+4+1+0}{9} = \frac{12}{9} = \frac{4}{3} \quad \text{this is not equal to } \sigma^2$$

- The average of variances of all samples calculated with $n-1$

$$\frac{0+2+8+2+0+2+8+2+0}{9} = \frac{24}{9} = \frac{8}{3} \quad \text{this is equal to } \sigma^2$$

- Sample variances calculated using $n-1$ are proven to be non-biased.

ANALYZE PHASE

17. UNDERSTANDING ANALYZE PHASE

The third phase of Six Sigma DMAIC project is the *Analyze phase*. As the name suggests, this phase focuses on analysing data from Measure phase to answer the questions for process improvement.

Let us begin the discussion on Analyze phase by reviewing the five phases of DMAIC and the $Y = f(X)$ formula.

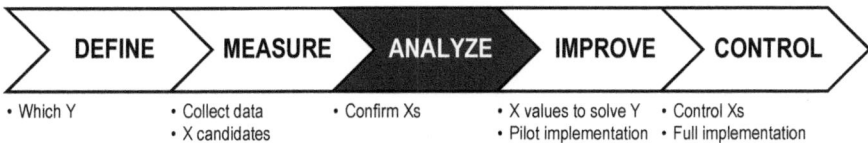

DEFINE	MEASURE	ANALYZE	IMPROVE	CONTROL
• Which Y	• Collect data • X candidates	• Confirm Xs	• X values to solve Y • Pilot implementation	• Control Xs • Full implementation

Figure 17-1 Analyze phase in DMAIC

In Analyze phase, the focus is to answer questions using data. Following the goal statement of a project, the main question that needs to be answered is: what are the confirmed X factors that impact the outcome of Y?

This question seems very similar to the question in Measure phase. However, there is one key difference: Measure phase uses the word <u>potential</u> factors (candidates); Analyze phase <u>confirms</u> the factors.

There are three ways to confirm X factors impacting Y:
- Use *visual analysis*. If an X candidate is already obvious as shown in visual representation of data, then there is no need to waste time and efforts, team can make conclusion and proceed with analysis of the next candidate.

- Use *Lean analysis*. If an X candidate is related to Lean measures (cycle time, lead time, takt time, value flow, etc) then perform Lean analysis to confirm X.
- Use *statistical analysis*. Descriptive statistics can be used if population data are available. Inferential statistics can be used if sample data are collected. Hypothesis testing is the most common form of inferential statistics. In this technique, hypothesis is made to answer questions about an X candidate, then use the data collected from Measure phase to confirm or reject the hypothesis.
- *Analyse solution risk*. After the X factors are confirmed, it is important to identify and analyse the risks that come with efforts to control such factors.

It is important to note that visual analysis or Lean analysis are not equal to gut feeling decision making. DMAIC is a data-driven process improvement methodology. Everything should be supported by data. The only difference is the level of processing that project team needs to work on to analyse the data. Some questions need deep analysis using inferential statistics, some need high-level analysis using Lean principles, some others are already obvious from the visual representation of data.

18. LEAN ANALYSIS

The basic principle of Lean is to deliver only what is needed at the right time. It classifies steps in a process as value-added, non-value-added and enabler activities. Please review Chapter 04 before continuing with this chapter.

Lean analysis allows DMAIC team to confirm some of the potential X candidates without going into complex statistical calculations. For example, a company producing perishable goods have an issue of distribution stores returning high number of products past expiry dates. Lean analysis on the company warehouse's inventory level shows that majority of products already stayed in the warehouse for too long before they were sent to distribution stores with not much time left to expiry dates. Looking at the measures from data, a Black Belt and project team may decide that there is no need to go further with inferential statistics, it can be concluded that the company has inventory problem as one of the X factors impacting Y.

Note that the decision to skip inferential statistics should never be a gut feeling decision. It should still be based on analysis of valid data, only with less processing.

The Nine Wastes of Lean

Lean identifies eight types of waste in a system or process.
- *Transportation waste*: excess movement of all parts, products, tools and equipment.
- *Inventory waste*: cost of storing products because production speed is higher than customer demand.

- *Motion waste*: excess movement of people, tools or machines involved in production.
- *Waiting waste*: process (or sub-process) cannot proceed with work because material or equipment is not ready, causing idle waiting time.
- *Overproduction waste*: production speed is higher than the rate of customer demand.
- *Overprocessing waste*: production system does more work than what is necessary according to customer demand.
- *Defect waste*: product or service has one or more aspects that fail to meet the requirement.
- *Skills underutilised waste*: waste of human potential.
- *Space waste*: physical space or digital storage does not add value for the customer.

With the exceptions of transportation and defect wastes, Lean wastes are often overlooked behind the piles of production data focused on other visible metrics. Transportation waste gets recorded properly because the process of transporting products or components usually involve direct costs. Defect waste is usually measured as part of inspection process or quality measurement.

Inventory costs are often considered as the unavoidable cost of running a production system. While eliminating the cost down to zero might not always be feasible, significant reduction can be achieved by aligning production speed with customer demand.

Motion waste does not usually associate with direct cost. It is easy to overlook the fact that workers spending time to move from one location to another multiple times a day is actually costing the company their productive time.

Waiting waste is usually captured as qualitative issue. Lean principles provide a mechanism to quantify this issue into measurable cost.

Overproduction waste is also known as inventory waste. There are 3 techniques to prevent minimise this:
- Calculate takt time and adjusting cycle time to match it.
- Use Kanban system to minimise the amount of WIP.
- Reduce batch size to reach *single piece flow*.

Overprocessing waste is often misperceived with as creating higher level of quality that translates into selling point. This could be true if the company manages to reach sufficient number of customers that appreciate extra feature and willing to pay for it. Otherwise, it will simply become wasteful activity because the current customer base does not consider it as value.

Skill-underutilised waste is one of the most difficult wastes to measure because human potential (and skills) are not always straightforward to be observed. There might be special occasions that bring the case about certain employees being underqualified or overqualified, but these are usually undetected during everyday normal activities.

Space waste could be related to physical space such as warehouse, or digital storage such as HDD or SSD in cloud or on-premise. Maintaining storage capacity that is larger than needed is generally associated with cost.

Lean Measures

Production process needs to have optimised workflow capable to generate outputs based on pull from customer demand. Lean uses three measurements to calculate this: cycle time, lead time and takt time.

Cycle time is the time needed to complete the production of a single count of product or service from start to finish. *Lead time* is the time needed to complete production of a single count of product or service from the time of customer demand until the product or service reaches the customer. Cycle time is a component inside lead time. *Takt time* is the time needed to satisfy the rate of customer demand, also known as the pull.

Lean principles aim to produce the right output at the first production attempt without any rework. Any defect produced by a system would always result in wasteful activities. *First Time Yield* (FTY) is the proportion of good units produced divided by the number of units went into production.

$$FTY = \frac{good\ units\ produced}{units\ at\ the\ start\ of\ production}$$

For a production system with multiple processes, the output from one process becomes the input for the following process. For every process, the number of good outputs is the number of inputs minus the number of rework and scrap. 100 units at the start of production and 100 good units at the end of production only shows an ideal production system if every unit is produced right (no defect) from the first attempt without the need of any rework of defect fixes.

Rolled Throughput Yield (RTY) is the probability of a unit to pass all processes without any defect. It is calculated as the multiplication of all local FTY of every process.

$$RTY = FTY(A) \times FTY(B) \times FTY(C) \times \cdots \times FTY(n)$$

Analysis of FTY from processes in a system helps to identify *bottlenecks*. Every bottleneck process is a strong potential candidate of X factors that may impact Y.

In most cases, production system involves multiple process that has complex relations instead of simple linear line. Every decision points and loops in process maps create *tangled flow*. Use visual analysis to walk the process and find the weak points in a system.

- Processes without predecessor (*dangler*) are potential disrupter because they are unpredictable.
- Processes without successor are classified as *waste* because they do not produce value that will reach customers.
- Process *loops* are negative contributors to RTY, costs and process flow because they cause units to flow backwards and repeating processes.

Any activity in production system that starts with "re" usually indicates problems from Lean perspective. Finding these words in process maps are usually indicators that the system fails to produce something right from the first go. Examples of "re" activities: rework, retest, remake, recall, reject and many others. For each of these activities, there should be a prior process that needs to be improved.

Value Stream Mapping

Value Stream Mapping (VSM) is Lean's version of process map. Instead of simply mapping the steps in a process, Value Stream Mapping maps the flow of value throughout a system. This tool requires quantitative data from Measure phase.

There are three main sections of VSM:

- *Information flow*. This part shows the flow of information between supplier, customer and production control.
- *Material flow*. This part shows the steps of making a product or service, who are responsible of each step and some high-level statistics about the steps. Usually, the high-level statistics include *First Time Yield* (FTY), number of scrap and rework, uptime percentage, number of operators and transport distance between steps.
- *Time flow*. This part shows cycle time for each step and lead time between steps.

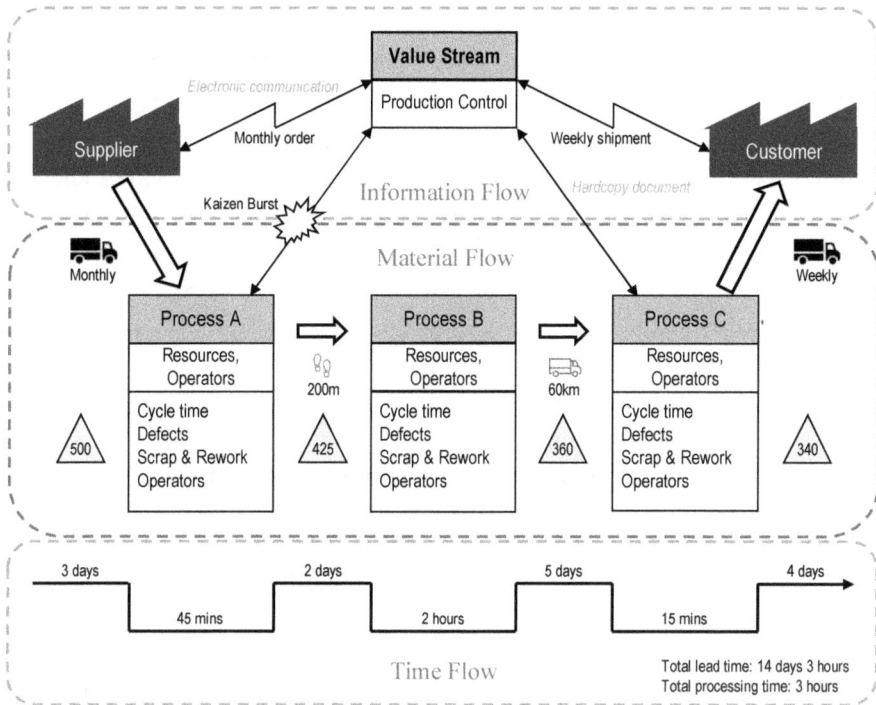

Figure 18-1 Value Stream Map

Supplier and customer in ***information flow*** section are represented in an abstract form that looks like a factory. Supplier is always located on the top-left corner and customer is always located on the top-right. Line with directional arrow represents hardcopy documents. Line with zigzag shows electronic communication. Spark symbol indicates Kaizen Burst, a Lean activity to resolve a problem.

Material flow starts with the frequencies of activities from supplier and to customer. The main part of this section lists all processes in a production system, each with information on resources and operators as well as production data. Lean measures such as cycle time, number of defects, number of scrap and rework, number of operators, percentage of uptime and takt rate can be presented for high-level analysis.

The movement of materials between processes is indicated by distance and symbol. In Figure 18-1, there is a 200 metres distance between the location for process A and B. The far distance (60 km) between location for process B and C requires materials to be transported in vehicles.

Triangles with numbers represents the amount of inventory being moved through production. It can be quickly observed that 500 units of inventory at the beginning of process A only produces 340 units at the end of process C. This could trigger further investigation by looking into the number of defects, scrap and rework in each process, along with the possible causes.

Time flow is the last section of VSM. It shows a time ladder with the amount of time spent in each process and between processes. This quickly indicates how much time is actually spent on the processes and how much time is spent in waiting. For example, the long 5 days of waiting time between process B and C might be caused from transportation optimisation issue.

There are other symbols can be used in VSM that are not currently used in Figure 18-1.

- Octagon shape with letter Q inside is used to mark particular process that has quality problem.
- Glasses symbol might be placed on area to prompt readers to see or observe more.
- If the number of inventory units flowing between processes is unknown, the triangles might have simple letter I inside to indicate inventory movement.
- Some people would differentiate the arrow for material movement with different colours for movement based on push and movement based on pull.

19. STATISTICAL DATA ANALYSIS

Statistical data analysis uses the theories of statistics to analyse and make conclusion about data. Two basic aspects of statistics are the measure of central tendency (mean, median, mode) and measure of variability (standard deviation, variance).

Before continuing with this chapter, it is strongly recommended to review the following chapters:
- Chapter 06 about Descriptive Statistics and Data Types
- Chapter 07 about Probability Distribution
- Chapter 16 about Data Collection and Sampling

Visual Analysis

Statistical analysis does not always have to involve complex mathematical calculation. Data can be presented using a lot of visual tools. Sometimes the visual representation of data could be sufficient to make a conclusion if the observed pattern is clear and obvious.

Visual analysis is the process of analysing data by observing their visual representation. This is the fastest and simplest method of data analysis but is only usable if the connection between factor and outcome is obvious from visual observation.

There are many ways of visual data representation. Some of the common ones include:
- Scatter plots

- Histograms
- Pareto charts
- Dot plots (strip charts)
- Box plots (box and whisker charts)

These visual tools have been discussed earlier in Chapter 08. Scatter plot represents the values of two different variables using x-axis and y-axis in a Cartesian plane. Histogram shows distribution of data using bar chart. Pareto chart is a visual tool showing frequencies in bars and cumulative percentage in line graph. Dot plot visualises data using dots to represent data points. Box plot is a tool to show the distribution and skewness of data. It presents mean, median, 25th & 75th percentile, range and outliers, allowing quick comparison between groups of data.

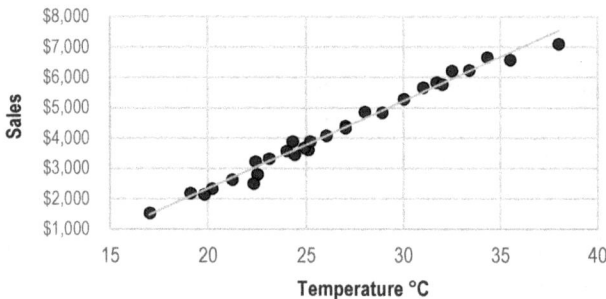

Figure 19-1 Scatter plot showing sales data of an ice cream shop

Figure 19-1 shows a scatter plot showing sales data of an ice cream shop in 30 days compared to the maximum temperature on each day. Sales number for the day is the Y variable. The maximum temperature on a day is an independent factor that was identified by Measure phase as potential X that impacts Y. Looking at the collected data, a Black Belt might decide that it is sufficient to decide this X candidate as confirmed factor.

Descriptive Statistics vs. Inferential Statistics

Descriptive statistics is a study of statistics to describe the summarised characteristics of data. This study describes data characteristics using measures of central tendency and measures of variability.

Measures of central tendency aims to give overall understanding on where most data points in a dataset are located. *Mean* is the average of all values in dataset. Median is the middle value in a sorted dataset. *Mode* is a value (or multiple values) that appears most often in dataset.

Measures of variability focuses on describing how different are the data in a dataset. *Range* is the difference between maximum and minimum values. *Variance* is the sum of squared difference between each value in a dataset and the mean, divided by the count of values. *Standard deviation* is the square root of variance, commonly used to describe how spread out the values in a dataset from its mean. *Skewness* measures the symmetry of value distribution on both sides of mode. If value distribution on the right side of mode looks identical to the value distribution on the left side of mode, it is said that such distribution is symmetrical, having skewness value of zero. *Kurtosis* is a measure of peakness and tailedness level of value distribution within a dataset.

Population in the set of data with every member in a particular topic of interest. When it is not feasible to collect all data from a population, statistical *sample* is collected using certain methods in such a way that the characteristics of sample data can be used to infer trends or patterns about a larger population.

Inferential statistics is a study of analysing sample data characteristics to make predictions about how those characteristics are related to the population where sample was collected from. Figure 19-2 shows the relationships between descriptive statistics and inferential statistics.

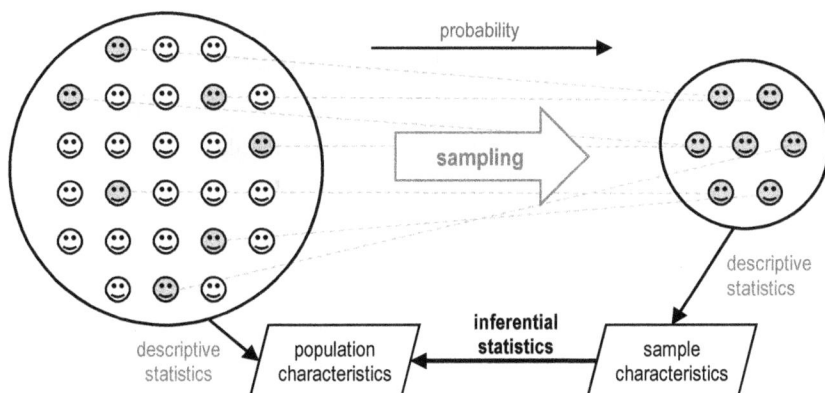

Figure 19-2 Inferential statistics in Central Dogma of Statistics

There are two major approaches of inferential statistics:
- Confidence Interval
- Hypothesis Testing

Confidence interval uses sample mean, standard deviation and Z score of normal distribution to estimate the value of population mean. Calculation of confidence interval is presented in the next part of this chapter. *Hypothesis Testing* is discussed in Chapters 20, 21, 22, 23 and 24.

Confidence Interval

Confidence interval is a statistical technique to estimate population mean from sample characteristics. It is applicable for sample data with normal distribution because it uses Z score to estimate the probability of true population mean is a value between certain limits in sample dataset.

There are four components of confidence interval:
- Sample mean
- Sample standard deviation
- Sample size
- Confidence level

X% confidence level means that statistical analysis is X% confident that the true mean of the population is located within sample mean's confidence interval.

$$CI = \{\bar{x} \pm w\}; \ \mu \in CI$$

w is the margin of error of confidence interval. This measure is comparable to precision in sample size calculation because it represents how far can values in sample data could be wrong in estimating values in population.

As refresher, sample size is calculated using the formula:

$$n = \left(\frac{Z \times \sigma}{\delta}\right)^2$$

The same formula can be used to calculate sample precision:

$$\delta = \frac{Z \times \sigma}{\sqrt{n}}$$

Margin of error (w) in confidence interval is calculated as:

$$w = \frac{Z \times S}{\sqrt{n}}$$

S is standard deviation of sample. n is sample size. Z is calculated from the expected confidence level. *Z score* is the distance in terms of standard deviation between a value and the mean of a dataset with normal distribution.

The most popular confidence level is 95%. Unless stated otherwise, this book uses 95% confidence level as the default assumption.

Values of Z for quick reference:
- 90% confidence level: Z = 1.65.
- 95% confidence level: Z = 1.96.
- 98% confidence level: Z = 2.33.
- 99% confidence level: Z = 2.58.

For all other values of confidence level, please refer to Z *table* in Chapter 38. This table shows the cumulative value of data points possibility from limit of Z score to the left. Please review Chapter 16 about Z score in normal distribution curve, middle area, left tail and right tail to understand more about reading *P* value from Z table.

To find Z for two-tailed problem with X% confidence level, find the first *P-value* in the table that is bigger than $X + (1 - X) / 2$. This can be simplified as $(X + 1) / 2$.

Full formula of confidence interval:

$$\mu \approx \bar{x} \pm Z_{\left(\frac{x+1}{2}\right)} \times \frac{S}{\sqrt{n}}$$

Example:
Sample with 100 data has standard deviation of 15 and mean of 120. What is the predicted population mean?
- $\bar{x} = 120$.
- $S = 15$.
- $n = 100$.
- $Z = 1.96$ because the default assumption is 95% confidence level.
- $\mu \approx 120 \pm 1.96 \times \frac{15}{\sqrt{100}}$
- $\mu \approx 120 \pm 2.94$
- Population mean is a value between 117.06 to 122.94.

Univariate, Bivariate and Multivariate Analysis

Univariate analysis is the act of describing one particular factor of data using descriptive or inferential statistics. When there are multiple factors, analysis is performed on one factor at a time. This is the simplest form statistical analysis.

Calculating a descriptive measure of one factor from a dataset, then comparing it with a standard value is a form of univariate analysis. This factor could be any column or category from data. For example, it is known that the acceptance rate of a top university is 28% from all applicants. Dean of Engineering and Science wants to know if the acceptance rate in his faculty is below or above that standard. Univariate analysis study counts the number of accepted applicants, divide it by the count of all applicants, then compare it with the standard value of 28%.

Working on two factors at the same time to find correlation is called *bivariate analysis*. This is a common type of analysis in Six Sigma project because it studies two sets of values, which are X and Y. X is the independent variable and the study needs to confirm if X impacts the outcome of dependent variable Y or not.

Bivariate analysis aims to find correlation and possible causation. The simplest form of bivariate analysis is a simple mapping of X and Y values in scatter plots. Other techniques include regression analysis and correlation coefficient. These concepts will be discussed later as part of Hypothesis Testing.

Multivariate analysis uses statistical analysis on more than two factors at the same time to find significance and relationships between the factors. There are many techniques of multivariate analysis, some of them will be discussed later as part of Design of Experiments chapters.

Common types of multivariate analysis:
- *Factor analysis*. This analysis is performed to discover the smallest number of factors that makes greatest contributions to outcome of Y. Pareto chart is a simple version of this technique.
- *Cluster analysis*. This analysis tries to group factors into clusters with similar statistical performance so that further analysis could be done on the clusters instead of individual factors. This technique helps to shorten the list of potential X factors when there are too many of them.
- *Discriminant analysis*. This study tries to determine why some groups exist and what factors are the best predictors of grouping results.
- *Multiple regression analysis*. This analysis calculates mathematical correlation between multiple X variables and the performance of Y using the formula of $Y = f(X1) + f(X2) + ... + f(Xn)$.

20. HYPOTHESIS TESTING PRINCIPLES

Hypothesis testing is the most common technique in inferential statistics. Some learning materials even refer to them as the same topic. Hypothesis testing is very useful in Analyze phase as a key technique to transform the list of potential X factors into shorter list of confirmed Xs.

Before continuing with this chapter, it is strongly recommended to review the following chapters:
- Chapter 06 about descriptive statistics and data types
- Chapter 07 about probability distribution
- Chapter 16 about data collection and sampling
- Chapter 19 about statistical data analysis and inferential statistics

Hypothesis testing is an inferential statistics technique to draw conclusion from collected data using hypothesis question. This technique starts from creating null and alternative hypothesis, then uses data analysis to statistically accept or reject the hypothesis.

Null hypothesis (H_0) is a hypothesis statement that there is nothing statistically significant from sample data. Any difference between sample and its comparison (target value, another sample or multiple other samples) are the results of random chance.

Alternative hypothesis (H_A) is the opposite of null hypothesis. This statement believes that the differences between sample and its comparison are statistically significant and they occur because of non-random causes. Alternative hypothesis is the statement that tester is trying to prove.

Executing hypothesis testing allows tester to *reject null hypothesis* if there is sufficient statistical evidence to do so. When null hypothesis is rejected, it means that testing results prefer the alternative hypothesis.

There is no such thing as accepting null hypothesis. When there is not enough statistical evidence, it is said that hypothesis testing *fails to reject null hypothesis*. If this happens, null hypothesis is chosen as the status quo.

Basic steps of performing hypothesis testing:
- Formulate the question
- Define null hypothesis and alternative hypothesis
- Select and perform test
- Analyse collected data
- Interpret results

Decision Errors: Alpha and Beta Risks

The decision made from hypothesis testing can have two types of errors:
- *Type I error* occurs when tester rejects null hypothesis (H_0) when it is actually true.
- *Type II error* occurs when tester fails to reject null hypothesis (H_0) when it is actually false.

	Do not reject H_0	Reject H_0
H_0 is true H_A is false	**Correct Decision** Confidence level	**Type I error** Alpha risk Significance level
H_0 is false H_A is true	**Type II error** Beta risk	**Correct Decision** Power

Figure 20-1 Decision errors in Hypothesis Testing

Alpha risk (α) or *significance level* is the maximum acceptable rate of Type I error. The most common value for Alpha is 5%. *Confidence level* is the probability of making the correct decision when null hypothesis is true (do not reject null hypothesis), it is calculated as $1 - \alpha$.

Beta risk (β) is the maximum acceptable rate of Type II error. The most common value of Beta is 10%. *Power* is the probability of making the correct decision when null hypothesis is false (reject null hypothesis), it is calculated as $1 - \beta$. *Average Run Length* (ARL) is $1 / (1 - \beta)$.

General patterns in adjusting Alpha and Beta risks:
- Efforts to reduce Alpha will usually increase Beta, and vice versa.
- Both Alpha and Beta risks can be reduced by increasing sample size.
- Beta risk can be reduced by increasing the difference between null hypothesis (H_0) and alternative hypothesis (H_A).

Test Statistics vs. Critical Value

Hypothesis testing works by comparing certain values calculated from sample data (test statistics) against the limits of rejection (critical value). Acceptable and rejection area are separated by one or two critical values. If test statistics is located inside rejection area, hypothesis test reject null hypothesis.

Right-tailed test has one critical value separating acceptable area on the left and rejection area on the right. Rejection area is the area under distribution curve with total area of α. In Figure 20-2, test statistics A fails to reject null hypothesis because it is located inside acceptable area. Test statistics B rejects null hypothesis because it is located in rejection area.

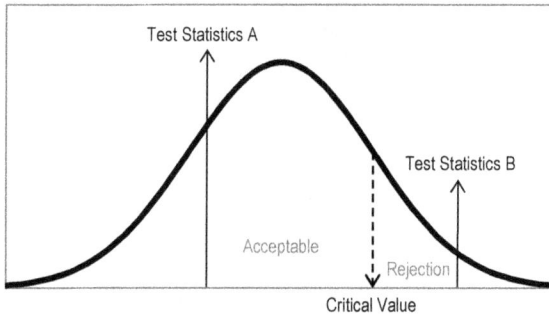

Figure 20-2 Test Statistics vs. Critical Value for right-tailed test

Left-tailed test has one critical value separating acceptable area on the right and rejection area on the left. Rejection area is the area under distribution curve with total area of α. In Figure 20-2, test statistics C rejects null hypothesis because it is located in rejection area; test statistics D fails to reject null hypothesis because it is located inside acceptable area.

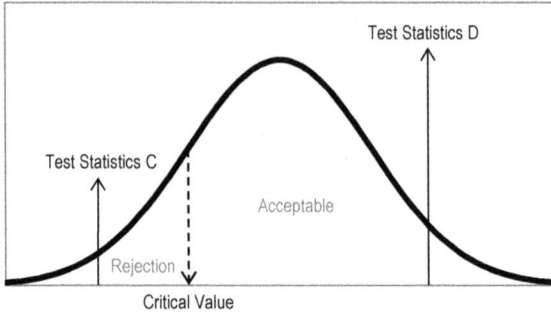

Figure 20-3 Test Statistics vs. Critical Value for left-tailed test

Two-tailed test has two critical values separating acceptable area in the middle from the left and right and rejection areas. Rejection areas are the areas under distribution curve with total area of α, which is the sum of areas on the left and right tails for normal distribution. If α is 0.05, then the left and right tails cover 0.025 area each. Figure 20-4 illustrates test statistics and critical value for two-tailed test. Test statistics E fails to reject null hypothesis, test statistics F rejects null hypothesis.

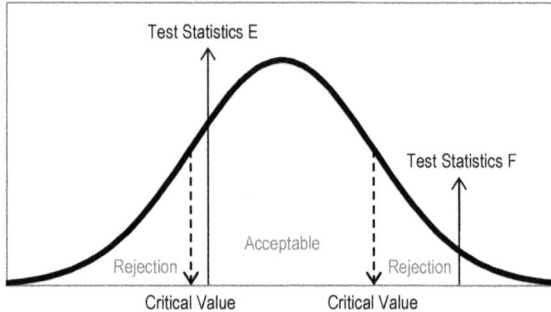

Figure 20-4 Test Statistics vs. Critical Value for two-tailed test

Note that not all distributions are symmetrical. For hypothesis testing with asymmetrical distributions, the critical values on left and right for two-tailed test must be calculated separately.

Example 20-1 (two-tailed problem):
A brand of soft drink product is supposed to have 35 gr of sugar inside each 600 ml bottle. Recent research wants to find out whether the products from certain batch meet the requirements. The average amount of sugar found inside random sample of 40 bottles is 34.3 gr with standard deviation of 2.3 gr. A researcher wants to use statistics to find out if this indicates a problem in

production system or not.
- H_0: $\mu = 35$ gr.
- H_A: $\mu \neq 35$ gr.
- This is a two-tailed problem because $\mu < 35$ and $\mu > 35$ would satisfy alternative hypothesis.
- Sample error has the formula $w = \frac{Z \times S}{\sqrt{n}}$
- *Z score* can be calculated by treating the difference between sample mean and population mean as sample error. This is the test statistics value.
- $Z_{test} = \frac{(\bar{x} - \mu) \times \sqrt{n}}{S} = \frac{(34.3 - 35) \times \sqrt{40}}{2.3} = -1.92$
- There is no information about α, default value of 0.05 is used.
- The lower critical value separates the area of 0.025 on the left from the acceptable area in the middle. *lower* $Z_{crit} = Z_{(\alpha/2)}$. Look at Z table to find the Z_{crit} for 0.025 is -1.96.
- The upper critical value separates the area of 0.025 on the right from the acceptable area in the middle. *upper* $Z_{crit} = Z_{(1-(\alpha/2))}$. Look at Z table to find the Z_{crit} for 0.975 is 1.96.
- *lower* $Z_{crit} < Z_{test} < upper\ Z_{crit}$
- $-1.96 < -1.92 < 1.96$
- Test statistics Z_{test} is located inside acceptable area. This test fails to reject null hypothesis.

Example 20-2 (left-tailed problem):
A top university claims that 80% of its graduates successfully get a full-time job within 2 years after graduation. Recent research wants to find out if this claim is true. From 100 respondents, 71 of them confirms that they did get a full-time job within 2 years after graduation. Is there statistically significant evidence that the university's claim is false?
- H_0: $p = 0.8$
- H_A: $p < 0.8$
- This is a left-tailed problem because alternative hypothesis tries to find evidence that the success rate to get a full-time job within 2 years is lower than the target rate of 0.8.
- Sample size formula for discrete or attribute data: n $= \left(\frac{Z \times \sqrt{(p)(1-p)}}{\delta} \right)^2$
- Same formula is used to calculate sample error: $w = \frac{Z \times \sqrt{(p)(1-p)}}{\sqrt{n}}$
- *Z score* can be calculated by treating the difference between sample value vs. standard value as sample error. This is the test statistics value.

- $Z_{test} = \frac{(\hat{p}-p)\times\sqrt{n}}{\sqrt{(p)(1-p)}} = \frac{(0.71-0.8)\times\sqrt{100}}{\sqrt{0.8\times0.2}} = -2.25$
- There is no information about α, default value of 0.05 is used.
- The critical value separates the area of 0.05 on the left from the acceptable area on the right. $Z_{crit} = Z_{(\alpha)}$. Look at Z table to find the Z_{crit} for 0.05 is -1.65.
- $Z_{test} < Z_{crit}$
- $-2.25 < -1.65$
- Test statistics Z_{test} is located inside rejection area. This test rejects null hypothesis.

Example 20-3 (right-tailed problem):
A city claims that its life expectancy is higher than nation-wide life expectancy of 83.35 years in a campaign to promote its healthy local cuisines. Sample of 70 people shows the average age at death is 84.15 years with standard deviation of 3.55 years. Does the research have sufficient evidence to show that the claim is true with 98% confidence level?

- H$_0$: $\mu = 83.35$ gr.
- H$_A$: $\mu > 84.15$ gr.
- This is a right-tailed problem because alternative hypothesis tries to find evidence that life expectancy is indeed above nation-wide average.
- $Z_{test} = \frac{(\bar{x}-\mu)\times\sqrt{n}}{s} = \frac{(84.15-83.35)\times\sqrt{70}}{3.55} = 1.89$
- For 98% confidence level, $\alpha = 0.02$.
- The critical value separates the area of 0.02 on the right from the acceptable area on the right. $Z_{crit} = Z_{(1-\alpha)}$. Look at Z table to find the Z_{crit} for 0.98 is 2.05.
- $Z_{test} < Z_{crit}$
- $1.89 < 2.05$
- Test statistics Z_{test} is located inside acceptable area. This test fails to reject null hypothesis.
- Note that if default $\alpha = 5\%$ is used, Z_{crit} becomes 1.65 and Z_{test} would fall inside rejection area.

P-Value

In hypothesis testing, *P-value* is the likelihood of observing more extreme test statistics than current sample, in the direction of alternative hypothesis, assuming that null hypothesis is true.

> Hypothesis testing rejects null hypothesis if *P-value* is smaller than α.

Example 20-4 (two-tailed problem):
A brand of soft drink product is supposed to have 35 gr of sugar inside each 600 ml bottle. Recent research wants to find out whether the products from certain batch meet the requirements. The average amount of sugar found inside random sample of 40 bottles is 34.3 gr with standard deviation of 2.3 gr. A researcher wants to use statistics to find out if this indicates a problem in production system or not.

- H_0: $\mu = 35$ gr.
- H_A: $\mu \neq 35$ gr.
- This is a two-tailed problem because $\mu < 35$ and $\mu > 35$ would satisfy alternative hypothesis.
- Sample error has the formula $w = \dfrac{z \times s}{\sqrt{n}}$
- *Z score* can be calculated by treating the difference between sample mean and population mean as sample error.
- $Z_{test} = \dfrac{(\bar{x}-\mu) \times \sqrt{n}}{s} = \dfrac{(34.3-35) \times \sqrt{40}}{2.3} = -1.92$
- Look at Z table, the *Z score* of –1.92 has cumulative probability of 0.027429, this represents the left tail of normal distribution curve.
- This is a two-tailed problem, so both left tail and right tail need to be considered.
- Normal distribution is symmetrical, so the right tail also has probability of 0.027429.
- *P-value* is 0.027429 + 0.027429 = 0.054858.
- There is no information about α, default value of 5% is used.
- 0.054858 > 0.05
- *P-value* is bigger than α, so the test fails to reject null hypothesis.

Example 20-5 (left-tailed problem):
A top university claims that 80% of its graduates successfully get a full-time job within 2 years after graduation. Recent research wants to find out if this claim is true. From 100 respondents, 71 of them confirms that they did get a full-time job within 2 years after graduation. Is there statistically significant evidence that the university's claim is false?

- H_0: $p = 0.8$
- H_A: $p < 0.8$
- This is a left-tailed problem because alternative hypothesis tries to find evidence that the success rate to get a full-time job within 2 years is lower than the target rate of 0.8.
- Sample size formula for discrete or attribute data: $n = \left(\frac{Z \times \sqrt{(p)(1-p)}}{\delta}\right)^2$
- Same formula is used to calculate sample error: $w = \frac{Z \times \sqrt{(p)(1-p)}}{\sqrt{n}}$
- Z score can be calculated by treating the difference between sample value vs. standard value as sample error.
- $Z_{test} = \frac{(\hat{p}-p) \times \sqrt{n}}{\sqrt{(p)(1-p)}} = \frac{(0.71-0.8) \times \sqrt{100}}{\sqrt{0.8 \times 0.2}} = -2.25$
- Look at Z table, the Z score of -2.25 has the cumulative probability of 0.012224, this represents the left tail of normal distribution curve.
- This is a left-tailed problem, so only left tail needs to be considered. P-Value = 0.012224.
- There is no information about α, default value of 5% is used.
- $0.012224 < 0.05$
- P-value is smaller than α, so the test rejects null hypothesis.

Example 20-6 (right-tailed problem):
A city claims that its life expectancy is higher than nation-wide life expectancy of 83.35 years in a campaign to promote its healthy local cuisines. Sample of 70 people shows the average age at death is 84.15 years with standard deviation of 3.55 years. Does the research have sufficient evidence to show that the claim is true with 98% confidence level?

- H_0: $\mu = 83.35$ gr.
- H_A: $\mu > 84.15$ gr.
- This is a right-tailed problem because alternative hypothesis tries to find evidence that life expectancy is indeed above nation-wide average.
- $Z = \frac{(\bar{x}-\mu) \times \sqrt{n}}{s} = \frac{(84.15-83.35) \times \sqrt{70}}{3.55} = 1.89$
- Look at Z table, the Z score of -1.92 has the P-value of 0.970621, this represents the left tail and middle area of normal distribution curve.

- This is a right-tailed problem, the P-value of right tail is calculated as $1 - 0.970621 = 0.029379$.
- For 98% confidence level, $\alpha = 2\%$. *P-value* $0.029379 > 0.02$.
- *P-value* is bigger than α, so the test fails to reject null hypothesis.
- Note that if default $\alpha = 5\%$ is used, *P-value* would be smaller than α.

Note that Example 20-4, Example 20-5 and Example 20-6 are identical to Example 20-1, Example 20-2 and Example 20-3 from the discussion of test statistics vs. critical value. This illustrates the two different approaches of interpreting the results of hypothesis testing. Comparing the *P-value* to α and comparing test statistics to critical value resulted in the same conclusions about null hypothesis.

Data Normality Test

Data normality test is often needed before applying other techniques of hypothesis testing. Many testing techniques in hypothesis testing assume that data has been confirmed to have normal distribution. Applying techniques for normal distribution on non-normal data will produce unreliable conclusion.

There are several different techniques to perform univariate data normality test. The most commonly used are *Anderson-Darling test* and *Shapiro-Wilk test*. Both techniques measure the level of normality using *P-value*.

Characteristics of data normality tests:
- Data normality test is performed to find evidence of non-normality characteristics. Therefore, the expected "good" result is when the calculation fails to show statistically significant evidence of non-normality, meaning the data is normally distributed.
- Null hypothesis: data is normally distributed.
- Alternative hypothesis: data is not normally distributed.
- Small *P-value* (smaller than α) means we reject null hypothesis; data is not normal.
- Big *P-value* (bigger than α) means we fail to reject null hypothesis; data is normal.

Test Selection

In hypothesis testing, different tests are needed for different types of data. Figure 20-5 shows simplified decision-making in choosing the tests for bivariate hypothesis testing to find connections between X and Y.

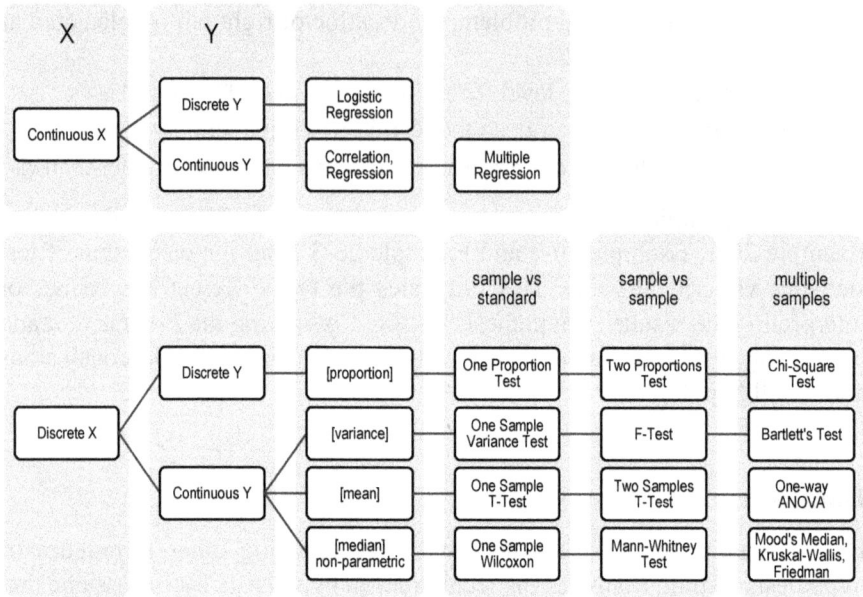

		sample vs standard	sample vs sample	multiple samples
Discrete Y	[proportion]	One Proportion Test	Two Proportions Test	Chi-Square Test
	[variance]	One Sample Variance Test	F-Test	Bartlett's Test
Continuous Y	[mean]	One Sample T-Test	Two Samples T-Test	One-way ANOVA
	[median] non-parametric	One Sample Wilcoxon	Mann-Whitney Test	Mood's Median, Kruskal-Wallis, Friedman

Figure 20-5 Hypothesis Testing

Regression is used to find mathematical correlation between continuous X and continuous Y. This topic will be discussed in Chapter 21.

Connection between continuous X and discrete Y can be analysed using logistic regression. This combination is rarely used in Six Sigma projects. Therefore, it will not be discussed in this book.

Proportion tests are used to perform hypothesis testing on discrete X and discrete Y. This topic will be discussed in Chapter 22.

Hypothesis testing on discrete X and continuous Y can be performed on different measures: mean, variance and median. The tests for mean and variance are generally applicable for normally distributed data. These will be discussed in Chapter 23. Non-parametric tests are used for non-normal data, focusing on median value. This topic will be discussed in Chapter 24.

Reference Tables: Z, T, F and Chi-Squared

Several techniques of hypothesis testing discussed in this book refer to one of the reference tables presented in Chapter 38. It is important to understand what are shown by the values in those tables and how to use them related to the calculations of test statistics and critical values.

Z table shows the cumulative value of all data points possibility from *Z score* to the left. The values in this table are calculated using NORM.S.DIST function in Excel.

- *P-Value* is calculated using NORM.S.DIST function with parameters: test statistics Z_{test} as z and *cumulative* set to *true*.
- *Critical value* Z_{crit} is calculated using NORM.S.INV function with *probability* as parameter, this could be α or $1 - \alpha$ or $\frac{\alpha}{2}$ or $1 - \frac{\alpha}{2}$ depending on the tests.

T table shows the *T scores* from combinations of probability and degrees of freedom. The values in this table are calculated using T.INV function in Excel.

- *P-Value* is calculated using T.DIST.RT function with parameters: test statistics T_{test} as x and degrees of freedom (*df*).
- *Critical value* T_{crit} is calculated using T.INV function with *probability* and degrees of freedom as parameters. Probability could be α or $1 - \alpha$ or $\frac{\alpha}{2}$ or $1 - \frac{\alpha}{2}$ depending on the tests.

Chi-squared distribution table shows the *chi-squared scores* from combinations of probability and degrees of freedom. The values in this table are calculated using CHISQ.INV.RT function in Excel.

- *P-Value* is calculated using CHISQ.DIST.RT function with parameters: test statistics $\chi^2{}_{test}$ as x, degrees of freedom (*df*) 1 and 2.
- *Critical value* $\chi^2{}_{crit}$ is calculated using CHISQ.INV.RT function with *probability* and degrees of freedom as parameters. Probability could be α or $1 - \alpha$ or $\frac{\alpha}{2}$ or $1 - \frac{\alpha}{2}$ depending on the tests.

F distribution table shows the *F scores* from combinations of probability, degrees of freedom 1 and degrees of freedom 2. The values in this table are calculated using F.INV.RT function in Excel.

- *P-Value* is calculated using F.DIST.RT function with parameters: test statistics F_{test} as x, degrees of freedom (*df*) 1 and 2.
- *Critical value* F_{crt} is calculated using F.INV.RT function with *probability*, degrees of freedom 1 and 2 as parameters. Probability could be α or $1 - \alpha$ or $\frac{\alpha}{2}$ or $1 - \frac{\alpha}{2}$ depending on the tests.

21. HYPOTHESIS TESTING: CONTINUOUS X AND Y

This chapter discusses hypothesis testing for continuous X and Y variables as illustrated in Figure 21-1. Before continuing with this chapter, it is strongly recommended to review Chapter 20 about the principles of hypothesis testing.

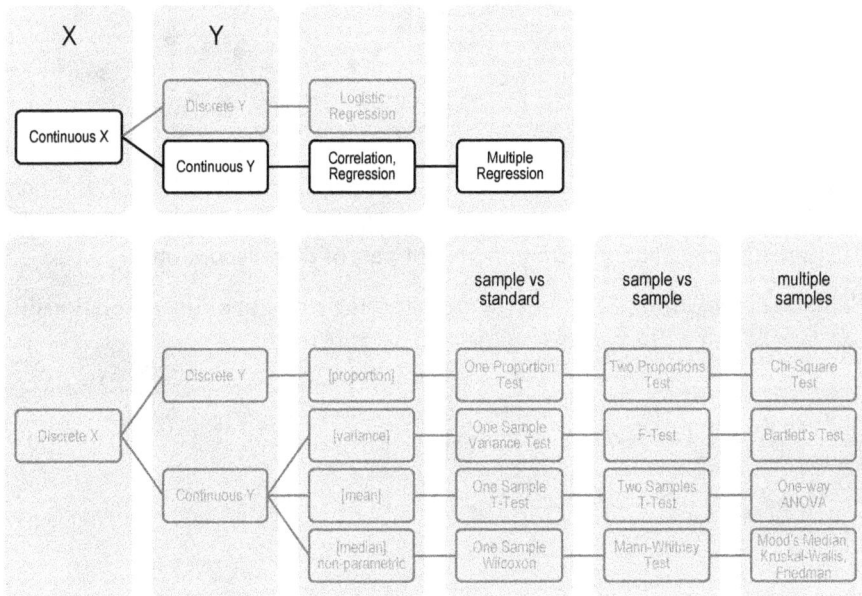

Figure 21-1 Hypothesis Testing for continuous X and Y

Correlation

In statistics, *correlation* between two variables is the mutual relationship between them. For Six Sigma DMAIC project, the two variables are X and Y. X is the variable of independent factor and Y is the variable of (possibly) dependent outcome. Correlation test aims to confirm if X is a variable that impacts Y.

Hypothesis for correlation test:
- Null hypothesis (H_0): no significant correlation between X and Y.
- Alternative hypothesis (H_A): there is significant correlation between X and Y.

Correlation does not always mean causal relation. Inversely, two variables with causal relationship does not always have correlation.

Positive correlation means if X goes up, Y goes up, and vice versa. The variables move together. *Negative correlation* means if X goes up, Y goes down, and vice versa. The variables move to the opposite direction.

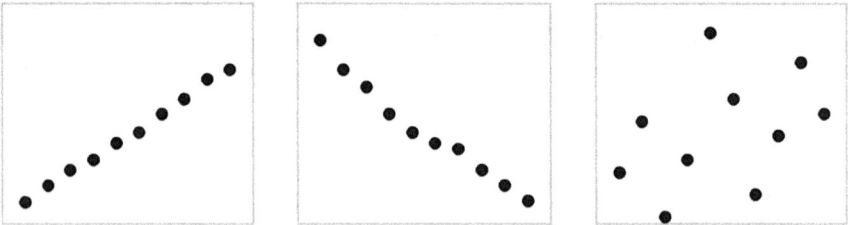

Figure 21-2 Correlation: positive (left), negative (middle), no correlation (right)

If relationship between X and Y can be illustrated with straight line, it is said that X and Y have *linear correlation*. Non-linear correlation is usually calculated using statistical tool and is not part of this discussion.

Pearson correlation coefficient (r) measures the strength of linear relationship between X and Y. It can have values from −1 to 1.

$r=-1$	Perfect negative correlation. Every change of X is certain to change Y to the opposite direction.
$-1 < r \leq -0.7$	Strong negative correlation.
$-0.7 < r \leq -0.4$	Moderate negative correlation.
$-0.4 < r < 0$	Weak negative correlation.
$r = 0$	No correlation.
$0 < r < 0.4$	Weak positive correlation.
$0.4 \leq r < 0.7$	Moderate positive correlation.
$0.7 \leq r < 1$	Strong positive correlation.
$r = 1$	Perfect negative correlation. Every change of X is certain to change Y in the same direction.

Table 21-A Possible values of Correlation Coefficient

Formula to calculate Pearson correlation coefficient:

$$r = \frac{\Sigma\left((x_i - \bar{x})(y_i - \bar{y})\right)}{\sqrt{\Sigma(x_i - \bar{x})^2 \times \Sigma(y_i - \bar{y})^2}}$$

This formula detects the relationship between X and Y in any order. X and Y can be swapped, and the correlation coefficient will stay the same. Outliers could significantly change the calculation, so it is recommended to visually identify outliers in the scatter plot before using the formula.

Coefficient of Determination (CoD) is the square of r. This measure describes how much the variance in X explains the variance in Y.

$$CoD = r^2$$

Example 21-1:
Calculate the correlation coefficient of X and Y.

X	1	2	3	4	5	6	7	8	9	10
Y	2	5	6	8	10	12	14	20	25	35

The following table is prepared to help with calculating the values needed for correlation coefficient formula.

x	y	$x - \bar{x}$	$y - \bar{y}$	$(x - \bar{x})(y - \bar{y})$	$(x - \bar{x})^2$	$(y - \bar{y})^2$
1	2	−4.5	−11.7	52.65	20.25	136.89
2	5	−3.5	−8.7	30.45	12.25	75.69
3	6	−2.5	−7.7	19.25	6.25	59.29
4	8	−1.5	−5.7	8.55	2.25	32.49
5	10	−0.5	−3.7	1.85	0.25	13.69
6	12	0.5	−1.7	−0.85	0.25	2.89
7	14	1.5	0.3	0.45	2.25	0.09
8	20	2.5	6.3	15.75	6.25	39.69
9	25	3.5	11.3	39.55	12.15	127.69
10	35	4.5	21.3	95.85	20.25	453.69
$\bar{x} = 5.5$	$\bar{y} = 13.7$		SUM	263.50	82.50	942.10

Putting calculated numbers into the formula:

- $r = \dfrac{263.5}{\sqrt{82.5 \times 942.1}} = 0.9452$
- Therefore, X and Y in this example has strong positive correlation.
- $CoD = (0.9452)^2 = 0.8933$

Linear Regression

Linear regression is a statistical process to analyse the relationship between two variables (X and Y) by fitting linear equation to the observed data. This linear equation (*regression line*) is a formula of Y expressed as a function of X with the calculation of intercept (*a*) and slope (*b*). *Intercept* is the value of Y when $X = 0$. *Slope* is steepness of the regression line.

Regression line formula:

$$y = a + bx$$

Both regression and correlation try to represent the relationship of X and Y using straight line. The difference is that correlation measures how consistent the observed data are following the straight line and regression measures the slope and intercept of that line.

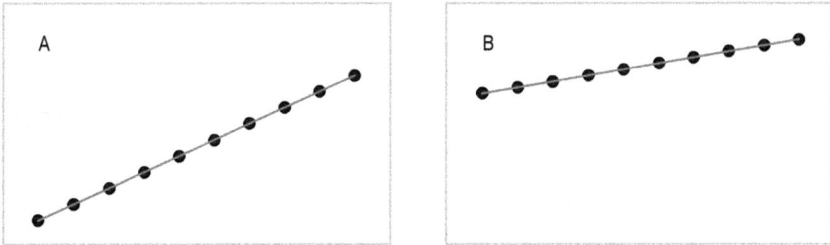

Figure 21-3 Same Correlation Coefficient, different Regression Line

Figure 21-3 shows two scatter plots (A and B) with data observations consistently aligned to straight lines. The scatter plot A has visibly different line from scatter plot B. The regression lines of A and B have different slopes and intercepts, but the correlation coefficient is the same because all observations are precisely on the line (perfect positive correlation).

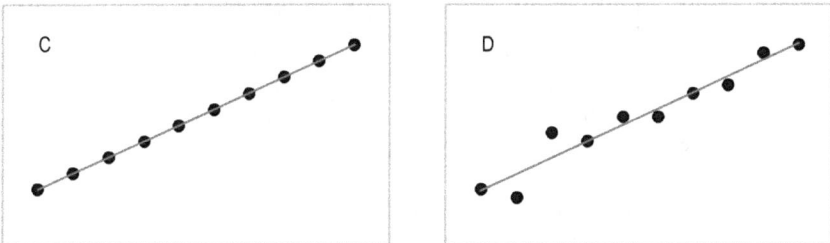

Figure 21-4 Same Regression Line, different Correlation Coefficient

Scatter plots C and D in Figure 21-4 have regression lines with the same slopes and intercepts. Scatter plot C has correlation coefficient of one because all observations perfectly match the straight line. However, scatter plot D has some values not perfectly aligned. Therefore, the correlation coefficient for scatter plot D is less than one.

Formula for calculating slope:

$$b = \frac{n\sum(xy) - (\sum x)(\sum y)}{n\sum(x^2) - (\sum x)^2}$$

Formula for calculating intercept:

$$a = \frac{\sum y - b\sum x}{n}$$

Example 21-2:

Calculate the regression line of X and Y.

X	1	2	3	4	5	6	7	8	9	10
Y	2	5	6	8	10	12	14	20	25	35

The following table is prepared to help with calculating the values needed for linear regression formula.

	x	y	x^2	y^2	xy
	1	2	1	4	2
	2	5	4	25	10
	3	6	9	36	18
	4	8	16	64	32
	5	10	25	100	50
	6	12	36	144	72
	7	14	49	196	98
	8	20	64	400	160
	9	25	81	625	225
	10	35	100	1225	350
SUM	55	137	385	2819	1017

Putting calculated numbers into the formula:

- Slope $b = \dfrac{(10 \times 1017) - (55 \times 137)}{(10 \times 385) - (55)^2} = 3.1939$

- Intercept $a = \dfrac{137 - (3.1939 \times 55)}{10} = -3.8667$

- Regression line: $y = -3.8667 + 3.1939\,x$.

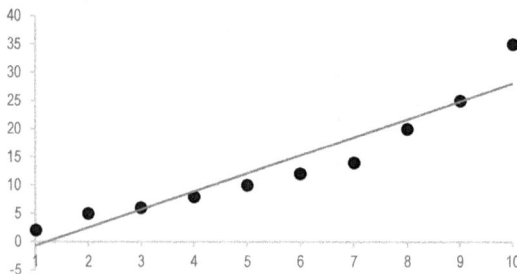

Figure 21-5 Scatter plot of example data

Residual is the difference between actual (observed) values and predicted values ($\hat{y}$) from regression formula. The sum of all residuals in a dataset should be zero.

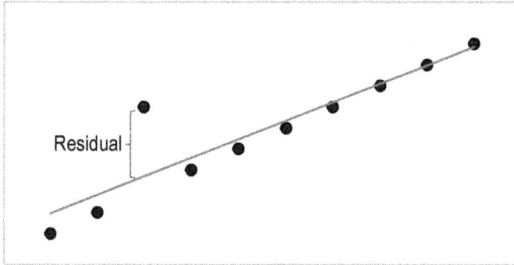

Figure 21-6 Regression Residual

Residual analysis is performed to confirm if linear relationship is the right regression type that has to be calculated for a pair of X and Y.

- Residual plot should show normal distribution.
- The mean of the normal distribution must be zero.
- Residual values should not show any pattern against Y.
- Residual plot should not have any obvious pattern.

If any of the criteria above is not met, X and Y might have non-linear relationship.

Using the formula of $y = -3.8667 + 3.1939\, x$, the sum of all residual values is equal to zero.

x	y	$\hat{y}$	Residual $y - \hat{y}$
1	2	-0.6727	2.6727
2	5	2.5212	2.4788
3	6	5.7152	0.2848
4	8	8.9091	-0.9091
5	10	12.1030	-2.1030
6	12	15.2979	-3.2970
7	14	18.4909	-4.4909
8	20	21.6848	-1.6848
9	25	24.8788	0.1212
10	35	28.0727	6.9273
			SUM = 0

Coefficient of Determination (r^2) can be calculated using regression line.

$$r^2 = \frac{SSR}{SST} = \frac{\sum(\hat{y} - \bar{y})^2}{\sum(y_i - \bar{y})^2}$$

SSR (*Sum Squares of Regression*) is the sum squares of the difference between expected y values and the average of y. SST (*Sum Squares of Total*) is the sum squares of the difference between actual y values and the average of y.

Calculation of r^2 using regression line:

x	y	$\hat{y}$	$\hat{y} - \bar{y}$	$(\hat{y} - \bar{y})^2$	$y_i - \bar{y}$	$(y_i - \bar{y})^2$
1	2	–0.6727	–14.3727	206.5753	–11.7	136.89
2	5	2.5212	–11.1788	124.9653	–8.7	75.69
3	6	5.7152	–7.9848	63.7578	–7.7	59.29
4	8	8.9091	–4.7909	22.9528	–5.7	32.49
5	10	12.1030	–1.5970	2.5503	–3.7	13.69
6	12	15.2979	1.5970	2.5503	–1.7	2.89
7	14	18.4909	4.7909	22.9528	0.3	0.09
8	20	21.6848	7.9848	63.7578	6.3	39.69
9	25	24.8788	11.1788	124.9653	11.3	127.69
10	35	28.0727	14.3727	206.5753	21.3	453.69
	$\bar{y} = 13.7$			$\Sigma = 841.6030$		$\Sigma = 942.10$

Putting calculated numbers into the formula:
- $r^2 = \dfrac{841.603}{942.1} = 0.8933$
- This is the same value as the one calculated earlier.

Non-Linear Regression

If the results of residual analysis show that linear regression is not the best fit to describe the relationship between X and Y, non-linear regression can be calculated and tested. *Non-linear regression* studies the relationship between two variables using higher order terms, or multiple Xs are being considered at the same time against Y in a multivariate analysis.

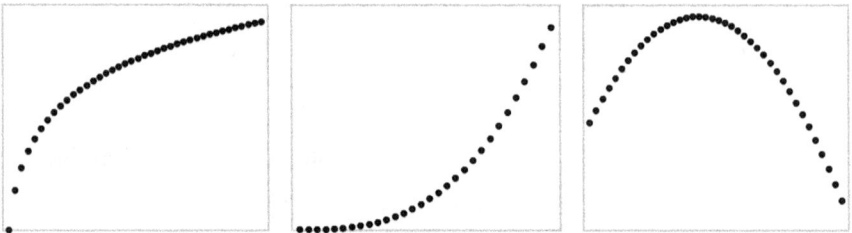

Figure 21-7 Non-linear relationships: logarithmic, exponential, quadratic

The most common method to apply higher order terms for non-linear regression is using *Box-Cox transformation*. This technique transforms X using the value of lambda (λ) and use the transformed results for regression calculation.

Box-Cox transformation formula:

$$x_{(\lambda)} = \begin{cases} \dfrac{x^\lambda - 1}{\lambda}, & \lambda \neq 0 \\ log(x), & \lambda = 0 \end{cases}$$

The value of lambda varies from –5 to 5. However, only values from –3 to 3 are commonly used.

This table presents simpler version of Box-Cox formula:

λ	3	2	1	0.5	0	–0.5	–1	–2	–3
Transformation	x^3	x^2	x	$\sqrt{x}$	$log(x)$	$\dfrac{1}{\sqrt{x}}$	$\dfrac{1}{x}$	$\dfrac{1}{x^2}$	$\dfrac{1}{x^3}$

Multiple transformations can be applied on the same X variable. For example: applying lambda 2 and 3 produces regression formula of $y = a + b_1 x^2 + b_2 x^3$.

Due to its complexity, non-linear regression analysis is usually calculated using statistical software. The analysis might take several attempts before the best fit is found. Manual calculation often requires more time and carries higher risk of mistakes, hence the strong preference of using statistical software.

Multiple Regression

Multiple regression is a multivariate analysis to find relationships between more than 2 variables. In the context of DMAIC project, this means between multiple X variables and the outcome of Y.

The simplest version of multiple regression is *multiple linear regression*. All X variables are evaluated with $\lambda = 1$. Regression analysis of n variables of X and the outcome of Y has the formula:

$$y = a + b_1 x_1 + b_2 x_2 + \ldots + b_n x_n$$

b_1, b_2, ... b_n are the relative importance of each X in determining Y. Since every X could have outliers and bias, involving many factors in multiple regression increases uncertainty. Calculation of multiple linear regression is part of the discussion in Chapters 27, 28 and 29 about *Design of Experiments*.

Theoretically, non-linear regression can also be performed with multiple X variables. This is called *multiple non-linear regression*. It brings further complications because each X can receive one or multiple transformations with different λ. For example:

$$y = a + b_{1A}x_1 + b_{1B}x_1{}^2 + b_{2A}x_2{}^3 + b_{2B}x_2{}^2 + \cdots$$

The calculation complexity and the level of uncertainty of multiple non-linear regression is significantly higher compared to the simpler models. Too many variables can mask the real relationships with random coincidences. For most cases, simpler models are sufficient.

22. HYPOTHESIS TESTING: DISCRETE X AND Y

This chapter discusses hypothesis testing for discrete X and Y variables as illustrated in Figure 22-1. Before continuing with this chapter, it is strongly recommended to review Chapter 20 about the principles of hypothesis testing.

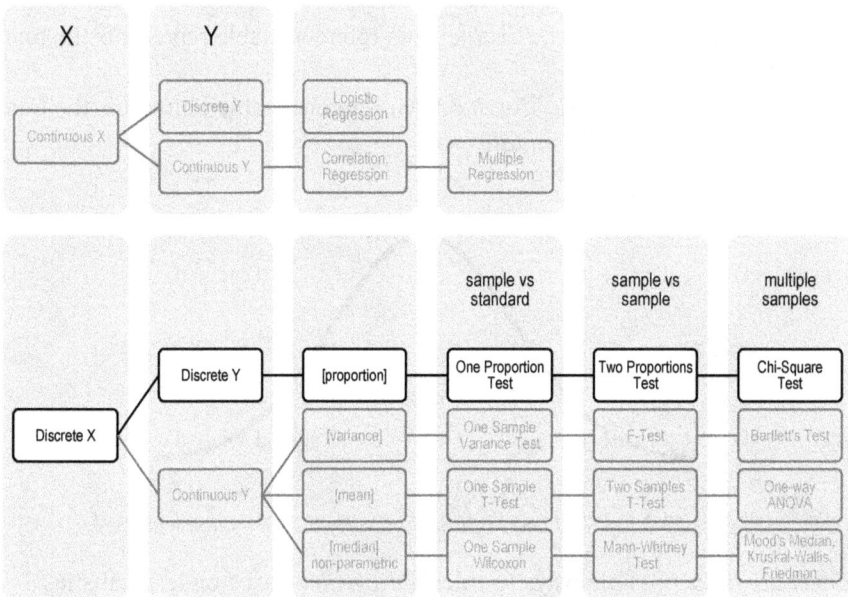

Figure 22-1 Hypothesis Testing for discrete X and Y

One Proportion Test

Proportion test focuses on analysing the proportion of items from discrete data against another proportion. *One proportion test* (also known as *one sample test of proportion*) is the simplest form of proportion test. It compares the proportion of items in a sample that have certain trait against a target value. Target value could come from various sources: such as known standard, government regulation, historical reference or other values of interest.

Hypothesis for one proportion test:
- Null hypothesis (H_0): p = target.
- Alternative hypothesis (H_A): $p \neq$ target or $p >$ target or $p <$ target.

One proportion test calculates the test statistics of Z using the formula:

$$Z_{test} = \frac{p - p_t}{\sqrt{\frac{p_t(1 - p_t)}{n}}}$$

p is the sample proportion. p_t is the target value. n is the sample size.

As refresher, Z table shows the *cumulative P* of all data points possibility <u>from Z score to the left</u>. The values in this table are calculated using NORM.S.DIST function in Excel.
- For negative Z score, *P-value* from reference table represents the total area of *left tail*.
- For positive Z score, *P-value* from reference table represents the total area of *left tail* plus *middle area*.

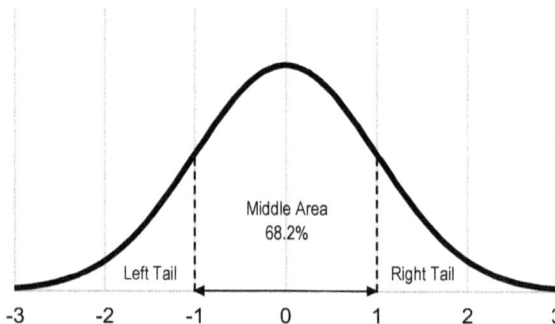

Figure 22-2 Left Tail and Right Tail of Normal Distribution with Z=1

There are three possible ways to calculate *P-value* based on test statistics:
- Use *Z table* in Chapter 38.

- Use NORM.S.DIST function in Excel with parameters: test statistics Z_{test} as z and *cumulative* set to *true*.
- Use statistical software of your choice.

In the context of one proportion test, *P-value* of hypothesis test is calculated based on the alternative hypothesis.

- If H_A is $p \neq$ target, then *P-value* for hypothesis testing is the total of *left tail* and *right tail*.
- If H_A is $p >$ target, then *P-value* for hypothesis testing is the *right tail*.
- If H_A is $p <$ target, then *P-value* for hypothesis testing is the *left tail*.

For maximum acceptable Alpha Risk of α, hypothesis testing rejects null hypothesis if *P-value* is smaller than α. Unless stated otherwise, this book assumes default $\alpha = 5\%$.

An alternative way to interpret one proportion test result is by comparing test statistics calculated from sample against critical values. Z_{crit} is calculated using NORM.S.INV function with *probability* as parameter.

- For right-tailed tests: $Z_{crit} = Z_{(1-\alpha)}$
- For left-tailed tests: $Z_{crit} = Z_{(\alpha)}$
- For two-tailed tests: $upper\ Z_{crit} = Z_{\left(1-\frac{\alpha}{2}\right)}$ and

$$lower\ Z_{crit} < Z_{\left(\frac{\alpha}{2}\right)}$$

Null hypothesis (H_0) is rejected if:

- $Z_{test} > Z_{crit}$ for right-tailed tests.
- $Z_{test} < Z_{crit}$ for left-tailed tests.
- $Z_{test} > upper\ Z_{crit}$ or $Z_{test} < lower\ Z_{crit}$ for two-tailed tests.

Example 22-1:
Certain hand sanitiser product claims to contain 75% isopropyl alcohol. Sample taken from 100 random units shows the average proportion of 66%. Does the hand sanitiser product contain isopropyl alcohol proportion different than 75%?

- $p = 0.73; p_t = 0.75$
- H_0 is $p = p_t$; H_A is $p \neq p_t$.
- $Z_{test} = \dfrac{0.66-0.75}{\sqrt{\frac{0.75\times0.25}{100}}} = \dfrac{-0.09}{0.0433} = -2.07$
- *P-value* from reference table is 0.019226. Since *Z score* is negative, this represents the *left tail*.
- H_A is $p \neq p_t$, this is a two-tailed problem. *P-value* for hypothesis test is the total of *left tail* and *right tail*.

- *P-value* = 0.019226 + 0.019226 = 0.038452.
- α = 5% and confidence level is 95% (default assumption)
- 0.038452 < 0.05
- *P-value* is smaller than α, therefore null hypothesis is rejected.
- The research concludes with 95% confidence that the hand sanitiser product does not contain 75% isopropyl alcohol.

Instead of using *P-value*, the same conclusion can be obtained by comparing test statistics against critical values:
- $p = 0.73$; $p_t = 0.75$
- H_0 is $p = p_t$; H_A is $p \neq p_t$.
- $Z_{test} = \dfrac{0.66-0.75}{\sqrt{\frac{0.75\times0.25}{100}}} = \dfrac{-0.09}{0.0433} = -2.07$
- There is no information about α, default value of 0.05 is used.
- The lower critical value separates the area of 0.025 on the left from the acceptable area in the middle. $lower\ Z_{crit} = Z_{\left(\frac{\alpha}{2}\right)}$. Look at Z table to find the $lower\ Z_{crit} = Z_{(0.025)} = -1.96$.
- The upper critical value separates the area of 0.025 on the right from the acceptable area in the middle. $upper\ Z_{crit} = Z_{\left(1-\frac{\alpha}{2}\right)}$. Look at Z table to find the $upper\ Z_{crit} = Z_{(0.975)} = 1.96$.
- $Z_{test} < lower\ Z_{crit} < upper\ Z_{crit}$
- $-2.07 < -1.96 < 1.96$
- Test statistics Z_{test} is located in rejection area. This test rejects null hypothesis.
- The research concludes with 95% confidence that the hand sanitiser product does not contain 75% isopropyl alcohol.

Two Proportions Test

Two proportions test (also known as *two samples test of proportion*) is a hypothesis test for discrete data comparing the proportions of two samples. The comparison could focus on equality or on finding which proportion is greater.

There are three possible sets of hypotheses for two proportions test:
- Set #1 H_0 is $p_1 = p_2$. H_A is $p_1 \neq p_2$.
- Set #2 H_0 is $p_1 \leq p_2$. H_A is $p_1 > p_2$.
- Set #3 H_0 is $p_1 \geq p_2$. H_A is $p_1 < p_2$.

Two proportions test calculates the test statistics of Z using the formula:

$$Z_{test} = \frac{p_1 - p_2}{\sqrt{\dfrac{p_1(1 - p_1)}{n_1} + \dfrac{p_2(1 - p_2)}{n_2}}}$$

p_1 and p_2 are the proportions of sample 1 and 2. n_1 and n_2 are the size of sample 1 and 2.

There are three possible ways to calculate *P-value* based on test statistics:
- Use *Z table* in Chapter 38.
- Use NORM.S.DIST function in Excel with parameters: test statistics Z_{test} as *z* and *cumulative* set to *true*.
- Use statistical software of your choice.

In the context of two proportions test, *P-value* of hypothesis test is calculated based on the alternative hypothesis.
- If H_A is $p_1 \neq p_2$, then *P-value* for hypothesis testing is the total of *left tail* and *right tail*.
- If H_A is $p_1 > p_2$, then *P-value* for hypothesis testing is the *right tail*.
- If H_A is $p_1 < p_2$, then *P-value* for hypothesis testing is the *left tail*.

An alternative way to interpret two proportions test result is by comparing test statistics calculated from sample against critical values. Z_{crit} is calculated using NORM.S.INV function with *probability* as parameter.
- For right-tailed tests: $Z_{crit} = Z_{(1-\alpha)}$
- For left-tailed tests: $Z_{crit} = Z_{(\alpha)}$
- For two-tailed tests: upper $Z_{crit} = Z_{\left(1-\frac{\alpha}{2}\right)}$ and

$$lower\ Z_{crit} < Z_{\left(\frac{\alpha}{2}\right)}$$

Null hypothesis (H_0) is rejected if:
- $Z_{test} > Z_{crit}$ for right-tailed tests.
- $Z_{test} < Z_{crit}$ for left-tailed tests.
- $Z_{test} > upper\ Z_{crit}$ or $Z_{test} < lower\ Z_{crit}$ for two-tailed tests.

Example 22-2:
Amy and Bec are teachers teaching different classes. They are comparing the results of final exam this year. After exam finishes, 82.6% of 23 students in Amy's class receive grade A. 71.4% of 21 students in Bec's class receive grade A. Does Amy's class have higher proportion of students achieving

grade A?
- Yes, Amy's class has higher proportion of students achieving grade A. No hypothesis testing is needed.
- This is a trick question. Hypothesis testing is needed when the population data are not available. Sample data are used to infer the characteristics of the population. This problem compares students' grades in two classes for final exam this year. All grades from both classes are available. Comparison can be made by simply comparing the proportions. 82.6% is higher than 71.4%.

Example 22-3:
Amy and Bec are teachers teaching different classes. A researcher compares former students graduated from their classes. 23 samples are chosen randomly from Amy's former students. 82.6% of them passed final exam with grade A. Similarly, 21 samples are chosen randomly from Bec's former students. 71.4% of them passed final exam with grade A. Does Amy's students have higher proportion of achieving grade A?
- Example 22-3 has the exact same numbers as Example 22-2, but the scenario is different. In Example 22-3, the study compares the former students already graduated. The whole population data of all former students are not available. Sample data is used to represent the population. Hypothesis testing is needed.
- $p_1 = 0.826$; $p_2 = 0.714$; $n_1 = 23$; $n_2 = 21$.
- H_0 is $p_1 \leq p_2$; H_A is $p_1 > p_2$.
- $Z_{test} = \dfrac{0.826 - 0.714}{\sqrt{\dfrac{0.826 \times 0.174}{23} + \dfrac{0.714 \times 0.286}{21}}} = \dfrac{0.112}{\sqrt{0.0062 + 0.0097}} = \dfrac{0.112}{0.1261} = 0.89$
- Cumulative probability from reference table is 0.813267. Since Z score is positive, this represents the *left tail* plus *middle area*.
- H_A is $p_1 > p_2$, this is a one-tailed problem. Rejection area for hypothesis test is the *right tail*.
- *P-value* $= 1 - 0.813267 = 0.186733$.
- $\alpha = 5\%$ and confidence level is 95% (default assumption)
- $0.186733 > 0.05$
- *P-value* is greater than α, therefore the experiment fails to reject null hypothesis.
- Alternatively, critical values for this test are $Z_{(0.025)} = -1.96$ and $Z_{(0.975)} = 1.96$.
- *lowe* $Z_{crit} < Z_{test} < upper\ Z_{crit}$
- $-1.96 < 0.89 < 1.96$; test statistics Z_{test} is located inside acceptable area. This test fails to reject null hypothesis.

- The research fails to conclude with 95% confidence that Amy's students have higher proportion of achieving grade A using the samples collected.

There is a different approach of calculating two proportions test using pooled proportion.

$$p_c = \frac{d_1 + d_2}{n_1 + n_2}$$

d_1 and d_2 are the amount of data is sample 1 and 2 having the expected trait.

Formula to calculate test statistics of Z using pooled proportion:

$$Z_{test} = \frac{p_1 - p_2}{\sqrt{p_c(1 - p_c)\left(\frac{1}{n_1} + \frac{1}{n_2}\right)}}$$

Calculation of Example 22-3 using Z formula with pooled proportion:
- $p_1 = 0.826$; $p_2 = 0.714$; $n_1 = 23$; $n_2 = 21$.
- 82.6% from 23 students got grade A = 19 students.
- 71.4% from 21 students got grade A = 15 students.
- $p_c = \frac{19+15}{23+21} = \frac{34}{44} = 0.7727$
- $Z_{test} = \frac{0.826-0.714}{\sqrt{0.7727 \times 0.2273 \times \left(\frac{1}{23}+\frac{1}{21}\right)}} = \frac{0.112}{\sqrt{0.0160}} = \frac{0.112}{0.1265} = 0.89$
- The same Z score is calculated using the pooled proportion formula.

Chi-Squared Test

Chi is the 22nd letter in Greek alphabet, pronounced as /ˈkaɪ/. *Chi-squared test* compares frequency distributions in multiple categories from a dataset against the expected distributions. This test requires random sample and can be applied on discrete or attribute data.

Main requirements for sample data to be compatible with chi-squared test:
- At least 80% of the categories have expected frequency of 5 or greater.
- No category has expected frequency of zero.

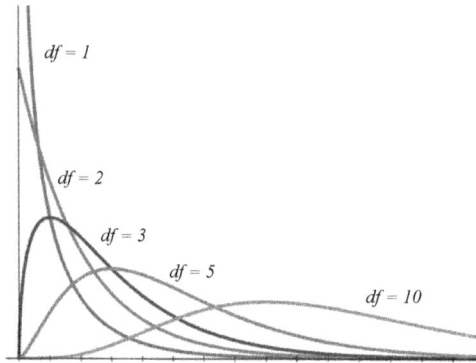

Figure 22-3 Chi-Squared distribution curves

Chi-squared tests refer to *chi-squared distribution curves* depending on degrees of freedom (*df*). Figure 22-3 shows different curves for degrees of freedom 1, 2, 3, 5 and 10. For each curve, the total area under the curve is equal to 1.

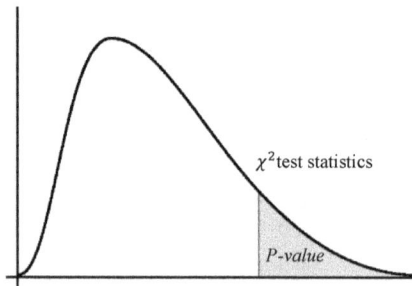

Figure 22-4 P-Value in Chi-Squared distribution

Figure 22-4 shows chi-squared distribution curve skewed to the right. Chi-squared value calculated from the formula (χ^2) is the test statistics. *P-value* in chi-squared test is the probability of obtaining values more extreme than critical value. Chi-squared tests discussed in this chapter are right tailed.

Chi-squared distribution table in Chapter 38 shows the *chi-squared scores* from combinations of probability and degrees of freedom. The values in this table are calculated using CHISQ.INV.RT function in Excel.

How to calculate the *P-value* of a chi-squared test?
- Use *chi-squared distribution table* in Chapter 38.
- Use CHISQ.DIST.RT function in Excel with parameters: test statistics χ^2_{test} as *x*, degrees of freedom (*df*) 1 and 2.
- Use statistical software of your choice.

If *P-value* is smaller than Alpha (α), null hypothesis (H_0) is rejected.

Critical value χ^2_{crit} is the value separating the rejection area (α) on the right and the acceptable area $(1 - \alpha)$ on the left. It is calculated using CHISQ.INV.RT function with α and degrees of freedom as parameters. If test statistics is greater than critical value, null hypothesis (H_0) is rejected.

$$\chi^2_{crit} = \chi^2_{(\alpha;\, df)}$$

There are two common implementations of chi-squared tests:
- *Chi-squared goodness of fit test* is a univariate analysis to calculate the similarity between observed distributions and expected proportions in one sample dataset. This is a one-way classification.
- *Chi-squared test of independence* is a hypothesis test performed to compare two or more random variables to infer whether they are independent or not. This test uses contingency table to perform two-ways classification.

For **chi-squared goodness of fit test**, degrees of freedom (*df*) is calculated as the number of categories (*k*) minus 1.

$$df = k - 1$$

The main formula of chi-squared test:

$$\chi^2_{test} = \sum \frac{(observed - expected)^2}{expected}$$

Example 22-4 (goodness of fit test):
A researcher wants to know if more babies are born in certain season compared to others. He collects data from 100 random respondents. 31 of them were born in summer, 28 were born in autumn, 18 were born in winter and 23 were born in spring.
- H_0: all categories (seasons) have equal distribution.
- H_A: the categories do not have equal distribution.
- For equal distribution, the expected values for each season: $e_{(summer)} = 25$, $e_{(autumn)} = 25$, $e_{(winter)} = 25$ and $e_{(spring)} = 25$.
- The observed values: $o_{(summer)} = 31$, $o_{(autumn)} = 28$, $o_{(winter)} = 18$ and $o_{(spring)} = 23$.
- $\chi^2_{test} = \frac{(31-25)^2}{31} + \frac{(28-25)^2}{28} + \frac{(18-25)^2}{18} + \frac{(23-25)^2}{23}$
- $\chi^2_{test} = \frac{36}{31} + \frac{9}{28} + \frac{49}{18} + \frac{4}{23} = 4.3789$
- Degrees of freedom (*df*) is $4 - 1 = 3$.

- $\alpha = 0.05$ (default assumption)
- Look at row 3 (*df*) in *chi-squared distribution table* from Chapter 38. The test statistics of 4.3789 is greater than 4.1083 from column 1 (0.25) and smaller than 4.6416 from column 2 (0.20). Therefore, the *P-value* for this sample is a value between 0.20 and 0.25.
- There is no need to get the precise *P-value* because any value between 0.20 and 0.25 is greater than α (0.05), so this experiment fails to reject null hypothesis.
- Even though it is not required to conclude hypothesis testing, we can still obtain precise *P-value* using Excel. The *P-value* is 0.2233.
- Alternatively, the critical value for this test is the value of row 3 (*df*) and column 0.05 (α) in reference table. $\chi^2{}_{crit} = \chi^2{}_{(0.05;\,3)} = 7.8147$.
- $\chi^2{}_{test} < \chi^2{}_{crit}$; $4.3789 < 7.8147$, it shows that test statistics is located inside acceptable area. This test fails to reject null hypothesis.
- This experiment fails to conclude with 95% confidence that more babies are born in certain season compared to others.
- If the researcher is willing to accept 25% alpha risk, then the *P-value* from sample data becomes smaller than α (0.25), making it sufficient to reject the null hypothesis. In other words, the experiment can conclude with 75% confidence that more babies are born in certain season compared to others.

Example 22-5 (goodness of fit test):
According to Australian Red Cross Blood Service, the percentage of blood group frequency in Australia is 49% for group O, 38% for group A, 10% for group B, 3% for group AB. A researcher wants to know if blood group percentage in a city is aligned with nationwide proportions. He collects data from 200 random respondents with the following results: 93 have type O blood, 71 have type A, 23 have type B and 13 have type AB.

- H_0: blood group proportions in that city is aligned with nationwide statistics.
- H_A: blood group proportions in that city is different from nationwide statistics.
- Expected values: $e_{(O)} = 98$, $e_{(A)} = 76$, $e_{(B)} = 20$ and $e_{(AB)} = 6$.
- Observed values: $o_{(O)} = 93$, $o_{(A)} = 71$, $o_{(B)} = 23$ and $o_{(AB)} = 13$.
- $\chi^2{}_{test} = \frac{(93-98)^2}{98} + \frac{(71-76)^2}{76} + \frac{(23-20)^2}{20} + \frac{(13-6)^2}{6}$
- $\chi^2{}_{test} = \frac{25}{98} + \frac{25}{76} + \frac{9}{20} + \frac{49}{6} = 9.2007$
- Degrees of freedom (*df*) is $4 - 1 = 3$.
- $\alpha = 0.05$ (default assumption)

- Look at row 3 in *chi-squared distribution table* from Chapter 38. The test statistics of 9.2007 is greater than 7.8147 from column 5 (0.050) and smaller than 9.3484 from column 6 (0.025). Therefore, the *P-value* for this sample is a value between 0.050 and 0.025.
- There is no need to get the precise *P-value* because any value between 0.050 and 0.025 is smaller than α (0.050), so this experiment rejects null hypothesis.
- Even though it is not required to conclude hypothesis testing, we can still obtain precise *P-value* using Excel. The *P-value* is 0.0267.
- Alternatively, the critical value for this test is the value of row 3 (*df*) and column 0.05 (α) in reference table. $\chi^2_{crit} = \chi^2_{(0.05;\ 3)} = 7.8147$.
- $\chi^2_{crit} < \chi^2_{test}$; 7.8147 < 9.2007, it shows that test statistics is located inside rejection area. This test rejects null hypothesis.
- This experiment concludes with 95% confidence that people in that specific city have different blood group distribution compared to nationwide statistics.

Chi-squared test of independence compares distributions of categories in two or more independent samples. Each sample represents Chi-squared test for discrete X, discrete Y and multiple samples listed in Figure 22-1 refers to chi-squared test of independence.

Two-ways table is used for chi-squared test of independence. The grouping variable and the outcome variable represented by samples are listed as rows and columns. The test analyses relationships between those variables.

Hypotheses for test of independence:
- Null hypothesis (H_0): the variables are independent
- Alternative hypothesis (H_A): the variables have relationships

Degrees of freedom for chi-squared test of independence:

$$df = (\#rows - 1) \times (\#columns - 1)$$

Expected value for each cell in the table:

$$e_{(row\ i;\ column\ j)} = \frac{total\ of\ row\ i \times total\ of\ column\ j}{grand\ total}$$

Example 22-6 (test of independence):
There are three major brands of certain consumer product: brand X, Y and Z. A researcher wants to know if these brands have the market shares in Sydney,

Melbourne, Brisbane and Perth. After collecting sample of 300 respondents, the distribution of favourite brands is presented in the table below:

		City			
		Sydney	Melbourne	Brisbane	Perth
Brand	X	50	43	26	25
	Y	29	22	17	19
	Z	21	15	27	6

The first step to perform hypothesis testing on these data is to calculate the total of each row and column of contingency table.

			City				TOTAL
			Sydney	Melbourne	Brisbane	Perth	
Brand	X	observed	50	43	26	25	144
		expected	$e_{(1,1)}$	$e_{(1,2)}$	$e_{(1,3)}$	$e_{(1,4)}$	
	Y	observed	29	22	17	19	87
		expected	$e_{(2,1)}$	$e_{(2,2)}$	$e_{(2,3)}$	$e_{(2,4)}$	
	Z	observed	21	15	27	6	69
		expected	$e_{(3,1)}$	$e_{(3,2)}$	$e_{(3,3)}$	$e_{(3,4)}$	
		TOTAL	100	80	70	50	300

Calculation of expected values:

- $e_{(1,1)} = \dfrac{total\ of\ row\ 1 \times total\ of\ column\ 1}{grand\ total} = \dfrac{100 \times 144}{300} = 48.00$

- $e_{(1,2)} = \dfrac{total\ of\ row\ 1 \times total\ of\ column\ 2}{grand\ total} = \dfrac{80 \times 144}{300} = 38.40$

- $e_{(1,3)} = \dfrac{total\ of\ row\ 1 \times total\ of\ column\ 3}{grand\ total} = \dfrac{70 \times 144}{300} = 33.60$

- $e_{(1,4)} = \dfrac{total\ of\ row\ 1 \times total\ of\ column\ 4}{grand\ total} = \dfrac{50 \times 144}{300} = 24.00$

- $e_{(2,1)} = \dfrac{total\ of\ row\ 2 \times total\ of\ column\ 1}{grand\ total} = \dfrac{100 \times 87}{300} = 29.00$

- $e_{(2,2)} = \dfrac{total\ of\ row\ 2 \times total\ of\ column\ 2}{grand\ total} = \dfrac{80 \times 87}{300} = 23.20$

- $e_{(2,3)} = \dfrac{total\ of\ row\ 2 \times total\ of\ column\ 3}{grand\ total} = \dfrac{70 \times 87}{300} = 20.30$

- $e_{(2,4)} = \dfrac{total\ of\ row\ 2 \times total\ of\ column\ 4}{grand\ total} = \dfrac{50 \times 87}{300} = 14.50$

- $e_{(3,1)} = \dfrac{total\ of\ row\ 3 \times total\ of\ column\ 1}{grand\ total} = \dfrac{100 \times 69}{300} = 23.00$

- $e_{(3,2)} = \dfrac{total\ of\ row\ 3 \times total\ of\ column\ 2}{grand\ total} = \dfrac{80 \times 69}{300} = 18.40$

- $e_{(3,3)} = \dfrac{total\ of\ row\ 3 \times toal\ of\ column\ 3}{grand\ total} = \dfrac{70 \times 69}{300} = 16.10$

- $e_{(3,4)} = \dfrac{total\ of\ row\ 3 \times total\ of\ column\ 4}{grand\ total} = \dfrac{50 \times 69}{300} = 11.50$

			City				TOTAL
			Sydney	Melbourne	Brisbane	Perth	
Brand	X	observed	50	43	26	25	144
		expected	48.00	38.40	33.60	24.00	
		contribution	$c_{(1,1)}$	$c_{(1,2)}$	$c_{(1,3)}$	$c_{(1,4)}$	
	Y	observed	29	22	17	19	87
		expected	29.00	23.20	20.30	14.50	
		contribution	$c_{(2,1)}$	$c_{(2,2)}$	$c_{(2,3)}$	$c_{(2,4)}$	
	Z	observed	21	15	27	6	69
		expected	23.00	18.40	16.10	11.50	
		contribution	$c_{(3,1)}$	$c_{(3,2)}$	$c_{(3,3)}$	$c_{(3,4)}$	
		TOTAL	100	80	70	50	300

The next step is calculating the contribution to chi-squared:

- $c_{(1,1)} = \dfrac{\left(o_{(1,1)} - e_{(1,1)}\right)^2}{e_{(1,1)}} = \dfrac{(50-48.00)^2}{48.00} = 0.08$

- $c_{(1,2)} = \dfrac{\left(o_{(1,2)} - e_{(1,2)}\right)^2}{e_{(1,2)}} = \dfrac{(43-38.40)^2}{38.40} = 0.55$

- $c_{(1,3)} = \dfrac{\left(o_{(1,3)} - e_{(1,3)}\right)^2}{e_{(1,3)}} = \dfrac{(26-33.60)^2}{33.60} = 1.72$

- $c_{(1,4)} = \dfrac{\left(o_{(1,4)} - e_{(1,4)}\right)^2}{e_{(1,4)}} = \dfrac{(25-24.00)^2}{24.00} = 0.04$

- $c_{(2,1)} = \dfrac{\left(o_{(2,1)} - e_{(2,1)}\right)^2}{e_{(2,1)}} = \dfrac{(29-29.00)^2}{29.00} = 0.00$

- $c_{(2,2)} = \dfrac{\left(o_{(2,2)} - e_{(2,2)}\right)^2}{e_{(2,2)}} = \dfrac{(22-23.20)^2}{23.20} = 0.06$

- $c_{(2,3)} = \dfrac{\left(o_{(2,3)} - e_{(2,3)}\right)^2}{e_{(2,3)}} = \dfrac{(17-20.30)^2}{20.30} = 0.54$

- $c_{(2,4)} = \dfrac{\left(o_{(2,4)} - e_{(2,4)}\right)^2}{e_{(2,4)}} = \dfrac{(19-14.50)^2}{14.50} = 1.40$

- $c_{(3,1)} = \dfrac{\left(o_{(3,1)} - e_{(3,1)}\right)^2}{e_{(3,1)}} = \dfrac{(21-23.00)^2}{23.00} = 0.17$

- $c_{(3,2)} = \dfrac{\left(o_{(3,2)} - e_{(3,2)}\right)^2}{e_{(3,2)}} = \dfrac{(15-18.40)^2}{18.40} = 0.63$

- $c_{(3,3)} = \dfrac{\left(o_{(3,3)} - e_{(3,3)}\right)^2}{e_{(3,3)}} = \dfrac{(27-16.10)^2}{16.10} = 7.38$

- $c_{(3,4)} = \dfrac{\left(o_{(3,4)} - e_{(3,4)}\right)^2}{e_{(3,4)}} = \dfrac{(6-11.50)^2}{11.50} = 2.63$

			City				TOTAL
			Sydney	Melbourne	Brisbane	Perth	
Brand	X	observed	50	43	26	25	144
		expected	48.00	38.40	33.60	24.00	
		contribution	0.08	0.55	1.72	0.04	
	Y	observed	29	22	17	19	87
		expected	29.00	23.20	20.30	14.50	
		contribution	0.00	0.06	0.54	1.40	
	Z	observed	21	15	27	6	69
		expected	23.00	18.40	16.10	11.50	
		contribution	0.17	0.63	7.38	2.63	
		TOTAL	100	80	70	50	300

Further calculations of test statistics and *P-value*:

- Chi-squared test statistics is the sum of all contribution values.
- $\chi^2_{test} = \sum \frac{(observed-expected)^2}{expected} = 15.20$
- Degrees of freedom (*df*) is (#rows – 1) × (#columns – 1) = 2 × 3 = 6.
- $\alpha = 0.05$ (default assumption)
- Look at row 6 in *chi-squared distribution table* from Chapter 38. The test statistics of 15.20 is greater than 14.4494 from column 6 (0.025) and smaller than 16.8119 from column 7 (0.010). Therefore, the *P-value* for this sample is a value between 0.025 and 0.010.
- There is no need to get the precise *P-value* because any value between 0.025 and 0.010 is smaller than α (0.050), so this experiment rejects null hypothesis.
- Even though it is not required to conclude hypothesis testing, we can still obtain precise *P-value* using Excel. The *P-value* is 0.0187.
- Alternatively, the critical value for this test is the value of row 6 (*df*) and column 0.05 (α) in reference table. $\chi^2_{crit} = \chi^2_{(0.05;\,6)} = 12.5916$.
- $\chi^2_{crit} < \chi^2_{test}$; 12.5916 < 15.20, this shows that test statistics is located inside rejection area. This test rejects null hypothesis.
- This experiment concludes with 95% confidence that the three major brands have different market shares in Sydney, Melbourne, Brisbane and Perth. In other words, at least one of those cities have significantly different distribution of market share.

Chi-squared contingency table is also useful to show which variable(s) cause the highest difference from others. The sum of all contribution values for Sydney is 0.08 + 0.00 + 0.17 = 0.26. Similarly, the sums for Melbourne, Brisbane and Perth are 1.24, 9.64 and 4.07. Brisbane has the largest contribution to chi-squared critical value, it means that it is the city having the most different market share compared to others.

Another experiment to check this conclusion can be performed by removing the variable(s) identified as the source of difference. In this case, the researcher removes data from Brisbane and then recalculates the contingency table.

			City			TOTAL
			Sydney	Melbourne	Perth	
Brand	X	observed	50	43	25	118
		expected	51.30	41.04	25.65	
		contribution	0.03	0.09	0.02	
	Y	observed	29	22	19	70
		expected	30.43	24.35	15.22	
		contribution	0.07	0.23	0.94	
	Z	observed	21	15	6	42
		expected	18.26	14.61	9.13	
		contribution	0.41	0.01	1.07	
		TOTAL	100	80	50	230

Calculations of critical value and *P-value* for Sydney, Melbourne and Perth:
- Recalculate all expected values. The expected values for each brand in Sydney, Melbourne and Perth must be recalculated after the removal of Brisbane data. This is because the total number of data in the sample changes. Therefore, the sum of every row also changes.
- Recalculate all contribution values.
- $\chi^2{}_{test} = \sum \frac{(observed-expected)^2}{expected} = 2.87$
- Degrees of freedom (*df*) is (#*rows* – 1) × (#*columns* – 1) = 2 × 2 = 4.
- $\alpha = 0.05$ (default assumption)
- Look at row 4 in *chi-squared distribution table* from Chapter 38. The test statistics of 2.87 is less than 5.3853 from column 1 (0.25). Therefore, the *P-value* for this sample is greater than 0.25.
- There is no need to get the precise *P-value* because any value greater than 0.25 is also greater than α (0.05), so this experiment fails to reject null hypothesis.
- Even though it is not required to conclude hypothesis testing, we can still obtain precise *P-value* using Excel. The *P-value* is 0.5798.
- Alternatively, the critical value for this test is the value of row 4 (*df*) and column 0.05 (α) in reference table. $\chi^2{}_{crit} = \chi^2{}_{(0.05;\,4)} = 9.4877$.

- $\chi^2_{test} < \chi^2_{crit}$; 2.87 < 9.4877, this shows that test statistics is located inside acceptable area. This test fails to reject null hypothesis.
- This experiment fails to conclude with 95% confidence that the three major brands have the different market shares in Sydney, Melbourne and Perth. In other words, they have same market shares in Sydney, Melbourne and Perth.

23. HYPOTHESIS TESTING: DISCRETE X, CONTINUOUS Y

This chapter discusses hypothesis testing of variance and mean for discrete X and continuous Y variables as illustrated in Figure 23-1. Before continuing with this chapter, it is strongly recommended to review Chapter 20 about the principles of hypothesis testing.

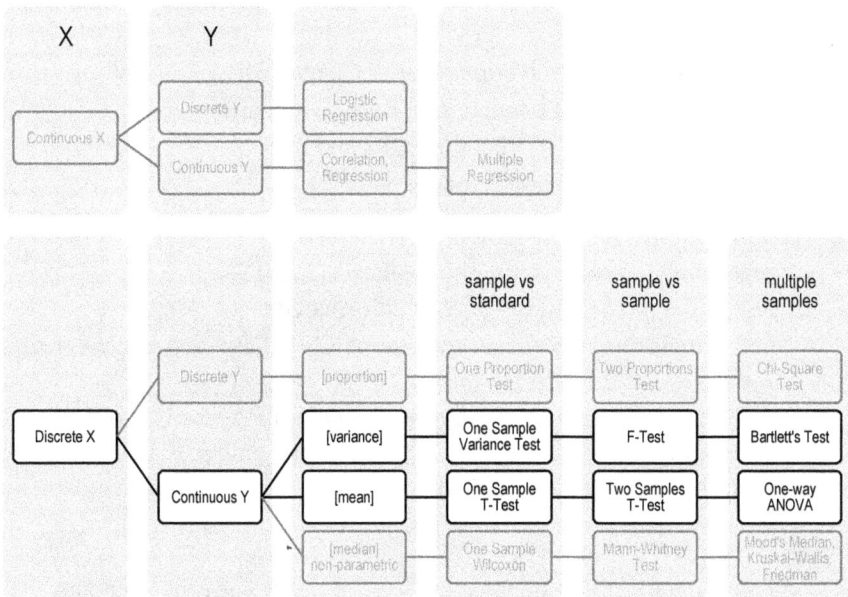

Figure 23-1 Hypothesis Testing for discrete X and continuous Y for variance and mean

One Sample Variance Test

One sample variance test is used to compare the variance of a sample with normal distribution against a given value (*m*). The comparison value could come from known historical variance or process requirement. Calculation of one sample variance test uses *chi-squared distribution*. Please refer to Chapter 22 for more explanation about chi-squared test.

Hypotheses for one sample variance test:
- H_0: $\sigma^2 = m$
- H_A: $\sigma^2 > m$ (right-tailed) or
  $\sigma^2 < m$ (left-tailed) or
  $\sigma^2 \neq m$ (two-tailed)

Test statistics for one sample variance test:

$$\chi^2{}_{test} = (n - 1) \times \frac{S^2}{m}$$

S^2 is sample variance. σ^2 is population variance that is inferred from sample. *m* is the target variance or the given value to be compared. *n* is the size of sample. Degrees of freedom (*df*) is $n - 1$.

P-value in chi-squared test is the probability of obtaining values more extreme than critical value. There are three possible ways to calculate *P-value* based on test statistics:
- Use *chi-squared distribution table* in Chapter 38.
- Use CHISQ.DIST.RT function in Excel with parameters: test statistics $\chi^2{}_{test}$ as *x*, degrees of freedom (*df*) 1 and 2.
- Use statistical software of your choice.

Interpretation of test result based on *P-value*:
- Right-tailed tests: reject null hypothesis (H_0) if *P-value* is less than α. This is the most common type of chi-squared tests.
- Left-tailed tests: reject null hypothesis (H_0) if *P-value* is greater than $1 - \alpha$.
- Two-tailed tests: reject null hypothesis (H_0) if *P-value* is less than $\alpha/2$ or *P-value* is greater than $1 - (\alpha/2)$. Remember that chi-squared distribution is not symmetrical.

Example 23-1:
A company manufactures metal planks. Five years ago, the company had measured that the length their 2 metres planks had standard deviation of 0.9

mm. They want to know if the current standard deviation is <u>worse than</u> five years ago. 56 random samples are collected and measured, showing standard deviation of 1.05 mm.

- $\sigma = 0.9$ mm. $S = 1.05$ mm.
- H_0: $\sigma^2 = m$
- H_A: $\sigma^2 > m$ (right-tailed)
- Degrees of freedom (df) is $56 - 1 = 55$.
- $\chi^2{}_{test} = 55 \times \frac{(1.05)^2}{(0.9)^2} = 74.8611$
- $\alpha = 0.05$ (default assumption)
- Look at the row for $df = 55$ in *chi-squared distribution table* from Chapter 38. The test statistics of 74.8611 is greater than 73.3115 from column 5 (0.050) and smaller than 77.3805 from column 6 (0.025). Therefore, the *P-value* for this sample is a value between 0.050 and 0.025.
- There is no need to get the precise *P-value* because any value between 0.050 and 0.025 is less than α (0.05), so this experiment rejects null hypothesis.
- Even though it is not required to conclude hypothesis testing, we can still obtain precise *P-value* using Excel. The *P-value* is 0.0387.
- This experiment concludes with 95% confidence that current standard deviation is greater than five years ago.

Example 23-2:
A company manufactures metal planks. Five years ago, the company had measured that the length their 2 metres planks had standard deviation of 0.9 mm. They want to know if the current standard deviation is <u>different from</u> five years ago. 56 random samples are collected and measured, showing standard deviation of 1.1 mm.

- $\sigma = 0.9$ mm. $S = 1.1$ mm. $df = 55$. $\alpha = 0.05$.
- H_0: $\sigma^2 = m$
- H_A: $\sigma^2 \neq m$ (two-tailed)
- $\chi^2 = 55 \times \frac{(1.05)^2}{(0.9)^2} = 74.8611$
- Look at the row for $df = 55$ in *chi-squared distribution table* from Chapter 38. The test statistics of 74.8611 is greater than 73.3115 from column 5 (0.050) and smaller than 77.3805 from column 6 (0.025). Therefore, the *P-value* for this sample is a value between 0.050 and 0.025.
- For two-tailed problem with $\alpha = 0.05$, we reject null hypothesis if *P-value* is smaller than 0.025 or greater than 0.975.

- There is no need to get the precise *P-value* because any value between 0.050 and 0.025 is neither less than 0.025 nor greater than 0.975. Therefore, this experiment fails to reject null hypothesis.
- This experiment fails to conclude with 95% confidence that current standard deviation is different from five years ago.
- Example 2 is different from example 1 because in two-tailed test, the 5% acceptable Alpha risk is split between left-tail and right-tail. *P-value* of 0.0387 is smaller than 0.05 but not smaller than 0.025.

Critical value χ^2_{crit} is the value separating the rejection and acceptable areas. It is calculated using CHISQ.INV.RT function with *probability* and degrees of freedom as parameters.

- For right-tailed tests: $\chi^2_{crit} = \chi^2_{(\alpha;\, df)}$
- For left-tailed tests: $\chi^2_{crit} = \chi^2_{(1-\alpha;\, df)}$
- For two-tailed tests: $upper\ \chi^2_{crit} = \chi^2_{\left(\frac{\alpha}{2};\, df\right)}$ and

$$lower\ \chi^2_{crit} < \chi^2_{\left(1-\frac{\alpha}{2};\, df\right)}$$

Critical value χ^2_{crit} is calculated using CHISQ.INV.RT function with *probability* and degrees of freedom as parameters. The critical value of $\chi^2_{(\alpha;\, df)}$ can be obtained from column α and row df in the reference table in Chapter 38.

One sample variance test rejects null hypothesis (H_0) if:

- $\chi^2_{test} > \chi^2_{crit}$ for right-tailed tests.
- $\chi^2_{test} < \chi^2_{crit}$ for left-tailed tests.
- $\chi^2_{test} > upper\ \chi^2_{crit}$ or $\chi^2_{test} < lower\ \chi^2_{crit}$ for two-tailed tests. Remember that *chi-squared distribution* is not symmetrical.

Using critical value to interpret test result in Example 23-1:

- Example 1 is a right-tailed problem.
- $\chi^2_{crit} = \chi^2_{(0.05;\, 55)} = 73.3115$, this is the value of row 55 (*df*) and column 0.05 in reference table.
- $\chi^2_{crit} < \chi^2_{test}$; $73.3115 < 74.8611$, it shows that test statistics is located inside rejection area. This test rejects null hypothesis.

Using critical value to interpret test result in Example 23-2:

- Example 2 is a two-tailed problem.
- $upper\ \chi^2_{crit} = \chi^2_{(0.025;\, 55)} = 77.3805$, this is the value of row 55 (*df*) and column 0.025 in reference table.

- *lower* $\chi^2_{crit} = \chi^2_{(0.975;\ 55)} = 36.3981$, this is the value of row 55 (*df*) and column 0.975 in reference table.
- *lower* $\chi^2_{crit} < \chi^2_{test} < upper\ \chi^2_{crit}$
- 36.3981 < 74.8611 < 77.3805, it shows that test statistics is located inside acceptable area. This test fails to reject null hypothesis.

To reach confidence level of X% where X = 1 − α, the limits of ***confidence interval*** can be calculated as:

Right-tailed problem	$Upper\ Limit = \dfrac{\sigma^2}{n-1} \times \chi^2_{crit}$
Left-tailed problem	$Lower\ Limit = \dfrac{\sigma^2}{n-1} \times \chi^2_{crit}$
Two-tailed problem	$Upper\ Limit = \dfrac{\sigma^2}{n-1} \times upper\ \chi^2_{crit}$ $Lower\ Limit = \dfrac{\sigma^2}{n-1} \times lower\ \chi^2_{crit}$

If sample variance is in the right tail (for right-tailed problem) or in the left tail (for left-tailed problem) or outside the boundaries of lower and upper limit of confidence interval (for two-tailed problem), null hypothesis is rejected because sample shows something more extreme than what is expected.

Confidence interval for Example 23-1:
- Example 1 is a right-tailed problem.
- $\chi^2_{crit} = \chi^2_{(0.05;\ 55)} = 73.3115$
- $Upper\ Limit = \dfrac{(0.9)^2}{55} \times 73.3115 = 1.0797$
- Sample variance $= (1.05)^2 = 1.1025$
- Sample variance is greater than upper limit of confidence interval, this experiment rejects null hypothesis.

Confidence interval for Example 23-2:
- Example 2 is a two-tailed problem.
- *upper* $\chi^2_{crit} = \chi^2_{(0.025;\ 55)} = 77.3805$
- $Upper\ Limit = \dfrac{(0.9)^2}{55} \times 77.3805 = 1.1396$
- *lower* $\chi^2_{crit} < \chi^2_{test} < upper\ \chi^2_{crit} = 36.3981$
- $Lower\ Limit = \dfrac{(0.9)^2}{55} \times 36.3981 = 0.5360$
- Sample variance $= (1.05)^2 = 1.1025$

- Sample variance is greater than lower limit and less than upper limit of confidence interval, this experiment fails to reject null hypothesis.

F-Test

F-test uses two samples from two populations and compares them to test if the variances of the populations are equal. It assumes data with normal distribution. Two-tailed F-test analyses if the variances of the two population are not equal. One-tailed F-test seeks to infer of one population has greater variance than the other.

Hypotheses for F-test:
- H_0: $\sigma_1{}^2 = \sigma_2{}^2$
- H_A: $\sigma_1{}^2 > \sigma_2{}^2$ (right-tailed) or

  $\sigma_1{}^2 < \sigma_2{}^2$ (left-tailed) or

  $\sigma_1{}^2 \neq \sigma_2{}^2$ (two-tailed)

Test statistics of F-test is calculated as:

$$F_{test} = \frac{S_1{}^2}{S_2{}^2}$$

$S_1{}^2$ and $S_2{}^2$ are variances of sample 1 and 2. Sample set with larger standard deviation becomes sample 1. F-test has two degrees of freedom (*df*), one from each sample. $df\,1 = n_1 - 1$. $df\,2 = n_2 - 1$. n_1 and n_2 are the amount of data in sample 1 and 2.

P-value in F-test is the probability of obtaining values more extreme than critical value. There are two possible ways to calculate *P-value* based on test statistics:
- Use F.DIST.RT function in Excel with parameters: test statistics F_{test} as x, degrees of freedom (*df*) 1 and 2.
- Use statistical software of your choice.

Note that using *F distribution table* in Chapter 38 is not one of the options to calculate *P-value* for F-test. This is different from Z table (one parameter) and chi-squared distribution (two parameters) discussed in earlier chapters. F distribution takes three parameters to calculate: test statistics, *df* (degrees of freedom) 1 and 2. The three-dimensional nature of the table makes it difficult to intuitively estimate *P-value* from the table.

Interpretation of F-test result using *P-value*:
- Right-tailed tests: reject null hypothesis (H_0) if *P-value* is less than α.
- Left-tailed tests: reject null hypothesis (H_0) if *P-value* is greater than $1 - \alpha$.
- Two-tailed tests: reject null hypothesis (H_0) if *P-value* is less than $\alpha/2$ or *P-value* is greater than $1 - (\alpha/2)$.

An alternative way to interpret F-test result is by comparing test statistics calculated from sample against critical values. F_{crit} is calculated using F.INV.RT function with *probability*, degrees of freedom 1 and 2 as parameters.
- For right-tailed tests: $F_{crit} = F_{(\alpha;\, df1;\, df2)}$
- For left-tailed tests: $F_{crit} = F_{(1-\alpha;\, df1;\, df2)}$
- For two-tailed tests: $upper\ F_{crit} = F_{\left(\frac{\alpha}{2};\, df1;\, df2\right)}$ and

$$lower\ F_{crit} < F_{\left(1-\frac{\alpha}{2};\, df1;\, df2\right)}$$

Null hypothesis (H_0) is rejected if:
- $F_{test} > F_{crit}$ for right-tailed tests.
- $F_{test} < F_{crit}$ for left-tailed tests.
- $F_{test} > upper\ F_{crit}$ or $F_{test} < lower\ F_{crit}$ for two-tailed tests.

Example 23-3:
A company manufactures metal planks with product length as its key requirement. 51 random sample data collected from batch 23568 have standard deviation of 1.16 mm. Another sample dataset is taken from batch 23569 with 56 data and standard deviation of 0.92 mm. They want to study if standard deviation of batch 23568 and 23569 are equal.
- Sample from batch 23568 has larger standard deviation so it becomes sample 1.
- $S_1 = 1.16$; $n_1 = 51$; $df\,1 = 50$
- $S_2 = 0.92$; $n_2 = 56$; $df\,2 = 55$
- H_0: $\sigma_1{}^2 = \sigma_2{}^2$
- H_A: $\sigma_1{}^2 \neq \sigma_2{}^2$ (two-tailed)
- $\alpha = 0.05$ (default assumption)
- $F_{test} = \dfrac{(1.16)^2}{(0.92)^2} = 1.5898$
- *P-value* = 0.0472, this is calculated from F.DIST.RT function in Excel.
- For two-tailed test: $\alpha/2 = 0.025$ and $1 - (\alpha/2) = 0.975$.
- *P-value* 0.0472 is greater than 0.025 and smaller than 0.975. Therefore, this experiment fails to reject null hypothesis.

- Another way to calculate the result uses the comparison between F_{test} against critical values of upper $F_{\left(\frac{\alpha}{2}; \, df1; \, df2\right)}$ and lower $F_{\left(1-\frac{\alpha}{2}; \, df1; \, df2\right)}$.
- Upper and lower critical values can be obtained from *F distribution table* in Chapter 38.
- $F_{(0.025; \, 50; \, 55)} = 1.7228$, this is the upper F_{crit}.
- $F_{(0.975; \, 50; \, 55)} = 0.5763$, this is the lower F_{crit}.
- *lower* $F_{crit} < F_{test} <$ *upper* F_{crit}
- $0.5763 < 1.5898 < 1.7228$, this shows that test statistics does not show extreme values (left tail or right tail) statistically sufficient to reject null hypothesis.
- This experiment fails to conclude with 95% confidence that standard deviations of batch 23568 and 23569 are different.

Example 23-4:

A company manufactures metal planks with product length as its key requirement. 51 random sample data collected from batch 23568 have standard deviation of 1.16 mm. Batch 23569 is the first production after process improvement from DMAIC project is implemented. Sample with 56 data have standard deviation of 0.92 mm. Does the process improvement reduce production variability?

- Sample from batch 23568 has larger standard deviation so it becomes sample 1.
- Reduced production variability means sample 2 should have smaller standard deviation compared to sample 1.
- $S_1 = 1.16$; $n_1 = 51$; $df\,1 = 50$
- $S_2 = 0.92$; $n_2 = 56$; $df\,2 = 55$
- $H_0: \sigma_1^2 = \sigma_2^2$
- $H_A: \sigma_1^2 > \sigma_2^2$ (right-tailed)
- $\alpha = 0.05$ (default assumption)
- $F_{test} = \frac{(1.16)^2}{(0.92)^2} = 1.5898$
- *P-value* $= 0.0472$, this is calculated from F.DIST.RT function in Excel.
- *P-value* 0.0472 is less than 0.05. Therefore, this experiment rejects null hypothesis.
- Another way to calculate the result uses the comparison between F_{test}, and critical value $F_{(\alpha; \, df1; \, df2)}$
- Critical value can be obtained from *F distribution table* in Chapter 38.
- $F_{(0.05; \, 50; \, 55)} = 1.5774$, this is the F_{crit}.
- $F_{crit} < F_{test}$

- 1.5774 < 1.5898, this shows that test statistics shows extreme values (right tail) statistically sufficient to reject null hypothesis.
- This experiment concludes with 95% confidence that standard deviation of batch 23569 is less than standard deviation of batch 23568.

Note that Example 23-3 and Example 23-4 use the same values of standard deviations and sample sizes but have different test conclusions. If Example 23-4 shows that sample 2 has less standard deviation than sample 1, why does Example 23-3 fail to conclude that the standard deviations of sample 1 and 2 are different? This is caused by the use of α. For one-tailed tests, *P-value* is compared with α (or $1 - \alpha$) because it only tries to observe right or left tail. For two-tailed tests, the same α has to be divided by 2 because it needs to cover both left tail and right tail.

Bartlett's Test

Bartlett's test compares multiple samples from multiple populations to test if the variances of the populations are equal. It uses chi-squared distribution to compare test statistics and assumes data with normal distribution.

Hypotheses for Bartlett's test:
- H_0: $\sigma_1^2 = \sigma_2^2 = \sigma_3^2 = \cdots = \sigma_k^2$
- H_A: at least one of the σ_i^2 is not equal to others.

Test statistics of Bartlett's test is calculated as:

$$B_{test} = \frac{(n - k) \ln S_p^2 - \sum_{i=1}^{k}(n_i - 1) \ln S_i^2}{1 + \frac{1}{3(k - 1)}\left(\sum_{i=1}^{k}\frac{1}{n_i - 1} - \frac{1}{n - k}\right)}$$

k is the number of sample datasets. n_i is the size of sample #i. n is the total amount of data in all samples. S_i^2 is variance of sample #i. Degrees of freedom (*df*) is $k - 1$. The formula might look a bit intimidating, but the actual calculation is easier than it seems.

S_p^2 is the pooled variance of all sample datasets. It is calculated as:

$$S_p^2 = \frac{\sum_{i=1}^{k}\left((n_i - 1) \times S_i^2\right)}{n - k}$$

P-value in Bartlett's test is the probability of obtaining values more extreme than critical value. There are three possible ways to calculate *P-value* based on test statistics:

- Use *chi-squared distribution table* in Chapter 38.
- Use CHISQ.DIST.RT function in Excel with parameters: test statistics χ^2_{test} as *x*, degrees of freedom (*df*) 1 and 2.
- Use statistical software of your choice.

Bartlett's test is a right-tailed test. Null hypothesis (*H$_0$*) is rejected if *P-value* is less than α.

Critical value χ^2_{crit} is calculated using CHISQ.INV.RT function with α and degrees of freedom as parameters. When using critical value, null hypothesis is rejected if test statistics is greater than critical value.

$$\chi^2_{crit} = \chi^2_{(\alpha;\,df)}$$

Example 23-5:
A company manufactures metal planks. Random samples are collected from different batches of 3 metres cable to find out if the standard deviations of those batches are equal.

Batch number	83570	83571	83572	83573
Sample size	20	20	25	20
Standard deviation	2.11 mm	2.15 mm	2.12 mm	2.67 mm

- H_0: $\sigma_1^2 = \sigma_2^2 = \sigma_3^2 = \sigma_4^2$
- H_A: at least one of the σ_i^2 is not equal to others.
- $\alpha = 0.05$ (default assumption)
- $k = 4$
- $S_p^2 = \dfrac{(19\times2.11^2)+(19\times2.15^2)+(24\times2.12^2)+(19\times2.67^2)}{85-4} = 5.1325$
- $B_{test} = \dfrac{(81\times ln\,5.1325)-\left((19\times ln\,2.11^2)+(19\times ln\,2.15^2)+(24\times ln\,2.12^2)+(19\times ln\,2.67^2)\right)}{1+\frac{1}{3\times3}\left(\frac{1}{19}+\frac{1}{19}+\frac{1}{24}+\frac{1}{19}-\frac{1}{81}\right)}$
- $B_{test} = \dfrac{132.4829-\left((19\times1.4934)+(19\times1.5309)+(24\times1.5028)+(19\times1.9642)\right)}{1+0.0208}$
- $B_{test} = \dfrac{132.4829-(28.3746+29.0871+36.0672+37.3190)}{1+0.0208}$
- $B_{test} = \dfrac{132.4829-130.8489}{1.0208} = 1.6008$
- Look at the row for *df* = 3 in *chi-squared distribution table* from Chapter 38. The test statistics of 1.6008 is less than 4.1083 from column 1 (0.25). Therefore, the *P-value* for this test is a value greater than 0.25.

- There is no need to get the precise *P-value* because any value greater than 0.25 is also greater than α (0.05), so this experiment fails to reject null hypothesis.
- Even though it is not required to conclude hypothesis testing, we can still obtain precise *P-value* using Excel. The *P-value* is 0.6592.
- Alternatively, the critical value for this test is the value of row 3 (*df*) and column 0.05 (α) in reference table. $B_{crit} = B_{(0.05;\ 3)} = 7.8147$.
- $B_{test} < B_{crit}$; $1.6008 < 7.8147$, it shows that test statistics is located inside acceptable area. This test fails to reject null hypothesis.
- This experiment fails to conclude with 95% confidence that at least one of the batches have standard deviation different than others.

Manual observation of sample data in example 1 would show that standard deviation of sample from batch 83573 seems to be quite different from other batches. Then why Bartlett's test fails to reject null hypothesis? Remember that the standard deviations of four batches presented in the example are calculated from sample data, not from the entire population of each batch. Increasing the number of collected data for the samples will change the result of hypothesis test.

Example 23-6:
A company manufactures metal planks. Random samples are collected from different batches of 3 metres cable to find out if the standard deviations of those batches are equal.

Batch number	83570	83571	83572	83573
Sample size	100	100	120	100
Standard deviation	2.11 mm	2.15 mm	2.12 mm	2.67 mm

- H_0: $\sigma_1{}^2 = \sigma_2{}^2 = \sigma_3{}^2 = \sigma_4{}^2$
- H_A: at least one of the $\sigma_i{}^2$ is not equal to others.
- $\alpha = 0.05$ (default assumption)
- $k = 4$
- $S_p{}^2 = \dfrac{(99\times2.11^2)+(99\times2.15^2)+(119\times2.12^2)+(99\times2.67^2)}{420-4} = 5.1418$
- $B_{test} = \dfrac{(416\times ln\ 5.1418)-\left((99\times ln\ 2.11^2)+(99\times ln\ 2.15^2)+(119\times ln\ 2.12^2)+(99\times ln\ 2.67^2)\right)}{1+\frac{1}{3\times3}\left(\frac{1}{99}+\frac{1}{99}+\frac{1}{119}+\frac{1}{99}-\frac{1}{416}\right)}$
- $B_{test} = \dfrac{681.1580-\left((99\times1.4934)+(99\times1.5309)+(119\times1.5028)+(99\times1.9642)\right)}{1+0.0040}$
- $B_{test} = \dfrac{681.1580-(147.8442+161.5626+178.8370+194.4515)}{1+0.0040}$
- $B_{test} = \dfrac{681.1580-672.6954}{1.0040} = 8.4286$

- Look at the row for $df = 3$ in *chi-squared distribution table* from Chapter 38. The test statistics of 8.4286 is greater than 7.8147 from column 5 (0.050) and smaller than 9.3484 from column 6 (0.025). Therefore, the *P-value* for this test is a value between 0.050 and 0.025.
- There is no need to get the precise *P-value* because any value between 0.050 and 0.025 is less than α (0.05), so this experiment rejects null hypothesis.
- Even though it is not required to conclude hypothesis testing, we can still obtain precise *P-value* using Excel. The *P-value* is 0.0379.
- Alternatively, the critical value for this test is the value of row 3 (*df*) and column 0.05 (α) in reference table. $B_{crit} = B_{(0.05;\ 3)} = 7.8147$.
- $B_{crit} < B_{test}$; $7.8147 < 8.4286$, it shows that test statistics is located inside rejection area. This test rejects null hypothesis.
- This experiment concludes with 95% confidence that at least one of the batches have standard deviation different than others.

Example 23-6 is similar to Example 23-5 with one key difference: the sample sizes are significantly larger. Larger samples allow inferential statistics to have higher confidence that the characteristics observed in sample dataset is close to the characteristics of the population.

One Sample T-Test

One sample T-test is used to compare the mean of a sample dataset against given value (*m*). The comparison value could come from known historical mean or process requirement. Calculation of one sample T-test uses *T distribution*.

Assumptions of T-test:
- Sample data follows normal distribution.
- Sample data are randomly selected from population.
- There is no significant outlier in sample data.
- Sample size is sufficient. This follows the general guide of inferential statistics.

Hypotheses for one sample T-test:
- H_0: $\mu = m$
- H_A: $\mu > m$ (right-tailed) or
  $\mu < m$ (left-tailed) or
  $\mu \neq m$ (two-tailed)

Test statistics for one sample T-test is calculated as:

$$T_{test} = \frac{|\bar{x} - m|}{S/\sqrt{n}}$$

S is sample standard deviation. $\bar{x}$ is sample mean. μ is the population mean inferred from sample. m is the comparison target value. n is the size of sample.

The result of one sample T-test is interpreted using the comparison of test statistics against critical values. T_{crit} is calculated using T.INV function with *probability* and degrees of freedom as parameters.

- For right-tailed tests: $T_{crit} = T_{(1-\alpha;\, n-1)}$
- For left-tailed tests: $T_{crit} = T_{(\alpha;\, n-1)}$
- For two-tailed tests: $upper\ T_{crit} = T_{\left(1-\frac{\alpha}{2};\, n-1\right)}$ and

  $lower\ T_{crit} < T_{\left(\frac{\alpha}{2};\, n-1\right)}$

To reach confidence level of X% where X = $1 - \alpha$, one sample T-test rejects null hypothesis (H_0) if:

- $T_{test} > T_{crit}$ for right-tailed tests.
- $T_{test} < T_{crit}$ for left-tailed tests.
- $T_{test} > upper\ T_{crit}$ or $T_{test} < lower\ T_{crit}$ for two-tailed tests.

P-value in T-test is the probability of obtaining values more extreme than critical value. There are three possible ways to calculate *P-value* based on test statistics:

- Use *T table* in Chapter 38.
- Use T.DIST.RT function in Excel with parameters: test statistics T_{test} as x and degrees of freedom (df).
- Use statistical software of your choice.

Note that the formula to calculate test statistics uses the absolute value so that the result is always positive. This can handle either left- and right-tailed tests because normal distribution is symmetrical. For two-tailed tests, the probability of obtaining values more extreme than critical value could go both ways because μ could be greater or less than m. Therefore, the *P-value* obtained from T.DIST.RT function needs to be multiplied by two to cover the right and left tails.

Example 23-7:
A company manufactures metal planks. Five years ago, the company had measured that the length their 2 metres plank had average length of 2002.35 mm. They want to know if the current average is different from five years ago.

76 random samples are collected and measured, showing average length of 1998.95 mm with standard deviation of 5.8 mm.

- $m = 2008.25$ mm. $\bar{x} = 1986.95$ mm. $S = 15.8$ mm. $n = 100$.
- H_0: $\mu = m$
- H_A: $\mu \neq m$ (two-tailed)
- $T_{test} = \frac{|1998.95 - 2002.35|}{15.8/\sqrt{76}} = \frac{3.4}{1.8124} = 1.8760$
- $\alpha = 0.05$ (default assumption)
- Critical values for this test are $T_{(0.025;\ 75)} = -1.9921$ and $T_{(0.975;\ 75)} = 1.9921$.
- $lower\ T_{crit} < T_{test} < upper\ T_{crit}$
- $-1.9921 < 1.8760 < 1.9921$; test statistics T_{test} is located inside acceptable area. This test fails to reject null hypothesis.
- Alternatively, we can calculate *P-value* using T.DIST.RT function in Excel. The *P-value* is $0.0323 \times 2 = 0.0646$, which is greater than α (0.05). There is no statistically sufficient evidence to reject null hypothesis.
- This experiment fails to conclude with 95% confidence that metal planks from current production have different length than five years ago.

If population standard deviation is known, **Z-test** can be performed instead of T-test to compare sample mean against given value of *m*. This is not commonly used in practice because when population standard deviation is known, there is a good chance that access to whole population data is possible, hence we can use descriptive statistics instead of inferential statistics.

Test statistics for one sample Z-test:

$$Z_{test} = \frac{\bar{x} - m}{\sigma/\sqrt{n}}$$

The calculations of critical value and *P-value* are quite similar to T-test, with obvious difference that we use Z table instead of T table. There are no degrees of freedom (*df*) in Z table.

Two Samples T-Test

Two samples T-test is used to compare the mean of two independent samples. Calculation of one sample T-test uses *T distribution*.

Assumptions of T-test:
- Sample data follows normal distribution.
- Sample data are randomly selected from population.
- There is no significant outlier in sample data.
- Sample size is sufficient. This follows the general guide of inferential statistics.

Hypotheses for two samples T-test:
- H_0: $\mu_1 = \mu_2$
- H_A: $\mu_1 \neq \mu_2$ (two-tailed)
- It is possible to do one-tailed two samples T-test, but two-tailed tests are far more common.

There are two scenarios of two samples T-test:
- *Equal variances*: the two samples are taken from two populations assumed to have equal variances.
- *Unequal variances*: the two samples are taken from two populations assumed to have different variances.

For **two samples T-test with equal variances**, we first calculate pooled standard deviation:

$$S_p = \sqrt{\frac{(n_1 - 1)S_1{}^2 + (n_2 - 1)S_2{}^2}{n_1 + n_2 - 2}}$$

Test statistics for two samples T-test with equal variances:

$$T_{test} = \frac{\bar{x}_1 - \bar{x}_2}{S_p \sqrt{\frac{1}{n_1} + \frac{1}{n_2}}}$$

Degrees of freedom (*df*) for two samples T-test with equal variances:

$$df = n_1 + n_2 - 2$$

For two samples T-test with unequal variances, the formula for test statistics:

$$T_{test} = \frac{\bar{x}_1 - \bar{x}_2}{\sqrt{\frac{S_1{}^2}{n_1} + \frac{S_2{}^2}{n_2}}}$$

Degrees of freedom (*df*) for two samples T-test with unequal variances:

$$df = \frac{\left(\dfrac{S_1^{\,2}}{n_1} + \dfrac{S_2^{\,2}}{n_2}\right)^2}{\dfrac{\left(S_1^{\,2}/n_1\right)^2}{n_1 - 1} + \dfrac{\left(S_2^{\,2}/n_2\right)^2}{n_2 - 1}}$$

S_1 and S_2 are standard deviations of samples. S_p is the pooled standard deviation. $\bar{x}_1$ and $\bar{x}_2$ are sample means. μ_1 and μ_2 are population means inferred from samples. n_1 and n_2 are sample sizes.

The result of two samples T-test is interpreted using the comparison of test statistics against critical values. T_{crit} is calculated using T.INV function with *probability* and degrees of freedom as parameters.

- For right-tailed tests: $T_{crit} = T_{(1-\alpha;\, df)}$
- For left-tailed tests: $T_{crit} = T_{(\alpha;\, df)}$
- For two-tailed tests: $upper\ T_{crit} = T_{\left(1-\frac{\alpha}{2};\, df\right)}$ and

$$lower\ T_{crit} < T_{\left(\frac{\alpha}{2};\, df\right)}$$

To reach confidence level of X% where X = $1 - \alpha$, two samples T-test rejects null hypothesis (H_0) if:

- $T_{test} > T_{crit}$ for right-tailed tests.
- $T_{test} < T_{crit}$ for left-tailed tests.
- $T_{test} > upper\ T_{crit}$ or $T_{test} < lower\ T_{crit}$ for two-tailed tests.

P-value in T-test is the probability of obtaining values more extreme than critical value. There are three possible ways to calculate *P-value* based on test statistics:

- Use *T table* in Chapter 38.
- Use T.DIST.RT function in Excel with parameters: test statistics T_{test} as *x* and degrees of freedom (*df*).
- Use statistical software of your choice.

For two-tailed tests, the probability of obtaining values more extreme than critical value could go both ways because μ_1 could be greater or less than μ_2. Therefore, the *P-value* obtained from T.DIST.RT function needs to be multiplied by two to cover the right and left tails.

Example 23-8
Company X wants to compare the length of bolts from production batches 20527 and 20528 to find out if the means are equal. Both batches are

manufactured in the same facility using the same machines. Therefore, they are assumed to have equal variance. 41 samples are collected from batch 20527, showing standard deviation of 0.9 mm and mean 37.2 mm. 46 samples are collected from batch 20528, showing standard deviation of 0.8 mm and mean 38.5 mm.

- $n_1 = 41$. $\bar{x}_1 = 38.4$ mm. $S_1 = 0.9$ mm.
- $n_2 = 46$. $\bar{x}_2 = 37.9$ mm. $S_2 = 1.4$ mm.
- H_0: $\mu_1 = \mu_2$
- H_A: $\mu_1 \neq \mu_2$ (two-tailed)
- $S_p = \sqrt{\dfrac{(40\times0.9^2)+(45\times1.4^2)}{41+46-2}} = \sqrt{\dfrac{32.4+88.2}{85}} = 1.1911$
- $T_{test} = \dfrac{38.4-37.9}{1.1911\times\sqrt{\frac{1}{41}+\frac{1}{46}}} = \dfrac{0.5}{0.2558} = 1.9544$
- $\alpha = 0.05$ (default assumption); $df = 85$.
- Critical values are $T_{(0.025;\ 85)} = -1.9883$ and $T_{(0.975;\ 85)} = 1.9883$.
- $lower\ T_{crit} < T_{test} < upper\ T_{crit}$
- $-1.9883 < 1.9544 < 1.9883$; test statistics T_{test} is located inside acceptable area. This test fails to reject null hypothesis.
- Alternatively, we can calculate *P-value* using T.DIST.RT function in Excel. The *P-value* is $0.0270 \times 2 = 0.0540$, which is greater than α (0.05). There is no statistically sufficient evidence to reject null hypothesis.
- This experiment fails to conclude with 95% confidence that bolts from batches 20527 and 20528 have different average length.

Example 23-9
Company X wants to compare the length of bolts from production batches 20527 and 31695 to find out if the means are equal. Both batches are manufactured in different facilities. Therefore, they are assumed to have unequal variances. 41 samples are collected from batch 20527, showing standard deviation of 1.1 mm and mean 37.2 mm. 46 samples are collected from batch 31695, showing standard deviation of 0.8 mm and mean 38.5 mm.

- $n_1 = 41$. $\bar{x}_1 = 38.4$ mm. $S_1 = 0.9$ mm.
- $n_2 = 46$. $\bar{x}_2 = 37.9$ mm. $S_2 = 1.4$ mm.
- H_0: $\mu_1 = \mu_2$
- H_A: $\mu_1 \neq \mu_2$ (two-tailed)
- $T_{test} = \dfrac{38.4-37.9}{\sqrt{\frac{0.9^2}{41}+\frac{1.4^2}{46}}} = \dfrac{0.5}{0.2497} = 2.0022$

- $df = \dfrac{\left(\frac{0.9^2}{41}+\frac{1.4^2}{46}\right)^2}{\frac{(0.9^2/41)^2}{40}+\frac{(1.4^2/46)^2}{45}} = \dfrac{0.00388937}{0.00005010} = 77.6289$, rounded to 78

- $\alpha = 0.05$ (default assumption)
- Critical values are $T_{(0.025;\,78)} = -1.9908$ and $T_{(0.975;\,78)} = 1.9908$.
- $lower\ T_{crit} < upper\ T_{crit} < T_{test}$
- $-1.9908 < 1.9908 < 2.0022$; test statistics T_{test} is located outside acceptable area (in right tail). This test rejects null hypothesis.
- Alternatively, we can calculate *P-value* using T.DIST.RT function in Excel. The *P-value* is $0.0244 \times 2 = 0.0488$, which is less than α (0.05). Such evidence is statistically sufficient to reject null hypothesis.
- This experiment concludes with 95% confidence that bolts from batches 20527 and 31695 have different average length.

Paired Sample T-Test

Paired sample T-test is a special case of two sample T-test. It compares two dependent (paired) samples instead of independent ones. On top of the normal assumptions of T-test, paired sample T-test means every data in sample 1 directly correspond to pair of data in sample 2.

Hypotheses for paired sample T-test:
- H_0: $\mu_1 = \mu_2$
- H_A: $\mu_1 \neq \mu_2$ (two-tailed)
- It is possible to do one-tailed paired samples T-test, but two-tailed tests are far more common.

Test statistics for paired sample T-test:

$$T_{test} = \frac{\bar{x}_{diff}}{S_{diff}/\sqrt{n}}$$

Degrees of freedom (*df*) for paired sample T-test with equal variances:

$$df = n - 1$$

$\bar{x}_{diff}$ is the means of the differences between two samples. S_{diff} is the standard deviation of the differences between paired samples. μ_1 and μ_2 are population means inferred from samples. n is sample size. There is no differentiation between the size of sample 1 and 2 because n_1 must be equal to n_2 for paired sample T-test.

The result of paired sample T-test is interpreted using the comparison of test statistics against critical values. T_{crit} is calculated using T.INV function with *probability* and degrees of freedom as parameters.

- For right-tailed tests: $T_{crit} = T_{(1-\alpha;\, df)}$
- For left-tailed tests: $T_{crit} = T_{(\alpha;\, df)}$
- For two-tailed tests: $upper\ T_{crit} = T_{\left(1-\frac{\alpha}{2};\, df\right)}$ and

$$lower\ T_{crit} < T_{\left(\frac{\alpha}{2};\, df\right)}$$

To reach confidence level of X% where $X = 1 - \alpha$, paired sample T-test rejects null hypothesis (H_0) if:

- $T_{test} > T_{crit}$ for right-tailed tests.
- $T_{test} < T_{crit}$ for left-tailed tests.
- $T_{test} > upper\ T_{crit}$ or $T_{test} < lower\ T_{crit}$ for two-tailed tests.

P-value in T-test is the probability of obtaining values more extreme than critical value. There are three possible ways to calculate *P-value* based on test statistics:

- Use *T table* in Chapter 38.
- Use T.DIST.RT function in Excel with parameters: test statistics T_{test} as *x* and degrees of freedom (*df*).
- Use statistical software of your choice.

For two-tailed tests, the *P-value* obtained from T.DIST.RT function needs to be multiplied by two to cover the right and left tails.

Example 23-10

10 samples are chosen from a batch of products. Two operators are assigned to measure the products. The measurement results are presented in the below table. Is there statistically sufficient evidence that the measurements of the two operators are not equal?

	Opr 1	Opr 2	Diff			Opr 1	Opr 2	Diff
1	56	61	−5		11	55	63	−8
2	45	54	−9		12	72	68	4
3	58	52	6		13	66	64	2
4	61	60	1		14	69	70	−1
5	59	65	−6		15	58	53	5
6	57	50	7		16	64	56	8
7	60	64	−4		17	63	69	−6
8	53	53	0		18	51	42	9
9	68	65	3		19	48	52	−4
10	73	71	2		20	62	65	7

- $n = 20$. $df = 19$.
- H_0: $\mu_1 = \mu_2$
- H_A: $\mu_1 \neq \mu_2$ (two-tailed)
- $\bar{x}_{diff} = \frac{\sum x_{diff}}{n} = 0.55$
- $S_{diff} = \sqrt{\frac{\sum(x_{diff} - \bar{x}_{diff})^2}{n-1}} = 5.6520$
- $T_{test} = \frac{0.55}{5.6520/\sqrt{20}} = 0.4352$
- $\alpha = 0.05$ (default assumption)
- Critical values are $T_{(0.025;\ 19)} = -2.0930$ and $T_{(0.975;\ 19)} = 2.0930$.
- lower T_{crit} < upper T_{crit} < T_{test}
- $-2.0930 < 0.4352 < 2.0930$; test statistics T_{test} is located inside acceptable area. This test fails to reject null hypothesis.
- Alternatively, we can calculate *P-value* using T.DIST.RT function in Excel. The *P-value* is $0.3342 \times 2 = 0.6683$, which is greater than α (0.05). There is no statistically sufficient evidence to reject null hypothesis.
- This experiment fails to conclude with 95% confidence that the measurements of the two operators are not equal.

One-way ANOVA

Analysis of Variance (ANOVA) is a collection of statistical techniques to analyse differences between groups of data. One-way ANOVA is the simplest form of ANOVA, comparing just one independent variable across multiple samples. N-way ANOVA, as the name suggests, compares N independent variables. MANOVA is ANOVA with multiple dependent variables.

Comparing employee salaries in multiple companies is an example of one-way ANOVA. It involves one dependent variable (salary) and one independent variable (company). Two-way ANOVA examines differences of salary (dependent variable) by company (independent variable 1) and gender (independent variable 2). N-way ANOVA is capable to include more independent variables that might impact salary, such as ethnicity, highest level of education and so on. Only one-way ANOVA is discussed in this chapter.

One-way ANOVA compares the mean of data from two or more independent samples using *F distribution*. For example: if dependent variable is salary and independent variable is company, sample data of employee salaries would be collected from different companies.

Assumptions of one-way ANOVA:
- Data is continuous with normal distribution.
- Sample data are randomly selected from population.
- Populations represented by samples have equal variances.
- Equal sample sizes.
- Sample size is sufficient. This follows the general guide of inferential statistics.

Hypotheses for one-way ANOVA:
- H_0: $\mu_1 = \mu_2 = \mu_3 = \cdots = \mu_k$ (population means are equal)
- H_A: population means are not equal

Rejecting null hypothesis indicates that one or more populations have different means, but one-way ANOVA could not directly point out which populations are the different ones.

Test statistics for one-way ANOVA:

$$F_{test} = \frac{SSB/(k-1)}{SSW/\left(\left(\sum_{i=1}^{k} n_i\right) - k\right)}$$

$$SST = SSB + SSW$$

k is the number of groups (sample datasets). n_i is the amount of data in each sample. The sum of all n_i is also known as N_k or the grand total of data count. *SSB* is sum of square between groups. *SSW* is sum of square within groups. *SST* is the total sum of square of the whole experiment.

$$N_k = \sum_{i=1}^{k} n_i$$

One-way ANOVA has two degrees of freedom: df for between (nominator) and df for within (denominator). It is important to note that these values are not interchangeable.

$$df1 = k - 1$$

$$df2 = N_k - k$$

The result of one-sample ANOVA is interpreted using the comparison of test statistics against critical values. F_{crit} is calculated using F.INV.RT function with *probability*, degrees of freedom 1 and degrees of freedom 2 as parameters.

$$F_{crit} = F_{(\alpha;\, df1;\, df2)}$$

To reach confidence level of X% where $X = 1 - \alpha$, one-way ANOVA rejects null hypothesis (H_0) if $F_{test} > F_{crit}$

P-value in one-way ANOVA is the probability of obtaining values more extreme than critical value. There are two possible ways to calculate *P-value* based on test statistics:
- Use F.DIST.RT function in Excel with parameters: test statistics F_{test} as x, degrees of freedom 1 and degrees of freedom 2.
- Use statistical software of your choice.

Example 23-11
Company X wants to compare the length of bolts from production batches 20550, 20551, 20552 and 20553 to find out if the means are equal. All batches are manufactured in the same facility using the same machines. Therefore, they are assumed to have equal variance. 5 samples are collected from each batch as shown in the below table.

	20550	20551	20552	20553
	37.5	38.1	37.7	37.8
	38.2	37.3	42.7	37.4
	38.9	38.6	38.7	38.8
	37.0	39.1	40.1	38.3
	37.4	37.9	40.3	38.2
Mean per sample	37.8	38.2	39.9	38.1
Grand mean	**38.5**			

- $k = 4$. $n_i = 5$. $N_k = 20$.
- $df1 = 3$. $df2 = 16$.

- H_0: $\mu_1 = \mu_2 = \mu_3 = \mu_4$
- H_A: population means are not equal

SST is calculated by subtracting each value with grand mean, then square the results.

20550	20551	20552	20553
$(37.5-38.5)^2 = 1.00$	$(38.1-38.5)^2 = 0.16$	$(37.7-38.5)^2 = 0.64$	$(37.8-38.5)^2 = 0.49$
$(38.2-38.5)^2 = 0.09$	$(37.3-38.5)^2 = 1.44$	$(42.7-38.5)^2 = 17.64$	$(37.4-38.5)^2 = 1.21$
$(38.9-38.5)^2 = 0.16$	$(38.6-38.5)^2 = 0.01$	$(38.7-38.5)^2 = 0.04$	$(38.8-38.5)^2 = 0.09$
$(37.0-38.5)^2 = 2.25$	$(39.1-38.5)^2 = 0.36$	$(40.1-38.5)^2 = 2.56$	$(38.3-38.5)^2 = 0.04$
$(37.4-38.5)^2 = 1.21$	$(37.9-38.5)^2 = 0.36$	$(40.3-38.5)^2 = 3.24$	$(38.2-38.5)^2 = 0.09$

Sum per sample	4.71	2.33	24.12	1.92
SST	**33.08**			

SSW is calculated by subtracting each value with sample mean, then square the results.

20550	20551	20552	20553
$(37.5-37.8)^2 = 0.09$	$(38.1-38.2)^2 = 0.01$	$(37.7-39.9)^2 = 4.84$	$(37.8-38.1)^2 = 0.09$
$(38.2-37.8)^2 = 0.16$	$(37.3-38.2)^2 = 0.81$	$(42.7-39.9)^2 = 7.84$	$(37.4-38.1)^2 = 0.49$
$(38.9-37.8)^2 = 1.21$	$(38.6-38.2)^2 = 0.16$	$(38.7-39.9)^2 = 1.44$	$(38.8-38.1)^2 = 0.49$
$(37.0-37.8)^2 = 0.64$	$(39.1-38.2)^2 = 0.81$	$(40.1-39.9)^2 = 0.04$	$(38.3-38.1)^2 = 0.04$
$(37.4-37.8)^2 = 0.16$	$(37.9-38.2)^2 = 0.09$	$(40.3-39.9)^2 = 0.16$	$(38.2-38.1)^2 = 0.01$

Sum per sample	2.26	1.88	14.32	1.12
SSW	**19.58**			

SSB is calculated by subtracting each sample mean with grand mean, then square the results.

20550	20551	20552	20553
$(37.8-38.5)^2 = 0.49$	$(38.2-38.5)^2 = 0.09$	$(39.9-38.5)^2 = 1.96$	$(39.9-38.5)^2 = 0.16$
$(37.8-38.5)^2 = 0.49$	$(38.2-38.5)^2 = 0.09$	$(39.9-38.5)^2 = 1.96$	$(39.9-38.5)^2 = 0.16$
$(37.8-38.5)^2 = 0.49$	$(38.2-38.5)^2 = 0.09$	$(39.9-38.5)^2 = 1.96$	$(39.9-38.5)^2 = 0.16$
$(37.8-38.5)^2 = 0.49$	$(38.2-38.5)^2 = 0.09$	$(39.9-38.5)^2 = 1.96$	$(39.9-38.5)^2 = 0.16$
$(37.8-38.5)^2 = 0.49$	$(38.2-38.5)^2 = 0.09$	$(39.9-38.5)^2 = 1.96$	$(39.9-38.5)^2 = 0.16$

Sum per sample	2.45	0.45	9.80	0.80
SSB	**13.50**			

Note that there is no need to calculate all three values (SST, SSW and SSB). After calculating SST and SSW, SSB can be calculated by simply subtracting SSW from SST. In this example: $33.08 - 19.58 = 13.50$.

After knowing the values of SSB and SSW:

- $F_{test} = \dfrac{13.50/3}{19.58/16} = \dfrac{4.5}{1.2238} = 3.6772$
- $\alpha = 0.05$ (default assumption)
- Critical value is $F_{(0.05;\,3;\,16)} = 3.2389$. This can be obtained from F distribution table for $\alpha = 0.05$ in column 3, row 16.
- $F_{crit} < F_{test}$
- $3.2389 < 3.6772$; test statistics. This test rejects null hypothesis.
- Alternatively, we can calculate *P-value* using F.DIST.RT function in Excel. The *P-value* is 0.0346, which is less than α (0.05). Such evidence is statistically sufficient to reject null hypothesis.
- This experiment concludes with 95% confidence that the average of bolt length in the tested batches are not equal.

24. HYPOTHESIS TESTING: NON-PARAMETRIC TESTS

This chapter discusses non-parametric tests: hypothesis tests that do not make assumption about sample data distribution. Before continuing with this chapter, it is strongly recommended to review Chapter 20 about the principles of hypothesis testing.

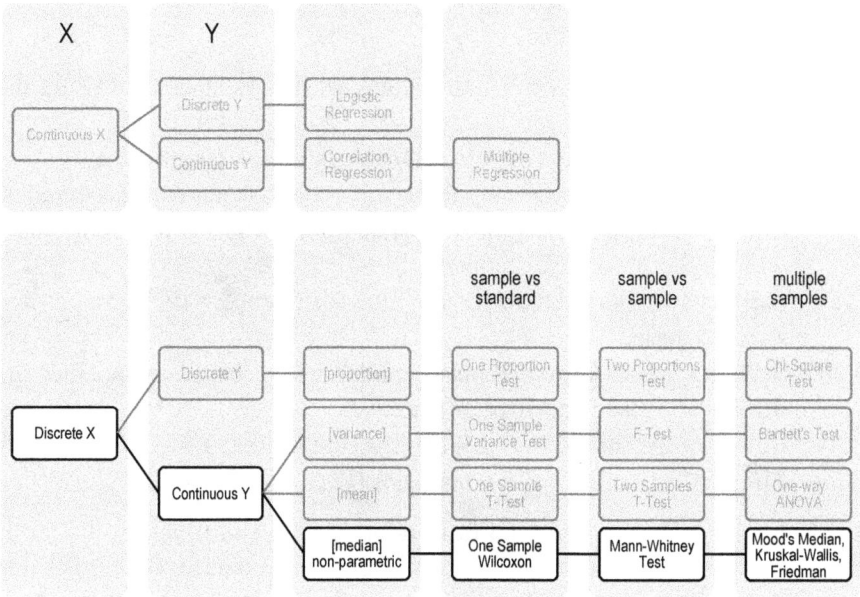

Figure 24-1 Hypothesis Testing (non-parametric tests)

Discussions in this chapter will focus more on small samples with less than 20 data. Using non-parametric hypothesis testing with large sample requires additional calculation because larger samples will gradually follow normal distribution (central limit theorem). Limiting the discussion to small sample size will help to understand the concepts of non-parametric techniques.

One Sample Wilcoxon Test

One sample Wilcoxon test is used to analyse a sample dataset to infer the median of population (η) and compare it against a given value (m). This technique is used instead of one sample T-test if data do not follow normal distribution.

Assumptions of one sample Wilcoxon test:
- Data do not need to be normally distributed.
- Sample data are randomly selected from population.
- Population has symmetric distribution. This can be observed by visual tool such as Boxplot.

Hypotheses for one sample Wilcoxon test:
- H_0: $\eta = m$
- H_A: $\eta > m$ (right-tailed) or
  $\eta < m$ (left-tailed) or
  $\eta \neq m$ (two-tailed)

Test statistics for sample with small amount of data is calculated using the following steps:
- Calculate the differences between each value and target value (m).
- Put rank 1 to n to each data. Rank 1 is given to data with the smallest difference without the signs (absolute value). Rank n is given to data with largest absolute difference.
- Skip data that is equal to target value (difference = 0), do not assign ranks to these.
- Separate the ranks into Ranks + and Ranks − based on whether the difference value is positive or negative.
- Calculate the sum of Ranks + and the sum of Ranks −
- The smallest sum is the test statistics (W_{test}) value.

Critical value (W_{crit}) is obtained from reference table in Chapter 38 with α, hypothesis type (one-tailed or two-tailed) and the amount of data in sample (n) as parameters. One sample Wilcoxon test rejects null hypothesis (H_0) if test statistics is greater than critical value.

Example 24-1

Random samples of 10 patients diagnosed with a particular disease are presented below, showing the age of each patient. Population data is assumed to be symmetrical. Is there sufficient statistical evidence to support hypothesis that the median value is not equal to 47?

Sample	1	2	3	4	5	6	7	8	9	10
Age	75	60	23	45	20	78	52	44	58	39

- $n = 10$. $m = 47$.
- H_0: $\eta = m$
- H_A: $\eta \neq 47$ (two-tailed test)
- $\alpha = 0.05$ (default assumption)

First, calculate the difference between each value and target value (m) of 47. To help with the next step, prepare the absolute values of those differences.

Sample	1	2	3	4	5	6	7	8	9	10
Age	75	60	23	45	20	78	52	44	58	39
Difference	28	13	−24	−2	−27	31	5	−3	11	−8
Diff (abs)	28	13	24	2	27	31	5	3	11	8

The next step is to rank the absolute values of differences from the smallest to the largest.

Sample	1	2	3	4	5	6	7	8	9	10
Age	75	60	23	45	20	78	52	44	58	39
Diff (abs)	28	13	24	2	27	31	5	3	11	8
Ranks	9	6	7	1	8	10	3	2	5	4

Split the ranks into ranks + and ranks − depending on the signs of difference.

Sample	1	2	3	4	5	6	7	8	9	10
Age	75	60	23	45	20	78	52	44	58	39
Difference	28	13	−24	−2	−27	31	5	−3	11	−8
Ranks +	9	6				10	3		5	
Ranks −			7	1	8			2		4

- The sum of all values in ranks + is 33.
- The sum of all values in ranks − is 22.
- The smallest sum is 22, this is the test statistics (W_{test}).

Critical value is obtained from Chapter 38. Table 24-A below shows relevant part of the reference table for easier use in this discussion.

n	One-tailed		Two-tailed	
	$\alpha = 0.01$	$\alpha = 0.05$	$\alpha = 0.01$	$\alpha = 0.05$
10	5	10	3	8
11	7	13	5	10
12	9	17	7	13
13	12	21	9	17
14	15	25	12	21

Table 24-A Critical values for Wilcoxon Signed Ranks Test

Example 24-1 is two-tailed problem because it seeks to find if the median is not equal to 47. Therefore, the critical value (W_{crit}) for this example is 8.
- Test statistics (22) is greater than critical value (8).
- This experiment rejects null hypothesis. It concludes with 95% confidence that median of patients' age is not equal to 47.

One Sample Sign Test

One sample sign test is used to analyse a sample dataset to infer the median of population (η) and compare it against a given value (m). This technique is very similar to one sample Wilcoxon test with one key difference: it does not require population with symmetrical distribution.

Hypotheses for one sample sign test:
- H_0: $\eta = m$
- H_A: $\eta > m$ (right-tailed) or
  $\eta < m$ (left-tailed) or
  $\eta \neq m$ (two-tailed)

Test statistics for sample with small amount of data is calculated using the following steps:
- Mark each value with + or − sign, depending on whether a value is greater or smaller than target value (m).
- Count the signs of + and − from the sample.
- For right-tailed problem, test statistics is the count of + signs.
- For left-tailed problem, test statistics is the count of − signs.
- For two-tailed problem, test statistics is the bigger one from the count of + and − signs.

Test acceptance is observed using the help of Binomial table, which can be obtained using BINOM.DIST function in Excel. This function takes four parameters: *number_s*, *trials*, *probability* and *cumulative*. The first parameter (*number_s*) is the sample size (n). The number of *trials* (x) is filled with values between 0 and n. *Probability* is set to 0.5 for one sample sign test. *Cumulative* is set to 1.

	1	2	3	4	5	6	7	8	9	10	11	12
0	0.5000	0.2500	0.1250	0.0625	0.0313	0.0156	0.0078	0.0039	0.0020	0.0010	0.0005	0.0002
1	1.0000	0.7500	0.5000	0.3125	0.1875	0.1094	0.0625	0.0352	0.0195	0.0107	0.0059	0.0032
2		1.0000	0.8750	0.6875	0.5000	0.3438	0.2266	0.1445	0.0898	0.0547	0.0327	0.0193
3			1.0000	0.9375	0.8125	0.6563	0.5000	0.3633	0.2539	0.1719	0.1133	0.0730
4				1.0000	0.9688	0.8906	0.7734	0.6367	0.5000	0.3770	0.2744	0.1938
5					1.0000	0.9844	0.9375	0.8555	0.7461	0.6230	0.5000	0.3872
6						1.0000	0.9922	0.9648	0.9102	0.8281	0.7256	0.6128
7							1.0000	0.9961	0.9805	0.9453	0.8867	0.8062
8								1.0000	0.9980	0.9893	0.9673	0.9270
9									1.0000	0.9990	0.9941	0.9807
10										1.0000	0.9995	0.9968
11											1.0000	0.9998
12												1.0000

Table 24-B Binomial Distribution for One Sample Sign Test

Table 24-B above shows the Binomial distribution table for one sample sign test. The columns in the table represent n, the amount of data in sample. The rows are the number of trials, they range from zero to n. For a particular test, data from one column will be observed. The number of trials showing values less than α are considered to be inside rejection region. Otherwise, they are considered to be inside acceptance region.

As an example, for sample size = 12, the number of trials (x) of 0, 1 and 2 have the values of 0.0002, 0.0032 and 0.0193. These values are less than α (default assumption is 0.05), so $x = 0$, 1 and 2 are considered as rejection region. Starting from 3 trials ($x = 3$), the value shown in the table is 0.0730, which is greater than α. Therefore, x = 3, 4, 5, 6, 7, 8, 9 and 10 are considered as acceptance region.

$x =$	0	1	2		3	4	5	6	7	8	9	10	11	12
	0.0002	0.0032	0.0193	0.0500	0.0730	0.1938	0.3872	0.6128	0.8062	0.9270	0.9807	0.9968	0.9998	1.0000
	rejection			α	acceptance									

One sample sign test rejects null hypothesis (H_0) if test statistics is one of the x values in reject region.

Example 24-2

Random samples of 10 patients diagnosed with a particular disease are presented below, showing the age of each patient. Population data might asymmetrical. Is there sufficient statistical evidence to support hypothesis that the median value is not equal to 47?

Sample	1	2	3	4	5	6	7	8	9	10
Age	75	60	23	45	20	78	52	44	58	39

- $n = 10$. $m = 47$.
- H_0: $\eta = m$
- H_A: $\eta \neq 47$ (two-tailed test)
- $\alpha = 0.05$ (default assumption)

Mark each value with $+$ or $-$ sign.

Sample	1	2	3	4	5	6	7	8	9	10
Age	75	60	23	45	20	78	52	44	58	39
Sign	+	+	−	−	−	+	+	−	+	−

- Count of $+$ signs: 5.
- Count of $-$ signs: 5.
- Test statistics $= \max(5, 5) = 5$.

For $n = 10$, the rejection and acceptance regions based on Binomial table:

$x =$	0	1		2	3	4	5	6	7	8	9	10
	0.0010	0.0107	0.0500	0.0547	0.1719	0.3770	0.6230	0.8281	0.9453	0.9893	0.9990	1.0000
	rejection		α					acceptance				

- Test statistics (5) is within acceptance region.
- This experiment fails to reject null hypothesis. It fails to conclude with 95% confidence that median of patients' age is not equal to 47.

Mann-Whitney Test

Mann-Whitney test is a non-parametric hypothesis testing used to compare the median of two populations (η_1 and η_2) based on two set of samples. This technique is often used for pilot studies to see if change in process have impact on performance.

Assumptions for Mann-Whitney test:
- Each sample is independent.

- Samples do not need to follow normal distribution.
- Samples do not need to have equal variances.
- Samples have same shape distribution.
- Sample data are randomly selected from population.

Hypotheses for Mann-Whitney test:
- H_0: $\eta_1 = \eta_2$ (two populations are equal)
- H_A: $\eta_1 \neq \eta_2$ (two populations are not equal)

Test statistics for sample with small amount of data is calculated using the following steps:
- Combine data from two samples, sort them in ascending order.
- The smallest value gets the rank of 1 and the largest value gets the rank of Y.
- For identical values, add the ranks of those values as if they are not identical, then calculate the average. Each value is assigned with the average rank.
- Separate values and assigned ranks back into two samples.
- Calculate test statistics U_{test}.

Formula to calculate test statistics for Mann-Whitney test:

$$U_1 = (n_1 \times n_2) + \left(0.5 \times n_1 \times (n_1 + 1)\right) - R_1$$

$$U_2 = (n_1 \times n_2) + \left(0.5 \times n_2 \times (n_2 + 1)\right) - R_2$$

$$U_{test} = min(U_1;\ U_2)$$

n_1 and n_2 are the size of sample 1 and 2. R_1 is the sum of all ranks in sample 1; R_2 is the sum of all ranks in sample 2. $U_1 + U_2$ is always equal to $n_1 \times n_2$.

Critical value (U_{crit}) is obtained from Mann-Whitney U Test table as presented in Table 24-C. Mann-Whitney test rejects null hypothesis (H_0) if test statistics is less than critical value.

n_2	n_1																	
	3	4	5	6	7	8	9	10	11	12	13	14	15	16	17	18	19	20
3	0	0	0	1	1	2	2	3	3	4	4	5	5	6	6	7	7	8
4	0	0	1	2	3	4	4	5	6	7	8	9	10	11	11	12	13	14
5	0	1	2	3	5	6	7	8	9	11	12	13	14	15	17	18	19	20
6	1	2	3	5	6	8	10	11	13	14	16	17	19	21	22	24	25	27
7	1	3	5	6	8	10	12	14	16	18	20	22	24	26	28	30	32	34
8	2	4	6	8	10	13	15	17	19	22	24	26	29	31	34	36	38	41
9	2	4	7	10	12	15	17	20	23	26	28	31	34	37	39	42	45	48
10	3	5	8	11	14	17	20	23	26	29	33	36	39	42	45	48	52	55

n_2									n_1									
	3	4	5	6	7	8	9	10	11	12	13	14	15	16	17	18	19	20
11	3	6	9	13	16	19	23	26	30	33	37	40	44	47	51	55	58	62
12	4	7	11	14	18	22	26	29	33	37	41	45	49	53	57	61	65	69
13	4	8	12	16	20	24	28	33	37	41	45	50	54	59	63	67	72	76
14	5	9	13	17	22	26	31	36	40	45	50	55	59	64	67	74	78	83
15	5	10	14	19	24	29	34	39	44	49	54	59	64	70	75	80	85	90
16	6	11	15	21	26	31	37	42	47	53	59	64	70	75	81	86	92	98
17	6	11	17	22	28	34	39	45	51	57	63	67	75	81	87	93	99	105
18	7	12	18	24	30	36	42	48	55	61	67	74	80	86	93	99	106	112
19	7	13	19	25	32	38	45	52	58	65	72	78	85	92	99	106	113	119
20	8	14	20	27	34	41	48	55	62	69	76	83	90	98	105	112	119	127

Table 24-C Mann-Whitney U Test Table for $\alpha = 0.05$

Example 24-3

Two samples of students' exam scores are taken from two different schools. A research team wants to find out if the medians of the two populations represented by the samples are different.

School A	78	75	56	89	92	78	76	64	80	78	65	77
School B	69	71	78	85	90	75	78	91	60	73		

- $n_1 = 12$. $n_2 = 10$.
- H_0: $\eta_1 = \eta_2$
- H_A: $\eta_1 \neq \eta_2$
- $\alpha = 0.05$ (default assumption)

First step is combining data from two samples and sort them in ascending order. Ranks are assigned to each value, starting from the lowest exam score.

Score	56	60	64	65	69	71	73	75	75	76	77	78	78	78	78	78	80	85	89	90	91	92
Sort	1	2	3	4	5	6	7	8	9	10	11	12	13	14	15	16	17	18	19	20	21	22
Rank	1	2	3	4	5	6	7	8.5	8.5	10	11	14	14	14	14	14	17	18	19	20	21	22

- For values (exam scores) with no duplicates, the sort order becomes the rank of that score. For values with duplicates, rank is the average of sort order of all exam scores of that value.
- There are two students in the samples with exam score 75. These scores have the sort order of 8 and 9. The average of 8 and 9 is 8.5. Therefore, each of the value of 75 gets the rank of 8.5.
- There are five students in the samples with exam score 78. These scores have the sort order of 12, 13, 14, 15 and 16. The average is (12 + 13 + 14 + 15 + 16) / 5 = 14. Therefore, each of the value of 78 gets the rank of 14.

After ranks are assigned to all exam scores, these scores are separated back into two samples.

School A		School B	
Scores	Ranks	Scores	Ranks
78	14	69	5
75	8.5	71	6
56	1	78	14
89	19	85	18
92	22	90	20
78	14	75	8.5
76	10	78	14
64	3	91	21
80	17	60	2
78	14	73	7
65	4		
77	11		
Total R_1	137.5	Total R_2	115.5

U_1 and U_2 can be calculated from the above tables:

- $U_1 = (12 \times 10) + (0.5 \times 12 \times 13) - 137.5 = 60.5$
- $U_2 = (12 \times 10) + (0.5 \times 10 \times 11) - 115.5 = 59.5$
- $U_{test} = min(60.5; 59.5) = 59.5$
- Critical value is 29. This value is obtained from column 12 (n_1) and row 10 (n_2) in Table 24-C.
- $U_{crit} < U_{test}$
- $29.0 < 59.5$; this experiment fails to reject null hypothesis. It fails to conclude with 95% confidence that median of two schools are different.

Mood's Median Test

Mood's Median test is a non-parametric hypothesis testing used to compare the median of multiple populations (η_1 to η_k) based on multiple samples. This technique is often seen as an extension of one sample sign test to handle multiple samples with the help of chi-squared test.

Common uses of Mood's median test include the measurement of customer satisfaction level between different account managers and comparing the median of production speed between different machines. This hypothesis test is robust with respect to outliers.

Assumptions for Mood's median test:
- Each sample is independent.
- Samples do not need to follow normal distribution.
- Sample data are randomly selected from population.
- Populations have same shape distribution.

Hypotheses for Mood's median test:
- H_0: $\eta_1 = \eta_2 = \eta_3 = \cdots = \eta_k$ (all populations are equal)
- H_A: not all populations are equal

Test statistics is calculated using the following steps:
- Calculate the grand median from all samples.
- For each sample, count how many observations are greater than grand median and how many are less than grand median.
- Create contingency table with k columns and 2 rows. k is the number of samples.
- Perform chi-squared test on the contingency table. If needed, please refer to Chapter 22 for discussion about this chi-squared test.
- Calculate χ^2_{test} and χ^2_{crit}
- Reject null hypothesis if $\chi^2_{crit} < \chi^2_{test}$

Example 24-4
Three samples of students' exam scores are taken from three different schools. A research team wants to find out if the medians of the three populations represented by the samples are different.

School A	78	75	56	89	92	78	76	64	80	78	65	77
School B	69	71	78	85	90	75	78	91	60	73		
School C	84	95	90	78	86	97	91	87	70	89	83	

- $n_1 = 12$. $n_2 = 10$. $n_3 = 11$. $k = 3$.
- H_0: all populations have equal median
- H_A: not all populations have equal median
- $\alpha = 0.05$ (default assumption)
- Total 33 observations are merged and sorted: 56, 60, 64, 65, 69, 70, 71, 73, 75, 75, 76, 77, 78, 78, 78, 78, 78, 78, 80, 83, 84, 85, 86, 87, 89, 89, 90, 90, 91, 91, 92, 95, 97.
- The median is the exam score at location #17 in the sorted list. It is the score of 78. This is the grand median of all samples.
- In sample from school A, there are 3 students with scores above grand median and there are 6 students with scores below grand median.
- In sample from school B, there are 3 students with scores above grand

median and there are 5 students with scores below grand median.
- In sample from school C, there are 9 students with scores above grand median and there is 1 student with scores below grand median.

The following contingency table is created:

		School A	School B	School C	Total
> median	observed	3	3	9	15
	expected	5.0000	4.4444	5.5556	
< median	observed	6	5	1	12
	expected	4.0000	3.5556	4.4444	
Total		9	8	10	27

- $\chi^2_{test} = \sum \frac{(observed - expected)^2}{expected}$
- $\chi^2_{test} = \frac{4}{5} + \frac{2.0864}{4.4444} + \frac{11.8642}{5.5556} + \frac{4}{4} + \frac{2.0864}{3.5556} + \frac{11.8642}{4.4444} = 7.6613$
- Degrees of freedom (df) is ($\#rows - 1$) × ($\#columns - 1$) = 2 × 1 = 2.
- Critical value is obtained from row 2 (df) and column 0.05 (α) in reference table from Chapter 38. $\chi^2_{crit} = \chi^2_{(0.05;\ 2)} = 5.9915$.
- $\chi^2_{crit} < \chi^2_{test}$; 5.9915 < 7.6613, this shows that test statistics is located inside rejection area. This test rejects null hypothesis.
- This experiment concludes with 95% confidence that not all of the three schools have equal median.

Kruskal-Wallis Test

Kruskal-Wallis test is a non-parametric hypothesis testing used to compare the median of multiple populations (η_1 to η_k) based on multiple samples. This technique is an alternative to Mood's median test.

Key comparison of Mood's median test and Kruskal-Wallis test:
- Mood's median test requires datasets to have same shape distribution, Kruskal Wallis test does not have this requirement.
- Mood's median test is robust to outliers. Kruskal-Wallis test is sensitive to outliers.
- Both Mood's median test and Kruskal-Wallis test use chi-squared distribution.

Assumptions for Kruskal-Wallis test:
- Each sample is independent.
- Samples do not need to follow normal distribution.
- Sample data are randomly selected from population.

Hypotheses for Kruskal Wallis test:
- H_0: $\eta_1 = \eta_2 = \eta_3 = \cdots = \eta_k$ (all populations are equal)
- H_A: not all populations are equal

Test statistics is calculated using the following steps:
- Combine data from all samples, sort them in ascending order.
- The smallest value gets the rank of 1 and the largest value gets the rank of Y.
- For identical values, add the ranks of those values as if they are not identical, then calculate the average. Each value is assigned with the average rank.
- Separate values and assigned ranks back into the samples.
- Calculate total ranks for each sample.
- Calculate test statistics H.

Formula to calculate test statistics for Kruskal Wallis test:

$$x^2{}_{test} = H = \left(\frac{12}{N(N+1)} \sum \frac{T_i{}^2}{n_i} \right) - 3(N+1)$$

n_i is the size of ith sample. N is total number of data (sum of all n_i) T_i is the sum of all ranks in i^{th} sample.

Critical value is obtained from *chi-squared distribution table*:

$$x^2{}_{crit} = x^2{}_{(\alpha;\, df)}$$

α is the Alpha risk of the experiment. If unknown, the default assumption is 0.05. Degrees of freedom (df) is the number of samples (k) minus 1.

Example 24-5
Three samples of students' exam scores are taken from three different schools. A research team wants to find out if the medians of the three populations represented by the samples are different.

School A	78	75	56	89	92	78	76	64	80	78	65	77
School B	69	71	78	85	90	75	78	91	60	73		
School C	84	95	90	78	86	97	91	87	70	89	83	

- $n_1 = 12$. $n_2 = 10$. $n_3 = 11$. $N = 33$. $k = 3$.
- H_0: all populations have equal median
- H_A: not all populations have equal median
- $\alpha = 0.05$ (default assumption)

First step is combining data from all samples and sort them in ascending order. Ranks are assigned to each value, starting from the lowest exam score.

Score	56	60	64	65	69	70	71	73	75	75	76	77	78	78	78	78	78
Sort	1	2	3	4	5	6	7	8	9	10	11	12	13	14	15	16	17
Rank	1	2	3	4	5	6	7	8	9.5	9.5	11	12	15.5	15.5	15.5	15.5	15.5

Score	78	80	83	84	85	86	87	89	89	90	90	91	91	92	95	97
Sort	18	19	20	21	22	23	24	25	26	27	28	29	30	31	32	33
Rank	15.5	19	20	21	22	23	24	25.5	25.5	27.5	27.5	29.5	29.5	31	32	33

- For values (exam scores) with no duplicates, the sort order becomes the rank of that score. For values with duplicates, rank is the average of sort order of all exam scores of that value.
- There are two students in the samples with exam score 75. These scores have the sort order of 9 and 10. The average of 9 and 10 is 9.5. Therefore, each of the value of 75 gets the rank of 9.5. Same calculations are applied to exam score 89, 90 and 91.
- There are six students in the samples with exam score 78. These scores have the sort order of 13, 14, 15, 16, 17 and 18. The average is (13 + 14 + 15 + 16 + 17 + 18) / 6 = 15.5. Therefore, each of the value of 78 gets the rank of 15.5.

After ranks are assigned to all exam scores, these scores are separated back into the samples.

														Total
School A	Score	78	75	56	89	92	78	76	64	80	78	65	77	
	Rank	15.5	9.5	1	25.5	31	15.5	11	3	19	15.5	4	12	**162.5**
School B	Score	69	71	78	85	90	75	78	91	60	73			
	Rank	5	7	15.5	22	27.5	9.5	15.5	29.5	2	8			**141.5**
School C	Score	84	95	90	78	86	97	91	87	70	89	83		
	Rank	21	32	27.5	15.5	23	33	29.5	24	6	25.5	20		**257.0**

H can be calculated from the above tables:

- $$\chi^2_{test} = H = \left(\frac{12}{33 \times 34} \times \left(\frac{162.5^2}{12} + \frac{141.5^2}{10} + \frac{257^2}{11} \right) \right) - 102 = 7.1679$$
- $k = 3$. $df = 2$.
- Critical value is obtained from row 2 (df) and column 0.05 (α) in reference table from Chapter 38. $\chi^2_{crit} = \chi^2_{(0.05; 2)} = 5.9915$
- $\chi^2_{crit} < \chi^2_{test}$; 5.9915 < 7.1679, this shows that test statistics is located inside rejection area. This test rejects null hypothesis.
- This experiment concludes with 95% confidence that not all of the three schools have equal median.

Friedman Test

Friedman test is another alternative of non-parametric hypothesis testing for comparing the results of repeated measurements of the same group. This technique requires three samples or more. Each sample represents one measurement, also known as treatment. Every observation within a sample must have direct connection to one observation in other samples.

Assumptions for Friedman test:
- One group is measured on three or more occasions.
- No interaction between blocks (rows) and treatments (columns).
- Samples do not need to follow normal distribution.
- Sample data are randomly selected from population.

Hypotheses for Friedman test:
- H_0: all treatments are equal
- H_A: not all treatments are equal

Test statistics is calculated using the following steps:
- Assign rank to each observation in a row, independent from other rows.
- Calculate the sums of each column, then square them.
- Calculate test statistics Q_{test}
- Obtain critical value Q_{crit}
- Reject null hypothesis if $Q_{crit} < Q_{test}$

Formula to calculate test statistics for Friedman test:

$$Q_{test} = \left(\frac{12}{nk(k+1)} \sum R_i^2\right) - 3n(k+1)$$

n is the size of each sample (the number of rows/blocks). k is the number of samples/groups/columns/treatments. R_i is the sum of ranks in i^{th} sample.

There are two different ways of obtaining critical value:
- If n is 20 or less and k is 6 or less, use Friedman table.
- If n is greater than 20 and/or k is greater than 6, critical value is obtained from *chi-squared distribution table* $\chi^2_{crit} = \chi^2_{(\alpha;\, df)}$ with $df = k - 1$.

n	1	2	3	4	5	6	7	8	9	10
$k = 3$	-	-	6.000	6.500	6.400	7.000	7.143	6.250	6.222	6.200
$k = 4$	-	6.000	7.400	7.800	7.800	7.600	7.800	7.650	7.667	7.680
$k = 5$	-	7.600	8.533	8.800	8.960	9.067	9.143	9.200	9.244	9.280
$k = 6$	-	9.143	9.857	10.29	10.49	10.57	10.67	10.71	10.78	10.80

n	11	12	13	14	15	16	17	18	19	20
$k = 3$	6.545	6.500	6.615	6.143	6.400	6.500	6.118	6.333	6.421	6.300
$k = 4$	7.691	7.700	7.800	7.714	7.720	7.800	7.800	7.733	7.863	7.800
$k = 5$	9.309	9.333	9.354	9.371	9.387	9.400	9.412	9.422	9.432	9.400
$k = 6$	10.84	10.86	10.89	10.90	10.92	10.96	10.95	10.95	11.00	11.00

Table 24-D Friedman Table for $\alpha = 0.05$

Example 24-6

Four production machines received minor repair in January. Three samples are taken from four production machines, measuring their operating temperature in January (before repair), February and March. A research team wants to find out if the repair changes the machines' temperature.

	Jan (Baseline)	Feb	Mar
Machine A	70.1°C	68.9°C	65.3°C
Machine B	65.2°C	59.7°C	62.5°C
Machine C	71.4°C	68.7°C	68.3°C
Machine D	75.6°C	75.4°C	72.1°C

- H_0: treatment has no impact
- H_A: treatment has impact
- $\alpha = 0.05$ (default assumption)
- $n = 4$. $k = 3$.

Ranks are assigned for each row/block:

	Jan (Baseline)		Feb		Mar	
	Temp	Rank	Temp	Rank	Temp	Rank
Machine A	70.1°C	3	68.9°C	2	65.3°C	1
Machine B	65.2°C	3	59.7°C	1.5	59.7°C	1.5
Machine C	71.4°C	3	68.7°C	2	68.3°C	1
Machine D	75.6°C	3	75.4°C	2	72.1°C	1
Total R_i		12		7.5		4.5

- $Q_{test} = \left(\frac{12}{12 \times 4} \times (12^2 + 7.5^2 + 4.5^2) \right) - (12 \times 4) = 7.125$

- Since $n < 20$ and $k < 6$, this experiment uses Friedman table instead of chi-squared table.
- $Q_{crit} = 6.500$ is obtained from Table 24-D.
- $Q_{crit} < Q_{test}$; $6.500 < 7.125$, this shows that there is statistically sufficient evidence to reject null hypothesis.
- This experiment concludes with 95% confidence that the repair changes the machines' temperature.

IMPROVE PHASE

25. UNDERSTANDING IMPROVE PHASE

The fourth phase of Six Sigma DMAIC project is the *Improve phase*. As the name suggests, this phase focused on improving the system outcome using the confirmed factors from Analyze phase.

Let us begin the discussion on Improve phase by reviewing the five phases of DMAIC and the $Y = f(X)$ formula.

DEFINE	MEASURE	ANALYZE	IMPROVE	CONTROL
• Which Y	• Collect data • X candidates	• Confirm Xs	• X values to solve Y • Pilot implementation	• Control Xs • Full implementation

Figure 25-1 Improve phase in DMAIC

Improve phase uses confirmed Xs factors from Measure phase and finds the values for X to improve Y. Following the goal statement of a project, the main question that needs to be answered is: what are the most optimal values of X factors to achieve best outcome of Y?

From Lean perspective, the improvement of Xs can be achieved through implementing workflow pulled by customer demand, error proofing (*poka yoke*) or other innovation techniques. These methods are generally applicable if subject matter expert is available with sufficient knowledge about X.

From Six Sigma perspective, the improvement of Xs is achieved using *Design of Experiments* (DOE) technique, a branch of applied statistics. It is a systematic approach to understand how a process and its parameters (X factors) affects the outcome variable (Y).

Higher value of X parameter does not necessarily bring improvement to Y. Baking pizza, for example, requires oven to be set on temperature from 250°C to 320°C for electric or gas oven. However, when wood oven is used, the result is obtained with temperature from 420°C to 500°C.

Simply raising oven temperature will not necessarily improve the result. Increasing temperature to 800°C does not make better pizza. Using wood oven temperature range for electric oven will also bring poor results, this is an example of how combination of factors impacts the end result of a production system.

Design of Experiment focuses on finding the set of values of multiple system parameters (X) that will bring better outcome of Y, assuming that some of the factors might have combined effects in determining results. Depending the data type of each factor, adding more factors into calculation might bring exponentially increased complexity.

Typical steps of Improve phase in DMAIC include:
- *Find (candidate) solutions* using Lean techniques or Design of Experiment (DOE).
- *Perform pilot implementation.* It is usually a wise idea to implement the solution on a limited scope before the bis-scale implementation. This will help to minimise setback if some factors were overlooked during the analysis process. This step should also help to identify potential implementation risks.
- *Analyse and verify the results of pilot implementation.* This step is a mini version of DMAIC Analyze phase. It can use the principles of hypothesis testing to confirm (or disprove) that the candidate solution is working as expected. Solution needs to actually solve the problem, have the characteristics of capable and stable process, adaptable to the organisational structure, suitable for operational procedures and does not cause safety issue.
- *Mitigate solution risks* that were identified during earlier phase. Lessons learned from pilot implementation are usually useful for risk mitigation. FMEA (see Chapter 14) can be used to help with prioritisation of risk mitigation.
- *Write documentation* on updated processes based on proposed solution. It is critically important to document the changes during this step because it is likely to be forgotten once the project enters the next phase.
- *Provide training.* After the new process is properly documented, the next logical step is to provide training to system users/operators before

the large-scale implementation of the improvement. This will ensure that new process is well understood from the beginning.

Improve phase might discover multiple possible solutions. These solutions could be complimentary or mutually exclusive.

- For *complimentary solutions*, each solution fixes the problem (could be partial), but when some solutions are implemented together, they help to achieve better results. Rank candidate solutions based on the expected contribution to improvement, cost and time to implement, resource availability and other constraints within the organisation to help with selection process.
- In *mutually exclusive solutions*, if one solution is selected, the others cannot be chosen anymore. Pilot implementation is critical for this situation because it allows an organisation to analyse a candidate solution with minimised risk.

Ideally, any organisation would like to find permanent solution to their problems. This permanent solution supports the long-term strategic goals of the organisation, it is often referred to as *strategic solution*.

A *tactical solution* can be chosen when the cost and resources required for a permanent solution is considered too high or there is not enough time to work on strategic solution. In theory, tactical (or interim) solution should have short lifespan yet still align with long-term strategic roadmap. It should be replaced with strategic solution as soon as possible, no later than the end of its limited lifespan.

Tactical solution is often confused with quick patch that does not really solve the primary cause of the problem, but able to help an organisation to achieve short-term goal. Having an interim solution is not a bad thing. However, continuing the use of interim solution beyond its limited lifetime could cause a number of unwanted consequences.

DMAIC methodology is more suited for finding strategic solution. However, it is theoretically possible to use it to discover tactical solution. Control Plan and Response Plan (deliverables from Control phase) should be applied to strategic solution instead of an interim one. A project to upgrade interim to permanent solution should take into account the necessary steps to remove the interim solution it replaces.

Last but not least, even the best process will not yield the expected results if the operators of the process do not fully understand it. The important (and often overlooked) steps in Improve phase are documentation and training. These two steps facilitate the gaps between theoretical improvement and an effective implementation.

26. LEAN IMPROVEMENT

Lean improvement allows DMAIC team to find optimal solution for the confirmed X factors without going into complex DOE calculations. For example, a company producing perishable goods have an issue of distribution stores returning high number of products past expiry dates. Lean analysis shows that majority of products already stayed in the warehouse for too long before they were sent to distribution stores. Lean improvement establishes pull-based production system so that goods are produced at the speed of customer demand, eliminating the need to store excess products in the warehouse.

Other principles of Lean improvement (error-proofing and six thinking hats) will be discussed briefly at the end of this chapter. Please review Chapter 04 about the basics of Lean principles if you need a refresher.

Pull-based System

The main concept of Lean is waste elimination. Anything that does not add value to a production system is a waste. There are 9 types of waste that Lean principles aim to eliminate: transportation, inventory, motion, waiting, overproduction, overprocessing, defect, skill underutilised and space.

Pull-based principle is a Lean technique to improve production process based on the speed of customer demand. Producing as many as possible will result in inventory, overproduction and space wastes. Transportation, motion and waiting wastes are often observable, depending on how the production system is built.

Lean uses three measurements to generate outputs based on pull from customer demand: cycle time, lead time and takt time.

- *Cycle time* is the time needed to complete the production of a single count of product or service from start to finish.
- *Lead time* is the time needed to complete production of a single count of product or service from the time of customer demand until the product or service reaches the customer. Cycle time is a subset of lead time.
- *Takt time* is the time needed to satisfy the rate of customer demand, also known as the pull.

A pull-based production system is achieved when *lead time* is equal to *takt time*. This will allow deliverables to be made only for actual demands (*Just-In-Time* principle, known as JIT) instead of pushing overproduction just in case there is a higher demand in the future (this is known as JIC, the opposite of JIT). The ideal solution is to reach *one piece plow*, or at least reduce *Work In Progress* (WIP) as much as possible. Please refer to Chapter 04 to review these concepts.

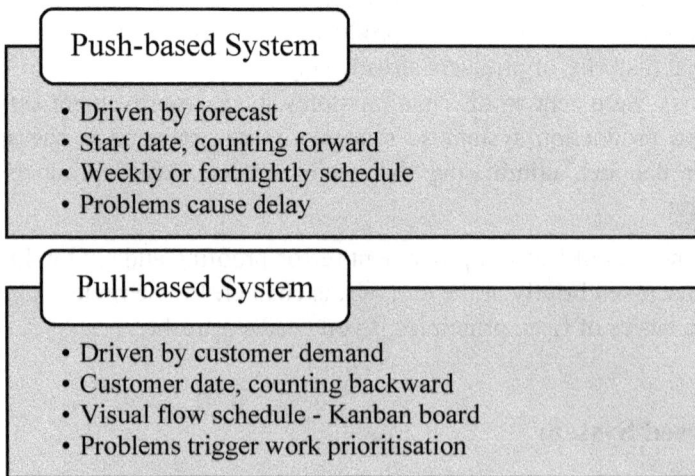

Push-based System

- Driven by forecast
- Start date, counting forward
- Weekly or fortnightly schedule
- Problems cause delay

Pull-based System

- Driven by customer demand
- Customer date, counting backward
- Visual flow schedule - Kanban board
- Problems trigger work prioritisation

Figure 26-1 Push-based and Pull-based comparison

It is easy to identify if a system is currently based on push or pull. A **push-based system** is driven by forecast. Things are planned with start date, then goes forward trying to achieve certain expected date. Schedule is made on a routine cycle, such as weekly or fortnightly. If problems occur during work, it forces delay from the original schedule.

On the other hand, ***pull-based system*** is driven by customer needs. Things are planned with the date from customer, then goes backwards to calculate the start date. Schedule is achieved using visual flow, such as Kanban. Therefore, there is no need to do any weekly or fortnightly schedule because work plan is being carried out all the time along with each movement of work items on Kanban board. Problems are addressed by changing priorities of work in pipeline.

Visual scheduling has multiple benefits in facilitating dynamic collaboration needed for pull-based system. It offers unobstructed view of detailed work, available for everyone involved. Each stakeholder will signal when something is ready without the need of complex communication that can always lead to misunderstanding. Everyone has the same view of problem and workload, making changes easier to achieve.

Heijunka is a technique often used to help with establishing pull-based system in Lean. This word is a Japanese word meaning "leveling". As the name suggests, this technique is used to reduce the unevenness in a production process. It is very useful to stop producing outputs in large batches.

There are two main methods of heijunka: leveling by volume and leveling by type. If the customer demand on each workday is different: Monday (300), Tuesday (250), Wednesday (220), Thursday (200) and Friday (305), *leveling by volume* means producing the average number each day (255) instead of producing different number of outputs every day. *Leveling by type* takes similar approach of producing the average number of customer demand, but it focuses on customer demand in each product type.

Error Proofing (Poka Yoke)

Error proofing (or mistake proofing) is a Lean technique designed to prevent errors from occurring. This technique is also known as *poka yoke*, a Japanese word that means inadvertent error prevention. If one of the identified factors of performance problem is operator mistakes, then Poka Yoke aims to eliminate those mistakes, or minimise them, or at least detect them immediately.

Three levels of *poka yoke*:
- *Prevention.* This is the highest level of *poka yoke* aimed to prevent mistake from happening.
- *Facilitation.* If mistakes cannot be fully prevented, then the next best thing to facilitate operator with visual clues to minimise mistakes.

- *Detection.* If neither prevention nor facilitation is feasible, then a system could be designed to automatically detect an error immediately after it happened.

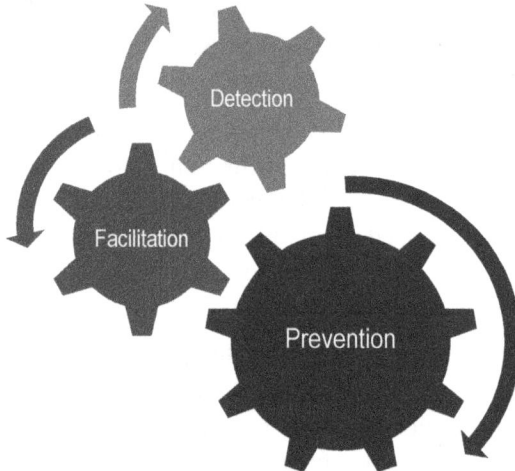

Figure 26-2 Levels of Poka Yoke

If you look at the back of your computer, you will find a number of different ports available for connection to different devices. Wired network is connected to the computer using RJ45 port. Monitor is connected using HDMI or DVI port. Various other accessories are connected using USB interface, either in the shape of USB-A (the conventional full-sized USB) or the newer USB-C. These ports are designed to have different shapes to prevent errors from happening. If a cable does not fit to a port, then it is not mean to be connected. Mistakes are prevented from happening.

Another good example of error prevention is the steps of withdrawing money from an ATM machine. Many years ago, an ATM machine would dispense the money before allowing customer to remove the ATM card from the machine. As a result, there used to be many cases of ATM cards left uncollected. Most modern ATMs will ask customers to retrieve their cards before dispensing the cash available. This helps to ensure that customers will not forget their cards because people would not leave an ATM machine before collecting the cash they withdraw.

Facilitation *poka yoke* can often be found in cash registers of fast-food restaurants. Buttons are equipped with pictures of menu items, making it easier to find the right button and minimise potential errors. Applying colour codes to work equipment is another example of *poka yoke* technique to facilitate operators to make fewer mistakes.

The last type of *poka yoke* is detection. Some cars have warning system to remind the driver to turn off front light if the engine is turned off while front light is still on. Another alert will sound if a driver opens the door without removing the car key. These alerts could not really prevent or facilitate a driver from committing errors in operating a car, but it detects as soon as incorrect sequence of action is detected.

Six Thinking Hats

Six thinking hats is a concept introduced by *Dr. Edward de Bono* in 1985. It is a powerful decision-making tool focused on looking at a problem from different point of views. As the name suggests, this technique uses hats with various colours as analogy to represents different point of views.

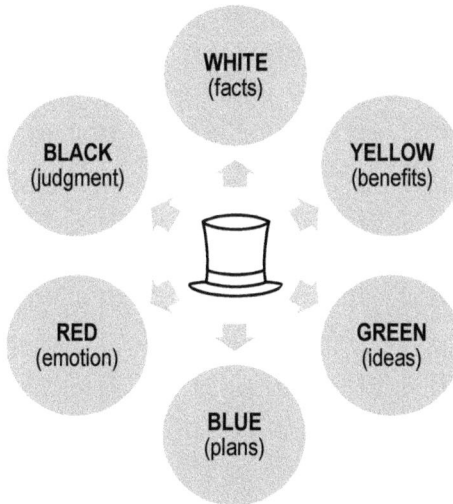

Figure 26-3 Six Thinking Hats

White hat is the foundation of all the other thinking hats. This hat focuses on gathering data. This is critically important to understand the problem and to ensure data-driven decision making.

Yellow hat represents optimism and positivity. It sees a problem as an opportunity to obtain values and benefits. This hat covers the point of view of hope, seeing things from the good aspects.

Green hat focuses on ideas and creativity. This point of view represents new concepts and perceptions. It attempts to see things out of the box and explore better ways of doing things.

Blue hat works on the planning and analysis. It takes the optimism from yellow hat and various ideas from green hats, then attempts to organise those into workable plan. This hat is supposed to manage and control all other hats.

Red hat views things from intuition and emotional perspective. This hat represents the gut feeling, hunches and other things that may or may not be directly reflected from the collected data.

Black hat is the judgment hat. It focuses on the logical negative of a problem. This hat aims to identify risks, potential dangers and other reasons why something might not work. Note that logical is the key word of using this hat so that we do not overuse it.

27. DESIGN OF EXPERIMENTS (DOE)

Design of Experiment (DOE) is a technique of applied statistics to investigate how the manipulation of controlled independent factors (X variables) impacts the results of dependent factor (Y). It attempts to identify cause and effect relationships between X and Y so that solutions can be made.

There are three main use cases of DOE:
- Design new product or service.
- Characterise new systems or processes after the introduction of new technology or approach.
- Determine the best settings of all independent variables in process improvement. This is the use case we are going to focus on for the purpose of DMAIC.

Different approaches of DOE can be grouped into five categories:
- Trial and Error (lucky guess)
- One Factor At A Time (OFAAT)
- Full Factorial Design (observes all possible combinations), this will be discussed in Chapter 28.
- Fractional Factorial Design, this will be discussed in Chapter 29.

Trial and Error

As the name suggests, trial and error approach to experimental design takes on a set of independent factors affecting a system, chooses one particular value combination of those factors, then performs experiment to see how the process output is impacted. This method does not have a methodical way to choose the value combination. It relies on being lucky that the optimal solution is one of early guesses.

Subject matter experts (SME) are often consulted in choosing the value combination, hoping to increase the chance of success. Depending on the expertise level of the SMEs and the complexity level of the problem to be solved, this approach could work and actually find acceptable solution within its first few attempts, costing the lowest compared to other approaches of DOE.

With highly capable SME, this approach could be the fastest approach with the lowest cost of DOE. However, it is also an approach with the highest risk and hardest to schedule and estimate. Finding one acceptable solution does not necessarily mean that the solution is an optimal solution because other possibilities have not even been explored.

A pizza restaurant purchased a new oven and would like to experiment on the ideal oven temperature to get the best pizza. A pizza chef is consulted. Based on his years of experience, he is able to suggest 300°C temperature for the first experiment, then 250°C and 270°C for the following experiments. Within a few experiments, an ideal temperature is discovered, and the experiment concludes. This is a simplified case with only one factor (temperature). In real process improvement problems, there are usually three or more factors impacting system outcome and selecting value combinations for experiment would not be as straightforward.

Example 27-1

Process improvement project has identified three independent factors (X1, X2 and X3) impacting the Y outcome. The goal of process improvement is to achieve Y value bigger than 4,000. Valid values for X1 are any value between 0 and 1. Valid values for X2 are any integer value from 250 to 400. Valid values for X3 are 5, 6, 7, 8 and 9. Perform DOE using Trial and Error.

- Experiment #1: SME suggests initial combination value of {X1=0.5, X2=300, X3=7}. These values produce process outcome of Y=2,372. It does not meet the required target for improvement.
- Experiment #2: SME suggests combination value of {X1=0.45, X2=370, X3=8}. These values produce process outcome of Y=2,577. It does not meet the required target for improvement.
- Experiment #3: SME suggests combination value of {X1=0.3, X2=310, X3=6}. These values produce process outcome of Y=4,016. This outcome meets the required target for improvement.
- Experiment accepts {X1=0.3, X2=310, X3=6} as the solution.

One Factor At A Time

One Factor At A Time (OFAAT) is an approach of DOE that aims to find the optimal value combination of multiple factors, one at a time. This approach can be estimated and managed properly because the maximum number of experiments can be calculated from the beginning. The system outcome will improve over time and there is a chance that experiment can be concluded early if the acceptable outcome is already obtained and deemed stable.

Steps of OFAAT:
- List all independent factors (Xs) impacting outcome (Y).
- Decide on the sequence of factors to be optimised. This step assigns sequence order (X1, X2, X3, ...) to the factors.
- Start with the first factor to be optimised (X1).
- All other factors are assigned default values, these values are held constant.
- Default values could be the current values in the existing process.
- Change the values of X1 throughout valid range and find which value brings the best result. This is called local optimal because other factors have not been considered.
- After the optimal value for X1 is found, move on to X2.
- When experimenting with possible values of X2, use the optimal value for X1 and use default values for all other factors, keep them constant.
- Change the values of X2, find its local optimal value.
- Move on to X3 and so on.

OFAAT approach can take a long time to complete if there are many factors impacting outcome and each of them has wide range of valid values. Factors with continuous values need to be observed based on *intervals*. For example, variable X1 has valid range between 0 and 1. We could not experiment on infinite number of possible values from 0 to 1 because 0.3, 0.33, 0.333, 0.3333, 0.33333 and so on are all valid values.

Smaller interval increases the number of experiments, which in turn will increase time and cost. However, it improves our ability to properly understand how a factor influence result. Bigger interval will speed up experiment time. However, it will increase the risk of missing the actual optimal value.

The sequence of factors to be optimised affects how fast OFAAT experiment can find acceptable result. It is generally preferred to start with factors that is expected to have the biggest impact on the system outcome first. The solution obtained by OFAAT is a set of local optimal values, not really the optimal solution for the whole set of factors. Interdependencies between factors are not fully observed.

Example 27-2

Process improvement project has identified three independent factors (X1, X2 and X3) impacting the Y outcome. The goal of process improvement is to achieve Y value bigger than 500. Valid values for X1 is any value between 0 and 1. Valid values for X2 are any integer value from 250 to 400. Valid values for X3 are 5, 6, 7, 8 and 9. Perform DOE using OFAAT.

- Interval for X1 is 0.2. This means that possible values for experiment are 0.0, 0.2, 0.4, 0.6, 0.8 and 1.0.
- Interval for X2 is 50. This means that possible values for experiment are 250, 300, 350 and 400.
- There is no need to decide interval for X3 because there is only limited number of valid values.
- Factor X2 is estimated to have the biggest impact for outcome Y, followed by X1 and then X3.
- Default value 0.6 is applied to X1.
- Default value 7 is applied to X3.
- Experiment #1: The first possible value of X2 is 250. Combination of {X1=0.6, X2=250, X3=7} is used for experiment. These values produce process outcome of Y=737.
- Experiment #2: The next possible value of X2 is 300. Combination of {X1=0.6, X2=300, X3=7} is used for experiment. These values produce process outcome of Y=1,301.
- Experiment #3: The next possible value of X2 is 350. Combination of {X1=0.6, X2=350, X3=7} is used for experiment. These values produce process outcome of Y=1,062.
- Experiment #4: The next possible value of X2 is 400. Combination of {X1=0.6, X2=400, X3=7} is used for experiment. These values produce process outcome of Y=498.
- Local optimal value for X2 is 300.
- Move on to the next phase by experimenting on the possible values of X1. This time, the constant value of X2 is 300 and the value of X3 remains the default value of 7.
- Experiment #5: The first possible value of X1 is 0.0. Combination of {X1=0.0, X2=300, X3=7} is used for experiment. These values produce process outcome of Y=762.

- Experiment #6: The next possible value of X1 is 0.2. Combination of {X1=0.2, X2=300, X3=7} is used for experiment. These values produce process outcome of Y=1,615.
- Experiment #7: The next possible value of X1 is 0.4. Combination of {X1=0.4, X2=300, X3=7} is used for experiment. These values produce process outcome of Y=13,407. This value meets the requirement for process improvement. Experiment can be concluded at this point with {X1=0.4, X2=300, X3=7} as the solution.
- This finding demonstrates that X1 has bigger impact to the outcome of Y. Therefore, the initial assumption that X2 has the biggest impact is incorrect.
- Alternatively, experiment can still continue to see if better solution can be found.
- Experiment #8: The next possible value of X1 is 0.6. Combination of {X1=0.6, X2=300, X3=7} is already used for experiment #2 with outcome Y=1,301. There is no need to repeat the experiment.
- Experiment #9: The next possible value of X1 is 0.8. Combination of {X1=0.8, X2=300, X3=7} is used for experiment. These values produce process outcome of Y=684.
- Experiment #10: The next possible value of X1 is 1.0. Combination of {X1=1.0, X2=300, X3=7} is used for experiment. These values produce process outcome of Y=464.
- Local optimal value for X1 is 0.4.
- Move on to the next phase by experimenting on the possible values of X3. This time, the constant values of X1 and X2 are 0.4 and 300.
- Experiment #11: The first possible value of X3 is 5. Combination of {X1=0.4, X2=300, X3=5} is used for experiment. These values produce process outcome of Y=13,686. This is a better result than experiment #7.
- Experiment #12: The next possible value of X3 is 6. Combination of {X1=0.4, X2=300, X3=6} is used for experiment. These values produce process outcome of Y=13,500.
- Experiment #13: The next possible value of X3 is 7. Combination of {X1=0.4, X2=300, X3=7} is already used for experiment #7 with outcome Y=13,407. There is no need to repeat the experiment.
- Experiment #14: The next possible value of X3 is 8. Combination of {X1=0.4, X2=300, X3=8} is used for experiment. These values produce process outcome of Y=13,360.

- Experiment #15: The next possible value of X3 is 9. Combination of {X1=0.4, X2=300, X3=9} is used for experiment. These values produce process outcome of Y=13,407.
- Selected solution is {X1=0.4, X2=300, X3=5}, from experiment #11.
- Note that the decision on interval reduces the number of possible values in experiment. Some values are not considered because they are not part of the interval. These omitted values could be part of the best possible combination.

28. DOE: FULL FACTORIAL DESIGN

This chapter discusses Full Factorial Experiments approach from Design of Experiments (DOE) technique. Before continuing with this chapter, it is strongly recommended to review Chapter 27 about DOE.

Full factorial design (also commonly known as *full factorial experiments*) is a DOE technique focused on finding the joint effects of multiple factors (Xs) on dependent variable (Y). To find the complete set of possible joint effects, an experiment needs to be performed for each possible value combinations of all factors. If X1, X2 and X3 have 3, 4 and 5 possible values, there are $3 \times 4 \times 5 = 60$ value combinations that need to be tested.

	X1=1				X1=2				X1=3			
	X2=1	X2=2	X2=3	X3=4	X2=1	X2=2	X2=3	X3=4	X2=1	X2=2	X2=3	X3=4
X3=1	#01	#02	#03	#04	#05	#06	#07	#08	#9	#10	#11	#12
X3=2	#13	#14	#15	#16	#17	#18	#19	#20	#21	#22	#23	#24
X3=3	#25	#26	#27	#28	#29	#30	#31	#32	#33	#34	#35	#36
X3=4	#37	#38	#39	#40	#41	#42	#43	#44	#45	#46	#47	#48
X3=5	#49	#50	#51	#52	#53	#54	#55	#56	#57	#58	#59	#60

Table 28-A Experiments for Full Factorial Design

Each of identifiers #01 to #60 in Table 28-A represents one group of experiments. If full factorial design does not have replication nor repetition, then one group of experiment is equal to one single experiment. Repetition and repeated measurement will be discussed in later part of this chapter.

In reality, many independent factors would have discrete or continuous data with many or infinite possible values. It is generally not feasible to test all combinations of these factors, as the time and cost for the experiments will grow exponentially.

Interval technique is used to reduce the number of possible values for an independent factor down to 2 or 3 *levels*. For 2 levels interval, the possible values are low and high values. 3 levels interval adds centre value.

Technically, intervals can be set with any number of levels. However, levels beyond 3 are considered expensive because they add significant number of required experiments and often do not contribute much to the quality of the obtained solution.

The selection of low and high values is critical to the whole calculation of full factorial design. Some possible sources for low and high:
- Minimum and maximum values within valid range of each factor.
- Historical data from current process.
- Customer requirement.
- Government regulation.

For full factorial design in 3 levels, centre value is a value in the middle of low and high values.

$$Centre = \frac{Low + High}{2}$$

The calculation model of full factorial design does not use the actual low and high values from independent factors. Instead, it uses *transformed values* -1 for low value and $+1$ for high value.

Transformation formula is used to convert low and high values into -1 and $+1$.

$$X' = \frac{X - Centre}{abs(X - Centre)}$$

If low and high values for an independent factor are 25 and 75, the transformation formula is $(X - 50) / |X - 50|$ because it transforms low value (25) into -1 and high value (75) into $+1$. Using the same formula, centre point (for the case of 3 levels) will be transformed to 0.

Full factorial design in 2 levels have 2^k possible value combinations (k is the number of factors). This is the most common type of full factorial design. Similarly, full factorial design with 3 levels have 3^k possible value combinations.

	X1 = −1		X1 = +1	
	X2 = −1	X2 = +1	X2 = −1	X2 = +1
X3 = −1	#01	#02	#03	#04
X3 = +1	#05	#06	#07	#08

Table 28-B Full Factorial Design with Standard Order (Type 1)

	X1	X2	X3
#01	−1	−1	−1
#02	+1	−1	−1
#03	−1	+1	−1
#04	+1	+1	−1
#05	−1	−1	+1
#06	+1	−1	+1
#07	−1	+1	+1
#08	+1	+1	+1

Table 28-C Full Factorial Design with Standard Order (Type 2)

Table 28-B and Table 28-C demonstrate different ways to present full factorial design in 2 levels with 3 factors. The technique shown in type 2 table is easier for large number of factors, and therefore is the more popular one.

To populate type 2 table, simply alternate between −1 and +1 for the first factor. Repeat the process for second factor but repeat each value twice. For the ith factor, repeat each value 2^i times, and so on. Note that $2^0 = 1$ and $2^1 = 2$.

Randomised Design and Centre Point

Randomisation is considered as best practice to minimise the possibility of biased experiments, especially if the experiment involves human operators and/or physical objects to be measured. As refresher, please review the discussion on accuracy and precision in Chapter 15 about Measurement System Analysis (MSA).

Standard Order	Random Order	X1	X2	X3
#01	03	−1	−1	−1
#02	05	+1	−1	−1
#03	07	−1	+1	−1
#04	01	+1	+1	−1
#05	04	−1	−1	+1
#06	08	+1	−1	+1
#07	02	−1	+1	+1
#08	06	+1	+1	+1

Table 28-D Full Factorial Design with random order

Centre point experiments (or *control runs*) can be added into full factorial design to help ensuring process stability and consistent variability. These experiments use the centre values from each factor. It is recommended to add 3 to 5 centre point experiments into full factorial design. They should not be randomised because their purpose is to detect process instability during experiments.

Random Order	Standard Order	X1	X2	X3
N/A	N/A	0	0	0
01	#04	+1	+1	−1
02	#07	−1	+1	+1
03	#01	−1	−1	−1
04	#05	−1	−1	+1
N/A	N/A	0	0	0
05	#02	+1	−1	−1
06	#08	+1	+1	+1
07	#03	−1	+1	−1
08	#06	+1	−1	+1
N/A	N/A	0	0	0

Table 28-E Full Factorial Design with centre points

There are two alternative methods of control runs:

- *Pseudo centre point experiments*. Pseudo centre point can be used if one or more of the factors have nominal value (see discussion on data types from Chapter 06). If actual centre could not be mathematically calculated, certain value could be considered as pseudo centre.
- *Oracle experiments*. This control run is possible for certain use cases where the standard result is known for particular combination of values.

Replication and Repetition

Replication and repetition are added into full factorial design to reduce the likelihood of bias and measurement errors. With these techniques, multiple experiments are being conducted on the same combination of factor levels. For example, experiment run #1 and #2 both uses high values for all three factors of X1, X2 and X3.

Replication creates multiple experiment runs using the same combination of factor levels. The instances of multiple experiments get different sequence number on randomised order. Each experiment run could use identical items, but not a reuse of exactly same item. For example, an experiment of making cake uses flour. Once flour is used, it becomes part of the cake and could not be reused to make the next cake. For the second experiment, same amount of flour from different batch is used, but they are considered identical (same type of flour from the same brand).

Repetition executes multiple measurements on experiment result, or repeating the experiment using exactly the same components. For example, instead of making another cake using same amount of flour, repeated measurement could record the result of different operator measuring the same cake that is already made from previous experiment.

In the setting of manufacturing industry:
- Operators set independent factors to the right values (following the high or low combinations from full factorial design), then start production to create one unit of product. Measure this outcome, then restart the production to create another unit. This is a *replication* of experiments.
- Operators set independent factors to the right values, then start production to create three units of product. Each unit is being measured and the results are recorded as *repetition*.

Each experiment run with replication is treated as different experiment. For full factorial design with randomisation, each experiment will receive different random order. For repeated measurement, each measurement is treated as part of one experiment.

Standard Order	Random Order	X1	X2	X3
#01		−1	−1	−1
#02		+1	−1	−1
#03		−1	+1	−1
#04		+1	+1	−1
#05		−1	−1	+1

Standard Order	Random Order	X1	X2	X3
#06		+1	−1	+1
#07		−1	+1	+1
#08		+1	+1	+1
#09		−1	−1	−1
#10		+1	−1	−1
#11		−1	+1	−1
#12		+1	+1	−1
#13		−1	−1	+1
#14		+1	−1	+1
#15		−1	+1	+1
#16		+1	+1	+1

Table 28-F Full Factorial Design with replication

Standard Order	Random Order	X1	X2	X3	Repeat
#01		−1	−1	−1	1
#01		−1	−1	−1	2
#02		+1	−1	−1	1
#02		+1	−1	−1	2
#03		−1	+1	−1	1
#03		−1	+1	−1	2
#04		+1	+1	−1	1
#04		+1	+1	−1	2
#05		−1	−1	+1	1
#05		−1	−1	+1	2
#06		+1	−1	+1	1
#06		+1	−1	+1	2
#07		−1	+1	+1	1
#07		−1	+1	+1	2
#08		+1	+1	+1	1
#08		+1	+1	+1	2

Table 28-G Full Factorial Design with repetition

Depending on the DOE objectives and constraints, it is possible to do both replication and repetition. It is also common to use replication and/or repetition with randomisation and centre point control runs.

Random Order	Standard Order	X1	X2	X3
N/A	N/A	0	0	0
01	#12	+1	+1	−1
02	#15	−1	+1	+1
03	#05	−1	−1	+1

Random Order	Standard Order	X1	X2	X3
04	#10	+1	−1	−1
05	#02	+1	−1	−1
06	#14	+1	−1	+1
07	#01	−1	−1	−1
08	#08	+1	+1	+1
N/A	N/A	0	0	0
09	#04	+1	+1	−1
10	#16	+1	+1	+1
11	#11	−1	+1	−1
12	#06	+1	−1	+1
13	#03	−1	+1	−1
14	#09	−1	−1	−1
15	#13	−1	−1	+1
16	#07	−1	+1	+1
N/A	N/A	0	0	0

Table 28-H Full Factorial Design with replication, random order and control runs

Random Order	Standard Order	X1	X2	X3	Repeat
N/A	N/A	0	0	0	
01	#04	+1	+1	−1	1
01	#04	+1	+1	−1	2
02	#07	−1	+1	+1	1
02	#07	−1	+1	+1	2
03	#01	−1	−1	−1	1
03	#01	−1	−1	−1	2
04	#05	−1	−1	+1	1
04	#05	−1	−1	+1	2
N/A	N/A	0	0	0	
05	#02	+1	−1	−1	1
05	#02	+1	−1	−1	2
06	#08	+1	+1	+1	1
06	#08	+1	+1	+1	2
07	#03	−1	+1	−1	1
07	#03	−1	+1	−1	2
08	#06	+1	−1	+1	1
08	#06	+1	−1	+1	2
N/A	N/A	0	0	0	

Table 28-I Full Factorial Design with repetition, random order and control runs

Cube Plot

Cube plot is a visualisation technique to represent design space of full factorial design with 3 factors and 2 levels in three-dimensional model. It uses X, Y and Z axis to visually show the movement of X1, X2 and X3 from high to low values.

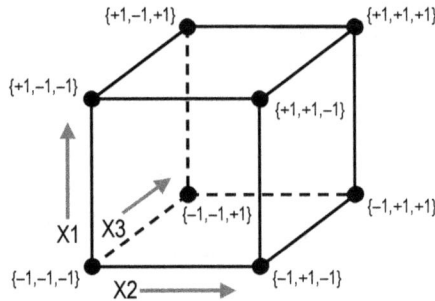

Figure 28-1 Cube Plot

Figure 28-1 shows a cube plot of full factorial design with 3 factors: X1, X2 and X3. X1 is represented by vertical axis. Therefore, each node located at the bottom side of the cube has low value for X1 and each node at the top surface has high value for X1. Similarly, X2 is represented by horizontal axis. Nodes on the left surface of the cube all have low values for X2, nodes on the right surface have high values, X3 is represented by the depth axis. All nodes on the front surface has low values for X3, all nodes on the back/behind surface has high values.

For full factorial design with 3 levels, middle points are added at every line on the cube. This adds complexity to the experiment. However, it also allows curvature detection.

Blocking

A key step before executing experiment is to identify external factors that might influence experiment outcome. External factors are factors other than the ones identified from earlier phase of DMAIC as confirmed contributing factors. *Blocking* is a common technique to isolate the systematic effects from external factor. Or it can also be used to accommodate real world constraints, such as the availability of operators to conduct experiments.

Blocking separates groups of runs based on environment and noise factors. It is almost always used together with randomised order of experiments. Centre point control runs are assigned for each block, as if the blocks are separate sets of experiment.

Simple example of blocking: it is already known that some material needed for experiments will come from different batches of production. Full factorial design with 3 factors, 2 levels and replication of 2 has 16 experiment runs. Blocking technique is applied to the experiments so that material from batch 1 and 2 are used in 8 experiments each.

There are many ways to design blocks within full factorial design. One of the simplest methods is *alternate corners* technique. This method uses cube plot to help with ensuring balance.

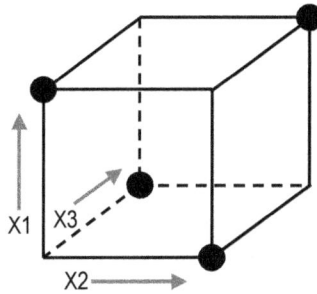

Figure 28-2 Blocking with alternate corners

In Figure 28-2, two blocks are indicated with the big dots placed on alternate corners. The corners with big dots belong to block #1, the other corners belong to block #2.

Standard Order	X1	X2	X3	Block
#01	−1	−1	−1	#2
#02	+1	−1	−1	#1
#03	−1	+1	−1	#1
#04	+1	+1	−1	#2
#05	−1	−1	+1	#1
#06	+1	−1	+1	#2
#07	−1	+1	+1	#2
#08	+1	+1	+1	#1

Table 28-J Full Factorial Design with blocking

More complex methods of blocking require further understanding of confounding effects, balanced selection and orthogonal design. These concepts will be discussed in Chapter 29.

Conducting Experiments

After creating the set of experiments based on the values (levels) of each factor, the next step is to prepare and conduct the actual experiments. Test sample preparation is often the part of full factorial design with highest cost. This is why decisions on replication and repetition had to take cost into consideration.

Some experiments are *destructive* test, meaning that material used in earlier runs of experiment could not be reused, causing the need to prepare many samples. It is considered as standard expectation that most of the products/outcome from experiment runs will not meet customer requirement to be sold as products. Therefore, most of the cost for materials will turn to waste, making it critically important for the experiment to yield valuable information for process improvement.

Let us refer back to Table 28-H of full factorial design with replication, random order and control runs. Suppose the experiment is about baking perfect pizza. X1 is the oven temperature, high value is 310°C and low value is 260°C. X2 is the duration of baking, high value is 15 minutes and low value is 10 minutes. X3 is the weight of the pizza before baking, high value is 350 grams and low value is 270 grams.

#	Temperature	Duration	Weight	Ref	X1	X2	X3
01	285°C	12.5 mins	310 grams	N/A	0	0	0
02	310°C	15.0 mins	270 grams	#12	+1	+1	−1
03	260°C	15.0 mins	350 grams	#15	−1	+1	+1
04	260°C	10.0 mins	350 grams	#05	−1	−1	+1
05	310°C	10.0 mins	270 grams	#10	+1	−1	−1
06	310°C	10.0 mins	270 grams	#02	+1	−1	−1
07	310°C	10.0 mins	350 grams	#14	+1	−1	+1
08	260°C	10.0 mins	270 grams	#01	−1	−1	−1
09	310°C	15.0 mins	350 grams	#08	+1	+1	+1
10	285°C	12.5 mins	310 grams	N/A	0	0	0
11	310°C	15.0 mins	270 grams	#04	+1	+1	−1
12	310°C	15.0 mins	350 grams	#16	+1	+1	+1
13	260°C	15.0 mins	270 grams	#11	−1	+1	−1
14	310°C	10.0 mins	350 grams	#06	+1	−1	+1
15	260°C	15.0 mins	270 grams	#03	−1	+1	−1
16	260°C	10.0 mins	270 grams	#09	−1	−1	−1
17	260°C	10.0 mins	350 grams	#13	−1	−1	+1

#	Temperature	Duration	Weight	Ref	X1	X2	X3
18	260°C	15.0 mins	350 grams	#07	−1	+1	+1
19	285°C	12.5 mins	310 grams	N/A	0	0	0

Table 28-K Execution plan of Full Factorial Design

The first column in Table 28-K represents the sequence of experiments that must be followed by operator. The temperature, duration and weight columns show the values of factors to be set for experiments. Ref column is for referencing a particular experiment back to the standard order before randomisation. X1, X2 and X3 columns show the levels for each factor. Operators do not need to see Ref, X1, X2 and S3 columns. They are presented here to help with explanation.

Mathematical Model

Mathematical model for full factorial design is represented as complex formula involving a set of independent factors (Xs) and Y outcome. Full factorial design with 2 levels allows the calculation of *linear model.*

Full factorial design linear model with 2 factors:

$$Y = \beta_0 + \beta_1 X_1 + \beta_2 X_2 + \beta_{12} X_1 X_2$$

Full factorial design linear model with 3 factors:

$$Y = \beta_0 + \beta_1 X_1 + \beta_2 X_2 + \beta_3 X_3 + \beta_{12} X_1 X_2 + \beta_{13} X_1 X_3 + \beta_{23} X_2 X_3 + \beta_{123} X_1 X_2 X_3$$

For more than 3 factors, the formula needs to include each individual factor and each possible combinations of the factors.

Let us use the following example to demonstrate the calculation of full factorial design mathematical model:

A company is producing tempered glass, making glass stronger by heating glass beyond its softening point (600°C), followed by rapid cooling process called quenching, that is applying high pressure cooling blasts through nozzles from various angles. For an experiment, 2 factors have been identified as the factors impacting the strength of produced glass: the top temperature during heating and the duration of quenching process. Tensile strength of glass is measured in megapascals (MPa)

Top heating temperature is X1 factor with low value of 615°C and high value of 635°C. Duration of quenching is X2 factor with low value of 3.5 seconds and high value of 8.5 seconds.

Two factors matrix is used to map the experiment results:

		X2 (Duration)					X2 (Duration)	
		−1	+1				3.5 s	8.5 s
X1	−1	−1, −1	−1, +1	→	X1	615°C	860 MPa	730 MPa
(Temp)	+1	+1, −1	+1, +1		(Temp)	635°C	980 MPa	790 MPa

Table 28-L Case example of tempered glass experiment

First, the transformation formula for X1 and X2:
- For X1, transformation formula is $X1' = (X1 − 625) / 10$
- 625 is the centre point of X1.
- This transformation formula transforms low value 615 into −1 and high value 635 into +1.
- For X2, transformation formula is $X2' = (X2 − 6.0) / 2.5$
- 6.0 is the centre point of X2.
- This transformation formula transforms low value 3.5 into −1 and high value 8.5 into +1.

Next step is to calculate the *main effects*. This is obtained from the average of all output values when the factor is set to high value, subtracted by the average of all output values when the factor is set to low value.
- Temperature effect = $(980 + 790) / 2 − (860 + 730) / 2 = 90$ MPa.
- Duration effect = $(730 + 790) / 2 − (860 + 980) / 2 = −160$ MPa.

Combination values of factors are grouped into positive or negative by multiplying the values of −1 or +1. Based on the groups, *interaction effects* are calculated from the average of all output values when the multiplication result is positive, subtracted by the average of all output values when the multiplication result is negative.
- 860 MPa belongs to group 1 because of −1 × −1 is positive.
- 730 MPa belongs to group 2 because of −1 × +1 is negative.
- 980 MPa belongs to group 2 because of +1 × −1 is negative.
- 790 MPa belongs to group 1 because of +1 × +1 is positive.
- Interaction effect for temperature and duration is calculated as: $(860 + 790) / 2 − (730 + 980) / 2 = −30$ MPa.

β_0 is the grand mean of all output values. Other β coefficients are calculated from the effects divided by 2. This is because the distance from −1 to +1 is 2.
- $\beta_0 = (860 + 730 + 980 + 790) / 4 = 840$.

- $\beta_1 = 90 / 2 = 45$.
- $\beta_2 = -160 / 2 = -80$.
- $\beta_{12} = -30 / 2 = -15$.

The mathematical model of X1 (temperature), X2 (duration) and Y (strength) can be expressed as:

- $Y = 840 + 45X_1{}' - 80X_2{}' - 15X_1{}'X_2{}'$
- However, this mathematical model uses X1' and X2' (values of –1 and +1) instead of the actual values in real world, which are 615°C and 635°C for X1; 3.5 seconds and 8.5 seconds for X2.
- To transform the mathematical model into real world values, the transformation formula is applied.
- $Y = 840 + 45 \left(\frac{(X_1 - 625)}{10} \right) - 80 \left(\frac{(X_2 - 6.0)}{2.5} \right) - 15 \left(\frac{(X_1 - 625)}{10} \right) \left(\frac{(X_2 - 6.0)}{2.5} \right)$
- $Y = -4030.5 + 8.1X_1 + 343X_2 - 0.6X_1X_2$

Lastly, to confirm the validity of calculated mathematical model:

- Substitute X1 with 615 and X2 with 3.5, Y = 860.
- Substitute X1 with 615 and X2 with 8.5, Y = 730.
- Substitute X1 with 635 and X2 with 3.5, Y = 980.
- Substitute X1 with 635 and X2 with 8.5, Y = 790.
- These Y values are consistent with experiment results from Table 28-L.

System outcome is impacted by main effects and interaction effects. Main effects represent impacts from individual factors and interaction effects represent impacts from value combinations. Instead of iteratively finding local optimal values for one factor at a time (OFAAT), full factorial design attempts to model the entire set of effects at the cost of reduced intervals for each factor. This approach is considered better if some factors are estimated to have linear impact.

Response Surface Design

Response surface design aims to find the best number of factor levels to be able to achieve mathematical model with acceptable fit. Earlier experiments with 2 levels for each factor have limited ability to detect linear relationships between factors and system outcome. Upgrading full factorial design to 3 levels allow quadratic relationship to be detected.

To detect quadratic relationships, the mathematical model of full factorial design is extended to:

$$Y = linear\ model + \beta_{11}X_1{}^2 + \beta_{22}X_2{}^2 + \cdots + \beta_{kk}X_k{}^2$$

Note that detecting quadratic relationship does not equal to finding the actual fit of quadratic effects. To calculate proper fit of quadratic effect, smaller interval allowing more combinations of values are needed, but this will exponentially increase the number of required experiments.

Quadratic model is sufficient for the vast majority of common cases in industrial applications. In the rare occasions when quadratic model is not enough, cubic model can be used:

$$Y = quadratic\ model + \beta_{111}X_1{}^3 + \beta_{222}X_2{}^3 + \cdots + \beta_{kkk}X_k{}^3$$

Cubic model requires minimum 4 levels of values for each factor, changing the total number of required experiments into 4^k. This could lead to significant increase in the time and cost of experiments. Therefore, it is rarely used unless in exceptional circumstances.

Benefits and Limitations

Main benefits of full factorial design:
- Allows the detection of interaction effects. This could not be achieved by Trial and Error or One Factor At A Time (OFAAT) techniques.
- More efficient compared to OFAAT because full factorial design could achieve better solution with smaller number of experiments.
- The number of required experiments can be calculated from early phase. This helps with planning and cost estimation.

Some limitations of full factorial design:
- Biggest benefit of small number of experiments is achieved only for small number of factors with 2 levels. Increasing the number or factors or the levels exponentially increase the number of required experiments. This is the main reason behind the next DOE technique: fractional factorial design, which will be discussed in Chapter 29.
- Full factorial design with 2 levels is only capable to detect linear relationship.
- The decision on low and high value greatly impacts the results of full factorial design.
- It requires measurement system with high precision and accuracy. This is a general limitation for all DOE techniques.

29. DOE: FRACTIONAL FACTORIAL DESIGN

This chapter discusses fractional factorial design approach from Design of Experiments (DOE) technique. Before continuing with this chapter, it is strongly recommended to review Chapter 27 about DOE and Chapter 28 about full factorial design.

As the name suggests, fractional factorial design does not include all possible value combinations into the list of experiments. Only a subset of the full factorial runs is conducted, and statistical analysis is performed to interpret the results.

Number of Factors	Full Factorial Runs	1 / 2 Fraction	1 / 4 Fraction	1 / 8 Fraction
3	$2^3 = 8$	$2^2 = 4$		
4	$2^4 = 16$	$2^3 = 8$	$2^2 = 4$	
5	$2^5 = 32$	$2^4 = 16$	$2^3 = 8$	$2^2 = 4$
6	$2^6 = 64$	$2^5 = 32$	$2^4 = 16$	$2^3 = 8$
7	$2^7 = 128$	$2^6 = 64$	$2^5 = 32$	$2^4 = 16$
8	$2^8 = 256$	$2^7 = 128$	$2^6 = 64$	$2^5 = 32$

Table 29-A Fractional Factorial Design for factors with 2 levels

There are three common reduction rates: half, one quarter and one eighth. If full factorial design has 128 runs, half factorial design will have 64 runs, quarter factorial design will have 32 runs and one eighth factorial will have 16 runs.

Half factorial design essentially means that researcher decides to confound one factor. Subsequently, quarter factorial design means 2 factors are confounded and one eighth factorial design confounds 3 factors. The number of fractional runs can be calculated as:

$$\#Runs = \#Level^{(\#Factor-\#Confounded)}$$

Number of Factors	Full Factorial Runs	1 / 3 Fraction	1 / 9 Fraction	1 / 27 Fraction
3	$3^3 = 27$	$3^2 = 9$		
4	$3^4 = 81$	$3^3 = 27$	$3^2 = 9$	
5	$3^5 = 243$	$3^4 = 81$	$3^3 = 27$	$3^2 = 9$
6	$3^6 = 729$	$3^5 = 243$	$3^4 = 81$	$3^3 = 27$
7	$3^7 = 2187$	$3^6 = 729$	$3^5 = 243$	$3^4 = 81$
8	$3^8 = 6561$	$3^7 = 2187$	$3^6 = 729$	$3^5 = 243$

Table 29-B   Fractional Factorial Design for factors with 3 levels

As shown in Table 29-B, the number of reduced runs becomes more significant for factorial design with higher number of levels.

A common reason to choose fractional factorial design is high number of independent factors from earlier phases of DMAIC (Measure and Analyze). Choosing only a subset of runs significantly reduces the time and cost required to handle many factors. However, it also risks of missing the interaction between factors. Referring to mathematical model of full factorial design, the interaction effects might not be captured properly. This could be a smaller problem if the main effects are dominant.

Fractional factorial design is conducted in three stages:
- *Screening*. This stage involves selection of runs and executing the experiment. Experiment on this stage normally does not include replication nor repetition oints.
- *Refining*. This stage involves identification of significant control factors, then perform second batch of tests on those factors. With the number of factors reduced, experiments on refining stage might include replication and repetition. This stage aims to predict the optimal values for the chosen factors.
- *Optimising*. This stage is performed to confirm the results of refining stage with factors set at optimal values. The focus is to validate of the optimal setting selected from the preceding stages.

Screening	Refining	Optimising
• 8 factors	• 3 factors	• 1 run with optimal values
• 2 levels	• 3 levels might be needed if the	• Replication as needed
• Full design = 256	factors are estimated to be non	• Repetition as needed
• Fractional design = 64	linear	• Result: confirmed optimal
• No replication	• Full design = 27	values
• No repetition	• Full replication	
• Control runs are optional	• Repetition as necessary	
• Result: 3 significant factors	• Control runs are recommended	
	• Result: set of optimal values	

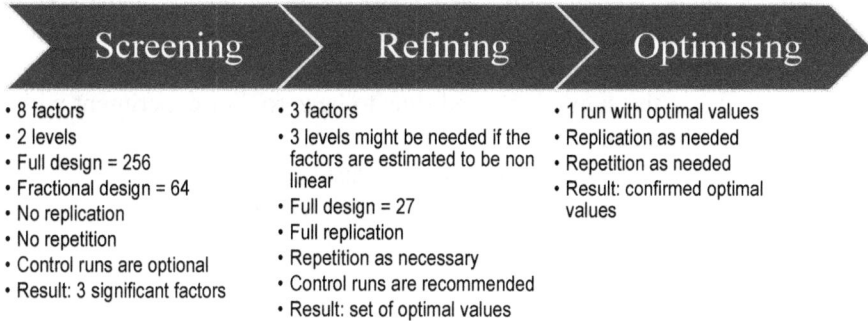

Figure 29-1 Fractional Factorial Design example with 8 factors

Figure 29-1 shows an example of running three stages of fractional factorial design for 8 factors. In the screening stage, 2 levels of values are assigned to all 8 levels. Quarter factorial design is decided, reducing the number of runs from 256 to 64. Replication and repetition are not needed. Screening stage is executed to identify significant factors. In this example, 3 factors are identified as significant.

Only the 3 significant factors are used in refining stage. Since they are assumed to have non-linear impact, 3 levels experiment is chosen. Full factorial design would have 27 runs, multiplied by the number of replication and/or repetition. Refining stage is identical to normal full factorial design. The end result is a set of optimal values, along with mathematical model to measure main and interaction effects.

In the optimising stage, one run is designed to confirm system outcome with optimal values from refining stage. Replication can be considered if there are multiple real-world settings for the same values of significant factors. Repetition is recommended if the measurement step of the result could produce bias.

Selection of Experiments (Balanced and Orthogonal)

To produce results that can be used for valid statistical analysis, selection of experiments for fractional factorial design needs to meet some criteria:

- *Balanced*: each factor is represented with same number of high and low values.
- *Orthogonal*: each factor can be analysed independently from other factors.

To achieve *balanced selection*, each factor must be represented by equal number of high and low values. Low values are transformed into −1 and high values are transformed into +1. Therefore, same number of high and low values will cause the sum of selected runs to be zero. For experiment with 3 factors X1, X2 and X3:

- The sum of X1 for all selected runs must be zero.
- The sum of X2 for all selected runs must be zero.
- The sum of X3 for all selected runs must be zero.

	Full Factorial			Fractional Factorial		
	X1	X2	X3	X1	X2	X3
#01	−1	−1	−1			
#02	+1	−1	−1	+1	−1	−1
#03	−1	+1	−1	−1	+1	−1
#04	+1	+1	−1			
#05	−1	−1	+1	−1	−1	+1
#06	+1	−1	+1			
#07	−1	+1	+1			
#08	+1	+1	+1	+1	+1	+1
			SUM	0	0	0

Table 29-C Balanced selection in Fractional Factorial Design

To achieve *orthogonal design*, the sum of values from factor interactions must be equal to zero. For experiment with 3 factors X1, X2 and X3:

- The sum of X1×X2 for all selected runs must be zero.
- The sum of X1×X3 for all selected runs must be zero.
- The sum of X2×X3 for all selected runs must be zero.

	Full Factorial			Fractional Factorial		
	X1	X2	X3	X1×X2	X1×X3	X2×X3
#01	−1	−1	−1			
#02	+1	−1	−1	−1	−1	+1
#03	−1	+1	−1	−1	+1	−1
#04	+1	+1	−1			
#05	−1	−1	+1	+1	−1	−1
#06	+1	−1	+1			
#07	−1	+1	+1			
#08	+1	+1	+1	+1	+1	+1
			SUM	0	0	0

Table 29-D Orthogonal design in Fractional Factorial Design

Note that the principles of balanced selection and orthogonal design can be applied to full factorial design separation of runs for the purpose of blocking. Please refer to Chapter 28 for more information.

Confounding Effects and Resolution

Fractional factorial design chooses only a subset of runs to be executed to save time and cost. A common side effect from partial execution is *confounding effect*, also known as *aliasing*. In confounding effect, certain factor effects could not be distinguished because they have identical set of high and low values. This often happens between main/primary and interaction effects.

	X1	X2	X3	X1×X2	X1×X3	X2×X3	X1×X2×X3
#02	+1	−1	−1	−1	−1	+1	+1
#03	−1	+1	−1	−1	+1	−1	+1
#05	−1	−1	+1	+1	−1	−1	+1
#08	+1	+1	+1	+1	+1	+1	+1

Table 29-E Confounding effects in Fractional Factorial Design

Table 29-E shows main effects (X1, X2 and X3) and interaction effects (X1×X2, X1×X3, X2×X3 and X1×X2×X3) of fractional factorial design with 3 factors. Confounding effects can be observed from:
- Main effect X1 has values of {+1, −1, −1, +1}. These are identical with the values of interaction effect X2×X3.
- Main effect X2 has values of {−1, +1, −1, +1}. These are identical with the values of interaction effect X1×X3.
- Main effect X3 has values of {−1, −1, +1, +1}. These are identical with the values of interaction effect X1×X2.

When interaction effect has identical value with main effect, fractional factorial design loses the ability to detect the actual effect of that interaction because all values are represented with identical set from one of the main effects.

Fractional factorial design could not analyse all possible factor interactions. 4 runs could analyse all interactions of 2 factors experiment (full factorial design), but it can only analyse main effects of 3 factors. Subsequently, 8 runs could analyse:
- All interactions of 3 factors experiment (full factorial design)
- Main effects plus some 2-factor interaction effects for 4 factors experiment.

- Main effects for experiments with 5, 6 or 7 factors.

Resolution is the ability to analyse interactions in fractional factorial design. Higher resolution has capability to measure more interactions. Roman numerals are used to express design resolution:

- III: experiment is capable to detect main effects only.
- IV: experiment is capable to detect main effects and some (but not all) 2-factor interaction effects.
- V: experiment is capable to detect main effects, all 2-factor interaction effects and some 3-factor interaction effects.
- VI: experiment is capable to detect main effects, all 2-factor interaction effects, all 3-factor interaction effects and some 4-factor interaction effects.

Resolution	Main Effects	X-factor Interaction Effects						
		2	3	4	5	6	7	8
III	all							
IV	all	some						
V	all	all	some					
VI	all	all	all	some				
VII	all	all	all	all	some			
VIII	all	all	all	all	all	some		
IX	all	all	all	all	all	all	some	

Table 29-F Resolution of Fractional Factorial Design

Higher number of runs will naturally increase the number of factors it can detect interactions from. Resolution III, IV and V are considered as the most common resolutions in real-world implementation.

For experiment with 3 factors, there are only 2 options: full factorial design with 8 runs or fractional factorial design with 4 runs that is only capable to detect the main effects because it has resolution III.

For experiment with 4 factors, choosing 16 runs will allow full factorial design (all interactions can be analysed). Choosing 8 runs will allow researcher to do fractional factorial design with resolution IV, which means it is capable to detect main effects and some 2-factor interaction effects. Choosing 4 runs for experiment with 4 factors will not even detect all main interactions.

Runs	Number of Factors								
	2	3	4	5	6	7	8	9	10
2^2	full	III							
2^3		full	IV	III	III	III			
2^4			full	V	IV	IV	IV	III	III
2^5				full	VI	IV	IV	IV	IV
2^6					full	VII	V	IV	IV
2^7						full	VIII	VI	V

Table 29-G Resolution for different number of runs

It is recommended to choose fractional factorial design with resolution IV or higher. Resolution III could be acceptable in some cases, particularly when the cost of performing each run is considered significant.

CONTROL PHASE

30. UNDERSTANDING CONTROL PHASE

The fifth phase of Six Sigma DMAIC project is the *Control phase*. As the name suggests, this phase focused on implementing the solution from Improve phase and establishing control to ensure that the improved process is maintained.

Let us begin the discussion on Improve phase by reviewing the five phases of DMAIC and the $Y = f(X)$ formula.

DEFINE	MEASURE	ANALYZE	IMPROVE	CONTROL
• Which Y	• Collect data • X candidates	• Confirm Xs	• X values to solve Y • Pilot implementation	• Control Xs • Full implementation

Figure 30-1 Control phase in DMAIC

Control phase learns from pilot implementation and addresses the solution risks identified throughout prior DMAIC phases. Then, it uses the optimal values of X factors (the solution) from Improve phase to execute full scale implementation and establish control.

From Lean perspective, control is already built into a system as pull-based production was established and process waste was eliminated. Lean takes the principle of prevention as control. As refresher, the *Standardise* and *Sustain* steps from *5S of Lean* aim to maintain and monitor the activities, and then integrate them as part of organisational culture.

From Six Sigma perspective, the control of improved process is achieved using *Statistical Process Control* (SPC) technique. It is a systematic approach to monitor and control a process using statistical principles to ensure that process is stable and capable.

Typical steps of Improve phase in DMAIC include:
- *Prepare Control Plan.* This step uses Statistical Process Control principles to detect special cause of variation in a process.
- *Prepare Response Plan.* This step defines steps to be taken when problem with process is detected.
- *Implementation planning* is a critical step to ensure that implementation is well thought, systematic and all relevant stakeholders are on the same page. If they are already involved throughout the journey of DMAIC, it should not be difficult to obtain their support on the proposed changes.
- *Implement the solution.* If all the previous steps were done correctly, the full-scale implementation of the solution is a straightforward process.
- *Cost and benefit analysis.* This step calculates the new Sigma Level after process improvement and compares the cost from DMAIC project against the benefits it brings after implementation.

Control Plan and Response Plan

Control plan is a document with description about a process and how to control the process. It is a key deliverable from Control phase and is usually prepared in pair with response plan.

Common parts of control plan include:
- Process name and brief description
- High level process map, including process inputs and outputs
- Process owner
- Process specifications, tolerance limits and performance criteria
- Measurement guidance
- Monitoring: sampling and reporting frequency
- Type of chart used for reporting (if applicable)
- Mechanism to detect problems

As critically important tool to ensure improved process is maintained, control plan needs to have the following characteristics:
- Easy to follow, no assumption about prior knowledge. Everyone without prior knowledge about the system should be able to understand this document.

- Clear and specific. Information within the document should not have anything that can have multiple different interpretations.
- Repeatable and reproducible. Anyone following the plan multiple times will get the same results.

Control Plan uses *Statistical Process Control* (SPC) to monitor and control a system to detect instability. As long as process outputs stay within control limits, system is considered stable and could proceed as per normal.

Response plan is another key deliverable of Control phase. It defines steps to be taken when problems are detected and who is responsible to ensure the response actions are being executed correctly.

Common parts of response plan include:
- Process name and brief description
- Process owner
- Designated person to address a problem
- Escalation mechanism
- Stakeholders to be notified
- Initial steps to do (first response)
- Next actions to do
- What to do if the initial steps could not help with a situation

Designated person to address a problem should be someone who can quickly perform response action when necessary. It should be someone from the place where actual production takes place. Or, in case of digital process, someone with 24/7 access to the system. Response plan will fail to deliver its critical function if the designated person is someone who lives in a different city, or someone in high position who is usually very busy and might not be able to swiftly act when needed.

Escalation mechanism describes what needs to be done if the designated person is not available or is not responding the situation as per required by response plan document. Common path of escalation usually involves direct manager of designated person or someone with general responsibility for the production site where problem occurred.

Possible actions for response plan:
- Notify someone and increase monitoring. This type of action is used when system performance is going close to the acceptable limits.
- Manual intervention. This type of action is used when human intervention could reduce the negative impact from continuing with the normal process.

- Stop the process so that corrective action can be done before process can resume.
- Stop the process and escalate the finding. This type of action is used when certain problems could not be resolved by designated person. It could also be used if the corrective action requires higher level of access or clearance.
- Special instruction other than the ones mentioned above.

Implementation Planning and Execution

Implementation planning is the key to successful execution. It needs to take various aspects of the solution into consideration, learn from pilot implementation, address solution risks (including implementation risks) and ensure that all relevant stakeholders understand (and support) the changes.

A solution for process improvement could involve following aspects:
- Product specification change
- System design change
- Work procedure change (this would require training)
- Equipment change (could be physical or digital tools)
- Management change

Each of these changes needs to be addressed separately with own resources and schedule. It is very important to make sure that resources will be available on the scheduled time of implementation and prepare backup plan if some key resources are not available.

Product specification and system design changes might be needed to adjust with the dynamic of customer demand. Implementation of equipment change might include parallel runs with old equipment for fixed amount of time to make sure that the new equipment is performing at least as good as the old equipment.

If certain aspects of the change impacts ongoing production system, then system would need to be stopped for the change to take place. The time required to perform change is considered downtime for the production system. It might be preferred to perform change on normal downtime. This could be during night-time for production systems normally run during business hours or scheduled maintenance window for 24/7 production system. Clear communication with all stakeholders about the milestones (stop, change, resume) is the key to avoid implementation issues.

Trainings need to be completed before full scale implementation to make sure that everyone is ready to use the improved process. Documentation of process changes should come together with documentation updates in impacted components.

Management change could be the most difficult change to implement unless the relevant stakeholders have been part of the journey from the beginning of DMAIC. Solid buy-in from stakeholders and strong support from company executive and project champion are critically important for any management change to be successful.

It is important to consider that management change could be closely related to structural impact and emotional aspect. Highlighting the positive impacts expected for a company/organisation needs to be balanced with positive impacts for the employees. By nature, human beings are reluctant to change.

Cost and Benefit Analysis

Cost and benefit analysis are performed at the end of Control phase to help with closure. As a refresher, business case in project charter from Define phase typically include some comparison of project cost vs. estimated benefit to justify the decision to start process improvement project.

With the solution already implemented, the process improvement goes back full circle by analysing the actual cost and benefits to replace prior estimations.

Cost and benefit analysis could be performed right after full implementation of the solution, or 12 months after implementation to obtain real data about financial benefits from the improved process.

Common components of ongoing cost:
- Rework and scrap costs
- Customer returns and warranty claims costs
- Material costs
- Non-value-added costs (including inventory and transportation costs, please refer to nine wastes of Lean from Chapter 18)
- Human resource costs
- Training costs
- Sales and marketing costs
- Control and maintenance costs

Each component of cost is also potential component of benefits because benefits are gained when costs are reduced or eliminated. Other benefits include higher customer satisfaction, which will lead to stronger brand power and increased market share.

Project cost is considered as one-off spending. Therefore, it is treated differently from ongoing costs. Common project costs include:
- Human resource costs from project leader and team members
- Costs associated with the involvement of project champion, process owners, subject matter experts and relevant stakeholders
- Materials used during DMAIC phases
- Tools and equipment used during project
- Administration costs
- Pilot and full implementation costs

Project benefits are achieved from project outcomes. Coming to the end of Control phase, it is important to understand the difference between output and outcome. *Output* is direct deliverable of a process (could be product or service). *Outcome* is the result achieved by stakeholder using the output. A particular output may or may not achieve the desired outcome. For example: even the best quality car will not be perceived as value for customers who wish to purchase helicopters.

Return on Investment (ROI) is a popular metric to measure profitability of a Lean Six Sigma project.

$$ROI = \frac{Return - Operational - Investment}{Investment}$$

Return is the total income earned as the result of a project. This could be increased or newly produced earnings, cost saving from efficiency gains, assets appreciation or other qualitative benefits measured in financial equivalent. *Operational* is the costs associated with earning the income. *Investment* is the total costs of a Lean Six Sigma project.

Return on Assets (ROA) is another metric to measure profitability by comparing income against the value of assets. It does not directly include the cost of project but comparing ROA before and after a project could help to measure the effectiveness of a project.

$$ROA = \frac{Net\ Return}{Assets}$$

Net Return is the company's total net income earned as the result of some assets. This is calculated from gross income minus operational and other associated costs. *Assets* is the total value of the current valuations of company's assets. Note that depreciation value might need to be applied on some physical assets.

Net Present Value (NPV) calculates the benefits of a project from multiple years of cash flow.

$$NPV = \sum_{t=1}^{n} \frac{R_t}{(1+d)^t}$$

t is the time of cash flow, usually measured in years. R_t is the net cash flow (income minus costs) in t^{th} year. d is the *discount rate*; it represents return that could be earned in alternative investment. The basic idea behind calculating discount rate is that one thousand dollars today is more valuable than one thousand dollars next year because the money from today could be used to earn income between today and next year.

As an example, a DMAIC project costs $300,000 to complete. The return values in the first three years are $380,000 (year 1), $400,000 (year 2) and $370,000 (year 3). Operational cost is $60,000 per year. Total value of assets used for production is $200,000. Discount rate is 8%.

- *Return on Investment* is usually measured using single value of return. For the purpose of easy illustration, only the first-year return is used to calculate ROI.
- $ROI = \frac{380k - 60k - 300k}{300k} = 6.67\%$
- Similarly, *Return on Assets* is usually measured using single value of return. For the purpose of easy illustration, only the first-year return is used to calculate ROA.
- $ROA = \frac{380k - 60k}{200k} = 160\%$
- *Net Present Value* is good to measure return across multiple years. The calculation below calculates the NPV for gross
- $NPV = \frac{380k - 60k}{1.08^1} + \frac{400k - 60k}{1.08^2} + \frac{370k - 60k}{1.08^3} = \$833,879.49$
- Note that NPV is pure measurement of net cash flow, it does not consider the investment value nor asset to achieve such cash flow.

Benefits are not limited to financial benefits. Measurements of the improved *process capability* and *sigma level* are often provided as part of cost and benefit analysis. As refresher, there are four indicators of process capability (please refer to Chapter 14):

- *Cp* is the best-case performance of a process using short-term data.
- *Cpk* is the actual performance of a process using short-term data.
- *Pp* is the best-case performance of a process using long-term data.
- *Ppk* is the actual performance of a process using long-term data.

After all project benefits are measured, documented and validated, the final step is to get acknowledgement from project sponsors that the benefits have been realised and project can be considered successful. Project team could celebrate after Project Champion signs off the final cost and benefit document for project completion.

31. STATISTICAL PROCESS CONTROL (SPC)

Statistical Process Control (SPC) is a statistical method to monitor and control a process to make sure that it remains stable and capable. A system is considered stable if it has predictable mean and standard deviation. It is considered capable if it produces outputs within specification requirements.

It is important to note that SPC is different from quality control. A process can still be within control even though it might occasionally produce outputs that fail to meet customer requirements. On the other hand, process could be identified as out of statistical control even if all of its outputs during observation meets requirement limits.

	All outcomes meet requirements	Some outcomes fail to meet requirements
Process within statistical control	All good, expected state	Low process capability
Process is outside statistical control	False perception of quality	Visible problems, need immediate actions

Table 31-A Four possible states of process performance

The ideal condition is to have a process operating within statistical control with all outcomes meet requirement limits. If some outcomes fail to meet requirements but the process is still within statistical control, then the process have low capability. Process improvement is required to improve process capability.

On the other hand, process outside statistical control could produce all outcomes within requirements. This is a sign that a process brings false perception of quality and bad outcomes could start appearing at any time. The worst combination is when a process is outside statistical control and the outcomes do not meet requirements. This situation needs immediate actions.

Finding out whether a process outcome meets specification limits or not is a straightforward case of measurement. What about statistical control limits? Different types of control charts have different ways to calculate the control limits. These will be discussed later in this chapter.

Common vs. Special Cause Variations

To understand the concept of statistical control limits, it is important to understand the differences between common cause vs. special cause variations. *Common cause variations* are normal variations expected to happen during normal everyday operations. This type of variation is predictable and cannot be avoided without significantly changing the process. An example of common cause variation is weather. Days with lower temperature or days with high humidity might impact production results to a certain degree.

Special cause variations are the unusual factors not part of everyday operations. They cannot be statistically predicted, but it can be detected using process control. An example of special cause variation is new operator joining production team before completing mandatory trainings. As a result, this operator might not follow the right process. Note that not following standard procedure may or may not produce outcome that fails to meet requirements.

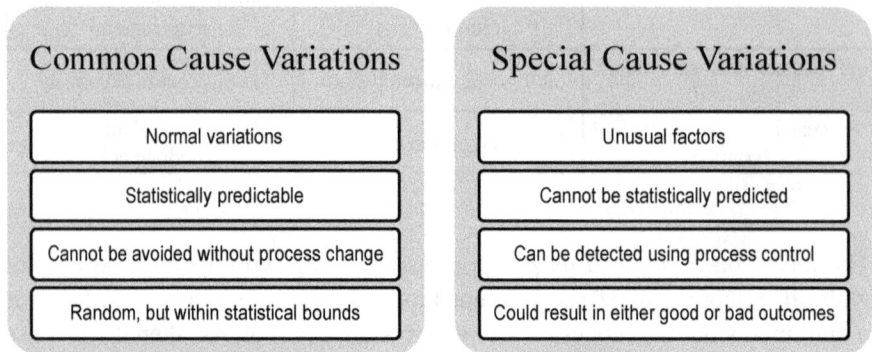

Common Cause Variations	Special Cause Variations
Normal variations	Unusual factors
Statistically predictable	Cannot be statistically predicted
Cannot be avoided without process change	Can be detected using process control
Random, but within statistical bounds	Could result in either good or bad outcomes

Figure 31-1 Common cause and special cause variations

It is important to note that special cause variations do not always result in bad outcome. Special cause variations bring unpredictable results outside the expected statistical range, it could be either positive or negative. Even if the result is positive, such result is not sustainable because it is not part of defined process.

Control limits are the boundaries between special cause and common cause variations. If certain variation is within control limits, it is considered as common cause variation. Otherwise, it is special cause variation, and its detection should be followed by executing Response Plan.

There are two kinds of control limit: upper and lower. The calculation of control limits is different for each type of control chart. It could be based on process mean, median, standard deviation, range or other statistical measures.

Example of control limits: process mean plus three times standard deviation (upper) and process mean minus three times standard deviation (lower). Sometimes there could be some real-life constraints that could change control limits because it is theoretically not possible to achieve observation point higher or lower than certain value.

As general guide, minimum 5 observation points are required to calculate control limits. The common practice is to have 30 observation points or more to obtain stable control limits. Observation points could be product characteristics (dimensions, toughness, weight, etc), processing times, time between events, number of occurrences something happens, number of incidents, number of defects, number of defective units. Some types of control charts require control limits to be recalculated with each addition of new data.

Process is considered stable if it has predictable mean and standard deviation. In other words, stable process only has common cause variations. For a process to be both stable and capable, control limits should be inside specification limits.

Control Chart in SPC

Control chart is a statistical tool to help operators to detect special cause variations indicating that process is out of statistical control. These charts were invented by *Walter Shewhart*, often known as *Shewhart chart*, and commonly used in control plan from Control phase of DMAIC.

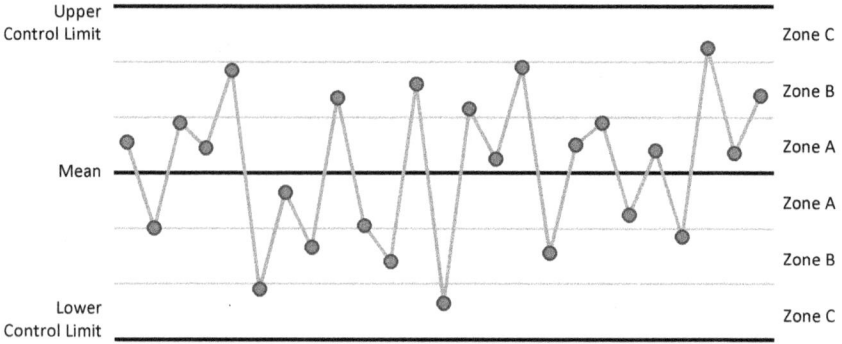

Figure 31-2 Anatomy of Control Chart

Figure 31-2 shows an example of control chart. All data points are located between upper and control limits. Control charts are divided into six equal zones. Three zones are located above the centre line (mean) and the other three are located below. The zones closest to centre line are called zone A, followed by zone B in the middle and zone C close to control limits. Areas outside control limits can be considered as zone D. For simple control chart with plus/minus three standard deviations as control limits, each zone represents one standard deviation.

Based on the six zones (plus zone D outside control limits), control chart detects special cause variations showing process out of statistical control. There are 8 basic patterns indicating special cause variations:

#	Name	Zone	Description
1	Beyond Limit	D	Any data point outside control limits.
2	Zone C	C	2 out of 3 consecutive data points are in zone C on the same side of centre line.
3	Zone BC	B,C	4 out of 5 consecutive data points are in zone B or C on the same side of centre line.
4	Zone ABC	A,B,C	8+ consecutive data points are in zone A, B or C on the same side of centre line.
5	Stratification	A	15+ consecutive data points are in zone A either sides of centre line.
6	Mixture	B,C	8+ consecutive data points are in zone B or C either sides of centre line.
7	Trend	A,B,C	7+ consecutive data points all increasing or all decreasing.
8	Over Control	A,B,C	14+ consecutive data points alternating up and down.

Table 31-B Control Chart patterns

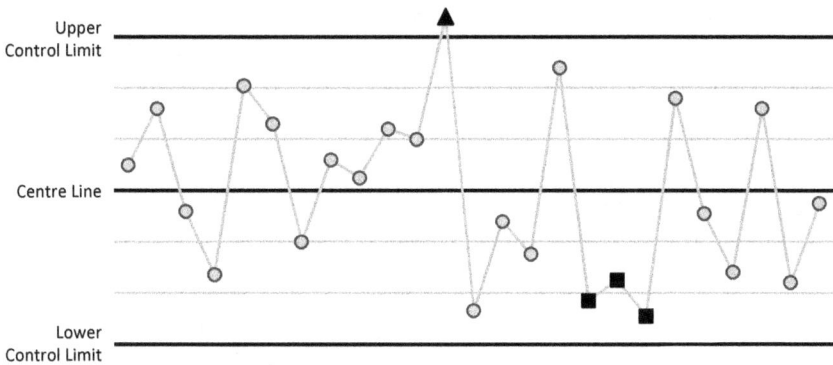

Figure 31-3 Beyond Limit and Zone C patterns in Control Chart

Beyond Limit is the first control chart pattern to indicate that a process is out of statistical control. As the name suggests, this pattern happens when there is any single data point outside control limit (zone D). This data point is shown with triangle marker in Figure 31-3.

Simply observing that no data is outside control limits does not mean that process is within statistical control. Other patterns from the chart could indicate special cause variations. *Zone C* pattern happens when at least 2 out of 3 consecutive data points are located in zone C on the same side of centre line. This can be observed in data points with square markers in Figure 31-3.

Both *Beyond Limit* and *Zone C* patterns represent large shift from centre line, which should not happen in process with only common cause variations. These could be caused by process steps not being followed properly, measurement error or problem with equipment.

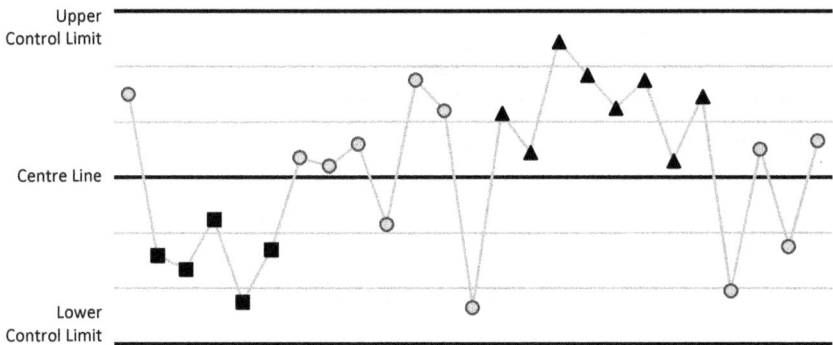

Figure 31-4 Zone BC and Zone ABC patterns in Control Chart

Zone BC pattern happens when at least 4 out of 5 consecutive data points are located in zone B or C on the same side of centre line. Five data points in Figure 31-4 have square markers. Four of them are located in zone B or C under centre line (same side).

Zone ABC pattern happens when 8 or more consecutive data points are located in zone A, B or C on the same side of centre line. Eight data points are shown in Figure 31-4 with triangle markers. All of them are located in zone A, B or C above centre line (same side).

Both *Zone BC* and *Zone ABC* patterns represent small shift from centre line in specific way that common cause variations are unlikely to produce. These could be caused by different measurement tools or recent change in the process.

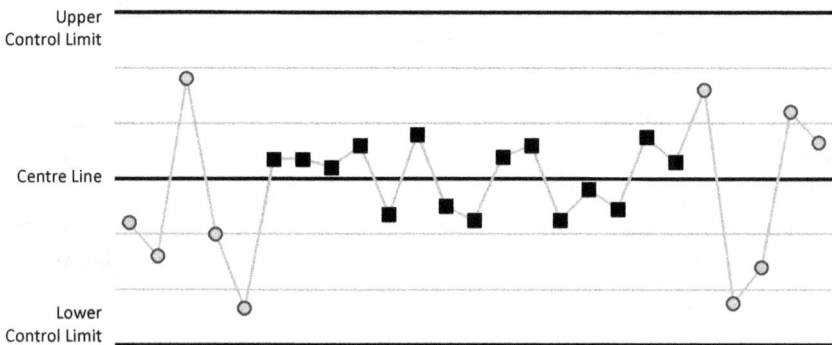

Figure 31-5 Stratification pattern in Control Chart

Stratification pattern is detected from 15 or more consecutive data points located in zone A either side of centre line. Data points with square markers in Figure 31-5 are all located in zone A above and under centre line. These could be caused by improved operators' skill, the use of higher quality raw material or recent process improvement. Stratification could also happen if control sample is taken systematically instead of randomly.

Special cause variations causing stratification pattern could be temporal or long term. If control chart consistently shows stratification pattern way beyond 15 consecutive point, there is a strong indication that process has improved, and control limits might need to be adjusted.

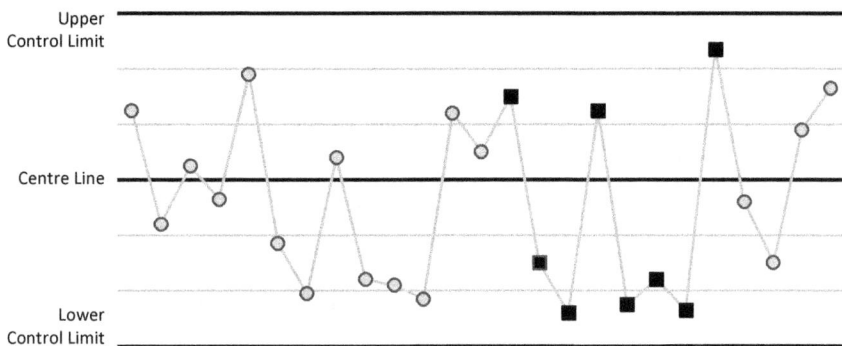

Figure 31-6 Mixture pattern in Control Chart

Mixture pattern is detected from 8 or more consecutive data points located in zone B or C either side of centre line. Data points with square markers in Figure 31-6Figure 31-5 are all located in zone B or C above and under centre line. These could happen when process under monitoring contains non-identical groups with different performances, such as different production machines and different groups of operators.

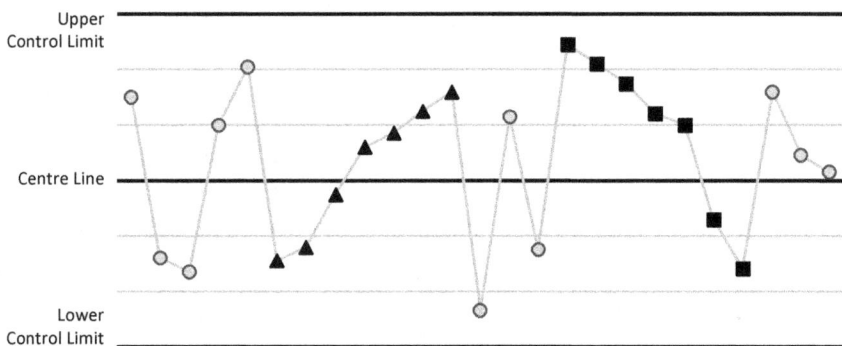

Figure 31-7 Trend Up and Trend Down patterns in Control Chart

Trend pattern is detected from 7 or more consecutive data points all increasing or all decreasing in zone A, B or C either side of centre line. Data points with triangle markers in Figure 31-7Figure 31-6Figure 31-5 show *trend up* pattern (all increasing). Similarly, data points with square markers show *trend down* pattern (all decreasing). These could be caused by equipment wear or environmental factors such as increasing or decreasing temperature during season change.

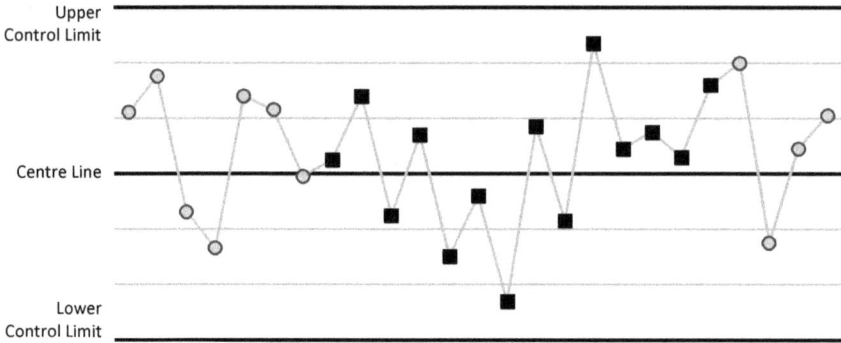

Figure 31-8 Over Control pattern in Control Chart

Over Control pattern is detected from 14 or more consecutive data points alternating up and down in zone A, B or C either side of centre line. Data points with square markers in Figure 31-8 show this pattern. These could be caused by alternating factor in the process (such as alternating raw materials or two operators taking turns) or tampering by operators.

Multiple patterns could be detected from the same control chart, even with overlapping data points. Best practice is to analyse each pattern one at a time, and then address the root cause.

Statistical Process Control requires data from production results to be monitored on a regular basis. Depending on the type of product (or service), measuring all process outputs might not be feasible and sampling technique could be used to represent the overall system performance. Sample data could be analysed individually, or they could be categorised into logical groups.

There are different types of control charts, grouped by the type of data being monitored. Control charts for continuous data will be discussed in Chapter 32:

- I-MR Chart
- Xbar-R Chart
- Xbar-S Chart

Control charts for discrete or attribute data will be discussed in Chapter 33:

- C Chart
- U Chart
- NP Chart
- P Chart

Time-weighted control charts are special types of control chart with ability to consider historical data. These charts will be discussed in Chapter 34:

- CuSum Chart
- EWMA Chart

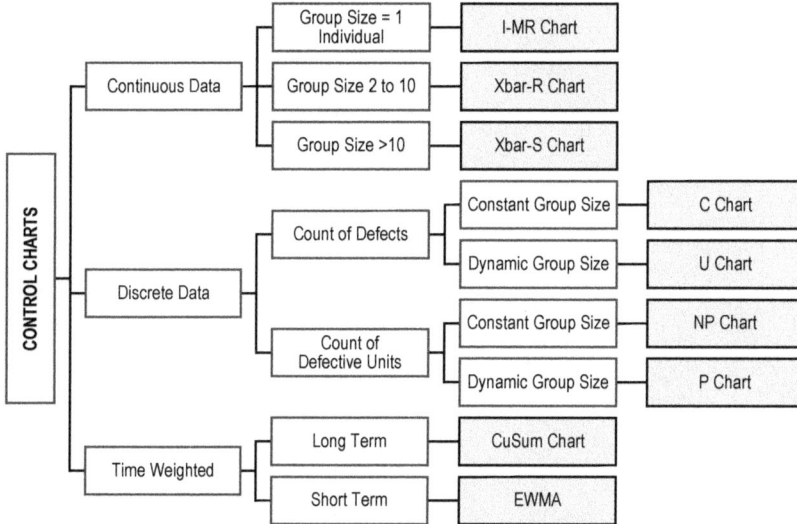

Figure 31-9 Control Chart selection

Different control charts have different ways to calculate control limits. Charts for variable data have different out-of-control patterns from charts for attribute data.

Control charts are powerful tool to compare system performance before and after change. This could be before and after process change through DMAIC project, or during normal system operation before and after special cause variation is addressed.

Not all factors and processes need control charts. Overusing control charts will reduce its usefulness because alerts triggered by non-important issues will hide the important ones.

32. CONTROL CHARTS FOR CONTINUOUS DATA

Continuous data is something that can be measured. Data from this type can take any value within a range and there is an infinite number of possible values. Before continuing with this chapter, it is strongly recommended to review Chapter 31 about Statistical Process Control.

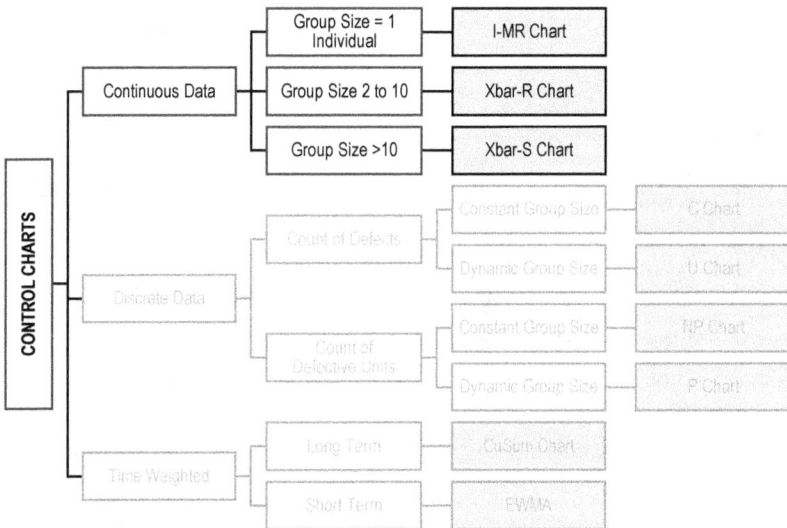

Figure 32-1 Control Charts for continuous data

There are three common control charts for continuous data:
- I-MR Chart (Individual and Moving Range) for direct observation of individual data.
- Xbar-R Chart (Mean and Range) for grouped data. Each group has 2 to 10 data points.
- Xbar-S Chart (Mean and Standard Deviation) for grouped data. Each group has more than 10 data points.

Control charts for continuous data plots time, units or groups of units as X. Values of Y could be the individual data points, average of values in each group, range of data points in each group or difference between two data points.

Special cause variations are detected from certain patterns from control chart. These patterns indicate that process is out of statistical control. For control charts with continuous data, the following patterns are observed:
- *Beyond Limit*: outside control limit.
- *Zone C*: 2 out of 3 data points on the same side.
- *Zone BC*: 4 out of 5 data points on the same side.
- *Zone ABC*: 8+ data points on the same side.
- *Stratification*: 15+ data points in zone A either side.
- *Mixture*: 8+ data points in zone B or C either side.
- *Trend*: 7+ data points all increasing or all decreasing.
- *Over Control*: 14+ data points alternating up and down.

I-MR Chart

I-MR chart is the simplest form of control chart. It contains two charts that always come as pair. The first chart is *individual* data points chart and the second one is *moving range* chart representing the differences (absolute value) between each data point in individual chart and its preceding value.

Data for I-MR chart could be obtained from full data or sampling (when full collection is not feasible or too expensive). Whole population data are usually used when the measurement system is automated or already built into the process. Sampling is usually chosen when data measurement requires manual additional efforts.

Unlike other control charts, I-MR chart does not implement data grouping. Each data point is observed individually for both individual and moving range charts. This type of monitoring is usually preferred if the number of produced units are relatively small compared to the possible sources of variations.

Steps of working with I-MR chart:

- Collect data.
- Create I (individual) chart based on collected data.
- Calculate moving range from each data point in individual chart.
- Create MR (moving range) chart based on calculated moving range.
- Calculate control limits for MR chart.
- Analyse MR chart.
- Calculate control limits for I chart.
- Analyse I chart.

To help with explanation, the following data will be used:

86	75	30	18	74	79	49	37	83	30
21	67	42	4	12	40	97	69	33	56

These data are mapped into individual chart:

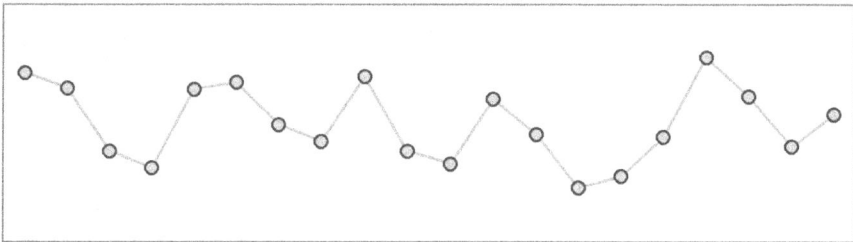

Figure 32-2 Draft of Individual Chart

There are 20 groups of data ($k = 20$), each is calculated from one data point. Group size (n) is 1. Individual chart in Figure 32-2 is still a draft because control limits have not been calculated. The calculation of control limits for individual chart requires data from moving range chart.

Moving range points are calculated from the absolute difference between each data point in individual chart and its preceding value. There is no moving range value for the first observation because the first value in individual chart has no previous value.

I	MR	I	MR	I	MR	I	MR
86		79	5	21	9	40	28
75	11	49	30	67	46	97	57
30	45	37	12	42	25	69	28
18	12	83	46	4	38	33	36
74	56	30	53	12	8	56	23

Moving range observations are mapped into moving range chart:

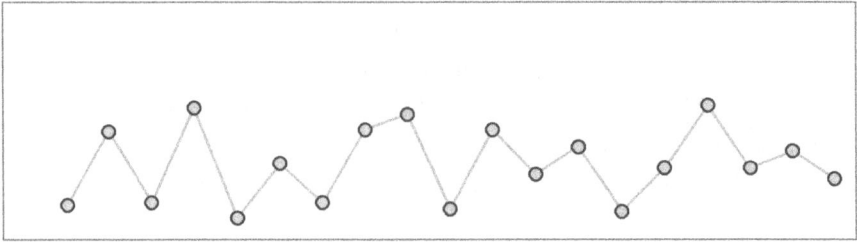

Figure 32-3 Draft of Moving Range Chart

Upper Control Limit (UCL) and *Lower Control Limit* (LCL) of MR chart are calculated using the following formula:

$$UCL = \bar{x}_{MR} \times D4$$

$$LCL = 0$$

$\bar{x}_{MR}$ is the average of moving range values. *D4* is a value from reference table. Table 32-A shows partial table with values required for I-MR chart. Full table can be obtained from Chapter 38.

n	2	3	4	5	6	7
D2	1.128	1.693	2.059	2.236	2.534	2.704
D4	3.267	2.575	2.282	2.114	2.004	1.924

Table 32-A Values of D2 and D4 for I-MR Chart

Even though each group in individual chart is calculated from one data point, $n = 2$ is used for the formula to calculate control limits because the nature of moving range chart compares a value with its preceding value.

Using the formula above:
- $UCL = \bar{x}_{MR} \times D4 = 29.8947 \times 3.267 = 97.6661$
- $LCL = 0$

With the calculated control limits, MR chart can be completed:

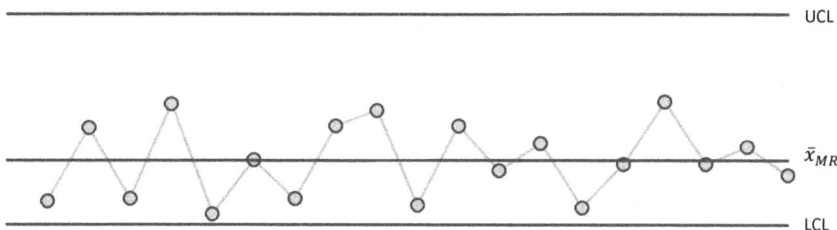

Figure 32-4 Moving Range Chart

UCL and LCL of individual chart are calculated using the following formula:

$$UCL = \bar{x}_I + \frac{3 \times \bar{x}_{MR}}{D2}$$

$$LCL = \bar{x}_I - \frac{3 \times \bar{x}_{MR}}{D2}$$

$\bar{x}_I$ is the average of individual values. $\bar{x}_{MR}$ is the average of moving range values. $D2$ is a value from reference table. Please refer to Table 32-A.

Using the formula above:

- $UCL = \bar{x}_I + \frac{3 \times \bar{x}_{MR}}{D2} = 50.1 + \frac{3 \times 29.8947}{1.128} = 129.6073$
- $LCL = \bar{x}_I - \frac{3 \times \bar{x}_{MR}}{D2} = 50.1 - \frac{3 \times 29.8947}{1.128} = -29.4073$

With the calculated control limits, I chart can be completed:

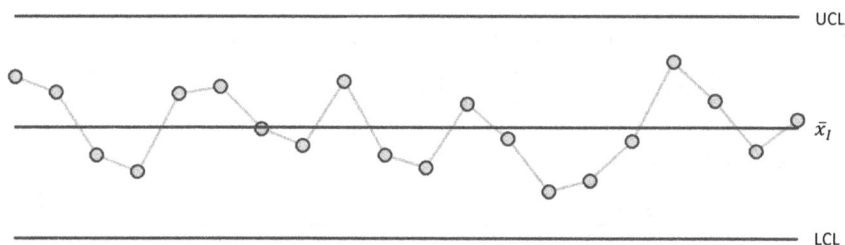

Figure 32-5 Individual Chart

If MR chart is out of statistical control, the control limits on I chart will be not accurate. We can only use I chart to detect process stability (no special cause variation) after confirming that MR chart is within statistical control.

Xbar-R Chart

Xbar-R chart was the most popular control chart before the digital era, mainly because this chart is the easiest to calculate without the help of computer. As the name suggests, Xbar-R chart contains two charts that always come as pair: *Xbar* chart and *Range* chart.

Data for Xbar-R chart are divided into groups. Grouping usually follows logical classifications based on the nature of data. For example, data can be grouped based on the operators taking the data, day/night shift, batch of raw material, or it could be based on simple sequence. For the simple sequence grouping, the first n data points are allocated into the first group, the following n data points go to the second group and so on.

Steps of working with Xbar-R chart:
- Collect data.
- Organise data into k groups, each having n data. Xbar-R chart is recommended for groups with n between 2 to 10.
- Calculate average and range values from each group.
- Create Xbar chart based on collected data. Each value in chart is the average of values within each group.
- Create Range chart based on calculated range. Each value in chart is the difference between maximum and minimum values in each group.
- Calculate control limits for Range chart.
- Analyse Range chart.
- Calculate control limits for Xbar chart.
- Analyse Xbar chart.

To help with explanation, the following data will be used:

Group	Measured Data				Xbar	R	Group	Measured Data				Xbar	R
	1	2	3	4				1	2	3	4		
1	44	21	52	42	39.75	31	11	63	68	50	29	52.50	39
2	72	10	29	68	44.75	62	12	16	24	20	22	20.50	8
3	43	41	95	68	61.75	54	13	75	80	78	81	78.50	6
4	61	60	55	57	58.25	6	14	56	8	25	22	27.75	48
5	11	51	23	71	39.00	60	15	56	79	20	53	52.00	59
6	33	70	56	75	58.50	42	16	33	55	38	10	34.00	45
7	23	75	88	35	55.25	65	17	71	80	75	85	77.75	14
8	16	20	25	16	19.25	9	18	35	80	71	3	47.25	77
9	40	83	92	29	61.00	63	19	69	56	45	89	64.75	44
10	19	79	84	79	65.25	65	20	23	33	70	13	34.75	57
											AVG	49.625	42.7

There are 20 groups of data ($k = 20$), each group has 4 measured data ($n = 4$). Xbar values are calculated as the average of 4 values within the same group. Range values are calculated as the difference between maximum and minimum of 4 values within a group.

The average values of all groups are mapped into Xbar chart:

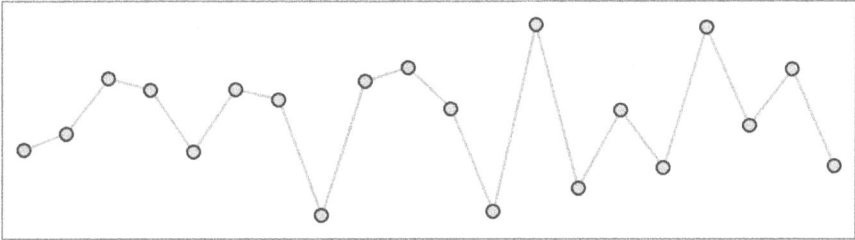

Figure 32-6 Draft of Xbar Chart for Xbar-R

Next, the range values of all groups are mapped into Range chart:

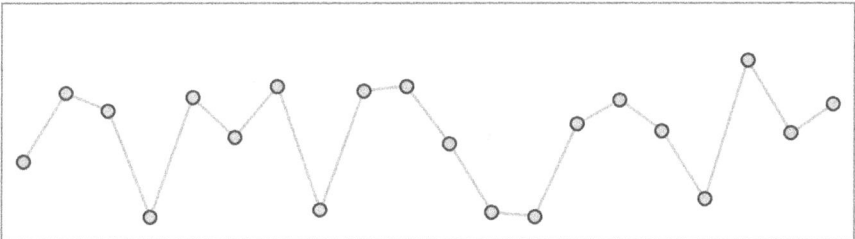

Figure 32-7 Draft of Range Chart for Xbar-R

Upper Control Limit (UCL) and *Lower Control Limit* (LCL) of Range chart are calculated using the following formula:

$$UCL = \bar{R} \times D4$$

$$LCL = \begin{cases} \bar{R} \times D3, & n > 7 \\ 0, & n \leq 7 \end{cases}$$

$\bar{R}$ is the average of range values. *D3* and *D4* are values from reference table. Table 32-B shows partial table with values required for Xbar-R chart. Full table can be obtained from Chapter 38. Note that the values of *D3* are zero for *n* less than 7.

n	2	3	4	5	6	7
A2	1.880	1.023	0.729	0.577	0.483	0.419
D3	0.000	0.000	0.000	0.000	0.000	0.076
D4	3.267	2.575	2.282	2.114	2.004	1.924

Table 32-B Values of A2, D3 and D4 for Xbar-R Chart

Using the formula above:

- $UCL = \bar{R} \times D4 = 42.7 \times 2.282 = 97.4414$
- $LCL = 0$

With the calculated control limits, Range chart can be completed:

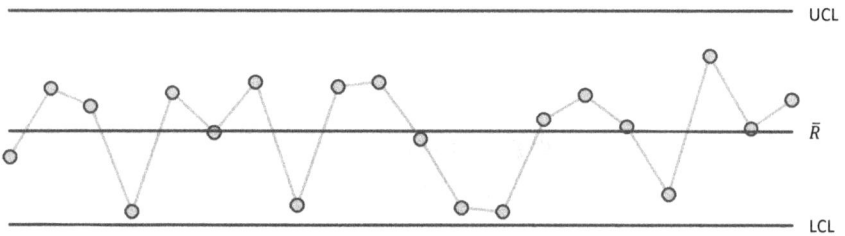

Figure 32-8 Range Chart for Xbar-R

UCL and LCL of Xbar chart are calculated using the following formula:

$$UCL = \overline{Xbar} + (A2 \times \bar{R})$$

$$LCL = \overline{Xbar} - (A2 \times \bar{R})$$

$\overline{Xbar}$ is the average of Xbar values (grand mean of all data). $\bar{R}$ is the average of range values. *A2* is value from reference table. Please refer to Table 32-B.

Using the formula above:

- $UCL = \overline{Xbar} + (A2 \times \bar{R}) = 49.625 + (0.729 \times 42.7) = 81.7533$
- $LCL = \overline{Xbar} - (A2 \times \bar{R}) = 49.625 + (0.729 \times 42.7) = 18.4967$

With the calculated control limits, Xbar chart can be completed:

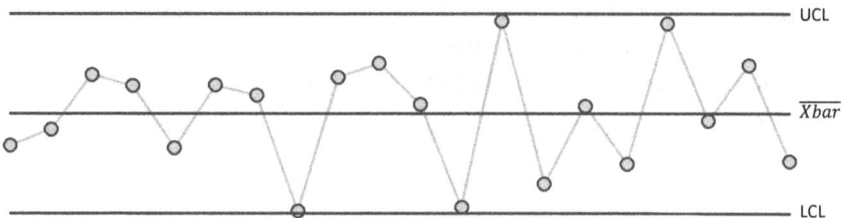

Figure 32-9 Xbar Chart for Xbar-R

If Range chart is out of statistical control, the control limits on Xbar chart will be not accurate. We can only use Xbar chart to detect process stability (no special cause variation) after confirming that Range chart is within statistical control.

Xbar-S Chart

Xbar-S chart is an alternative version of Xbar-R chart designed to handle groups with larger size. As the name suggests, Xbar-S chart contains two charts that always come as pair: *Xbar* chart and *Standard Deviation* chart.

Data for Xbar-S chart are divided into groups, similar to groups in Xbar-R chart. Each group in Xbar-S chart needs to have more than 10 data values. Instead of range, the second chart uses standard deviation.

Steps of working with Xbar-S chart:
- Collect data.
- Organise data into k groups, each having n data. Xbar-S chart is recommended for groups with n greater than 10.
- Calculate average and standard deviation values from each group.
- Create Xbar chart based on collected data. Each value in chart is the average of values within each group.
- Create Standard Deviation chart based on calculated range. Each value in chart is the standard deviation values from each group.
- Calculate control limits for Standard Deviation chart.
- Analyse Standard Deviation chart.
- Calculate control limits for Xbar chart.
- Analyse Xbar chart.

To help with explanation, the following data will be used:

Group	Measured Data				Xbar	S	Group	Measured Data				Xbar	S
	1	2	3	4				1	2	3	4		
1	44	21	52	42	39.75	13.23	11	63	68	50	29	52.50	17.41
2	72	10	29	68	44.75	30.21	12	16	24	20	22	20.50	3.42
3	43	41	95	68	61.75	25.34	13	75	80	78	81	78.50	2.65
4	61	60	55	57	58.25	2.75	14	56	8	25	22	27.75	20.24
5	11	51	23	71	39.00	27.13	15	56	79	20	53	52.00	24.29
6	33	70	56	75	58.50	18.81	16	33	55	38	10	34.00	18.57
7	23	75	88	35	55.25	31.16	17	71	80	75	85	77.75	6.08
8	16	20	25	16	19.25	4.27	18	35	80	71	3	47.25	35.33
9	40	83	92	29	61.00	31.14	19	69	56	45	89	64.75	18.91
10	19	79	84	79	65.25	30.92	20	23	33	70	13	34.75	24.88
											AVG	49.625	19.34

There are 20 groups of data ($k = 20$), each group has 4 measured data ($n = 4$). Xbar values are calculated as the average of 4 values within the same group. Standard deviation values are calculated from 4 values within each group.

The average values of all groups are mapped into Xbar chart:

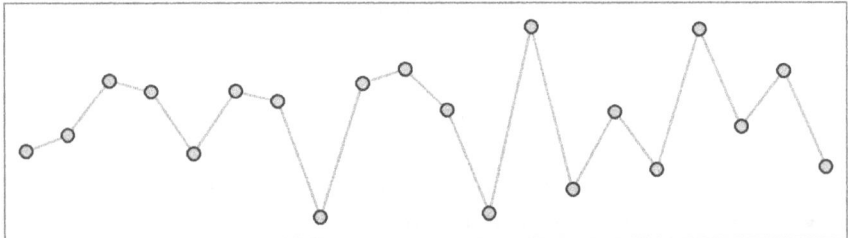

Figure 32-10 Draft of Xbar Chart for Xbar-S

Next, the range values of all groups are mapped into Range chart:

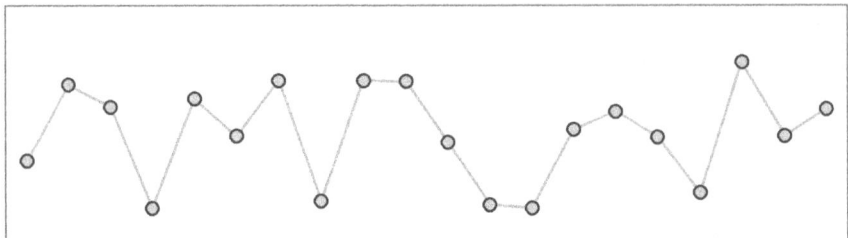

Figure 32-11 Draft of Standard Deviation Chart for Xbar-S

Upper Control Limit (UCL) and *Lower Control Limit* (LCL) of Standard Deviation chart are calculated using the following formula:

$$UCL = \bar{S} \times B4$$

$$LCL = \begin{cases} \bar{S} \times B3, & n > 6 \\ 0, & n \leq 6 \end{cases}$$

$\bar{S}$ is the average of standard deviation values. *B3* and *B4* are values from reference table. Table 32-C shows partial table with values required for Xbar-S chart. Full table can be obtained from Chapter 38. Note that the values of *B3* are zero for *n* less than 6.

n	2	3	4	5	6	7
A3	2.659	1.954	1.628	1.427	1.287	1.182
B3	0.000	0.000	0.000	0.000	0.030	0.118
B4	3.267	2.568	2.266	2.089	1.970	1.882

Table 32-C Values of A3, B3 and B4 for Xbar-S Chart

Using the formula above:
- $UCL = \bar{S} \times B4 = 19.3364 \times 2.266 = 43.8162$
- $LCL = 0$

With the calculated control limits, Standard Deviation chart can be completed:

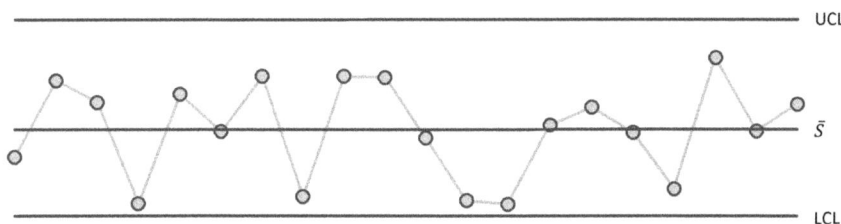

Figure 32-12 Standard Deviation Chart for Xbar-S

UCL and LCL of Xbar chart are calculated using the following formula:

$$UCL = \overline{Xbar} + (A3 \times \bar{S})$$

$$LCL = \overline{Xbar} - (A3 \times \bar{S})$$

$\overline{Xbar}$ is the average of Xbar values (grand mean of all data). $\bar{S}$ is the average of standard deviation values. *A3* is value from reference table. Please refer to Table 32-C.

Using the formula above:

- $UCL = \overline{Xbar} + (A3 \times \overline{S}) = 49.625 + (1.628 \times 19.34) = 81.1046$
- $LCL = \overline{Xbar} - (A3 \times \overline{S}) = 49.625 + (1.628 \times 19.34) = 18.1454$

With the calculated control limits, Xbar chart can be completed:

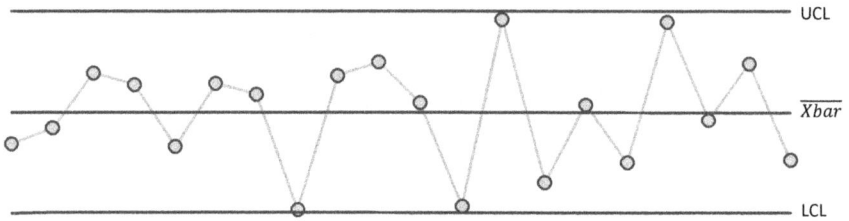

Figure 32-13 Xbar Chart for Xbar-R

If Standard Deviation chart is out of statistical control, the control limits on Xbar chart will be not accurate. We can only use Xbar chart to detect process stability (no special cause variation) after confirming that Standard Deviation chart is within statistical control.

33. CONTROL CHARTS FOR DISCRETE DATA

Discrete data is something that can be counted. For Statistical Process Control, it is a common practice to monitor count of defects and count of defective units. A defect is any aspect of a product or service that fails to meet requirements. One unit of product or service is considered defective if it contains one or more defects. Before continuing with this chapter, it is strongly recommended to review Chapter 31 about Statistical Process Control.

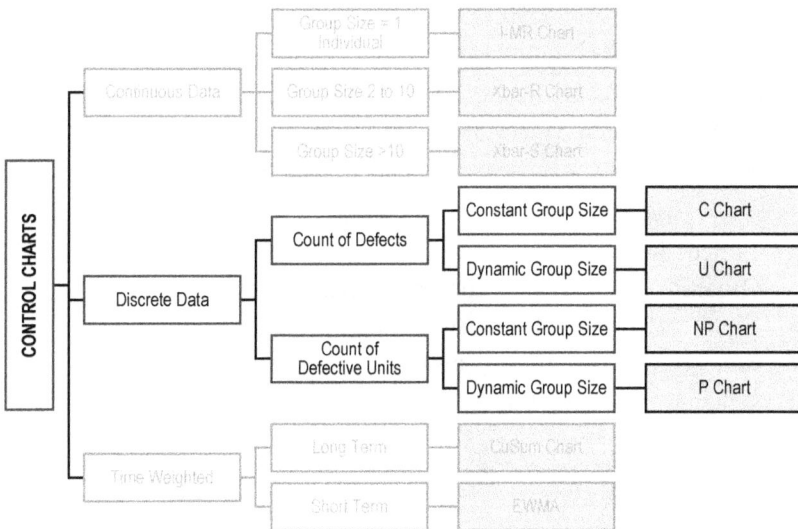

Figure 33-1 Control Charts for discrete data

There are four common control charts for discrete data:
- C Chart for count of defects with constant group size.
- U Chart for count of defects with dynamic group size.
- NP Chart for count of defective units with constant group size.
- P Chart for count of defective units with dynamic group size.

Control charts for discrete data plots time or grouped units as X. Values of Y could be proportion or count of data.

Special cause variations are detected from certain patterns from the chart. These patterns indicate that process is out of statistical control. For control charts with discrete data, the following patterns are observed:
- *Beyond Limit*: outside control limit.
- *Zone ABC*: 8+ data points on the same side.
- *Trend*: 7+ data points all increasing or all decreasing.
- *Over Control*: 14+ data points alternating up and down.

C Chart

C chart is a control chart for attribute data. It counts the number of defects within each group. This chart is commonly used to monitor count of data that happens regularly with large number of opportunities but small number of actual occurrences. For example: how many customer returns received every week, or how many times certain production machine needs to be readjusted every month.

Data for C chart are divided into groups. Each group must have equal size of 2 or greater. The average of all count values from every group must be greater than 2. Group criteria is normally based on time or constraints within a process.

Steps of working with C chart:
- Collect data.
- Organise data into k groups, each having n data.
- Count occurrences from each group.
- Plot <u>count of occurrences</u> into C chart.
- Calculate control limits for C chart.
- Analyse C chart.

To help with explanation, the following data will be used:

Group	Count		Group	Count		Group	Count		Group	Count
1	11		6	6		11	14		16	17
2	15		7	27		12	18		17	29
3	26		8	24		13	10		18	7
4	25		9	9		14	22		19	23
5	28		10	5		15	12		20	16

There are 20 groups of data ($k = 20$). The average of all counts is 17.2.

The count values of all groups are mapped into C chart:

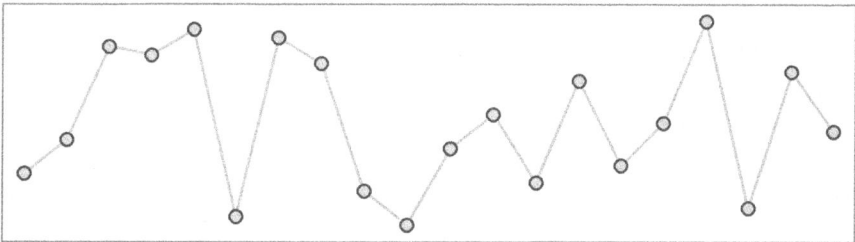

Figure 33-2 Draft of C Chart

Upper Control Limit (UCL) and *Lower Control Limit* (LCL) of C chart are calculated using the following formula:

$$UCL = \bar{c} + \left(3 \times \sqrt{\bar{c}}\right)$$

$$LCL = max\left(\bar{c} - \left(3 \times \sqrt{\bar{c}}\right); 0\right)$$

Using the formula above:
- $UCL = \bar{c} + \left(3 \times \sqrt{\bar{c}}\right) = 29.6419$
- $LCL = max\left(\bar{c} - \left(3 \times \sqrt{\bar{c}}\right); 0\right) = max(4.7581; 0) = 4.7581$

With the calculated control limits, C chart can be completed:

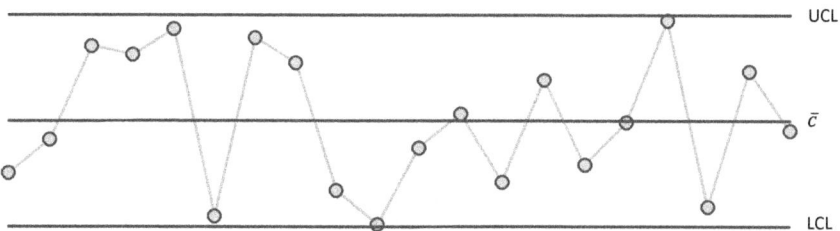

Figure 33-3 C Chart

325

U Chart

U chart is a control chart for attribute data with dynamic group size. It counts the number of defects within each group. Data for C chart are divided into groups with different sizes. The size of each group should be large enough to have at least 5 defects.

Steps of working with U chart:
- Collect data.
- Organise data into k groups with different sizes.
- Count occurrences and calculate U ratio from each group.
- Plot U ratio values into U chart.
- Calculate control limits for U chart.
- Analyse U chart.

To help with explanation, the following data will be used:

Group	Size	Count	Group	Size	Count	Group	Size	Count	Group	Size	Count
1	25	9	6	34	12	11	18	7	16	20	10
2	37	21	7	32	17	12	32	13	17	37	7
3	7	8	8	38	10	13	24	14	18	19	11
4	17	11	9	24	11	14	22	5	19	46	19
5	21	10	10	40	18	15	36	21	20	33	6

There are 20 groups of data ($k = 20$). For each group, calculate the U ratio of that group using the formula:

$$u_i = \frac{c_i}{n_i}$$

u_i is the U ratio for i^{th} group. c_i is the count of occurrences in i^{th} group. n_i is the size of ith group.

U ratio is different from proportions because the value can be greater than one. It is possible to observe more defects than the number of units if there are multiple defects per unit.

The calculation of U ratios:
- $u_1 = \frac{c_1}{n_1} = \frac{9}{25} = 0.3600$
- $u_2 = \frac{c_2}{n_2} = \frac{21}{37} = 0.5676$
- $u_3 = \frac{c_3}{n_3} = \frac{8}{7} = 1.1429$ (note that this U ratio is greater than 1)
- $u_4 = \frac{c_4}{n_4} = \frac{11}{17} = 0.6471$

- $u_5 = \dfrac{c_5}{n_5} = \dfrac{10}{21} = 0.4762$
- Do the same for u_6 to u_{20}.

U ratio values for all groups:

Group	Size	Count	U ratio	LCL	UCL
1	25	8	0.36		
2	37	21	0.57		
3	10	9	1.14		
4	17	11	0.65		
5	21	10	0.48		
6	34	12	0.35		
7	32	17	0.53		
8	38	10	0.26		
9	24	11	0.46		
10	40	18	0.45		

Group	Size	Count	U ratio	LCL	UCL
11	18	7	0.39		
12	32	13	0.41		
13	24	14	0.58		
14	22	5	0.23		
15	36	21	0.58		
16	20	10	0.50		
17	37	7	0.19		
18	19	11	0.58		
19	46	19	0.41		
20	33	6	0.18		

Map the U ratios of all groups into U chart:

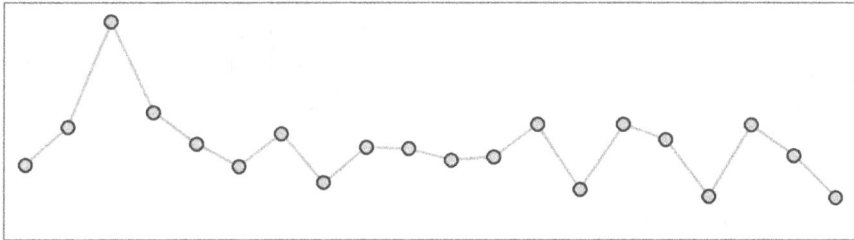

Figure 33-4 Draft of U Chart

Next, calculate U-bar (grand U ratio):

$$\bar{u} = \frac{\sum c}{\sum n}$$

Total number of counts from all groups is 240. The sum of all group sizes is 562. Therefore, the U-bar is $\bar{u} = \dfrac{240}{562} = 0.4270$.

Each U ratio value in U chart has different *Upper Control Limit* (UCL) and *Lower Control Limit* (LCL):

$$UCL_i = \bar{u} + \left(3 \times \sqrt{\bar{u}/n_i}\right)$$

$$LCL_i = max\left(\bar{u} - \left(3 \times \sqrt{\bar{u}/n_i}\right); 0\right)$$

$\bar{u}$ is the grand U ratio from all groups. n_i is the size of ith group. LCL could not be less than zero but UCL can be greater than one.

Calculations of UCL and LCL:

- $UCL_1 = \bar{u} + \left(3 \times \sqrt{\bar{u}/25}\right) = 0.82$
- $LCL_1 = max\left(\bar{u} - \left(3 \times \sqrt{\bar{u}/25}\right); 0\right) = max(0.03; 0) = 0.03$
- $UCL_2 = \bar{u} + \left(3 \times \sqrt{\bar{u}/37}\right) = 0.75$
- $LCL_2 = max\left(\bar{u} - \left(3 \times \sqrt{\bar{u}/37}\right); 0\right) = max(0.10; 0) = 0.10$
- $UCL_3 = \bar{u} + \left(3 \times \sqrt{\bar{u}/7}\right) = 1.17$
- $LCL_3 = max\left(\bar{u} - \left(3 \times \sqrt{\bar{u}/7}\right); 0\right) = max(-0.31; 0) = 0.00$
- Do the same for UCL_4 to UCL_{20} and LCL_4 to LCL_{20}.

UCL and LCL for all groups:

Group	Size	Count	U ratio	UCL	LCL
1	25	9	0.36	0.82	0.03
2	37	21	0.57	0.75	0.10
3	7	8	1.14	1.17	0.00
4	17	11	0.65	0.90	0.00
5	21	10	0.48	0.85	0.00
6	34	12	0.35	0.76	0.09
7	32	17	0.53	0.77	0.08
8	38	10	0.26	0.75	0.11
9	24	11	0.46	0.83	0.03
10	40	18	0.45	0.74	0.12

Group	Size	Count	U ratio	UCL	LCL
11	18	7	0.39	0.89	0.00
12	32	13	0.41	0.77	0.08
13	24	14	0.58	0.83	0.03
14	22	5	0.23	0.85	0.01
15	36	21	0.58	0.75	0.10
16	20	10	0.50	0.87	0.00
17	37	7	0.19	0.75	0.10
18	19	11	0.58	0.88	0.00
19	46	19	0.41	0.72	0.14
20	33	6	0.18	0.77	0.09

With the calculated control limits, U chart can be completed:

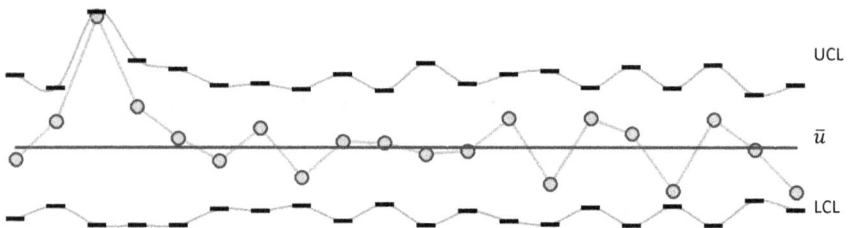

Figure 33-5 U Chart

Calculating different control limits for every data point is necessary to decrease the risk of false positive detection. For comparison, static UCL and

LCL are calculated as:

$$UCL = \bar{u} + \left(3 \times \sqrt{\bar{u}/\bar{n}}\right)$$

$$LCL = max\left(\bar{u} - \left(3 \times \sqrt{\bar{u}/\bar{n}}\right); 0\right)$$

$\bar{u}$ is the grand U ratio from all groups. $\bar{n}$ is average of group the sizes. UCL could not be greater than one and LCL could not be less than zero.

Calculations of static UCL and LCL:

- $\bar{n} = \frac{\Sigma n}{k} = \frac{562}{20} = 28.1$
- $UCL = \bar{u} + \left(3 \times \sqrt{\bar{u}/\bar{n}}\right) = 0.80$
- $LCL = max\left(\bar{u} - \left(3 \times \sqrt{\bar{u}/\bar{n}}\right); 0\right) = max(0.06; 0) = 0.06$

With the static control limits, U chart can be completed:

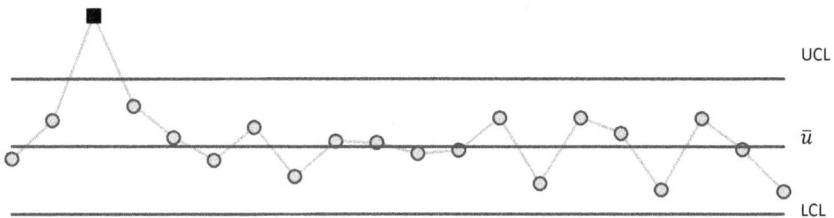

Figure 33-6 U Chart with Static Control Limits

As demonstrated in Figure 33-6, static control limits falsely detect U ratio for third group (shown in rectangle marker) as special cause variation. This happens because static control limits fail to consider that third group has small amount of data.

NP Chart

NP chart is a control chart for pass/fail attribute data. It counts the number of defective units within each group. How is it different from counting the number of defects?

One defective unit might have one or multiple defects. Even though a defective unit with one defect and another unit with ten defects might end up to the same pile of scrap, ten defects show more variations compared to one defect. Counting the number of defects is considered as the preferred way to measure system performance. Counting the number of defective units is often used to measure the financial impact to the organisation. Please review the discussions on defect opportunity from Chapter 03.

Unit A1	Unit A2	Unit A3	Unit A4	Unit A5	Unit A6	Unit A7
		D · D		· · D		
	· · D	D · D		· · D		

Unit B1	Unit B2	Unit B3	Unit B4	Unit B5	Unit B6	Unit B7
				· · D		
	D · ·		· · D			

Unit C1	Unit C3	Unit C3	Unit C4	Unit C5	Unit C6	Unit C7
		D · ·				· · D
	· · D		· · D		D · ·	

Table 33-A Defects vs. defective units

Table 33-A shows three groups of data: A, B and C. Each group has 7 units. Each unit has 4 defect opportunities. Defect opportunities are shown as boxes attached to units. Defects are indicated by letter D inside a box. One unit is considered as defective if it has at least one defect.

- Group A has 7 defects, but only has 3 defective units because unit A3 has 3 defects and unit A5 has 2 defects.
- Group B has 3 defects and 3 defective units.
- Group C has 5 defects and 5 defective units.
- Group A has more defects than group B, but the count of defective units will show that group A has the same count as group B.
- Group C has less defects compared to group A, but the count of defective units actually shows higher amount.

NP chart is commonly used to count pass or fail without going into details on how bad the failure is. For example: how many products are scrapped every week, how many defective units in a fixed-size batch, or how many unique visitors are coming every month (multiple visits from the same visitor is counted as one).

Data for NP chart are divided into groups. Each group must have equal size of n. Minimum group size must satisfy these requirements:
- n times the average of proportion must be greater than 5.
- n times [one minus the average of proportion] must be greater than 5.

Steps of working with NP chart:
- Collect data.
- Organise data into k groups, each having n data.
- Count occurrences and calculate proportions from each group.

- Plot <u>group size times proportions</u> (np) into NP chart.
- Calculate control limits for NP chart.
- Analyse NP chart.

To help with explanation, the following data will be used:

Group	Count
1	22
2	30
3	14
4	20
5	12

Group	Count
6	16
7	26
8	22
9	30
10	14

Group	Count
11	29
12	23
13	11
14	24
15	15

Group	Count
16	27
17	29
18	18
19	15
20	28

There are 20 groups of data ($k = 20$). Each group has the same size ($n = 50$).

Proportion for each group can be calculated as:

$$p_i = \frac{c_i}{n}$$

Count of occurrences (c_i) are also known as np_i values because:

$$c_i = np_i$$

The calculation of proportions:

- $p_1 = \frac{c_1}{n} = \frac{22}{50} = 0.44$
- $p_2 = \frac{c_2}{n} = \frac{30}{50} = 0.60$
- $p_3 = \frac{c_3}{n} = \frac{14}{50} = 0.28$
- Do the same for p_4 to p_{20}.

Proportion values for all groups:

Group	Size (n)	np_i	p_i
1	50	22	0.44
2	50	30	0.60
3	50	14	0.28
4	50	20	0.40
5	50	12	0.24
6	50	16	0.32
7	50	26	0.52
8	50	22	0.44
9	50	30	0.60
10	50	14	0.28

Group	Size (n)	np_i	p_i
11	50	29	0.58
12	50	23	0.46
13	50	11	0.22
14	50	24	0.48
15	50	15	0.30
16	50	27	0.54
17	50	29	0.58
18	50	18	0.36
19	50	15	0.30
20	50	28	0.56
AVG		21.25	0.43

The np_i values of all groups are mapped into NP chart:

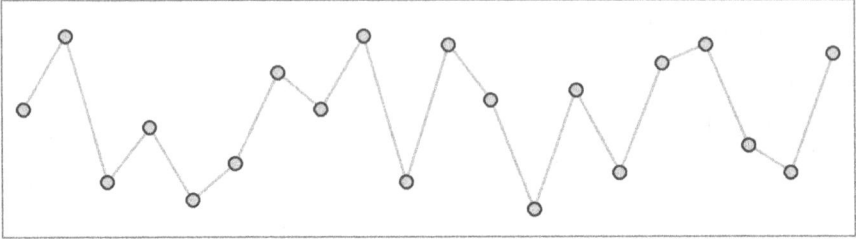

Figure 33-7 Draft of NP Chart

The minimum requirement of group size:
- Average of proportions $(\bar{p})$ is 0.43. n is 50.
- $50 \times 0.43 = 21.25$. This is greater than 5.
- $50 \times (1 - 0.43) = 28.75$. This is greater than 5.
- Both requirements are met.

Upper Control Limit (UCL) and *Lower Control Limit* (LCL) of NP chart are calculated using the following formula:

$$UCL = \overline{np} + \left(3 \times \sqrt{\overline{np} \times (1 - \bar{p})}\right)$$

$$LCL = \overline{np} - \left(3 \times \sqrt{\overline{np} \times (1 - \bar{p})}\right)$$

$\overline{np}$ is the average of np_i. $\bar{p}$ is the average of p_i.

Calculations of UCL and LCL:
- $UCL = 21.25 + \left(3 \times \sqrt{21.25 \times (1 - 0.43)}\right) = 31.74$
- $LCL = 21.25 - \left(3 \times \sqrt{21.25 \times (1 - 0.43)}\right) = 10.76$

With the calculated control limits, NP chart can be completed:

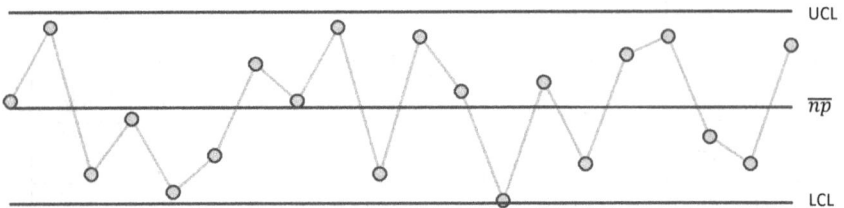

Figure 33-8 NP Chart

P Chart

P chart is a control chart for pass/fail attribute data with dynamic group size. It counts the number of defective units within each group in a similar way to NP chart.

Steps of working with P chart:
- Collect data.
- Organise data into k groups with different sizes.
- Count occurrences and calculate proportions from each group.
- Plot <u>proportion</u> values into P chart.
- Calculate control limits for P chart.
- Analyse P chart.

P chart is the only control chart using proportions. The mapped values could not be less than zero and could not be greater than one. This is not to be confused with U ratio from U chart, which can have values greater than one.

To help with explanation, the following data will be used:

Group	Size	Count	Group	Size	Count	Group	Size	Count	Group	Size	Count
1	43	31	6	19	10	11	16	11	16	15	12
2	28	21	7	12	9	12	25	8	17	43	16
3	42	15	8	44	19	13	34	19	18	29	17
4	40	19	9	15	8	14	28	20	19	15	9
5	18	16	10	45	33	15	22	16	20	39	14

There are 20 groups of data ($k = 20$). For each group, proportion can be calculated as:

$$p_i = \frac{c_i}{n_i}$$

p_i is the proportion for i^{th} group. c_i is the count of occurrences in i^{th} group. n_i is the size of ith group.

The calculation of proportions:
- $p_1 = \frac{c_1}{n_1} = \frac{31}{43} = 0.7209$
- $p_2 = \frac{c_2}{n_2} = \frac{21}{28} = 0.7500$
- $p_3 = \frac{c_3}{n_3} = \frac{15}{42} = 0.3571$
- Do the same for p_4 to p_{20}.

Proportion values for all groups:

Group	Size	Count	p_i	LCL	UCL
1	43	31	0.72		
2	28	21	0.75		
3	42	15	0.36		
4	40	19	0.48		
5	18	16	0.89		
6	19	10	0.53		
7	12	9	0.75		
8	44	19	0.43		
9	15	8	0.53		
10	45	33	0.73		

Group	Size	Count	p_i	LCL	UCL
11	16	11	0.69		
12	25	8	0.32		
13	34	19	0.56		
14	28	20	0.71		
15	22	16	0.73		
16	15	12	0.80		
17	43	16	0.37		
18	29	17	0.59		
19	15	9	0.60		
20	39	14	0.36		

Map the proportion values of all groups into P chart:

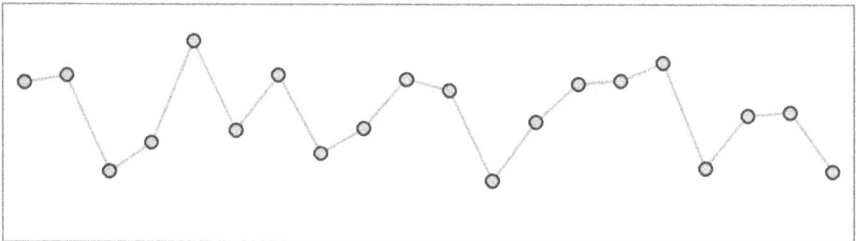

Figure 33-9 Draft of P Chart

Next, calculate the average of p:

$$\bar{p} = \frac{\Sigma c}{\Sigma n}$$

Total number of counts from all groups is 323. The sum of all group sizes is 572. Therefore, $\bar{p} = \frac{323}{572} = 0.5647$.

Minimum group size for P chart:
- n times the average of proportion must be greater than 5.
- The smallest n from all groups is 12.
- $12 \times 0.5647 = 6.7762$. This meets the requirement.
- n times [one minus the average of proportion] must be greater than 5.
- $12 \times (1 - 0.5647) = 5.2238$. This meets the requirement.

Each proportion value in P chart has different *Upper Control Limit* (UCL) and *Lower Control Limit* (LCL):

$$UCL_i = min\left[\bar{p} + \left(3 \times \sqrt{\bar{p} \times (1 - \bar{p})/n_i}\right); 1\right]$$

$$LCL_i = max\left[\bar{p} - \left(3 \times \sqrt{\bar{p} \times (1 - \bar{p})/n_i}\right); 0\right]$$

$\bar{p}$ is the average of proportion values. n_i is the size of ith group. UCL could not be greater than one and LCL could not be less than zero.

Calculations of UCL and LCL:

- $UCL_1 = min\left[\bar{p} + \left(3 \times \sqrt{\bar{p} \times (1 - \bar{p})/43}\right); 1\right] = 0.79$
- $LCL_1 = max\left[\bar{p} - \left(3 \times \sqrt{\bar{p} \times (1 - \bar{p})/43}\right); 0\right] = 0.34$
- $UCL_2 = min\left[\bar{p} + \left(3 \times \sqrt{\bar{p} \times (1 - \bar{p})/28}\right); 1\right] = 0.85$
- $LCL_2 = max\left[\bar{p} - \left(3 \times \sqrt{\bar{p} \times (1 - \bar{p})/28}\right); 0\right] = 0.28$
- Do the same for UCL_3 to UCL_{20} and LCL_3 to LCL_{20}.

UCL and LCL for all groups:

Group	Size	Count	U ratio	UCL	LCL
1	43	31	0.72	0.79	0.34
2	28	21	0.75	0.85	0.28
3	42	15	0.36	0.79	0.34
4	40	19	0.48	0.80	0.33
5	18	16	0.89	0.92	0.21
6	19	10	0.53	0.91	0.22
7	12	9	0.75	0.99	0.14
8	44	19	0.43	0.79	0.34
9	15	8	0.53	0.95	0.18
10	45	33	0.73	0.79	0.34

Group	Size	Count	U ratio	UCL	LCL
11	16	11	0.69	0.94	0.19
12	25	8	0.32	0.86	0.27
13	34	19	0.56	0.82	0.31
14	28	20	0.71	0.85	0.28
15	22	16	0.73	0.88	0.25
16	15	12	0.80	0.95	0.18
17	43	16	0.37	0.79	0.34
18	29	17	0.59	0.84	0.29
19	15	9	0.60	0.95	0.18
20	39	14	0.36	0.80	0.33

With the calculated control limits, P chart can be completed:

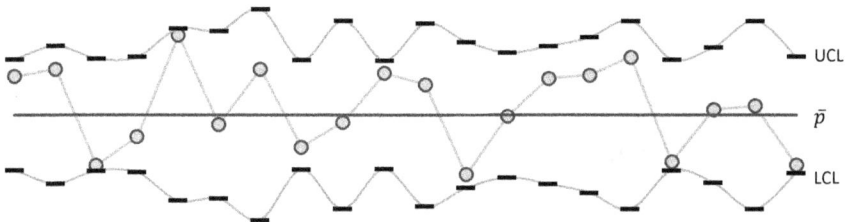

Figure 33-10 P Chart

Calculating different control limits for every data point is necessary to decrease the risk of false positive detection. For comparison, static UCL and LCL are calculated as:

$$UCL = min\left[\bar{p} + \left(3 \times \sqrt{\bar{p} \times (1 - \bar{p})/\bar{n}}\right); 1\right]$$

$$LCL = max\left[\bar{p} - \left(3 \times \sqrt{\bar{p} \times (1 - \bar{p})/\bar{n}}\right); 0\right]$$

$\bar{p}$ is the average of proportion values. $\bar{n}$ is average of group the sizes. UCL could not be greater than one and LCL could not be less than zero.

Calculations of static UCL and LCL:

- $\bar{n} = \frac{\Sigma n}{k} = \frac{572}{20} = 28.6$
- $UCL = min\left[\bar{p} + \left(3 \times \sqrt{\bar{p} \times (1 - \bar{p})/28.6}\right); 1\right] = 0.84$
- $LCL = max\left[\bar{p} - \left(3 \times \sqrt{\bar{p} \times (1 - \bar{p})/28.6}\right); 0\right] = 0.29$

With the static control limits, U chart can be completed:

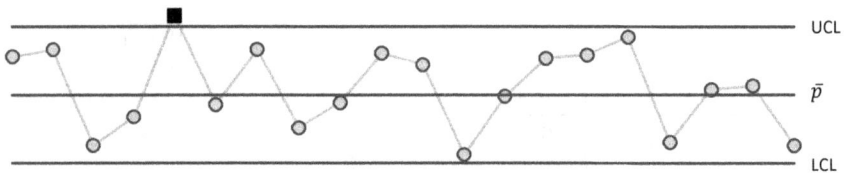

Figure 33-11 P Chart with static control limits

As demonstrated in Figure 33-11, static control limits falsely detect proportion for fifth group (shown in rectangle marker) as special cause variation. Calculation of different control limits for each proportion value is considered as best practice.

34. TIME-WEIGHTED CONTROL CHARTS

Time-weighted control charts are special types of control charts for continuous data. Instead of mapping one value to one point in the chart, each point in the chart is calculated with a formula involving historical values. These charts are more sensitive to small variations in the process and less sensitive to large variations. Before continuing with this chapter, it is strongly recommended to review Chapter 31 about Statistical Process Control.

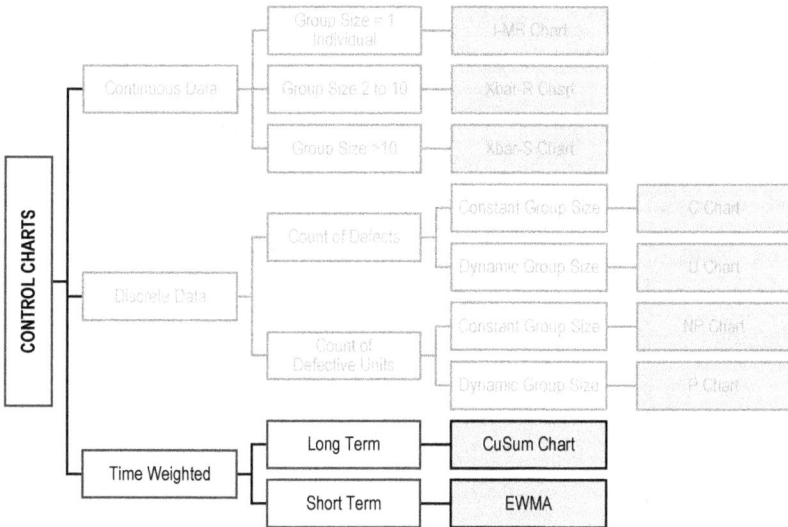

Figure 34-1 Time Weighted Control Charts

There are two time-weighted control charts discussed in this book:
- CuSum Chart (Cumulative Sum).
- EWMA Chart (Exponentially Weighted Moving Average).

Units or groups are mapped as X. Values of Y could be the individual data observations or average of values from groups with the same size.

CuSum Chart

Cumulative Sum chart is a type of time-weighted control chart focused on historical deviations from target value. It can be used with individual values or average of groups, but individual values (group size of one) will produce better results. CuSum chart does not have the ability to track range variation. Therefore, it is recommended to use CuSum chart together with Xbar-R charts.

There are two kinds of CuSum chart:
- *One-sided analysis* plots two sets of data (above and below) in one control chart.
- *Two-sided analysis* has control limit shaped like sideways V. This technique is also known as *V-Mask* method.

Steps of working with one-sided CuSum chart:
- Collect data.
- Organise data into k groups, each having n data.
- Decide target (T), sensitivity level (v) and threshold (h) values.
- Calculate estimated standard deviation.
- Calculate above and below cumulative sums.
- Plot <u>above and below cumulative sums</u> into CuSum chart.
- Calculate control limits for CuSum chart.
- Analyse CuSum chart.

Target value (T) is normally the process mean. Default value of sensitivity level (v) is 0.5. Default value of threshold (h) is 4.

Estimated standard deviation for individual data ($n = 1$):

$$\sigma_e = \frac{\bar{x}_{MR}}{D2}$$

Estimated standard deviation for grouped data ($n > 1$):

$$\sigma_e = \frac{\bar{S}_t/C4}{D2}$$

$\bar{x}_{MR}$ is the average of moving range values. $\bar{S}_t$ is the average of the standard deviations from each group. *D2* and *C4* are values from reference table. Table 34-A shows partial table with values required for CuSum chart. Full table can be obtained from Chapter 38.

n	1	2	3	4	5	6	7
D2	1.128	1.128	1.693	2.059	2.236	2.534	2.704
C4	–	0.798	0.886	0.921	0.940	0.951	0.959

Table 34-A Values of D2 and C4 for CuSum Chart

Allowable slack (*K*) is calculated from sensitivity level and estimated standard deviation:

$$K = v \times \sigma_e$$

There are two sets of cumulative sum values: above (*ACS*) and below (*BCS*):

$$ACS_i = max[0; ACS_{i-1} + x_i - T - K]$$

$$BCS_i = min[0; BCS_{i-1} + x_i - T + K]$$

ACS_i is the ith value of cumulative sum (above). BCS_i is the ith value of cumulative sum (below). x_i is the ith individual value; for grouped data, this could be replaced with the mean of ith group. *T* is target value. *K* is allowable slack. *ACS* could never be less than zero. *BCS* could never be greater than zero.

Control limits of one-sided CuSum chart:

$$UCL = h \times \sigma_e$$

$$LCL = -h \times \sigma_e$$

Example 34-1: One-sided CuSum chart with individual data

93	55	73	54	82	97	123	51	81	88
52	85	59	29	90	64	48	56	70	58

There are 20 groups of data (*k* = 20), each is calculated from one data point. Group size (*n*) is 1. Target value (*T*) is 70. Sensitivity level (*v*) is 0.5. Threshold (*h*) is 3.

Moving range values are calculated from the absolute difference between each data point and its preceding value. There is no moving range value for the first observation because the first data point has no previous value.

Data	MR
93	
55	38
73	18
54	19
82	28

Data	MR
97	15
123	26
51	72
81	30
88	7

Data	MR
52	36
85	33
59	26
29	30
90	61

Data	MR
64	26
48	16
56	8
70	14
58	12

Calculations of estimated standard deviation and allowable slack:
- Average of moving range values $\bar{x}_{MR} = 27.105$.
- Estimated standard deviation $\sigma_e = \dfrac{27.1053}{1.128} = 24.029$.
- Allowable slack $K = 0.5 \times 24.029 = 12.015$.

The next step is calculating above and below cumulative sum values:
- For the first ACS and BCS, the previous values are zero.
- $ACS_1 = max[0; 0 + 93 - 70 - 12.015] = max[0; 10.985] = 10.985$
- $BCS_1 = min[0; 0 + 93 - 70 + 12.015] = min[0; 35.015] = 0$
- $ACS_2 = max[0; 10.985 + 55 - 70 - 12.015] = max[0; -16.029] = 0$
- $BCS_2 = min[0; 0 + 55 - 70 + 12.015] = min[0; -2.985] = -2.985$
- $ACS_3 = max[0; 0 + 73 - 70 - 12.015] = max[0; -9.015] = 0$
- $BCS_3 = min[0; -2.985 + 73 - 70 + 12.015] = min[0; 12.029] = 0$
- $ACS_4 = max[0; 0 + 54 - 70 - 12.015] = max[0; -28.015] = 0$
- $BCS_4 = min[0; 0 + 54 - 70 + 12.015] = min[0; -3.985] = -3.985$
- Continue with calculations for ACS_5 to ACS_{20} and BCS_5 to BCS_{20}.

Values of ACS and BCS:

#	Data	ACS	BCS
1	93	10.985	0.000
2	55	0.000	-2.985
3	73	0.000	0.000
4	54	0.000	-3.985
5	82	0.000	0.000
6	97	14.985	0.000
7	123	55.971	0.000
8	51	24.956	-6.985
9	81	23.941	0.000
10	88	29.926	0.000

#	Data	ACS	BCS
11	52	0.000	-5.985
12	85	2.985	0.000
13	59	0.000	0.000
14	29	0.000	-28.985
15	90	7.985	0.000
16	64	0.000	0.000
17	48	0.000	-9.985
18	56	0.000	-11.971
19	70	0.000	0.000
20	58	0.000	0.000

ACS and BCS values are mapped into CuSum chart:

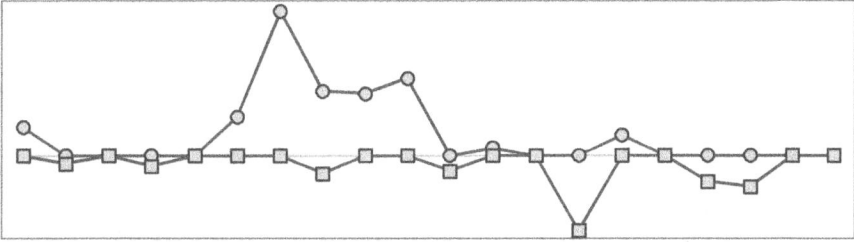

Figure 34-2 Draft of CuSum Chart with individual data

Control limits are calculated as:
- $UCL = 3 \times 24.029 = 72.088$
- $LCL = -3 \times 24.029 = -72.088$

Complete CuSum chart with control limits:

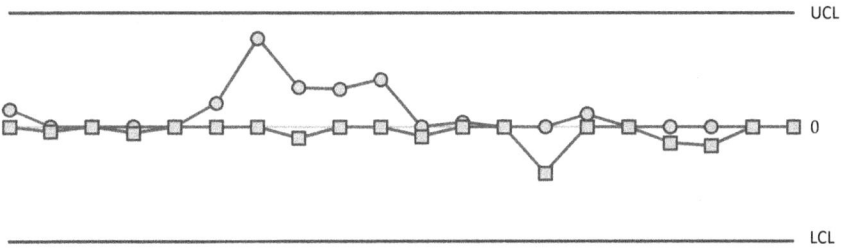

Figure 34-3 CuSum Chart with individual data

Example 34-2: One-sided CuSum chart with grouped data

Group	Measured Data				Xbar	S	Group	Measured Data				Xbar	S
	1	2	3	4				1	2	3	4		
1	44	21	52	42	39.75	13.23	11	63	68	50	29	52.50	17.41
2	72	10	29	68	44.75	30.21	12	16	24	20	22	20.50	3.42
3	43	41	95	68	61.75	25.34	13	75	80	78	81	78.50	2.65
4	61	60	55	57	58.25	2.75	14	56	8	25	22	27.75	20.24
5	11	51	23	71	39.00	27.13	15	56	79	20	53	52.00	24.29
6	33	70	56	75	58.50	18.81	16	33	55	38	10	34.00	18.57
7	23	75	88	35	55.25	31.16	17	71	80	75	85	77.75	6.08
8	16	20	25	16	19.25	4.27	18	35	80	71	3	47.25	35.33
9	40	83	92	29	61.00	31.14	19	69	56	45	89	64.75	18.91
10	19	79	84	79	65.25	30.92	20	23	33	70	13	34.75	24.88
											AVG	49.625	19.336

There are 20 groups of data ($k = 20$), each group has 4 measured data ($n = 4$). Xbar values are calculated as the average of 4 values within the same group.

341

Standard deviation values are calculated from 4 values within each group. Target value (T) is 50. Sensitivity level (v) is 0.5. Threshold (h) is 3.

Calculations:

- Average of group standard deviations $\overline{S}_t = 19.336$.
- Find the values of D2 and C4 from Table 34-A.
- Estimated standard deviation $\sigma_e = \dfrac{19.336/0.921}{2.059} = 10.197$.
- Allowable slack $K = 0.5 \times 10.197 = 5.098$.
- For the first ACS and BCS, the previous values are zero.
- $ACS_1 = max[0; 0 + 39.75 - 50 - 5.098] = max[0; -15.348] = 0$
- $BCS_1 = min[0; 0 + 39.75 - 50 + 5.098] = min[0; -5.152] = -5.152$
- $ACS_2 = max[0; 10.985 + 44.75 - 50 - 5.098] = max[0; -10.348] = 0$
- $BCS_2 = min[0; -5.152 + 44.75 - 50 + 5.098] = min[0; -0.152] = -0.152$
- $ACS_3 = max[0; 0 + 61.75 - 50 - 5.098] = max[0; 6.652] = 6.652$
- $BCS_3 = min[0; -0.152 + 61.75 - 50 + 5.098] = min[0; 16.848] = 0$
- $ACS_4 = max[0; 6.652 + 58.25 - 50 - 5.098] = max[0; 9.803] = 9.803$
- $BCS_4 = min[0; 0 + 58.25 - 50 + 5.098] = min[0; 20.000] = 0$
- Continue with calculations for ACS_5 to ACS_{20} and BCS_5 to BCS_{20}.
- $UCL = 3 \times 10.197 = 30.590$
- $LCL = -3 \times 10.197 = -30.590$

All values of ACS and BCS:

Group	ACS	BCS	Group	ACS	BCS
1	0.000	−5.152	11	13.455	0.000
2	0.000	−0.152	12	0.000	−10.947
3	6.652	0.000	13	23.402	0.000
4	9.803	0.000	14	0.000	0.000
5	0.000	0.000	15	0.000	0.000
6	3.402	0.000	16	0.000	−10.902
7	3.553	0.000	17	22.652	0.000
8	0.000	−22.098	18	14.803	0.000
9	5.902	0.000	19	24.455	0.000
10	16.503	0.000	20	4.107	0.000

Complete CuSum chart:

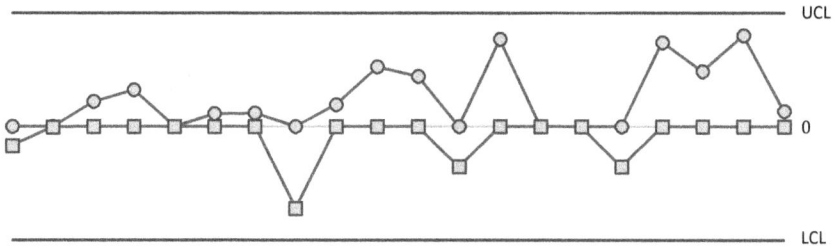

Figure 34-4 CuSum Chart with grouped data

Two-sided CuSum chart uses the cumulative sum of deviation from target value. Control limits in the form of sideways V-mask are used to check whether process is within statistical control. Any single data outside control limits indicates special cause variation.

V-mask starts from a data point in control chart. Two straight lines are drawn above and below that point, converging into one point on the left.

The distance from data point to converging point:

$$d = \left(\frac{2}{\delta^2}\right) \ln\left(\frac{1-\beta}{\alpha}\right)$$

$$\theta = tan^{-1}\left(\frac{\delta}{2A}\right)$$

$$\delta = \frac{\Delta}{\sigma_{\bar{x}}}$$

α is the probability of false positive, finding that process is out of statistical control when in fact it is still within statistical control. β is the probability of false negative, finding that there is no special cause variation (process is within statistical control) when in fact the process is out of statistical control. δ is the detection level, expressed in how many standard deviations.

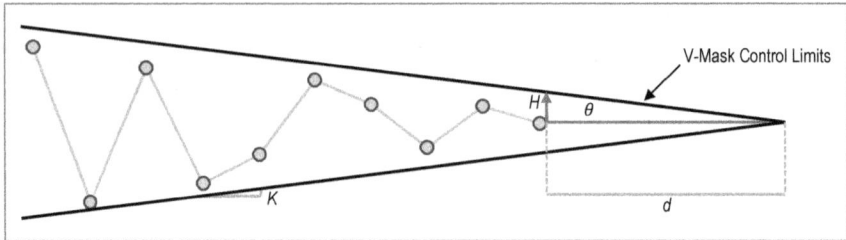

Figure 34-5 CuSum Chart with V-Mask

H is the rise of the control line corresponding to distance d. K is the rise of the control line corresponding to one unit of X-axis.

EWMA Chart

Exponentially Weighted Moving Average (EWMA) chart is a type of time-weighted control chart using moving average of data values. Data for EWMA chart must be ordered by time. Even though EWMA works better with grouped data (n > 1), it is also capable to handle individual data.

The importance of historical data is set by parameter λ, which must satisfy $0 > \lambda \geq 1$. Setting $\lambda = 1$ will produce individual chart for individual data, or Xbar chart for grouped data. Smaller λ gives higher importance of historical data, making it sensitive to small variations. Bigger λ gives higher importance of current data, making it more sensitive to slightly larger variations.

It is recommended to use EWMA chart when:
- Data from the entire life of a process is available.
- The focus of control is to detect small variations.
- There is a need to smooth out noise effect.

Steps of working with EWMA chart:
- Collect data.
- Organise data into k groups, each having n data.
- Calculate mean of each group and grand mean.
- Decide λ value.
- Calculate EWMA values (Z_i).
- Plot <u>EWMA values</u> into EWMA chart.
- Calculate control limits for EWMA chart.
- Analyse EWMA chart.

EWMA value (z_i) is calculated using the formula:

$$Z_i = (\lambda \times \bar{x}_i) + \big((1 - \lambda) \times z_{i-1}\big)$$

$\bar{x}_i$ is the mean of ith group, or i^{th} data if $n = 1$. Z_{i-1} is the previous EWMA value. z_0 is the grand mean of all data.

Formula to calculate EWMA chart control limits:

$$UCL_i = \bar{\bar{x}} + m\frac{\bar{S}}{\sqrt{n}} \times \sqrt{\frac{\lambda}{2 - \lambda} \times [1 - (1 - \lambda)^{2i}]}$$

$$LCL_i = \bar{\bar{x}} - m\frac{\bar{S}}{\sqrt{n}} \times \sqrt{\frac{\lambda}{2 - \lambda} \times [1 - (1 - \lambda)^{2i}]}$$

$\bar{\bar{x}}$ is the grand mean. m is a parameterised multiplier, commonly set as 2.7 or 3. $\bar{S}$ is the average of standard deviations of all groups. Control limits for EWMA chart has different values for each data points. They usually start slightly narrow, gradually widen and then stabilise.

Example 34-3: EWMA chart

Group	Measured Data				$\bar{x}_i$	S	Group	Measured Data				$\bar{x}_i$	S
	1	2	3	4				1	2	3	4		
1	44	21	52	42	39.75	13.23	11	63	68	50	29	52.50	17.41
2	72	10	29	68	44.75	30.21	12	16	24	20	22	20.50	3.42
3	43	41	95	68	61.75	25.34	13	75	80	78	81	78.50	2.65
4	61	60	55	57	58.25	2.75	14	56	8	25	22	27.75	20.24
5	11	51	23	71	39.00	27.13	15	56	79	20	53	52.00	24.29
6	33	70	56	75	58.50	18.81	16	33	55	38	10	34.00	18.57
7	23	75	88	35	55.25	31.16	17	71	80	75	85	77.75	6.08
8	16	20	25	16	19.25	4.27	18	35	80	71	3	47.25	35.33
9	40	83	92	29	61.00	31.14	19	69	56	45	89	64.75	18.91
10	19	79	84	79	65.25	30.92	20	23	33	70	13	34.75	24.88
											AVG	49.625	19.336

There are 20 groups of data ($k = 20$), each group has 4 measured data ($n = 4$). $\bar{x}_i$ and S values are calculated as the average and standard deviation of values within the same group. $\lambda = 0.7$ and $m = 3$.

Z values calculation:
- Grand mean is 49.625, this is the centre line for EWMA chart.
- Average of group standard deviations $\bar{S} = 19.336$.

- $Z_0 = 49.625$
- $Z_1 = (0.7 \times 39.75) + (0.3 \times 49.625) = 42.713$
- $Z_2 = (0.7 \times 44.75) + (0.3 \times 42.713) = 44.139$
- $Z_3 = (0.7 \times 61.75) + (0.3 \times 44.139) = 56.467$
- $Z_4 = (0.7 \times 58.25) + (0.3 \times 56.467) = 57.715$
- $Z_5 = (0.7 \times 39.00) + (0.3 \times 57.715) = 44.614$
- Continue with calculations for Z_6 to Z_{20}.

All values of Z:

Group	EWMA (Z)	UCL	LCL
1	42.713		
2	44.139		
3	56.467		
4	57.715		
5	44.614		
6	54.334		
7	54.975		
8	29.968		
9	51.690		
10	61.182		

Group	EWMA (Z)	UCL	LCL
11	55.105		
12	30.881		
13	64.214		
14	38.689		
15	48.007		
16	38.202		
17	65.886		
18	52.841		
19	61.177		
20	42.678		

EWMA (Z) values are mapped into EWMA chart:

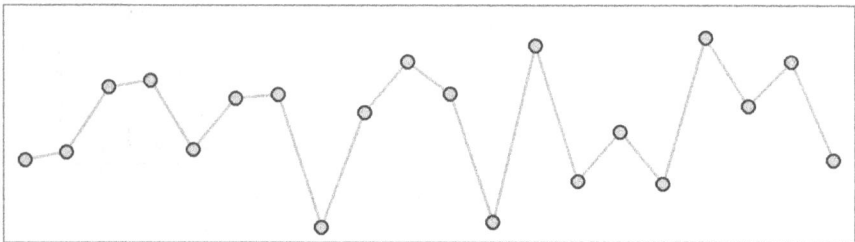

Figure 34-6 Draft of EWMA Chart

Control limits calculation:

- $UCL_1 = 49.625 + 3\frac{19.336}{\sqrt{4}} \times \sqrt{\frac{0.7}{1.3} \times [1 - (0.3)^2]} = 69.928$

- $LCL_1 = 49.625 - 3\frac{19.336}{\sqrt{4}} \times \sqrt{\frac{0.7}{1.3} \times [1 - (0.3)^2]} = 29.322$

- $UCL_2 = 49.625 + 3\frac{19.336}{\sqrt{4}} \times \sqrt{\frac{0.7}{1.3} \times [1 - (0.3)^4]} = 70.822$

- $LCL_2 = 49.625 - 3\frac{19.336}{\sqrt{4}} \times \sqrt{\frac{0.7}{1.3} \times [1 - (0.3)^4]} = 28.428$

- $UCL_3 = 49.625 + 3\frac{19.336}{\sqrt{4}} \times \sqrt{\frac{0.7}{1.3} \times [1 - (0.3)^6]} = 70.901$

- $LCL_3 = 49.625 - 3\frac{19.336}{\sqrt{4}} \times \sqrt{\frac{0.7}{1.3} \times [1 - (0.3)^6]} = 28.349$

- Continue with calculations for UCL_4 to UCL_{20} and LCL_4 to LCL_{20}.

All values of UCL and LCL:

Group	EWMA (Z)	UCL	LCL	Group	EWMA (Z)	UCL	LCL
1	42.713	69.928	29.322	11	55.105	70.909	28.341
2	44.139	70.822	28.428	12	30.881	70.909	28.341
3	56.467	70.901	28.349	13	64.214	70.909	28.341
4	57.715	70.908	28.342	14	38.689	70.909	28.341
5	44.614	70.908	28.342	15	48.007	70.909	28.341
6	54.334	70.909	28.341	16	38.202	70.909	28.341
7	54.975	70.909	28.341	17	65.886	70.909	28.341
8	29.968	70.909	28.341	18	52.841	70.909	28.341
9	51.690	70.909	28.341	19	61.177	70.909	28.341
10	61.182	70.909	28.341	20	42.678	70.909	28.341

EWMA chart from calculated values:

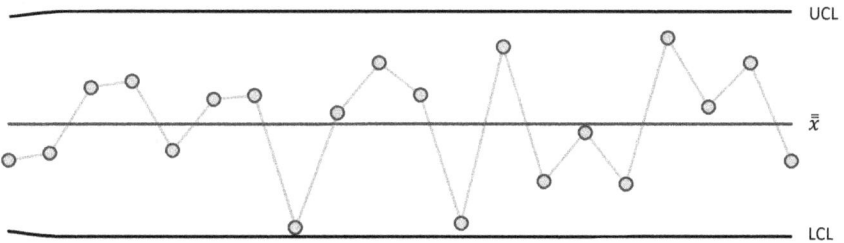

Figure 34-7 EWMA Chart

OTHER TOPICS

35. DMAIC SUMMARY

DMAIC is a Six Sigma process improvement methodology with five phases: *Define, Measure, Analyze, Improve* and *Control*. Chapter 09 to 34 discuss the concepts, topics and techniques of each phase. Lean Six Sigma with DMAIC combines the power of Lean principles to reduce waste and the power of Six Sigma to reduce variations.

Six Sigma formula takes the form of $Y = f(X)$. Y is the outcome from a function of X. The five phases of DMAIC are the steps of a methodical journey to improve Y (process improvement) by controlling X.

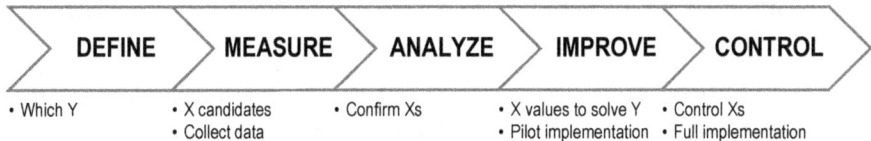

DEFINE	MEASURE	ANALYZE	IMPROVE	CONTROL
• Which Y	• X candidates • Collect data	• Confirm Xs	• X values to solve Y • Pilot implementation	• Control Xs • Full implementation

Figure 35-1 Five phases of DMAIC

The journey of DMAIC process improvement starts from project selection Several factors such as cost and benefit analysis, degree of urgency, alignment with company goals, alignment with customers' perceived value, estimated completion time, safety impact, operational impact, resource impact and data availability need to be considered. A selected project needs project sponsors, project champion and project leader. With these three components, project can enter the first phase of DMAIC.

Define phase focuses on Project Charter as its main deliverable. Problem Statement and Goal Statement in Project Charter represent the Y outcome that needs to be improved. This goal needs to be specific, measurable, attainable, relevant and time bound. It is important to remember that project goal should be driven by Voice of the Customer (VOC) and Critical to Quality (CTQ). Topics in Define phase also include stakeholder and risk management.

Process mapping is the next step after defining the problem and goal. It helps to obtain general understanding about the current process. Common types of process mapping in Define phase are High Level Process Map, Detailed Process Map, Swimlane Process Map and SIPOC Diagram.

Measure phase focuses on collecting data from the current process. Specific data are collected to discover what are the possible X factors that impact the outcome Y.

The first step of Measure phase is as-is process review. This is critical to help understanding performance gap related to Y and identifying a list of possible candidates of X factors that might impact the Y outcome.

There are two preconditions of data collection. One: team needs to perform Measurement System Analysis (MSA) to ensure that valid data can be collected with acceptable accuracy and precision. Two: data collection plan needs to be created to perform data collection efficiently while minimising potential issues. Data collection plan includes calculation of sample size and data collection technique.

Measure factors does not aim to confirm which X factors have actual impact on Y because this phase does not perform in-depth analysis of the collected data. Instead, Measure phase uses As-Is process review to remove factors that are clearly have no impact to Y. This phase produces a list of X candidates along with collected data related to these Xs.

Analyze phase takes the list of possible X factors and their related data to perform in-depth analysis and then come up with a list of actual X factors statistically proven as independent factors impacting Y. Measure phase identifies potential factors; Analyze phase confirms the factors.

There are three ways to confirm X factors: visual analysis, Lean analysis and statistical analysis. Statistical analysis used descriptive statistics to explain the characteristics of data, or inferential statistics if only a subset of data (sample) are collected. Hypothesis testing is the most common form of inferential statistics. It analyses what tester is trying to prove (alternative hypothesis) against status quo (null hypothesis) and make conclusion based on acceptable confidence level.

Improve phase aims to find the optimal values of X factors to achieve the best possible Y outcome. From Lean perspective, the improvement of Xs can be achieved through pull-based workflow, error proofing or other innovation techniques. From Six Sigma perspective, the improvement of Xs is achieved using Design of Experiments (DOE) technique, a systematic approach to understand how a process and its parameters affects the outcome variable.

After finding the optimal values for Xs, pilot implementation is conducted to validate the solution and identify implementation risks. Risk mitigation, documentation and training are the next steps in Improve phase.

Control phase is the final phase of DMAIC. It starts with preparing Control Plan and Response Plan. Control Plan helps to detect special cause variations in the process using Statistical Process Control (SPC) technique. Response Plan defines what to do when problems are detected and who is responsible to carry out the response.

Implementation planning, and then full-scale implementation takes place after all other preparations are completed. Cost and benefit analysis are performed after process improvement is completed, usually involving comparison of process capability before and after improvement as well as financial benefits within 12 months after implementation.

36. KAIZEN EVENT

Kaizen is a Japanese word meaning *change for the better*. Kaizen event is a Lean technique for process improvement using a facilitated and structured event. This technique is powerful if drivers of performance can be obtained using collective knowledge of certain people in the organisation. Please review Chapter 05 about choosing the right framework for Lean Six Sigma.

DMAIC framework is based on data analysis. Kaizen is based on Subject Matter Expert (SME) expertise. Kaizen event could be one-day to one-week workshop involving the right experts within the organisation to improve certain aspect of the process.

Other names of Kaizen event:
- Kaizen workshop
- Kaizen Blitz
- Kaizen Burst
- Focused group workshop
- Accelerated improvement workshop

Kaizen event is a one-off improvement event to resolve or improve something, However, some organisation conduct Kaizen event on a regular basis and refer to it as continuous improvement workshop.

Various Lean tools and techniques could be used during Kaizen event. This event combines traditional brainstorming session with structure and facilitation to capitalise on expert knowledge so that solution could be achieved in a timely manner.

Common deliverables of Kaizen event:
- As Is Process Map
- List of non-value-added activities in the process
- Detailed Process Map with improvements
- List of recommended actions
- Revised operational standards
- Implementation plan
- Management presentation

Preparation

A productive Kaizen event starts from preparation. Normally, preparation needs to begin 3 to 4 weeks before the event. Even the preparation requires dedicated time and efforts because non-productive Kaizen event is a waste of collective time from multiple decision makers and SMEs within an organisation.

Steps for Kaizen event preparation:
- Define improvement goal and scope.
- Obtain buy-in and commitment from executive and management.
- Establish team.
- Measure As-Is performance. Collect data as required.
- Define required expertise.
- Communicate with invited experts and managers.
- Appoint facilitator.
- Create event schedule.
- Decide on event venue.
- Conduct pre-event training if necessary.

Any process improvement needs to have clear *goal* that meets *SMART* (specific, measurable, attainable, relevant and time-bound) requirements. Specific goal means it defines what it is trying to resolve, not other things. This helps to set the *scope* of Kaizen event. Measurable goal means the success criteria must be something that can be measured objectively after event completion. Attainable goal indicates that goal is achievable given agreed time frame, available resources, support from project sponsors and other constraints. Relevant goal means that a goal needs to be aligned with the business goals. Time bound goal provides the connection between event goal and time frame when such goal needs to be achieved.

The next step for Kaizen event preparation is obtaining *buy-in* and full *commitment* from top executive and management. This is critically important because Kaizen event relies on the expertise of subject matter experts, people who typically have many other responsibilities. Requesting them to spend significant time on Kaizen event means they will not be able to carry out their usual tasks during the event.

After goal and scope are defined and the necessary buy-ins are obtained, small *team* is formed to carry out the subsequent work from planning to execution. Ideally, this team needs to have someone with leadership experience and green belt skill level or higher.

To help with problem solving during Kaizen event, it is important to have proper *analysis* and *measurement* on the system's As-Is performance. Depending on the nature of the improvement to achieve, it might be necessary to collect data before the event.

With the analysis of current process, high level process map is used to identify the list of expertise required to solve a particular problem. Team needs to *communicate* with relevant stakeholders with the identified expertise and get their support.

Kaizen event needs *facilitator* to run the event. Facilitator is a crucial role to enforce event structure and help participants to stay focused. If no one within the organisation has experience as facilitator, team can decide to hire professional facilitator. The cost of non-effective event from wasting everyone's time is usually higher than the cost of facilitator.

Any good event requires clear *schedule* that is communicated with participants prior to execution day. If an SME is required in two out of five session, there is no point of having this expert involved in all five. A good schedule makes sure all key stakeholders know when they are expected to be involved and what kind of preparation they need to make before the session.

In the modern world, event *venue* could be on site or virtual using online conference tool. If meeting is planned on site, event venue needs to be a place that is easily accessible by all participants. If virtual meeting is planned, there needs to be prior test to make sure that all participants are able to access the tool.

The final step of preparation is to consider whether or not *pre-event training* is needed. If a Kaizen event is planned to have various discussions using quality tools (such as cause-and-effect diagram, control chart, pareto chart, etc) then team needs to make sure that participants are already equipped with the skill to understand those tools. Pre-event training could be a trainer-led session (could be from the facilitator who will lead the event), or it could be simple reading material sent to participants.

Execution

There is no detailed formal rule on what the agenda of Kaizen event should look like. However, as general guide, Kaizen event agenda usually follow five phases:

- Orientation.
- Understand current state.
- Develop solution candidates.
- Make the improvements.
- Report and celebrate.

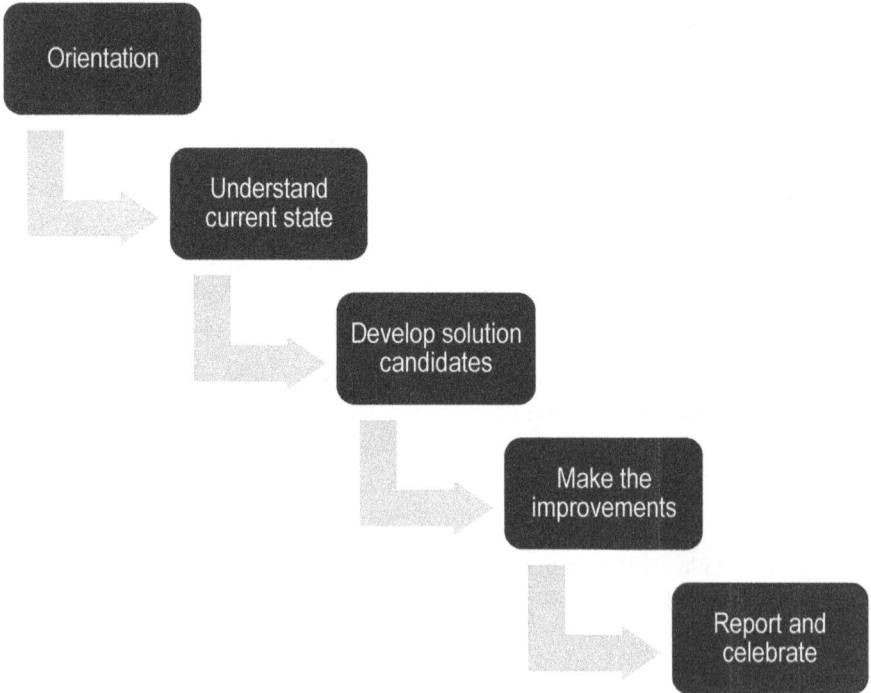

Figure 36-1 Kaizen Event agenda

Orientation is the first phase of Kaizen event. This phase includes opening session, introduction, and initial speech or presentation to set expectations. Initial speech usually involves someone from top management to give directions and guidance. This will help to establish authority of the event. If participants have not received training on the tools that will be used during Kaizen event, short training might be provided after initial speech. The next part of orientation is to conduct another short session to identify the processes, customers and values.

If event is planned for multiple days, daily opening/briefing session is needed at the beginning of each day. Daily brief sessions from day 2 onwards is focused on brief recap on previous day achievement, followed by general plan for the day. Any session could take between 30 minutes to 3 hours. Longer sessions usually become less effective as participants are getting tired and losing focus.

For multi-day event, it is recommended to conduct quick *debrief* session at the end of each day. Ask participants to write feedback in two sticky notes. One is a list of things that went well that day, the other is a list of things that need to be improved. This will help to catch problem early so that actions could be taken when possible.

Understand current state is about reviewing As-Is processes using process map, value stream map, SIPOC diagram or other tools. Participants discuss the current state and identify non-value-added steps in the process, identifying process waste.

Data collection (could be sampling) and data analysis are used to further understand the current state and establish common understanding, supported by data. Various charts and diagrams could be used during analysis sessions.

Losing focus during data and process analysis is a common problem, especially because these sessions are very likely to lead to the discoveries of other problems. There is nothing wrong about finding other problems to fix, but anything outside the original scope of the event must be discussed separately, perhaps in future Kaizen event. It is very important to ensure that the current event achieves its original goal without getting side-tracked.

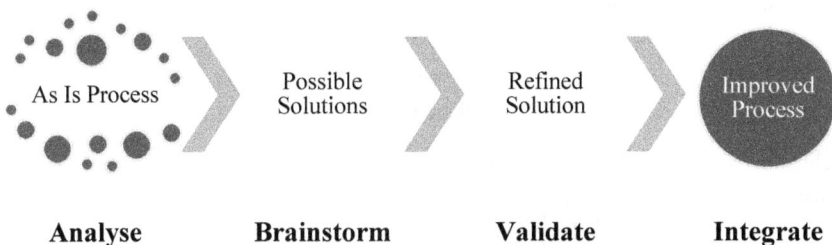

| Analyse | Brainstorm | Validate | Integrate |

Figure 36-2 Process improvement with Kaizen Event

Develop solution candidates phase initiates the actual work of improvement with focus on future state design. It can be started by brainstorming session to perform *root cause analysis* and discuss *possible solutions*. This is when experts are using their knowledge to fix a problem or improve process. Various techniques such as 5S, Lean waste, XY matrix, multi-voting, FMEA, error proofing and six thinking hats could be used to help with this step.

After the list of possible solutions is obtained, participants continue with *solution prioritisation*. A few solution candidates are chosen for *further refinement*.

Participants need to agree on one refined solution. The next step is to *make the improvement* by integrating the agreed solution into *operational standard*. Depending on the type of solution, it might be necessary to try out the solution by running some *simulations*. Solution design might be tweaked as necessary based on the result of simulations.

It is important to estimate the *potential impact* of the solution, both from the perspective of cost and benefits. This estimation will become the baseline to evaluate the effectiveness of Kaizen event after event completion, using real implementation data.

Implementing a solution is a change. Any change needs *risk assessment*. Risks need to be identified, classified and mitigated. Failure Modes and Effects Analysis (FMEA) with Risk Priority Number (RPN) is a great tool for this step. Using RPN, risks can be prioritised based on severity, occurrence (likelihood) and detection probability.

Training material must be prepared to enable effective implementation of the solution. Participants in the Kaizen event are both the creators and the initial trainees of the updated processes. If applicable, *control plan* and *response plan* need to be prepared to ensure that improved process is monitored and maintained.

The final phase is *report and celebrate*. At the end of Kaizen event, team needs to prepare and then *presents the solution* to executive and management. This presentation helps to wrap up the event findings, makes sure everyone has the same interpretation and seeks *approval* from management.

Celebration aspect from an event is often ignored. It is not an easy task to come up with a workable solution for a systematic problem in a few days. Simple appreciation such as short social session with pizza or finger food would help everyone to remember the event in a positive note. This will greatly improve their involvement in future Kaizen events.

Last but not least, it is often forgotten that any performance improvement needs to achieve measurable goal. More often than not, the measurement of results needs to happen after event completion. It remains the team's responsibility to *measure* the results of improvement (both from system and financial perspective) and then compile a report to properly conclude the work.

37. DESIGN FOR SIX SIGMA (DFSS)

Design for Six Sigma (DFSS) is a Six Sigma framework to design a new product, service or process. The most popular framework for DFSS is DMADV: *Define*, *Measure*, *Analyze*, *Design* and *Verify*. The main difference between DMAIC and DMADV is the fact that DMAIC focuses on improving something that already exists whilst DMADV is a framework for creation.

Different organisations might have different approach to implement DFSS. This chapter discusses the basic principles of DMADV using some terms and tools that are already explained in previous chapters of this book, followed by some other alternative frameworks for DFSS.

DMADV Framework

Similar to DMAIC, DMADV is a data-driven framework based on Six Sigma principles. Both frameworks share the same first three phases with some differences on what are being defined, measured and analysed. The fourth phase is Design phase instead of Improve phase because, naturally, there is nothing to improve when we are creating something new that did not exist before.

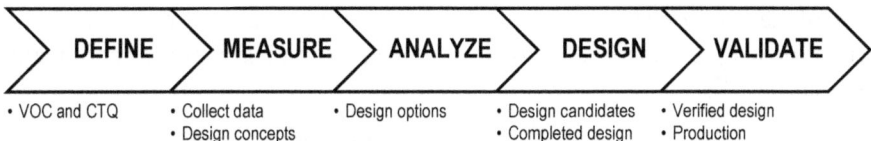

DEFINE	MEASURE	ANALYZE	DESIGN	VALIDATE
• VOC and CTQ	• Collect data • Design concepts	• Design options	• Design candidates • Completed design	• Verified design • Production

Figure 37-1 Five phases of DMADV

DMADV uses $Y = f(X)$ formula in a slightly different way from DMAIC. The Y outcome is the expected new product, service or process. The X factors are the evolution of design, starting from *design concepts* in Measure phase, *design options* in analyse phase and *design candidates* in Design phase.

Define phase in DMADV is quite similar to Define phase in DMAIC. It starts with project selection, followed by Project Charter document. Project name, problem statement, goal statement, business case, project scope, project impacts and timeline are defined in Project Charter.

In DMADV, more efforts are spent in understanding Voice of the Customer (VOC) and Critical to Quality (CTQ). Existing product, service or process usually have more established understanding of VOC and CTQ whilst designing new product, service or process would require team to identify VOC and CTQ from a blank state.

It is usually not feasible to design product, service or process that satisfy all customer requirements because there is always constraint between complexity and cost. The next step after understanding customer requirements is to prioritise those requirements.

After selecting requirements to meet, team moves on the next step to establish measurable targets and tolerances. If a new product, service or process require the use of existing resources and infrastructures, team needs to evaluate the capability of existing system to produce the new output. Perform gap analysis to learn gaps in current systems that will block or reduce the capability to deliver the new product, service or process.

If this is not the first time an organisation is designing a new product, service or process, this phase is a good time to review lessons learnt from previous work. For the first DMADV project, make sure to set proper precedents for the future.

Measure phase in DMADV focuses on establishing baseline measurements for the designed product, service or process in order to formulate the initial set of *design concepts*. Objects of measurement could be customer needs (market size), competitors, perceived value (for pricing decision) and quality targets.

Similar to DMAIC, standard steps of Measurement System Analysis (MSA) need to be completed before the start of data collection. Data obtained from this phase will be used to finalise CTQ specifications. Based on CTQ, current system capability and gap analysis, team should be able to estimate the sigma level of the new design.

Analyze phase in DMADV aims to obtain sufficient level of understanding about a new product, service or process so that team can transform initial design concepts from Measure phase into *design options* to meet requirements from Define phase.

Using the $Y = f(X)$ formula, this phase analyses how different design concepts impact the Y outcome, what needs to change so that better Y is obtained, and which component of design concept has the most significant impact to Y. Alternatives are considered if needed. Best practices in the industry are used as benchmark.

Hypothesis testing can be utilised to help team with understanding the correlations between design concepts and projected outcomes. It is important to note that this phase mainly works with estimations since the actual product, service or process is not yet available.

Design phase capitalises on design options produced from the previous phase to perform the main activities to develop new product, service or process. The end goal of this phase is a design that meets CTQ with acceptable cost, quality and production time.

Possible steps in Design phase:
- Consider design options. Find out if some of them successfully satisfy all requirements.
- Develop design candidates based on selected design options.
- Develop alternative design candidates if applicable.
- For product design, develop relevant designs for the manufacturing process.
- Review design candidates using *Failure Modes and Effects Analysis* (FMEA) tool.
- Select few design candidates.
- Refine the shortlisted designs. This could be done by expert discussion or running simulations using computer model or statistical analysis.
- Run pilot tests.
- Estimate process performance.
- Perform risk analysis.
- Evaluate and select the best design.

- It is important to note that iterative design is fairly common in DMAV. If no design is identified as acceptable after the first run, team goes back to find more alternatives of design candidates and begins a new iteration of design steps.
- Use *Design of Experiment* principles to improve selected design.
- For product design, select and prepare materials and manufacturing tools.
- Implement the completed design.

Verify phase takes on completed design from Design phase and begins production on limited scale to prove that it is able to meet customer requirements. This could be performed by prototype production or offering service to selected customer group.

With the beginning of actual production, team is now able to measure the actual process capability, sigma level and other metrics required to verify a product, service or process. Minor adjustments can still be made in Verify phase if needed. However, if major changes are required, project needs to return back to Design phase.

After design is verified, the next step is to implement *Statistical Process Control* (SPC) to create Control Plan and Response Plan. This help to ensure that production will continue to follow the verified design.

Similar to DMAIC, post-project cost-and-benefit analysis is also needed for DMADV. Return of Investment (ROI) is usually measured using profit reports within certain period after the start of production.

Alternative Frameworks

Design for Six Sigma (DFSS) is a relatively new field. Even though DMADV is considered as the most common standard, some organisations choose different implementation models for DFSS.

Other popular frameworks for DFSS:
- IDOV: Identify, Design, Optimize, Verify
- DMADOV: Define, Measure, Analyze, Design, Optimize, Verify
- DMADIC: Define, Measure, Analyze, Design, Implement, Control
- RCI: Requirements, Concepts, Improvements

IDOV framework is popular within manufacturing industry. It starts with identification of customer specifications and translate them into Critical to Quality (CTQ). Design phase creates the first iteration of product, service or process design. Optimize phase uses statistical tools to model performance. Finally, the Validate phase focuses on ensuring that design meets all points from CTQ.

DMADOV is a variation of DMADV. Instead of bundling the process of design and optimisation into one phase, DMADOV separates the activities to create design candidates and the activities to improve the selected design.

DMADIC is another variation of DMADV. This framework merges the activities for design, optimisation and validation into Design phase. Then it has dedicated phases for implementation and control.

RCI framework has three main phases: requirements, concepts and improvements. It takes unique approach to have full steps from define to develop for each phase, which translates into:
- Define and develop requirements
- Define and develop concepts
- Define and develop improvements

38. REFERENCE TABLES

This final chapter presents reference tables for the topics discussed in this book. Each table has different use. Please refer to the relevant chapters to review the use of these tables.

- Z table
- T table
- Chi-squared distribution table
- F distribution table
- Wilcoxon critical value table
- Binomial table
- Constants table for control charts

Z table shows the cumulative value of all data points possibility from Z score to the left. This table can be obtained using NORM.S.DIST function in Excel with *cumulative* parameter set to *true*.

T table is used for T-Test in in hypothesis testing. It is obtained using T.INV function in Excel. Rows indicate degrees of freedom (*df*) and columns indicate alpha risk (α).

Chi-squared distribution table maps the critical value from test statistics to *P-values*. Rows indicate degrees of freedom (*df*), table contents show the critical value and column titles indicate *P-value* to be compared with α. This table shows the values of Chi-square inverse and can be obtained using CHISQ.INV.RT function in Excel.

F distribution table is used for F-Test. It is obtained using F.INV.RT function in Excel with three parameters: probability, *df* (degrees of freedom) 1 and 2. Columns indicate degrees of freedom 1 and rows indicate degrees of freedom 2. Alpha risk 0.05 is used for probability value.

Binomial table is used for test acceptance in one sample sign test. This table is obtained using BINOM.DIST function in Excel with four parameters: *number_s*, *trials*, *probability* and *cumulative*. Sample size (*n*) is shown as columns, this is the *number_s* parameter for the function. The number of *trials* (*x*) is filled with values between 0 and *n*, shown as rows. *Probability* is set to 0.5 for one sample sign test. *Cumulative* is set to *true*.

Z Table

Z	0.00	0.01	0.02	0.03	0.04	0.05	0.06	0.07	0.08	0.09
- 4.9	0.000000	0.000000	0.000000	0.000000	0.000000	0.000000	0.000000	0.000000	0.000000	0.000000
- 4.8	0.000001	0.000001	0.000001	0.000001	0.000001	0.000001	0.000001	0.000001	0.000001	0.000001
- 4.7	0.000001	0.000001	0.000001	0.000001	0.000001	0.000001	0.000001	0.000001	0.000001	0.000001
- 4.6	0.000002	0.000002	0.000002	0.000002	0.000002	0.000002	0.000002	0.000002	0.000001	0.000001
- 4.5	0.000003	0.000003	0.000003	0.000003	0.000003	0.000003	0.000003	0.000002	0.000002	0.000002
- 4.4	0.000005	0.000005	0.000005	0.000005	0.000004	0.000004	0.000004	0.000004	0.000004	0.000004
- 4.3	0.000009	0.000008	0.000008	0.000007	0.000007	0.000007	0.000007	0.000006	0.000006	0.000006
- 4.2	0.000013	0.000013	0.000012	0.000012	0.000011	0.000011	0.000010	0.000010	0.000009	0.000009
- 4.1	0.000021	0.000020	0.000019	0.000018	0.000017	0.000017	0.000016	0.000015	0.000015	0.000014
- 4.0	0.000032	0.000030	0.000029	0.000028	0.000027	0.000026	0.000025	0.000024	0.000023	0.000022
- 3.9	0.000048	0.000046	0.000044	0.000042	0.000041	0.000039	0.000037	0.000036	0.000034	0.000033
- 3.8	0.000072	0.000069	0.000067	0.000064	0.000062	0.000059	0.000057	0.000054	0.000052	0.000050
- 3.7	0.000108	0.000104	0.000100	0.000096	0.000092	0.000088	0.000085	0.000082	0.000078	0.000075
- 3.6	0.000159	0.000153	0.000147	0.000142	0.000136	0.000131	0.000126	0.000121	0.000117	0.000112
- 3.5	0.000233	0.000224	0.000216	0.000208	0.000200	0.000193	0.000185	0.000178	0.000172	0.000165
- 3.4	0.000337	0.000325	0.000313	0.000302	0.000291	0.000280	0.000270	0.000260	0.000251	0.000242
- 3.3	0.000483	0.000466	0.000450	0.000434	0.000419	0.000404	0.000390	0.000376	0.000362	0.000349
- 3.2	0.000687	0.000664	0.000641	0.000619	0.000598	0.000577	0.000557	0.000538	0.000519	0.000501
- 3.1	0.000968	0.000935	0.000904	0.000874	0.000845	0.000816	0.000789	0.000762	0.000736	0.000711
- 3.0	0.001350	0.001306	0.001264	0.001223	0.001183	0.001144	0.001107	0.001070	0.001035	0.001001
- 2.9	0.001866	0.001807	0.001750	0.001695	0.001641	0.001589	0.001538	0.001489	0.001441	0.001395
- 2.8	0.002555	0.002477	0.002401	0.002327	0.002256	0.002186	0.002118	0.002052	0.001988	0.001926
- 2.7	0.003467	0.003364	0.003264	0.003167	0.003072	0.002980	0.002890	0.002803	0.002718	0.002635
- 2.6	0.004661	0.004527	0.004396	0.004269	0.004145	0.004025	0.003907	0.003793	0.003681	0.003573
- 2.5	0.006210	0.006037	0.005868	0.005703	0.005543	0.005386	0.005234	0.005085	0.004940	0.004799
- 2.4	0.008198	0.007976	0.007760	0.007549	0.007344	0.007143	0.006947	0.006756	0.006569	0.006387
- 2.3	0.010724	0.010444	0.010170	0.009903	0.009642	0.009387	0.009137	0.008894	0.008656	0.008424
- 2.2	0.013903	0.013553	0.013209	0.012874	0.012545	0.012224	0.011911	0.011604	0.011304	0.011011
- 2.1	0.017864	0.017429	0.017003	0.016586	0.016177	0.015778	0.015386	0.015003	0.014629	0.014262
- 2.0	0.022750	0.022216	0.021692	0.021178	0.020675	0.020182	0.019699	0.019226	0.018763	0.018309
- 1.9	0.028717	0.028067	0.027429	0.026803	0.026190	0.025588	0.024998	0.024419	0.023852	0.023295
- 1.8	0.035930	0.035148	0.034380	0.033625	0.032884	0.032157	0.031443	0.030742	0.030054	0.029379
- 1.7	0.044565	0.043633	0.042716	0.041815	0.040930	0.040059	0.039204	0.038364	0.037538	0.036727
- 1.6	0.054799	0.053699	0.052616	0.051551	0.050503	0.049471	0.048457	0.047460	0.046479	0.045514
- 1.5	0.066807	0.065522	0.064255	0.063008	0.061780	0.060571	0.059380	0.058208	0.057053	0.055917
- 1.4	0.080757	0.079270	0.077804	0.076359	0.074934	0.073529	0.072145	0.070781	0.069437	0.068112
- 1.3	0.096800	0.095098	0.093418	0.091759	0.090123	0.088508	0.086915	0.085343	0.083793	0.082264
- 1.2	0.115070	0.113139	0.111232	0.109349	0.107488	0.105650	0.103835	0.102042	0.100273	0.098525
- 1.1	0.135666	0.133500	0.131357	0.129238	0.127143	0.125072	0.123024	0.121000	0.119000	0.117023
- 1.0	0.158655	0.156248	0.153864	0.151505	0.149170	0.146859	0.144572	0.142310	0.140071	0.137857
- 0.9	0.184060	0.181411	0.178786	0.176186	0.173609	0.171056	0.168528	0.166023	0.163543	0.161087
- 0.8	0.211855	0.208970	0.206108	0.203269	0.200454	0.197663	0.194895	0.192150	0.189430	0.186733
- 0.7	0.241964	0.238852	0.235762	0.232695	0.229650	0.226627	0.223627	0.220650	0.217695	0.214764
- 0.6	0.274253	0.270931	0.267629	0.264347	0.261086	0.257846	0.254627	0.251429	0.248252	0.245097

Z	0.00	0.01	0.02	0.03	0.04	0.05	0.06	0.07	0.08	0.09
-0.5	0.308538	0.305026	0.301532	0.298056	0.294599	0.291160	0.287740	0.284339	0.280957	0.277595
-0.4	0.344578	0.340903	0.337243	0.333598	0.329969	0.326355	0.322758	0.319178	0.315614	0.312067
-0.3	0.382089	0.378280	0.374484	0.370700	0.366928	0.363169	0.359424	0.355691	0.351973	0.348268
-0.2	0.420740	0.416834	0.412936	0.409046	0.405165	0.401294	0.397432	0.393580	0.389739	0.385908
-0.1	0.460172	0.456205	0.452242	0.448283	0.444330	0.440382	0.436441	0.432505	0.428576	0.424655
0.0	0.500000	0.503989	0.507978	0.511966	0.515953	0.519939	0.523922	0.527903	0.531881	0.535856
0.1	0.539828	0.543795	0.547758	0.551717	0.555670	0.559618	0.563559	0.567495	0.571424	0.575345
0.2	0.579260	0.583166	0.587064	0.590954	0.594835	0.598706	0.602568	0.606420	0.610261	0.614092
0.3	0.617911	0.621720	0.625516	0.629300	0.633072	0.636831	0.640576	0.644309	0.648027	0.651732
0.4	0.655422	0.659097	0.662757	0.666402	0.670031	0.673645	0.677242	0.680822	0.684386	0.687933
0.5	0.691462	0.694974	0.698468	0.701944	0.705401	0.708840	0.712260	0.715661	0.719043	0.722405
0.6	0.725747	0.729069	0.732371	0.735653	0.738914	0.742154	0.745373	0.748571	0.751748	0.754903
0.7	0.758036	0.761148	0.764238	0.767305	0.770350	0.773373	0.776373	0.779350	0.782305	0.785236
0.8	0.788145	0.791030	0.793892	0.796731	0.799546	0.802337	0.805105	0.807850	0.810570	0.813267
0.9	0.815940	0.818589	0.821214	0.823814	0.826391	0.828944	0.831472	0.833977	0.836457	0.838913
1.0	0.841345	0.843752	0.846136	0.848495	0.850830	0.853141	0.855428	0.857690	0.859929	0.862143
1.1	0.864334	0.866500	0.868643	0.870762	0.872857	0.874928	0.876976	0.879000	0.881000	0.882977
1.2	0.884930	0.886861	0.888768	0.890651	0.892512	0.894350	0.896165	0.897958	0.899727	0.901475
1.3	0.903200	0.904902	0.906582	0.908241	0.909877	0.911492	0.913085	0.914657	0.916207	0.917736
1.4	0.919243	0.920730	0.922196	0.923641	0.925066	0.926471	0.927855	0.929219	0.930563	0.931888
1.5	0.933193	0.934478	0.935745	0.936992	0.938220	0.939429	0.940620	0.941792	0.942947	0.944083
1.6	0.945201	0.946301	0.947384	0.948449	0.949497	0.950529	0.951543	0.952540	0.953521	0.954486
1.7	0.955435	0.956367	0.957284	0.958185	0.959070	0.959941	0.960796	0.961636	0.962462	0.963273
1.8	0.964070	0.964852	0.965620	0.966375	0.967116	0.967843	0.968557	0.969258	0.969946	0.970621
1.9	0.971283	0.971933	0.972571	0.973197	0.973810	0.974412	0.975002	0.975581	0.976148	0.976705
2.0	0.977250	0.977784	0.978308	0.978822	0.979325	0.979818	0.980301	0.980774	0.981237	0.981691
2.1	0.982136	0.982571	0.982997	0.983414	0.983823	0.984222	0.984614	0.984997	0.985371	0.985738
2.2	0.986097	0.986447	0.986791	0.987126	0.987455	0.987776	0.988089	0.988396	0.988696	0.988989
2.3	0.989276	0.989556	0.989830	0.990097	0.990358	0.990613	0.990863	0.991106	0.991344	0.991576
2.4	0.991802	0.992024	0.992240	0.992451	0.992656	0.992857	0.993053	0.993244	0.993431	0.993613
2.5	0.993790	0.993963	0.994132	0.994297	0.994457	0.994614	0.994766	0.994915	0.995060	0.995201
2.6	0.995339	0.995473	0.995604	0.995731	0.995855	0.995975	0.996093	0.996207	0.996319	0.996427
2.7	0.996533	0.996636	0.996736	0.996833	0.996928	0.997020	0.997110	0.997197	0.997282	0.997365
2.8	0.997445	0.997523	0.997599	0.997673	0.997744	0.997814	0.997882	0.997948	0.998012	0.998074
2.9	0.998134	0.998193	0.998250	0.998305	0.998359	0.998411	0.998462	0.998511	0.998559	0.998605
3.0	0.998650	0.998694	0.998736	0.998777	0.998817	0.998856	0.998893	0.998930	0.998965	0.998999
3.1	0.999032	0.999065	0.999096	0.999126	0.999155	0.999184	0.999211	0.999238	0.999264	0.999289
3.2	0.999313	0.999336	0.999359	0.999381	0.999402	0.999423	0.999443	0.999462	0.999481	0.999499
3.3	0.999517	0.999534	0.999550	0.999566	0.999581	0.999596	0.999610	0.999624	0.999638	0.999651
3.4	0.999663	0.999675	0.999687	0.999698	0.999709	0.999720	0.999730	0.999740	0.999749	0.999758
3.5	0.999767	0.999776	0.999784	0.999792	0.999800	0.999807	0.999815	0.999822	0.999828	0.999835
3.6	0.999841	0.999847	0.999853	0.999858	0.999864	0.999869	0.999874	0.999879	0.999883	0.999888
3.7	0.999892	0.999896	0.999900	0.999904	0.999908	0.999912	0.999915	0.999918	0.999922	0.999925
3.8	0.999928	0.999931	0.999933	0.999936	0.999938	0.999941	0.999943	0.999946	0.999948	0.999950
3.9	0.999952	0.999954	0.999956	0.999958	0.999959	0.999961	0.999963	0.999964	0.999966	0.999967
4.0	0.999968	0.999970	0.999971	0.999972	0.999973	0.999974	0.999975	0.999976	0.999977	0.999978

Z	0.00	0.01	0.02	0.03	0.04	0.05	0.06	0.07	0.08	0.09
4.1	0.999979	0.999980	0.999981	0.999982	0.999983	0.999983	0.999984	0.999985	0.999985	0.999986
4.2	0.999987	0.999987	0.999988	0.999988	0.999989	0.999989	0.999990	0.999990	0.999991	0.999991
4.3	0.999991	0.999992	0.999992	0.999993	0.999993	0.999993	0.999993	0.999994	0.999994	0.999994
4.4	0.999995	0.999995	0.999995	0.999995	0.999996	0.999996	0.999996	0.999996	0.999996	0.999996
4.5	0.999997	0.999997	0.999997	0.999997	0.999997	0.999997	0.999997	0.999998	0.999998	0.999998
4.6	0.999998	0.999998	0.999998	0.999998	0.999998	0.999998	0.999998	0.999998	0.999999	0.999999
4.7	0.999999	0.999999	0.999999	0.999999	0.999999	0.999999	0.999999	0.999999	0.999999	0.999999
4.8	0.999999	0.999999	0.999999	0.999999	0.999999	0.999999	0.999999	0.999999	0.999999	0.999999
4.9	1.000000	1.000000	1.000000	1.000000	1.000000	1.000000	1.000000	1.000000	1.000000	1.000000

T Table

T	0.005	0.010	0.025	0.050	0.100	0.150	0.200	0.250
1	63.656741	31.820516	12.706205	6.313752	3.077684	1.962611	1.376382	1.000000
2	9.924843	6.964557	4.302653	2.919986	1.885618	1.386207	1.060660	0.816497
3	5.840909	4.540703	3.182446	2.353363	1.637744	1.249778	0.978472	0.764892
4	4.604095	3.746947	2.776445	2.131847	1.533206	1.189567	0.940965	0.740697
5	4.032143	3.364930	2.570582	2.015048	1.475884	1.155767	0.919544	0.726687
6	3.707428	3.142668	2.446912	1.943180	1.439756	1.134157	0.905703	0.717558
7	3.499483	2.997952	2.364624	1.894579	1.414924	1.119159	0.896030	0.711142
8	3.355387	2.896459	2.306004	1.859548	1.396815	1.108145	0.888890	0.706387
9	3.249836	2.821438	2.262157	1.833113	1.383029	1.099716	0.883404	0.702722
10	3.169273	2.763769	2.228139	1.812461	1.372184	1.093058	0.879058	0.699812
11	3.105807	2.718079	2.200985	1.795885	1.363430	1.087666	0.875530	0.697445
12	3.054540	2.680998	2.178813	1.782288	1.356217	1.083211	0.872609	0.695483
13	3.012276	2.650309	2.160369	1.770933	1.350171	1.079469	0.870152	0.693829
14	2.976843	2.624494	2.144787	1.761310	1.345030	1.076280	0.868055	0.692417
15	2.946713	2.602480	2.131450	1.753050	1.340606	1.073531	0.866245	0.691197
16	2.920782	2.583487	2.119905	1.745884	1.336757	1.071137	0.864667	0.690132
17	2.898231	2.566934	2.109816	1.739607	1.333379	1.069033	0.863279	0.689195
18	2.878440	2.552380	2.100922	1.734064	1.330391	1.067170	0.862049	0.688364
19	2.860935	2.539483	2.093024	1.729133	1.327728	1.065507	0.860951	0.687621
20	2.845340	2.527977	2.085963	1.724718	1.325341	1.064016	0.859964	0.686954
21	2.831360	2.517648	2.079614	1.720743	1.323188	1.062670	0.859074	0.686352
22	2.818756	2.508325	2.073873	1.717144	1.321237	1.061449	0.858266	0.685805
23	2.807336	2.499867	2.068658	1.713872	1.319460	1.060337	0.857530	0.685306
24	2.796940	2.492159	2.063899	1.710882	1.317836	1.059319	0.856855	0.684850
25	2.787436	2.485107	2.059539	1.708141	1.316345	1.058384	0.856236	0.684430
26	2.778715	2.478630	2.055529	1.705618	1.314972	1.057523	0.855665	0.684043
27	2.770683	2.472660	2.051831	1.703288	1.313703	1.056727	0.855137	0.683685
28	2.763262	2.467140	2.048407	1.701131	1.312527	1.055989	0.854647	0.683353
29	2.756386	2.462021	2.045230	1.699127	1.311434	1.055302	0.854192	0.683044
30	2.749996	2.457262	2.042272	1.697261	1.310415	1.054662	0.853767	0.682756
31	2.744042	2.452824	2.039513	1.695519	1.309464	1.054064	0.853370	0.682486
32	2.738481	2.448678	2.036933	1.693889	1.308573	1.053504	0.852998	0.682234
33	2.733277	2.444794	2.034515	1.692360	1.307737	1.052979	0.852649	0.681997
34	2.728394	2.441150	2.032245	1.690924	1.306952	1.052485	0.852321	0.681774
35	2.723806	2.437723	2.030108	1.689572	1.306212	1.052019	0.852012	0.681564
36	2.719485	2.434494	2.028094	1.688298	1.305514	1.051580	0.851720	0.681366
37	2.715409	2.431447	2.026192	1.687094	1.304854	1.051165	0.851444	0.681178
38	2.711558	2.428568	2.024394	1.685954	1.304230	1.050772	0.851183	0.681001
39	2.707913	2.425841	2.022691	1.684875	1.303639	1.050399	0.850935	0.680833
40	2.704459	2.423257	2.021075	1.683851	1.303077	1.050046	0.850700	0.680673
41	2.701181	2.420803	2.019541	1.682878	1.302543	1.049710	0.850476	0.680521
42	2.698066	2.418470	2.018082	1.681952	1.302035	1.049390	0.850263	0.680376
43	2.695102	2.416250	2.016692	1.681071	1.301552	1.049085	0.850060	0.680238
44	2.692278	2.414134	2.015368	1.680230	1.301090	1.048794	0.849867	0.680107

T	0.005	0.010	0.025	0.050	0.100	0.150	0.200	0.250
45	2.689585	2.412116	2.014103	1.679427	1.300649	1.048516	0.849682	0.679981
46	2.687013	2.410188	2.012896	1.678660	1.300228	1.048250	0.849505	0.679861
47	2.684556	2.408345	2.011741	1.677927	1.299825	1.047996	0.849336	0.679746
48	2.682204	2.406581	2.010635	1.677224	1.299439	1.047752	0.849174	0.679635
49	2.679952	2.404892	2.009575	1.676551	1.299069	1.047519	0.849018	0.679530
50	2.677793	2.403272	2.008559	1.675905	1.298714	1.047295	0.848869	0.679428
55	2.668216	2.396081	2.004045	1.673034	1.297134	1.046298	0.848205	0.678977
60	2.660283	2.390119	2.000298	1.670649	1.295821	1.045469	0.847653	0.678601
65	2.653604	2.385097	1.997138	1.668636	1.294712	1.044768	0.847186	0.678283
70	2.647905	2.380807	1.994437	1.666914	1.293763	1.044169	0.846786	0.678011
75	2.642983	2.377102	1.992102	1.665425	1.292941	1.043649	0.846440	0.677775
80	2.638691	2.373868	1.990063	1.664125	1.292224	1.043195	0.846137	0.677569
85	2.634914	2.371022	1.988268	1.662978	1.291591	1.042795	0.845870	0.677387
90	2.631565	2.368497	1.986675	1.661961	1.291029	1.042440	0.845633	0.677225
95	2.628576	2.366243	1.985251	1.661052	1.290527	1.042122	0.845421	0.677081
100	2.625891	2.364217	1.983972	1.660234	1.290075	1.041836	0.845230	0.676951
110	2.621265	2.360726	1.981765	1.658824	1.289295	1.041342	0.844901	0.676727
120	2.617421	2.357825	1.979930	1.657651	1.288646	1.040932	0.844627	0.676540
130	2.614177	2.355375	1.978380	1.656659	1.288098	1.040584	0.844395	0.676382
140	2.611403	2.353278	1.977054	1.655811	1.287628	1.040287	0.844196	0.676246
150	2.609003	2.351465	1.975905	1.655076	1.287221	1.040029	0.844024	0.676129
200	2.600634	2.345137	1.971896	1.652508	1.285799	1.039128	0.843422	0.675718

Chi-Squared Distribution Table – Right Tail

χ^2	0.250	0.200	0.150	0.100	0.050	0.025	0.010	0.001
1	1.3233	1.6424	2.0723	2.7055	3.8415	5.0239	6.6349	10.8276
2	2.7726	3.2189	3.7942	4.6052	5.9915	7.3778	9.2103	13.8155
3	4.1083	4.6416	5.3170	6.2514	7.8147	9.3484	11.3449	16.2662
4	5.3853	5.9886	6.7449	7.7794	9.4877	11.1433	13.2767	18.4668
5	6.6257	7.2893	8.1152	9.2364	11.0705	12.8325	15.0863	20.5150
6	7.8408	8.5581	9.4461	10.6446	12.5916	14.4494	16.8119	22.4577
7	9.0371	9.8032	10.7479	12.0170	14.0671	16.0128	18.4753	24.3219
8	10.2189	11.0301	12.0271	13.3616	15.5073	17.5345	20.0902	26.1245
9	11.3888	12.2421	13.2880	14.6837	16.9190	19.0228	21.6660	27.8772
10	12.5489	13.4420	14.5339	15.9872	18.3070	20.4832	23.2093	29.5883
11	13.7007	14.6314	15.7671	17.2750	19.6751	21.9200	24.7250	31.2641
12	14.8454	15.8120	16.9893	18.5493	21.0261	23.3367	26.2170	32.9095
13	15.9839	16.9848	18.2020	19.8119	22.3620	24.7356	27.6882	34.5282
14	17.1169	18.1508	19.4062	21.0641	23.6848	26.1189	29.1412	36.1233
15	18.2451	19.3107	20.6030	22.3071	24.9958	27.4884	30.5779	37.6973
16	19.3689	20.4651	21.7931	23.5418	26.2962	28.8454	31.9999	39.2524
17	20.4887	21.6146	22.9770	24.7690	27.5871	30.1910	33.4087	40.7902
18	21.6049	22.7595	24.1555	25.9894	28.8693	31.5264	34.8053	42.3124
19	22.7178	23.9004	25.3289	27.2036	30.1435	32.8523	36.1909	43.8202
20	23.8277	25.0375	26.4976	28.4120	31.4104	34.1696	37.5662	45.3147
21	24.9348	26.1711	27.6620	29.6151	32.6706	35.4789	38.9322	46.7970
22	26.0393	27.3015	28.8225	30.8133	33.9244	36.7807	40.2894	48.2679
23	27.1413	28.4288	29.9792	32.0069	35.1725	38.0756	41.6384	49.7282
24	28.2412	29.5533	31.1325	33.1962	36.4150	39.3641	42.9798	51.1786
25	29.3389	30.6752	32.2825	34.3816	37.6525	40.6465	44.3141	52.6197
26	30.4346	31.7946	33.4295	35.5632	38.8851	41.9232	45.6417	54.0520
27	31.5284	32.9117	34.5736	36.7412	40.1133	43.1945	46.9629	55.4760
28	32.6205	34.0266	35.7150	37.9159	41.3371	44.4608	48.2782	56.8923
29	33.7109	35.1394	36.8538	39.0875	42.5570	45.7223	49.5879	58.3012
30	34.7997	36.2502	37.9903	40.2560	43.7730	46.9792	50.8922	59.7031
35	40.2228	41.7780	43.6399	46.0588	49.8018	53.2033	57.3421	66.6188
40	45.6160	47.2685	49.2439	51.8051	55.7585	59.3417	63.6907	73.4020
45	50.9849	52.7288	54.8105	57.5053	61.6562	65.4102	69.9568	80.0767
50	56.3336	58.1638	60.3460	63.1671	67.5048	71.4202	76.1539	86.6608
55	61.6650	63.5772	65.8550	68.7962	73.3115	77.3805	82.2921	93.1675
60	66.9815	68.9721	71.3411	74.3970	79.0819	83.2977	88.3794	99.6072
65	72.2848	74.3506	76.8071	79.9730	84.8206	89.1771	94.4221	105.9881
70	77.5767	79.7146	82.2554	85.5270	90.5312	95.0232	100.4252	112.3169
75	82.8581	85.0658	87.6877	91.0615	96.2167	100.8393	106.3929	118.5991
80	88.1303	90.4053	93.1058	96.5782	101.8795	106.6286	112.3288	124.8392
90	98.6499	101.0537	103.9041	107.5650	113.1453	118.1359	124.1163	137.2084
100	109.1412	111.6667	114.6588	118.4980	124.3421	129.5612	135.8067	149.4493

Chi-Squared Distribution Table – Left Tail

χ^2	0.750	0.800	0.850	0.900	0.950	0.975	0.990	0.999
1	0.1015	0.0642	0.0358	0.0158	0.0039	0.0010	0.0002	0.0000
2	0.5754	0.4463	0.3250	0.2107	0.1026	0.0506	0.0201	0.0020
3	1.2125	1.0052	0.7978	0.5844	0.3518	0.2158	0.1148	0.0243
4	1.9226	1.6488	1.3665	1.0636	0.7107	0.4844	0.2971	0.0908
5	2.6746	2.3425	1.9938	1.6103	1.1455	0.8312	0.5543	0.2102
6	3.4546	3.0701	2.6613	2.2041	1.6354	1.2373	0.8721	0.3811
7	4.2549	3.8223	3.3583	2.8331	2.1673	1.6899	1.2390	0.5985
8	5.0706	4.5936	4.0782	3.4895	2.7326	2.1797	1.6465	0.8571
9	5.8988	5.3801	4.8165	4.1682	3.3251	2.7004	2.0879	1.1519
10	6.7372	6.1791	5.5701	4.8652	3.9403	3.2470	2.5582	1.4787
11	7.5841	6.9887	6.3364	5.5778	4.5748	3.8157	3.0535	1.8339
12	8.4384	7.8073	7.1138	6.3038	5.2260	4.4038	3.5706	2.2142
13	9.2991	8.6339	7.9008	7.0415	5.8919	5.0088	4.1069	2.6172
14	10.1653	9.4673	8.6963	7.7895	6.5706	5.6287	4.6604	3.0407
15	11.0365	10.3070	9.4993	8.5468	7.2609	6.2621	5.2293	3.4827
16	11.9122	11.1521	10.3090	9.3122	7.9616	6.9077	5.8122	3.9416
17	12.7919	12.0023	11.1249	10.0852	8.6718	7.5642	6.4078	4.4161
18	13.6753	12.8570	11.9463	10.8649	9.3905	8.2307	7.0149	4.9048
19	14.5620	13.7158	12.7727	11.6509	10.1170	8.9065	7.6327	5.4068
20	15.4518	14.5784	13.6039	12.4426	10.8508	9.5908	8.2604	5.9210
21	16.3444	15.4446	14.4393	13.2396	11.5913	10.2829	8.8972	6.4467
22	17.2396	16.3140	15.2788	14.0415	12.3380	10.9823	9.5425	6.9830
23	18.1373	17.1865	16.1219	14.8480	13.0905	11.6886	10.1957	7.5292
24	19.0373	18.0618	16.9686	15.6587	13.8484	12.4012	10.8564	8.0849
25	19.9393	18.9398	17.8184	16.4734	14.6114	13.1197	11.5240	8.6493
26	20.8434	19.8202	18.6714	17.2919	15.3792	13.8439	12.1981	9.2221
27	21.7494	20.7030	19.5272	18.1139	16.1514	14.5734	12.8785	9.8028
28	22.6572	21.5880	20.3857	18.9392	16.9279	15.3079	13.5647	10.3909
29	23.5666	22.4751	21.2468	19.7677	17.7084	16.0471	14.2565	10.9861
30	24.4776	23.3641	22.1103	20.5992	18.4927	16.7908	14.9535	11.5880
35	29.0540	27.8359	26.4604	24.7967	22.4650	20.5694	18.5089	14.6878
40	33.6603	32.3450	30.8563	29.0505	26.5093	24.4330	22.1643	17.9164
45	38.2910	36.8844	35.2895	33.3504	30.6123	28.3662	25.9013	21.2507
50	42.9421	41.4492	39.7539	37.6886	34.7643	32.3574	29.7067	24.6739
55	47.6105	46.0356	44.2448	42.0596	38.9580	36.3981	33.5705	28.1731
60	52.2938	50.6406	48.7587	46.4589	43.1880	40.4817	37.4849	31.7383
65	56.9903	55.2620	53.2926	50.8829	47.4496	44.6030	41.4436	35.3616
70	61.6983	59.8978	57.8443	55.3289	51.7393	48.7576	45.4417	39.0364
75	66.4168	64.5466	62.4119	59.7946	56.0541	52.9419	49.4750	42.7573
80	71.1445	69.2069	66.9938	64.2778	60.3915	57.1532	53.5401	46.5199
90	80.6247	78.5584	76.1954	73.2911	69.1260	65.6466	61.7541	54.1552
100	90.1332	87.9453	85.4406	82.3581	77.9295	74.2219	70.0649	61.9179

F Distribution Table

F	1	2	3	4	5	6	7	8	9	10
1	161.4476	199.5000	215.7073	224.5832	230.1619	233.9860	236.7684	238.8827	240.5433	241.8817
2	18.5128	19.0000	19.1643	19.2468	19.2964	19.3295	19.3532	19.3710	19.3848	19.3959
3	10.1280	9.5521	9.2766	9.1172	9.0135	8.9406	8.8867	8.8452	8.8123	8.7855
4	7.7086	6.9443	6.5914	6.3882	6.2561	6.1631	6.0942	6.0410	5.9988	5.9644
5	6.6079	5.7861	5.4095	5.1922	5.0503	4.9503	4.8759	4.8183	4.7725	4.7351
6	5.9874	5.1433	4.7571	4.5337	4.3874	4.2839	4.2067	4.1468	4.0990	4.0600
7	5.5914	4.7374	4.3468	4.1203	3.9715	3.8660	3.7870	3.7257	3.6767	3.6365
8	5.3177	4.4590	4.0662	3.8379	3.6875	3.5806	3.5005	3.4381	3.3881	3.3472
9	5.1174	4.2565	3.8625	3.6331	3.4817	3.3738	3.2927	3.2296	3.1789	3.1373
10	4.9646	4.1028	3.7083	3.4780	3.3258	3.2172	3.1355	3.0717	3.0204	2.9782
11	4.8443	3.9823	3.5874	3.3567	3.2039	3.0946	3.0123	2.9480	2.8962	2.8536
12	4.7472	3.8853	3.4903	3.2592	3.1059	2.9961	2.9134	2.8486	2.7964	2.7534
13	4.6672	3.8056	3.4105	3.1791	3.0254	2.9153	2.8321	2.7669	2.7144	2.6710
14	4.6001	3.7389	3.3439	3.1122	2.9582	2.8477	2.7642	2.6987	2.6458	2.6022
15	4.5431	3.6823	3.2874	3.0556	2.9013	2.7905	2.7066	2.6408	2.5876	2.5437
16	4.4940	3.6337	3.2389	3.0069	2.8524	2.7413	2.6572	2.5911	2.5377	2.4935
17	4.4513	3.5915	3.1968	2.9647	2.8100	2.6987	2.6143	2.5480	2.4943	2.4499
18	4.4139	3.5546	3.1599	2.9277	2.7729	2.6613	2.5767	2.5102	2.4563	2.4117
19	4.3807	3.5219	3.1274	2.8951	2.7401	2.6283	2.5435	2.4768	2.4227	2.3779
20	4.3512	3.4928	3.0984	2.8661	2.7109	2.5990	2.5140	2.4471	2.3928	2.3479
21	4.3248	3.4668	3.0725	2.8401	2.6848	2.5727	2.4876	2.4205	2.3660	2.3210
22	4.3009	3.4434	3.0491	2.8167	2.6613	2.5491	2.4638	2.3965	2.3419	2.2967
23	4.2793	3.4221	3.0280	2.7955	2.6400	2.5277	2.4422	2.3748	2.3201	2.2747
24	4.2597	3.4028	3.0088	2.7763	2.6207	2.5082	2.4226	2.3551	2.3002	2.2547
25	4.2417	3.3852	2.9912	2.7587	2.6030	2.4904	2.4047	2.3371	2.2821	2.2365
26	4.2252	3.3690	2.9752	2.7426	2.5868	2.4741	2.3883	2.3205	2.2655	2.2197
27	4.2100	3.3541	2.9604	2.7278	2.5719	2.4591	2.3732	2.3053	2.2501	2.2043
28	4.1960	3.3404	2.9467	2.7141	2.5581	2.4453	2.3593	2.2913	2.2360	2.1900
29	4.1830	3.3277	2.9340	2.7014	2.5454	2.4324	2.3463	2.2783	2.2229	2.1768
30	4.1709	3.3158	2.9223	2.6896	2.5336	2.4205	2.3343	2.2662	2.2107	2.1646
35	4.1213	3.2674	2.8742	2.6415	2.4851	2.3718	2.2852	2.2167	2.1608	2.1143
40	4.0847	3.2317	2.8387	2.6060	2.4495	2.3359	2.2490	2.1802	2.1240	2.0772
45	4.0566	3.2043	2.8115	2.5787	2.4221	2.3083	2.2212	2.1521	2.0958	2.0487
50	4.0343	3.1826	2.7900	2.5572	2.4004	2.2864	2.1992	2.1299	2.0734	2.0261
55	4.0162	3.1650	2.7725	2.5397	2.3828	2.2687	2.1813	2.1119	2.0552	2.0078
60	4.0012	3.1504	2.7581	2.5252	2.3683	2.2541	2.1665	2.0970	2.0401	1.9926
65	3.9886	3.1381	2.7459	2.5130	2.3560	2.2417	2.1541	2.0844	2.0274	1.9798
70	3.9778	3.1277	2.7355	2.5027	2.3456	2.2312	2.1435	2.0737	2.0166	1.9689
75	3.9685	3.1186	2.7266	2.4937	2.3366	2.2221	2.1343	2.0644	2.0073	1.9594
80	3.9604	3.1108	2.7188	2.4859	2.3287	2.2142	2.1263	2.0564	1.9991	1.9512
85	3.9532	3.1038	2.7119	2.4790	2.3218	2.2072	2.1193	2.0493	1.9919	1.9440
90	3.9469	3.0977	2.7058	2.4729	2.3157	2.2011	2.1131	2.0430	1.9856	1.9376
95	3.9412	3.0922	2.7004	2.4675	2.3102	2.1955	2.1075	2.0374	1.9799	1.9318
100	3.9361	3.0873	2.6955	2.4626	2.3053	2.1906	2.1025	2.0323	1.9748	1.9267
110	3.9274	3.0788	2.6871	2.4542	2.2969	2.1821	2.0939	2.0236	1.9661	1.9178
120	3.9201	3.0718	2.6802	2.4472	2.2899	2.1750	2.0868	2.0164	1.9588	1.9105

F	11	12	13	14	15	16	17	18	19	20
1	242.9835	243.9060	244.6898	245.3640	245.9499	246.4639	246.9184	247.3232	247.6861	248.0131
2	19.4050	19.4125	19.4189	19.4244	19.4291	19.4333	19.4370	19.4402	19.4431	19.4458
3	8.7633	8.7446	8.7287	8.7149	8.7029	8.6923	8.6829	8.6745	8.6670	8.6602
4	5.9358	5.9117	5.8911	5.8733	5.8578	5.8441	5.8320	5.8211	5.8114	5.8025
5	4.7040	4.6777	4.6552	4.6358	4.6188	4.6038	4.5904	4.5785	4.5678	4.5581
6	4.0274	3.9999	3.9764	3.9559	3.9381	3.9223	3.9083	3.8957	3.8844	3.8742
7	3.6030	3.5747	3.5503	3.5292	3.5107	3.4944	3.4799	3.4669	3.4551	3.4445
8	3.3130	3.2839	3.2590	3.2374	3.2184	3.2016	3.1867	3.1733	3.1613	3.1503
9	3.1025	3.0729	3.0475	3.0255	3.0061	2.9890	2.9737	2.9600	2.9477	2.9365
10	2.9430	2.9130	2.8872	2.8647	2.8450	2.8276	2.8120	2.7980	2.7854	2.7740
11	2.8179	2.7876	2.7614	2.7386	2.7186	2.7009	2.6851	2.6709	2.6581	2.6464
12	2.7173	2.6866	2.6602	2.6371	2.6169	2.5989	2.5828	2.5684	2.5554	2.5436
13	2.6347	2.6037	2.5769	2.5536	2.5331	2.5149	2.4987	2.4841	2.4709	2.4589
14	2.5655	2.5342	2.5073	2.4837	2.4630	2.4446	2.4282	2.4134	2.4000	2.3879
15	2.5068	2.4753	2.4481	2.4244	2.4034	2.3849	2.3683	2.3533	2.3398	2.3275
16	2.4564	2.4247	2.3973	2.3733	2.3522	2.3335	2.3167	2.3016	2.2880	2.2756
17	2.4126	2.3807	2.3531	2.3290	2.3077	2.2888	2.2719	2.2567	2.2429	2.2304
18	2.3742	2.3421	2.3143	2.2900	2.2686	2.2496	2.2325	2.2172	2.2033	2.1906
19	2.3402	2.3080	2.2800	2.2556	2.2341	2.2149	2.1977	2.1823	2.1683	2.1555
20	2.3100	2.2776	2.2495	2.2250	2.2033	2.1840	2.1667	2.1511	2.1370	2.1242
21	2.2829	2.2504	2.2222	2.1975	2.1757	2.1563	2.1389	2.1232	2.1090	2.0960
22	2.2585	2.2258	2.1975	2.1727	2.1508	2.1313	2.1138	2.0980	2.0837	2.0707
23	2.2364	2.2036	2.1752	2.1502	2.1282	2.1086	2.0910	2.0751	2.0608	2.0476
24	2.2163	2.1834	2.1548	2.1298	2.1077	2.0880	2.0703	2.0543	2.0399	2.0267
25	2.1979	2.1649	2.1362	2.1111	2.0889	2.0691	2.0513	2.0353	2.0207	2.0075
26	2.1811	2.1479	2.1192	2.0939	2.0716	2.0518	2.0339	2.0178	2.0032	1.9898
27	2.1655	2.1323	2.1035	2.0781	2.0558	2.0358	2.0179	2.0017	1.9870	1.9736
28	2.1512	2.1179	2.0889	2.0635	2.0411	2.0210	2.0030	1.9868	1.9720	1.9586
29	2.1379	2.1045	2.0755	2.0500	2.0275	2.0073	1.9893	1.9730	1.9581	1.9446
30	2.1256	2.0921	2.0630	2.0374	2.0148	1.9946	1.9765	1.9601	1.9452	1.9317
35	2.0750	2.0411	2.0117	1.9858	1.9629	1.9424	1.9240	1.9073	1.8922	1.8784
40	2.0376	2.0035	1.9738	1.9476	1.9245	1.9037	1.8851	1.8682	1.8529	1.8389
45	2.0088	1.9745	1.9446	1.9182	1.8949	1.8740	1.8551	1.8381	1.8226	1.8084
50	1.9861	1.9515	1.9214	1.8949	1.8714	1.8503	1.8313	1.8141	1.7985	1.7841
55	1.9675	1.9329	1.9026	1.8760	1.8523	1.8311	1.8120	1.7946	1.7788	1.7644
60	1.9522	1.9174	1.8870	1.8602	1.8364	1.8151	1.7959	1.7784	1.7625	1.7480
65	1.9393	1.9044	1.8739	1.8470	1.8231	1.8017	1.7823	1.7648	1.7488	1.7342
70	1.9283	1.8932	1.8627	1.8357	1.8117	1.7902	1.7708	1.7531	1.7371	1.7223
75	1.9188	1.8836	1.8530	1.8259	1.8018	1.7802	1.7607	1.7430	1.7269	1.7121
80	1.9105	1.8753	1.8445	1.8174	1.7932	1.7716	1.7520	1.7342	1.7180	1.7032
85	1.9031	1.8679	1.8371	1.8099	1.7856	1.7639	1.7443	1.7265	1.7102	1.6953
90	1.8967	1.8613	1.8305	1.8032	1.7789	1.7571	1.7375	1.7196	1.7033	1.6883
95	1.8909	1.8555	1.8246	1.7973	1.7729	1.7511	1.7314	1.7134	1.6971	1.6821
100	1.8857	1.8503	1.8193	1.7919	1.7675	1.7456	1.7259	1.7079	1.6915	1.6764
110	1.8767	1.8412	1.8101	1.7827	1.7582	1.7363	1.7164	1.6984	1.6819	1.6667
120	1.8693	1.8337	1.8026	1.7750	1.7505	1.7285	1.7085	1.6904	1.6739	1.6587

F	21	22	23	24	25	26	27	28	29	30
1	248.3094	248.5791	248.8256	249.0518	249.2601	249.4525	249.6309	249.7966	249.9510	250.0951
2	19.4481	19.4503	19.4523	19.4541	19.4558	19.4573	19.4587	19.4600	19.4613	19.4624
3	8.6540	8.6484	8.6432	8.6385	8.6341	8.6301	8.6263	8.6229	8.6196	8.6166
4	5.7945	5.7872	5.7805	5.7744	5.7687	5.7635	5.7586	5.7541	5.7498	5.7459
5	4.5493	4.5413	4.5339	4.5272	4.5209	4.5151	4.5097	4.5047	4.5001	4.4957
6	3.8649	3.8564	3.8486	3.8415	3.8348	3.8287	3.8230	3.8177	3.8128	3.8082
7	3.4349	3.4260	3.4179	3.4105	3.4036	3.3972	3.3913	3.3858	3.3806	3.3758
8	3.1404	3.1313	3.1229	3.1152	3.1081	3.1015	3.0954	3.0897	3.0844	3.0794
9	2.9263	2.9169	2.9084	2.9005	2.8932	2.8864	2.8801	2.8743	2.8688	2.8637
10	2.7636	2.7541	2.7453	2.7372	2.7298	2.7229	2.7164	2.7104	2.7048	2.6996
11	2.6358	2.6261	2.6172	2.6090	2.6014	2.5943	2.5877	2.5816	2.5759	2.5705
12	2.5328	2.5229	2.5139	2.5055	2.4977	2.4905	2.4838	2.4776	2.4718	2.4663
13	2.4479	2.4379	2.4287	2.4202	2.4123	2.4050	2.3982	2.3918	2.3859	2.3803
14	2.3768	2.3667	2.3573	2.3487	2.3407	2.3333	2.3264	2.3199	2.3139	2.3082
15	2.3163	2.3060	2.2966	2.2878	2.2797	2.2722	2.2652	2.2587	2.2525	2.2468
16	2.2642	2.2538	2.2443	2.2354	2.2272	2.2196	2.2125	2.2059	2.1997	2.1938
17	2.2189	2.2084	2.1987	2.1898	2.1815	2.1738	2.1666	2.1599	2.1536	2.1477
18	2.1791	2.1685	2.1587	2.1497	2.1413	2.1335	2.1262	2.1195	2.1131	2.1071
19	2.1438	2.1331	2.1233	2.1141	2.1057	2.0978	2.0905	2.0836	2.0772	2.0712
20	2.1124	2.1016	2.0917	2.0825	2.0739	2.0660	2.0586	2.0517	2.0452	2.0391
21	2.0842	2.0733	2.0633	2.0540	2.0454	2.0374	2.0299	2.0229	2.0164	2.0102
22	2.0587	2.0478	2.0377	2.0283	2.0196	2.0116	2.0040	1.9970	1.9904	1.9842
23	2.0356	2.0246	2.0144	2.0050	1.9963	1.9881	1.9805	1.9734	1.9668	1.9605
24	2.0146	2.0035	1.9932	1.9838	1.9750	1.9668	1.9591	1.9520	1.9453	1.9390
25	1.9953	1.9842	1.9738	1.9643	1.9554	1.9472	1.9395	1.9323	1.9255	1.9192
26	1.9776	1.9664	1.9560	1.9464	1.9375	1.9292	1.9215	1.9142	1.9074	1.9010
27	1.9613	1.9500	1.9396	1.9299	1.9210	1.9126	1.9048	1.8975	1.8907	1.8842
28	1.9462	1.9349	1.9244	1.9147	1.9057	1.8973	1.8894	1.8821	1.8752	1.8687
29	1.9322	1.9208	1.9103	1.9005	1.8915	1.8830	1.8751	1.8677	1.8608	1.8543
30	1.9192	1.9077	1.8972	1.8874	1.8782	1.8698	1.8618	1.8544	1.8474	1.8409
35	1.8657	1.8540	1.8432	1.8332	1.8239	1.8152	1.8071	1.7995	1.7923	1.7856
40	1.8260	1.8141	1.8031	1.7929	1.7835	1.7746	1.7663	1.7586	1.7513	1.7444
45	1.7953	1.7833	1.7722	1.7618	1.7522	1.7432	1.7348	1.7270	1.7195	1.7126
50	1.7709	1.7588	1.7475	1.7371	1.7273	1.7183	1.7097	1.7017	1.6942	1.6872
55	1.7511	1.7388	1.7275	1.7169	1.7071	1.6979	1.6893	1.6812	1.6736	1.6664
60	1.7346	1.7222	1.7108	1.7001	1.6902	1.6809	1.6722	1.6641	1.6564	1.6491
65	1.7207	1.7082	1.6967	1.6860	1.6759	1.6666	1.6578	1.6496	1.6419	1.6345
70	1.7088	1.6962	1.6846	1.6738	1.6638	1.6543	1.6455	1.6372	1.6294	1.6220
75	1.6985	1.6859	1.6742	1.6633	1.6532	1.6437	1.6348	1.6265	1.6186	1.6112
80	1.6895	1.6768	1.6651	1.6542	1.6440	1.6345	1.6255	1.6171	1.6092	1.6017
85	1.6815	1.6688	1.6571	1.6461	1.6358	1.6263	1.6173	1.6088	1.6009	1.5934
90	1.6745	1.6618	1.6499	1.6389	1.6286	1.6190	1.6100	1.6015	1.5935	1.5859
95	1.6682	1.6554	1.6435	1.6325	1.6222	1.6125	1.6034	1.5949	1.5869	1.5793
100	1.6626	1.6497	1.6378	1.6267	1.6163	1.6067	1.5976	1.5890	1.5809	1.5733
110	1.6528	1.6399	1.6279	1.6167	1.6063	1.5966	1.5874	1.5788	1.5706	1.5630
120	1.6447	1.6317	1.6197	1.6084	1.5980	1.5881	1.5789	1.5703	1.5621	1.5543

Wilcoxon Critical Value Table

	One-tailed		Two-tailed	
	0.01	0.05	0.01	0.05
5	--	0	--	--
6	--	2	--	0
7	0	3	--	2
8	1	5	0	3
9	3	8	1	5
10	5	10	3	8
11	7	13	5	10
12	9	17	7	13
13	12	21	9	17
14	15	25	12	21
15	19	30	15	25
16	23	35	19	29
17	27	41	23	34
18	32	47	27	40
19	37	53	32	46
20	43	60	37	52
21	49	67	42	58
22	55	75	48	65
23	62	83	54	73
24	69	91	61	81
25	76	100	68	89
26	84	110	75	98
27	92	119	83	107
28	101	130	91	116
29	110	140	100	126
30	120	151	109	137

Binomial Table

	1	2	3	4	5	6	7	8	9	10	11	12
0	0.5000	0.2500	0.1250	0.0625	0.0313	0.0156	0.0078	0.0039	0.0020	0.0010	0.0005	0.0002
1	1.0000	0.7500	0.5000	0.3125	0.1875	0.1094	0.0625	0.0352	0.0195	0.0107	0.0059	0.0032
2		1.0000	0.8750	0.6875	0.5000	0.3438	0.2266	0.1445	0.0898	0.0547	0.0327	0.0193
3			1.0000	0.9375	0.8125	0.6563	0.5000	0.3633	0.2539	0.1719	0.1133	0.0730
4				1.0000	0.9688	0.8906	0.7734	0.6367	0.5000	0.3770	0.2744	0.1938
5					1.0000	0.9844	0.9375	0.8555	0.7461	0.6230	0.5000	0.3872
6						1.0000	0.9922	0.9648	0.9102	0.8281	0.7256	0.6128
7							1.0000	0.9961	0.9805	0.9453	0.8867	0.8062
8								1.0000	0.9980	0.9893	0.9673	0.9270
9									1.0000	0.9990	0.9941	0.9807
10										1.0000	0.9995	0.9968
11											1.0000	0.9998
12												1.0000

Constants for Control Charts

n	For Xbar Chart			For R Chart		For S Chart	
	A2	A3	D2	D3	D4	B3	B4
2	1.880	2.659	1.128	0.000	3.267	0.000	3.267
3	1.023	1.954	1.693	0.000	2.575	0.000	2.568
4	0.729	1.628	2.059	0.000	2.282	0.000	2.266
5	0.577	1.427	2.326	0.000	2.114	0.000	2.089
6	0.483	1.287	2.534	0.000	2.004	0.030	1.970
7	0.419	1.182	2.704	0.076	1.924	0.118	1.882
8	0.373	1.099	2.847	0.136	1.864	0.185	1.815
9	0.337	1.032	2.970	0.184	1.816	0.239	1.761
10	0.308	0.975	3.078	0.223	1.777	0.284	1.716
11	0.285	0.927	3.173	0.256	1.744	0.321	1.679
12	0.266	0.886	3.258	0.283	1.717	0.354	1.646
13	0.249	0.850	3.336	0.307	1.693	0.382	1.618
14	0.235	0.817	3.407	0.328	1.672	0.406	1.594
15	0.223	0.789	3.472	0.347	1.653	0.428	1.572
16	0.212	0.763	3.532	0.363	1.637	0.448	1.552
17	0.203	0.739	3.588	0.378	1.622	0.466	1.534
18	0.194	0.718	3.640	0.391	1.609	0.482	1.518
19	0.187	0.698	3.689	0.404	1.596	0.497	1.503
20	0.180	0.680	3.735	0.415	1.585	0.510	1.490
21	0.173	0.663	3.778	0.425	1.575	0.523	1.477
22	0.167	0.647	3.819	0.435	1.565	0.534	1.466
23	0.162	0.633	3.858	0.443	1.557	0.545	1.455
24	0.157	0.619	3.895	0.452	1.548	0.555	1.445
25	0.153	0.606	3.931	0.459	1.541	0.565	1.435

REFERENCES

C.S. Peirce. *A Theory of Probably Inference*. Little, Brown and Co. 1883.

ASQ Certified Six Sigma Black Belt Body of Knowledge. American Society for Quality. 2015.

N. Kano, N. Seraku, F. Takahashi, S. Tsuji. *Attractive Quality and Must-be Quality*. Journal of the Japanese Society for Quality Control. 1984.

S. Chowdhury. *Design for Six Sigma: The Revolutionary Process for Achieving Extraordinary Profits*. Prentice Hall. 2002.

K. Ishikawa. *Guide to Quality Control*. Tokyo: JUSE. 1968.

J.K. Patel and C.B. Read. *Handbook of the Normal Distribution*. New York: Dekker. 1982.

S. Haghsheno, M. Binninger, J. Dlouhy, S. Sterlike. *History and Theoretical Foundations of Takt Planning and Takt Control*. 24th Annual Conference of the International Group for Lean Construction. 2016.

IASSC Lean Six Sigma Black Belt Body of Knowledge. International Association for Six Sigma Certification. 2017.

F.W. Breyfogle III. *Implementing Six Sigma: Smarter Solutions Using Statistical Methods*. New York: John Wiley & Sons. 1999.

A.N. Christopher. *Interpreting and Using Statistics in Psychological Research*. 2017.

D.C. Montgomery. *Introduction to Statistical Quality Control*. John Wiley & Sons. 2013.

J.A. De Feo and W. Barnard. *JURAN Institute's Six Sigma Breakthrough and Beyond - Quality Performance Breakthrough Methods*. McGraw-Hill. 2005.

M. Imai. *Kaizen: The Key to Japan's Competitive Success*. New York: Random House. 1986.

G. Blue and R. Howes. *Lean Six Sigma - The McGraw-Hill 36-Hour Course*. McGraw-Hill. 2006.

R. Sheen. *Lean Six Sigma - Black Belt*. GoSkills Course. 2018.

J.P. Womack. *Lean Thinking: Banish Waste and Create Wealth in Your Corporation*. New York: Free Press. 2003.

B. Wheat, C. Mills, M. Carnell. *Leaning into Six Sigma: The Path to Integration of Lean Enterprise and Six Sigma*. 2001.

Measurement System Analysis, MSA (4th Edition). Automotive Industry Action Group. 2010.

R. Chua. *Operational Excellence Foundations*. LinkedIn Learning Course. 2018.

J. Harrington. *Poor-Quality Cost*. American Society for Quality. 1987.

A. Stagliano. *Rath & Strong's Six Sigma Advanced Tools Pocket Guide*. McGraw-Hill. 2004.

T. Bertels. *Rath & Strong's Six Sigma Leadership Handbook*. John Wiley & Sons. 2003.

R. Chua. *Six Sigma Foundations*. LinkedIn Learning Course. 2020.

R. Chua. *Six Sigma: Black Belt*. LinkedIn Learning Course. 2017.

A. Laureani, J. Anthony. *Standards for Lean Six Sigma Certification*. International Journal of Productivity and Performance Management. 2011.

M. Rosenthal. *The Essence of Jidoka*. SME Lean Directions Newsletter. 2002.

F. Herzberg, B. Mausner, B.B. Snyderman. *The Motivation to Work (2nd Edition)*. New York: Wiley. 1959.

N.R. Tague. *The Quality Toolbox*. American Society for Quality. 2004

T. Pyzdek and P.A. Keller. *The Six Sigma Handbook, Third Edition*. McGraw-Hill. 2009.

T. Ohno. *Toyota Production System*. Productivity Press. 1988.

T. Manos. *Value Stream Mapping - An Introduction*. American Society for Quality. 2006.

W. Cleveland. *Visualizing Data*. Hobart Press. 1993.

S. Gaskin, et al. *Voice of the Customer*. Massachusetts Institute of Technology. 2018.

INDEX

ABOUT THE AUTHOR

Robert Setiadi is an author, proud father, technology enthusiast, project manager, service delivery manager and Certified Lean Six Sigma Black Belt (ICBB). With a passion for business and a love of information technology, Robert has over 15 years of experience as an IT professional. He is a big believer in data-driven processes and decision making, which makes him dedicated to providing readers with down-to-earth, practical guide to the Lean Six Sigma process, helping entrepreneurs and industry professionals supercharge their businesses by mastering this highly effective framework. Robert has a PhD in software testing and quality assurance, as well as a master's degree in software systems engineering.

For more information, visit: www.robertsetiadi.com

www.ingramcontent.com/pod-product-compliance
Lightning Source LLC
Chambersburg PA
CBHW072044020426
42334CB00017B/1379